Marital Violence

C000270062

This book exposes the 'hidden' history of marital violence and explores its place in English family life between the Restoration and the mid-nineteenth century. In a time before divorce was easily available and when husbands were popularly believed to have the right to beat their wives, Elizabeth Foyster examines the variety of ways in which women, men and children responded to marital violence. For contemporaries this was an issue that raised central questions about family life: the extent of men's authority over other family members, the limitations of married women's property rights, the different roles of mothers and fathers in the upbringing of their children, and the problems of access to divorce and child custody. Opinion about the legitimacy of marital violence continued to be divided, but by the nineteenth century the basis of ideas about what was intolerable or cruel violence had changed significantly. This accessible study will be invaluable reading for anyone interested in gender studies, feminism, social history and family history.

ELIZABETH FOYSTER is Lecturer in History at Clare College, Cambridge. She previously published *Manhood in Early Modern England: Honour, Sex and Marriage* (1999).

Marital Violence

An English Family History, 1660–1857

Elizabeth Foyster

Clare College, Cambridge

CAMBRIDGE
UNIVERSITY PRESS

CAMBRIDGE UNIVERSITY PRESS
Cambridge, New York, Melbourne, Madrid, Cape Town, Singapore, São Paulo

Cambridge University Press
The Edinburgh Building, Cambridge, CB2 2RU, UK

Published in the United States of America by Cambridge University Press,
New York

www.cambridge.org
Information on this title: www.cambridge.org/9780521619127

First published 2005

Printed in the United Kingdom at the University Press, Cambridge

A catalogue record for this publication is available from the British Library

Library of Congress Cataloguing in Publication data

Foyster, Elizabeth A., 1968–
    Marital violence: an English family history, 1660–1875/Elizabeth Foyster.
    p. cm.
    Includes bibliographical references and index.
    ISBN 0-521-83451-1
    1. Family violence – England – History.   2. Wife abuse –
England – History.   3. Women – Violence against – England –
History.   4. Family – England – History.   I. Title.

HV6626.23.G7F69 2005
362.82′92′09420903 – dc22   2005045785

ISBN-13 978-0-521-83451- 3 hardback
ISBN-10 0-521-83451- 1 hardback
ISBN-13 978-0-521-61912- 7 paperback
ISBN-10 0-521-61912- 2 paperback

For Peter

Contents

Preface

'One in 5 women live with the constant threat of domestic abuse'. This was the shocking headline of a Scottish government campaign against domestic violence undertaken while I was writing this book. Along with posters that asked 'Which type of woman is most often abused?', and answered 'The female type', the '1 in 5' statistic appeared on billboards by roads and at bus-stops, on television advertisements, in magazines and newspapers, and on a new website offering information and advice. Yet, within three months of launching this campaign, the Advertising Standards Authority (the national advertising watchdog) had forced a government rethink. The ASA had received two main sources of complaint. The first was that the campaign was biased because it only showed female victims of domestic abuse. This was not upheld by the ASA. But the second complaint was that the government had no proof to support its '1 in 5' claim. Where was their evidence? The government pointed the ASA to a recent survey that had been based on 5,000 households, and had shown that one in five women had experienced domestic abuse at some point in their lives. That, argued the ASA, did not support the claim that one in five women lived in 'constant threat of domestic abuse'. The campaign as it stood was discredited and had to be withdrawn.[1]

As a historian, this campaign taught me a number of lessons about domestic violence, present and past. First, that domestic violence does not yield evidence that can be readily translated into reliable numbers or statistics. Even today, when domestic violence is a crime, and we have a professional police force and modern systems of recording crime, we cannot be certain about the numbers of people it affects. Historians sometimes talk about the 'dark figure' of unrecorded crime, or the number of offences that were not reported because of fear, intimidation, a lack of time or resources. Domestic violence has always been the archetype of this form of offence. Whereas most historians agree that

---

[1] As reported in *The Scotsman* (27 March 2002), and *Scotland on Sunday* (31 March 2002).

domestic violence was likely to be reported if it became so severe that death was the result, the extent of the more common and non-lethal forms of domestic violence is unknown. As a result we can make no confident assertions about whether the levels or incidence of domestic violence have increased or decreased over time.

Second, the advertising campaign and the dispute that followed convinced me that what I was discovering in the archives about marital violence in the past were the roots of many of our present-day ideas about domestic violence. Undoubtedly, marital violence in the period between the Restoration and the mid-nineteenth century took place in a very different legal and socio-economic context. Most importantly, husbands and fathers were widely believed to have a right to 'chastise' their wives and children using physical means. But, as this book will show, it was also in this period that the English government first passed legislation that it hoped would tackle the problem of marital violence. Popular condemnation of violent husbands was voiced in newspapers and other forms of print, in church during sermons, in fictional literature, particularly novels, and in the ballads or songs that were sung on street corners and in taverns and pubs. The common causes of marital violence had been identified: male drunkenness, sexual frustration or jealousy, and economic insecurity. In this period there was also recognition that marital violence could be directed against husbands as well as wives, although most attention was paid to extreme forms of female violence. Ironically, given the nature of the complaint upheld by the ASA, there was even debate in the eighteenth and nineteenth centuries about whether living with the threat of violence was as damaging to a woman's health as the experience of actual violence. By the mid-nineteenth century, the lawyers and judges who heard women's evidence were prepared to admit and take account of threats, in addition to actual incidents of violence.

Yet some one-hundred-and-fifty years after the end of this study, and well beyond the point when men's right to beat their wives had been formally rejected, domestic violence was still enough of a problem to attract a government campaign. This history can offer some answers to the question 'why?'. For it was in the period between c.1660–1857 that our most powerful misconceptions and prejudices about domestic violence were forged. The idea that domestic violence only affected certain 'types' of people emerged, and this book will show how the labels of the typical wife-beater and his victim came to be attached to particular sectors of the working class. These cultural stereotypes have proved hard to counter, as has the conviction that domestic violence is a 'private' matter for resolution just by the family themselves, with help from professionals only if requested directly. The belief that much current domestic violence remains 'Behind Closed Doors', as the song that accompanied the television advert relayed, is often seen today as the consequence of a breakdown in 'traditional' social relations. Families, it is argued, now live in isolation from their communities. Non-family members who intervene in occasions of violence, or who report it, are liable to be seen as interfering in matters that are none of their business. But this book will show that there is little evidence that there was a long-term privatization of family life, which bore significance for dealing with domestic violence. Personal relationships remained a public concern from the seventeenth to the mid-nineteenth century. I will argue that it was when the issue of domestic violence started to be regarded as so problematic that only 'professionals' could deal with it satisfactorily, a point which began to be reached by the mid-nineteenth century, that the shift away from community responsibility for handling domestic violence began.

This book is a study of domestic violence that focuses on marital violence. It shows how children and other family members could be victims of marital violence, even though they were not its chief targets. On the whole, the stories of violence that were examined for this book were not ones that ended with murder. While evidence about domestic homicide may be more readily available, it does not tell us as much about attitudes towards violence as non-lethal instances. Not only was non-lethal violence a more routine form of violence, it also provoked considerable uncertainty, debate and division among contemporaries about its legitimacy. It is violence that was intended to be part of an ongoing relationship, not end it, which interests me. This was violence that could be subject to negotiation and accommodation within marriages. During the period of this study the notion that violence in marriage could be regarded as acceptable was deeply embedded into thinking about relationships between men and women, even within those where violence never occurred. By exposing and exploring differing views and levels of tolerance, this history of domestic violence will reveal the fundamental patterns of how many people governed, experienced and managed their daily married lives.

This book has not been an easy one to research or write, and the accounts of marital violence that I have discovered may make uncomfortable reading. The pages that follow contain descriptions of violence that are both disturbing and depressing. My aim, however, was not to shock or provide any lengthy catalogue of human misery, but to demonstrate how and when in history marital violence could produce resistance, objection, protest and outrage. There are stories of courage, resilience, escape and recovery throughout the book. The first court case I read in which a wife pleaded to be separated from her violent husband, made me feel compelled to write this book. It is a 'hidden history' of women's and men's lives that has to be confronted and told.

The research for this book was funded by a British Academy Postdoctoral Fellowship, a Carnegie Trust grant, and an AHRB Research Leave award. It is based upon work conducted in a number of archives and libraries, and I am particularly grateful to Melanie Barber and the team at Lambeth Palace Library, and Ruth Paley and Amanda Bevan at the National Archives for their assistance. For five years I was lucky enough to work alongside a group of inspiring teachers, researchers and staff in the Department of History at the University of Dundee. They were friends as well as colleagues, and I benefited greatly from their interest and support. I began, and then returned to complete this book, as a Fellow at Clare College, Cambridge, and I would like to thank the Master and Fellows for welcoming me back.

Many historians have been generous with their time, expertise and ideas. I owe special thanks to Jonathan Andrews, Bernard Capp, Louisa Cross, Jeremy Gregory, Bob Harris, Tim Hitchcock, Steve King, Tim Stretton, Ceri Sullivan, Rosemary Sweet, David Turner and Chris Whatley. Students at Dundee and Cambridge Universities have had the useful habit of asking me some of the most pertinent and difficult questions about my work, and I hope this book will answer at least some of them. I am grateful to the anonymous readers at Cambridge University Press for providing helpful comments and to Michael Watson and Isabelle Dambricourt at the Press for all their assistance. It is Anthony Fletcher and Helen Berry who have helped me most with this book. Both have read and commented upon the entire draft and they have given me much important encouragement. Anthony has shown a commitment and interest in my work that has long outlived his original role as my PhD supervisor, and his advice has been invaluable as my career has taken me in new directions. Helen is my favourite critic, whom I greatly admire for her unique blend of intellectual rigour, sensitivity and good humour. Without her input completing this book would have been a far more difficult enterprise.

Margaret, Richard, Rachel, Kate and Chris are my family who have kept me happy while writing this book, and I would like to thank them very much. My life has been transformed since I met and married Peter Jackson. Peter's enthusiasm for history rivals my own, and his interest in my work has meant much to me. He has coped admirably with the inevitable curiosity that has arisen when others have discovered that his wife is researching marital violence, and I know that sharing the first year of married life with a book that needed finishing has not been easy. While I have been uncovering so much sadness and pain in the historical past, Peter has been the reminder of the great affection and love that can be found in human relationships. This book is dedicated to him.

Abbreviations and conventions

For ease of comprehension, spellings and punctuation from court records have been modernised.

Baring-Gould	Sabine Baring-Gould Collection of Ballads, 10 vols., c.1800–c.1870, British Library, London
Bell Collection	Thomas Bell Collection of Ballads, c.1780–c.1820, British Library, London
CCRO	Cambridgeshire County Record Office, Shire Hall, Cambridge
CUL	Cambridge University Library, Cambridge
English Reports	*English Reports: Ecclesiastical, Admiralty, Probate and Divorce*, Edinburgh and London, 1917–21
Hansard	Hansard's Parliamentary Debates, 3rd series
LMA	London Metropolitan Archives, London
LPL	Lambeth Palace Library, London
Madden	Madden Collection of Ballads, 26 vols., for the period c.1775–c.1850, Cambridge University Library, Cambridge
NA	National Archives, Kew
Pepys	W. G. Day (ed.), *The Pepys Ballads* 5 vols., Cambridge, 1987
Roxburghe	W. Chappell (ed.), *The Roxburghe Ballads* vols. I–III, London, 1871–80, and J. W. Ebsworth (ed.), *The Roxburghe Ballads* vols. IV–IX, London, 1883–99

Introduction

Let me start by introducing two married women: Rachael Norcott and Mary Veitch. They both lived near London; Rachael in Barking, Essex and Mary in Richmond, Surrey. They were of comparable social status. Rachael's husband, John, earned enough from the rents of the houses he owned to support a comfortable middle-class lifestyle. James Veitch, Mary's husband, was a member of the Royal College of Physicians, received an annual pension for being a surgeon to the Royal Navy, and had inherited a considerable sum of money upon the death of his father. Like Rachael, Mary was supported in her household tasks by the presence of a number of live-in servants. Both women were mothers as well as wives. Rachael had given birth to at least two sons, but only one of the children born to Mary and James had lived beyond its infancy. Mary was a widow when she met James and she brought one child from her previous marriage into her new home. The wealth, income and occupations of their husbands, their role as managers of households with servants, shared histories of motherhood, and lives cut short by infant and premature mortality, made these women typical of the middle classes of their generation.[1]

But we only know about these women because they experienced a level and type of violence from their husbands that became so unbearable that they both went to the same law court to seek a marriage separation. The records that survive from this court tell us that each woman endured physical, verbal and sexual violence from their

---

[1] Rachael brought her husband a portion of £500, and in 1666 John had a yearly income of £70 in rents. In 1837 James Veitch earned an annual income of at least £380 as a doctor, and had inherited between £8,000 to £14,000 from his father. Although James disputed these sums, as these were used to determine alimony, they place both couples within the wealth and income brackets that historians have agreed were shared by the middle class. See, for example, P. Earle, *The Making of the English Middle Class: Business, Society and Family Life in London 1660–1730* (London, 1989), pp. 14–15, and L. Davidoff and C. Hall, *Family Fortunes: Men and Women of the English Middle Class 1780–1850* (London, 1987), pp. 23–24.

husbands, which was exacerbated by forms of economic deprivation. The range of violence that John and James inflicted included hitting, threatening, swearing, forced confinement of Mary in her home, threats of confinement to a madhouse, separation from children and deprival of adequate money for basic survival. In this book the term 'cruel violence' will be used to define behaviour of any of these kinds that contemporaries agreed was unacceptable or intolerable. Both Rachael and Mary had lived with years of this treatment before they took the legal steps to end their marriages. Rachael and John had been married for twenty-three years when she approached the courts; Mary waited thirteen years.

Rachael's and Mary's final solution to marital violence was the same, yet their stories were heard in different centuries. Rachael fought for separation from her husband in 1666 and Mary Veitch followed the same course of action in 1837.[2] As this book will show, what was different about their marriages, was not the forms of violence that Rachael and Mary endured, but how they were interpreted. Although there was a continuity of division in opinion about the place of violence in married life, this was accompanied by a shift in the meanings that were given to violence when it occurred. It was not just judges and lawyers who were important in deciding how marital violence should be interpreted. Instead, the ordinary people who surrounded Rachael and Mary, their servants, children, neighbours, friends and other family members all had views that contributed to how and when they responded to their husband's violence. The reaction and responses of this wider audience to marital violence provides us with vital clues about popular attitudes towards this kind of domestic violence. In the process of responding to marital violence, people revealed their opinions about the ideal roles of women and men in marriage, understandings of the place of servants and children in family life, and thoughts about the best relationship between family and community. Thus, while in many ways this book is a study of violence in the lives of two women, and we will return to Rachael and Mary in each of the chapters that follow, their stories serve as just the starting point for opening up a much wider history of gender and household relations, changing ideas of parenting and childhood, and the varying balance of responsibility for family welfare between the individual, community, professional and state.

---

[2] LPL, CA, Case 6659 (1666), Eee2, ff.94v–99r, 101–124v; LPL, CA, Case 9440 (1837), H550/ 1–18.

Histories of marital violence

This kind of history book would have been unthinkable until recently. Before the 1970s marital violence and the 'battered' woman were little discussed by sociologists, psychologists or criminologists, let alone historians. Since then, thanks largely to the feminist movement and the emergence of women's history, the issue of marital violence has received some historical attention. In seeking to recover women from the past, some of the earlier studies provided an overly simplified history of marital violence that was intended to expose the brutalities of male oppression and female subjection.[3] But a more enduring approach emerged, influenced by the work of sociologists (particularly Rebecca and Russell Dobash), which is the search for the causes of marital violence in the past.[4] Believing that the reasons for marital violence are historically contingent, or shaped by the social, economic, political and cultural conditions of each period, more recently a group of historians has explored the historical roots of violence, hoping to explain its occurrence.[5]

These studies have shown that the motives for violence were sexual jealousy, frustration or insecurity, concerns over money or the management of economic resources, and excessive consumption of alcohol, which could also exacerbate the other causes. While the triggers to this violence may have depended on the particular social and economic circumstances of each period, the same combination of factors have remained the causes of violence across time and space. There is little that would have surprised contemporaries about these studies. Throughout our period there was much concern about the influence of the 'demon drink' upon male behaviour, and as we shall see, by the

---

[3] See, for example, T. Davidson, 'Wifebeating: a recurring phenomenon throughout history', in M. Roy (ed.), *Battered Women: A Psychosociological Study of Domestic Violence* (New York, 1977), pp. 2–23.

[4] R. and R. Dobash, *Violence Against Wives: A Case Against the Patriarchy* (New York, 1979), and *Women, Violence and Social Change* (London, 1992).

[5] See, for example, N. Tomes, 'A "torrent of abuse": crimes of violence between working-class men and women in London, 1840–1875', *Journal of Social History* 11, 3 (1978), 331–5; E. Ross, '"Fierce questions and taunts": married life in working-class London, 1870–1914', *Feminist Studies* 8 (1982), 581–2; L. Abrams, 'Companionship and conflict: the negotiation of marriage relations in the nineteenth century', in L. Abrams and E. Harvey (eds.), *Gender Relations in German History: Power, Agency and Experience from the Sixteenth to the Twentieth Century* (London, 1996), pp. 108–16; L. Leneman, "A tyrant and tormentor': violence against wives in eighteenth- and early nineteenth-century Scotland', *Continuity and Change* 12, 1 (1997), 39–42; R. Trumbach, *Sex and the Gender Revolution: Volume One. Heterosexuality and the Third Gender in Enlightenment London* (Chicago, 1998), chapter 10; and J. Warner and A. Lunny, 'Marital violence in a martial town: husbands and wives in early modern Portsmouth, 1653–1781', *Journal of Family History* 28, 2 (2003), 269–71.

nineteenth century there was a close association between poverty and certain types of marital violence. The 'green-eyed monster' haunted many married couples. Onlookers frequently asked husbands why they were violent to their wives, because if it could be proved that there had been some failure in wifely duty, violence could be viewed as a legitimate form of correction. But there was also a recognition that marital violence did not always have a cause, a point missed by these historians. Witnesses who spoke for Rachael Norcott, for example, emphasized that John was 'causelessly' violent to her.[6]

There are limitations to an approach to violence which begins with its causation. There is a danger of uncritically reproducing the arguments deployed by violent men to justify, defend, or at the very least excuse their behaviour. Historians can be drawn into a process by which they shift attention and responsibility for violence onto external factors, such as economic conditions, over which individual men can be said to have little control. This does not answer the question of why, when men were poverty-stricken, sexually frustrated, drunk and so on, they directed their violence against their wives rather than their work colleagues, drinking companions or neighbours? We have to look at contemporary ideas about marriage, and men's and women's roles within it, to find answers. Without understanding these ideas, we cannot retrieve the meanings that those living in the past gave to violent behaviour. Influenced by modern-day attitudes towards marital violence, which see it as a social 'problem' to be regulated and controlled, historians assume that they can find identifiable causes for this behaviour in the past. But, crucially, in the period of this study, violence in marriage was not always seen as deviant behaviour, and could be viewed instead as a feature of a 'normal', functioning relationship.

Other historians have examined marital violence as part of surveys on the history of divorce.[7] The most well known historian in this field is Lawrence Stone. Stone was interested in charting the emergence of modern-day divorce, and he regarded the Divorce Act of 1857, which this book takes as its end point, as a measure of women's improved position within the family and society. In contrast, during the seventeenth and eighteenth centuries, Stone believed, wives could suffer violence of the most brutal kind. Stone certainly had an eye for the sensational and he relished telling stories of marriage breakdown.[8] But

---

[6] LPL, CA, Case 6659 (1666), Eee2, ff.95,124r.

[7] R. Phillips, *Putting Asunder: A History of Divorce in Western Society* (Cambridge, 1988); and L. Stone, *Road to Divorce: England 1530–1987* (Oxford, 1990).

[8] See, for example, L. Stone, 'Money, sex and murder in eighteenth-century England', in I. P. H. Duffy (eds.), *Women and Society in the Eighteenth Century* (Bethlehem, PA, 1983),

these were often selected from printed law reports and parliamentary papers, which meant that he neglected studying the primary sources detailing the more mundane, and perhaps more typical marital disputes involving violence. The marriages of those below the social elite were given little attention, and he assumed that the upper and middling social ranks were always the standard bearers of new ideals of marital conduct. Furthermore, Stone was deeply suspicious of the methods of women's history, once pompously writing a list of ten commandments that he believed all historians of women should follow.[9] He gave scant regard to analysing women's views in the law cases he studied, and he did not consider how he might recover the experiences of the many women who did not reach the stage of telling their stories formally in the courts.

More balanced and focused studies of marital violence have been written by legal historians. These have shown when and how the legal concept of marital cruelty developed. Maeve E. Doggett, in particular, considers why the principle of female subjection to men continued to have importance long after the right of husbands to beat their wives was rejected in the courts.[10] These studies have influenced the writing of this book, as has the work by the social historians Anna Clark and A. James Hammerton. Clark's book on working-class marriage from the late eighteenth century until the mid-nineteenth century demonstrates just what Stone missed by concentrating only on the upper and middle social classes. Following her example, the lives of working women who endured marital violence are examined in this book using evidence from petty and quarter sessions, police courts, reports in newspapers, and views of this violence as reflected in popular ballads. Clark showed how the histories of gender and class were intertwined, and this book will develop that theme by demonstrating that ideas of class became increasingly important for determining what forms of marital violence were seen as unacceptable and cruel. However, this study has found no evidence to support Clark's thesis that the extent of marital violence varied with occupation. Clark argued that the wives of artisans employed in traditional trades were more likely to be beaten than wives of the new textile workers. Married men in the former group faced an uncertain economic future, and feeling threatened they reasserted their

pp. 15–28, and *Uncertain Unions and Broken Lives: Intimate and Revealing Accounts of Marriage and Divorce in England* (Oxford, 1995).

[9] L. Stone, 'Only women', *The New York Review of Books* (11 April 1985), 21.

[10] M. E. Doggett, *Marriage, Wife-Beating and the Law in Victorian England* (Columbia, South Carolina, 1993); see also, J. M. Biggs, *The Concept of Matrimonial Cruelty* (London, 1962).

masculinity by returning to a bachelor culture of hard drinking and violent misogyny. But as well as resorting to a causation theory that places workplace stress at its core, Clark's conclusions are problematic because she assumes that the number of prosecutions for assault brought by wives against their violent husbands reflected the actual incidence of marital violence. This assumption is a false one because we cannot tell how often marital violence occurred and was not prosecuted. As Joanne Bailey has recently remarked, the willingness to prosecute could depend as much upon the proximity of couples to a magistrate or law court as the incidence of violence within particular social groups.[11]

Hammerton's work is unusual because he has examined marital violence in both the working and middle classes. Taking his starting point from where this book ends, he has used the records of the new Divorce Court established after 1857, and those of the magistrates' courts to build a picture of violence in late Victorian marriage. His argument that the ideals of patriarchal and companionate marriage coexisted is convincing, and he shows how this meant that there was never universal condemnation of marital violence. He is sensitive to the continuing difference between the articulation of domestic ideals and the realities of men's and women's behaviour in married life.

Nevertheless, Hammerton makes claims about marital violence in the period of his study, which this book will challenge. Put simply, this book presents a weight of evidence that questions the chronology of change that underpins many of Hammerton's arguments. Hammerton believes that public interest in the issue of marital violence was unprecedented in the nineteenth century, but this book will show that there had been extensive debate about this matter since at least the start of the seventeenth century. This makes it difficult to compare levels of popular intolerance for marital violence over time, and impossible to prove Hammerton's theory that intolerance was increasing in the nineteenth century. Second, Hammerton, along with Martin Wiener, who has focused on domestic violence that led to murder, has argued that the Victorian period saw new pressures on men to control their use of violence. Manliness was being measured by domestic as well as public conduct. However, work on the ideals for early-modern masculinity reveals that there was little that was novel about these requirements. Third, Hammerton believes that the myth created by the Victorians about marital violence, which was that it was a problem confined to

---

[11] A. Clark, *The Struggle for the Breeches: Gender and the Making of the British Working Class* (London, 1995), especially pp. 74–83, 260–2; J. Bailey, *Unquiet Lives: Marriage and Marriage Breakdown in England, 1660–1800* (Cambridge, 2003), pp. 96–7.

the working classes, meant that the middle classes did not face up to the issue of its incidence in their own social circles until the end of the nineteenth century. But there is overwhelming evidence, from the cases of marital violence brought to the courts by middle-class wives such as Mary Veitch, the interest in reading reports of marital violence in daily newspapers, and the necessity for middle-class officials and professionals to deal with its consequences, that maintaining any collective blindness to this issue was practicably impossible. Finally, Hammerton argues that in the early years of the new Divorce Court, the concept of matrimonial cruelty was widened to include more than just physical violence, and to take account of the consequences of violence as well as the nature of the violent incident itself. This book will show, however, that well before the mid-nineteenth century, the definition of cruel violence was one that was often dependent on more than physical violence, and was assessed according to its effects upon the women involved. As Chapter 1 will demonstrate, it is crucial that we understand how ordinary people, outside as well as within the courtroom setting, defined and described the violence they experienced or witnessed, before we analyse how they judged it in any formal capacity.[12]

Despite the recent publication of scholarly work that focuses specifically on marital violence, it is noticeable how this is divided between studies that examine the early-modern period, which usually means the period up to the outbreak of the Civil War, and those like Hammerton's, which examine the mid to late Victorian period.[13] While it raises some crucial issues that will be discussed in this book, the most important study of marital violence in the eighteenth century, by Margaret Hunt, draws upon a sample of just ten cases drawn over a two-year period.[14] Based on the period from the Restoration until 1857, this book addresses the gap in our knowledge about marital violence in the 'long' eighteenth century. By providing a much needed longer perspective on the history of marital violence, it questions the originality of many Victorian ideals for married life, and shows how their attitudes towards

[12] A. James Hammerton, 'Victorian marriage and the law of matrimonial cruelty', *Victorian Studies* 33, 3 (1990), 269–92, and *Cruelty and Companionship: Conflict in Nineteenth-Century Married Life* (London, 1992); M. J. Wiener, 'The Victorian criminalization of men', in P. Spierenburg (ed.), *Men and Violence: Gender, Honor, and Rituals in Modern Europe and America* (Ohio, 1998), pp. 197–212, and *Men of Blood: Violence, Manliness, and Criminal Justice in Victorian England* (Cambridge, 2004).

[13] For an example of work on the earlier period see, S. D. Amussen, '"Being stirred to much unquietness": Violence and domestic violence in early modern England', *Journal of Women's History* 6, 2 (1994), 70–89.

[14] M. Hunt, 'Wife beating, domesticity and women's independence in eighteenth-century London', *Gender and History* 4, 1 (1992), 10–33.

marital violence were derived from debates that had been ongoing for centuries. The problematisation of male violence was no innovation of the nineteenth century, but had antecedents in the seventeenth and eighteenth centuries. Crossing the divide between early modern and modern social history reveals what people living in these periods held in common. In contrast to previous studies, this book will demonstrate the many continuities in ideas about marital violence in the past. The most fundamental of these was an intolerance for this form of marital conduct. This was enduring, and not mounting or increasing over time, as it has been suggested. As Chapter 1 will show, however, this criticism of marital violence was always circumstantial, depending on the characteristics of the couple involved. Across our period, there was a point at which marital violence became intolerable: it was not unacceptable per se. Thus critical comment about marital violence was accompanied by a long-term acceptance that there were occasions when husbands did have a right to use violence to correct their wives. The popular judgement of incidents of marital violence was subjective, but the common terms of reference that people used to reach their viewpoints altered less than many historians have led us to believe.

This emphasis upon continuity does not mean that discussion of changes in the definition or responses to marital violence will be absent from this book. Instead it will be shown that as the period progressed, class became more influential in shaping the types of violence that contemporaries thought would be experienced in each social group. The ways in which wives could respond to their husband's violence also changed as ideas about what constituted ideal femininity developed along new lines. In the final chapters of the book, the continuities of neighbourhood intervention will be contrasted with the early attempts by the professionals, including the 'new police', to deal with the consequences of marital violence. Legislation to deal with the problem of marital violence, passed in 1803, 1828 and 1853, also marked the beginning of parliamentary attempts to deal with its occurrence.

A further common theme to emerge from previous studies on marital violence is their concentration upon male violence. The violence of wives has been largely ignored. In part this is because historians have defined marital violence as physical violence, and have given less consideration to its other forms. As Chapters 1 and 2 will show, taking the same wider definition of violence as people in the past allows us to discuss when and how women used violence in their relationships with their husbands. Violence could be exchanged within marriage, rather than simply being one-way.

By seeing marital violence as an important part of family history, this book is taking a new approach to the subject. It is an extraordinary reflection of the distance between historians of gender relations and those of the family, that consideration of the impact of violence between men and women upon other family members has never been attempted.[15] In particular, children have been the 'missing persons' in all previous histories of marital violence. Yet there is ample evidence of their presence during marital quarrels, and that they were immediately affected by what they saw and heard. Important changes in the law on child custody occurred during the period of this book, and along with children's responses to parental violence they will be discussed in Chapter 3.

Despite the criticisms that have been outlined above, there is still much to learn from the histories of marital violence that have been written since the 1970s, and this book will engage with many of their findings. Drawing upon evidence of conflict in marriage across the social scale, and placing marital violence in the context of familial as well as gender and social relations, this study will examine both marital behaviour and ideas about it over a two hundred-year period. To make sense of what the book will reveal, however, it is vital that first we place the institution of marriage in its historical context.

Married life c. 1660–1857

When Rachael Norcott and Mary Veitch married they entered an institution and stage in their lives that brought status, rights, duties and obligations. Marriage, and motherhood that was assumed to follow, were goals for middle-class women in a society where spinsterhood and widowhood held so many economic and social uncertainties. But while being a wife signalled adulthood, authority and usually governance over a household, it also required a woman to assume a gender role of subjection and obedience to her husband. The institution of marriage was intended to be the bedrock of the patriarchal ideal where women were subordinated to men, and husbands ruled over and dominated their wives.

Women's inferior position to men was supported in scriptural, political, medical and legal thought across our period. Ordinary women and men learned about their gender roles through popular culture and

---

[15] The different directions of research often undertaken by historians of gender and the family have been noted by Megan Doolittle in, 'Close relations? Bringing together gender and family in English history', *Gender and History* 11, 3 (1999), 542–54.

custom, and from a range of prescriptive and advice literature. All tended to support the idea that the organizing principle of gender relations within marriage should be that of 'separate spheres'. In other words, the lives of wives should be confined to the 'private' sphere of the home, where they carried out their domestic tasks, and men should be active in the 'public' sphere of work and politics outside it. Wives and husbands were prescribed particular gender roles for their lives in these spheres, which were based on what were perceived to be the natural qualities for each sex. Wives were to be carers and managers of their families and homes, because they had the female characteristics of compassion, patience, tenderness and charity. Their more emotional natures and lack of reason made them less suited than men to the competitive and challenging world of business and politics. It was men's greater intellectual capacities, ambition and determination that gave them the ability to survive, and, more importantly, prosper in the public sphere. The main duty for husbands was to provide economic sustenance for their wives and families.

Historians initially believed that the ideal of separate spheres in married life emerged in the late eighteenth century, and that it was their attempts to achieve this state of gender relations, which were crucial to middle-class formation and identity.[16] Subsequently, however, it has been shown that many aspects of this ideal were shared by men and women living in the sixteenth, seventeenth and early to mid-eighteenth centuries, so that Victorian notions of ideal gender relations represented more a refashioning than a radical new model. It is now thought that it was ideals such as those of separate spheres which enabled patriarchal beliefs to adapt and endure over time. What was perhaps more novel by the nineteenth century was that changes in the economy meant that the ideal of wives remaining in the home while their husbands went out to work became within the sights of working-class as well as middle-class couples. Victorian concepts of respectability in family life placed much importance on women's economic dependence upon their husbands. Nevertheless, as many historical studies have shown, from the sixteenth to the nineteenth centuries, there could be an important difference between ideals and practice. In reality, wives and husbands crossed the boundaries between the private and public spheres on a daily basis, and many households continued to rely upon the economic contribution of both sexes. Thus as an analytical tool for historians, the concept of separate spheres does not capture the complexities or range of women's

---

[16] Davidoff and Hall, *Family Fortunes*, passim.

or men's experiences. For many couples, of whatever social position, living in separate spheres was a goal that was never fully realised.[17]

Equally, those who are interested in the quality of married life in the past are now agreed that it is mistaken to assume that patriarchal beliefs and structures precluded companionship between wives and husbands. Rather than this period witnessing a transition in marriage from relations characterised by violence and cruelty to those of intimacy and affection, as Stone argued, case studies of marriages have revealed how the experience of marriage continued to offer infinite variety between the extremes of happiness and misery.[18] Men were able to exercise power over their wives within loving relationships. Indeed, husbands were instructed that without love, they were tyrannical rulers. Women's inferior and unequal position to men did not prevent them from having the potential to be valued companions for their husbands. Instead, in our period the ideals of femininity and masculinity were constructed so that each complemented the other. Success and contentment in marriage, it was believed, depended upon both marriage partners playing their part.[19]

The study of violence in marriage provides unique opportunities for examining these ideas, and for comparing contemporary ideals for marriage with practice. It was during and following occasions of violence, when individuals were under great stress, or when relationships were at breaking point, that people were most articulate about what was important to them in married life. Demonstrably, marital relationships could not be confined to the 'private' sphere. Quarrels between couples were often about more than domestic matters, were located outside the home, and led to the involvement or intervention of non-family members. To those in positions of public authority, the stability of marriage was far too vital a matter to be left to just husbands and wives to decide. Private relationships were a public issue. Hence marital violence was of concern to many more individuals than just those who directly experienced it. Marriage, as one judge put it, 'is a contract formed with a view, not only to the benefit of the parties themselves, but to the benefit of third parties; to the benefit of their common offspring, and to the moral order of civil society'.[20] The health and discipline of familial and social life

---

[17] A. Vickery, 'Golden age to separate spheres? A review of the categories and chronology of English women's history', *Historical Journal* 36, 2 (1993), 383–414; and R. B. Shoemaker, *Gender in English Society 1650–1850: The Emergence of Separate Spheres?* (London, 1998).

[18] L. Stone, *The Family, Sex and Marriage in England 1500–1800* (London, 1977); for a recent study of marriage in this period see, Bailey, *Unquiet Lives*.

[19] A. Fletcher, *Gender, Sex and Subordination in England 1500–1800* (London, 1995), chapters 8, 9, 16 and 19.

[20] *Evans v. Evans* (1790), *English Reports* vol. 161, p. 496.

depended upon the institution of marriage, according to this line of thinking. The analogy between relations in the family and in the state, made explicit in the seventeenth century, continued to hold political currency. By the nineteenth century, for example, it was only husbands who could demonstrate good order in their marriages, who were seen as deserving of the franchise.[21]

Most obviously, research into attitudes towards marital violence reveals what contemporaries believed should be the limits of a husband's patriarchal authority. As we will see, across our period there was much official and popular acceptance that husbands should be able to correct their wives using physical means. At least in law, this male right was not denied until a landmark decision in 1891.[22] But there remained considerable debate about how far husbands could discipline their wives. At what point did violence become so severe that it was no longer legitimate? It was an indication of the desperate, yet unsatisfactory attempts to address this question that the most dubious of all authorities, 'the rule of thumb', took hold of the popular imagination. According to myth, Sir Francis Buller, who was a judge of the Court of King's Bench from 1778, had said that a husband could beat his wife, as long as it was with a stick that was no thicker than his thumb. There is absolutely no proof that Buller, who became known as 'Judge Thumb', ever made this statement in any formal capacity, and it did not become a legal precedent. But, as a good example of how statements supposedly made by legal authorities could be adopted and adapted to suit popular needs, the idea of the rule of thumb stuck. Three cartoons depicting Buller, one by James Gillray, appeared in print during 1782, and popular ballads repeated the thumb rule.[23] The thumb rule also had an impact on the complaints that women made to the authorities. Wives and their witnesses could be eager to detail the size of the implement that had been used by their husbands against them. As late as 1836, a magistrate in the Marylebone police courts asked a witness how thick the stick had been that was used by a husband to beat his wife. The answer was a chilling, 'as thick as my wrist'.[24] Since, of course, the size of men's thumbs was infinitely variable, the irony of 'the rule of thumb' was, as Doggett has remarked, that it was 'no rule at all'.[25] It left men's rights over their wives open

[21] S. D. Amussen, *An Ordered Society: Gender and Class in Early Modern England* (Oxford, 1988); and Clark, *Struggle for the Breeches*.

[22] Doggett takes this decision as her starting point in, *Marriage, Wife-Beating*.

[23] H. A. Kelly, 'Rule of thumb and the folklaw of the husband's stick', *Journal of Legal Education* 44, 3 (1994), 341–65; Clark, *Struggle for the Breeches*, p. 70.

[24] *The Times* (15 December 1836), 6d.

[25] Doggett, *Marriage, Wife-Beating*, p. 8.

to individual choice and challenge, and it is how these rights were negotiated and contested that is the subject of this book.

While this will be a history of men and ideas of masculinity that focuses on their personal and family lives, it is also a study of gender relations in conflict. The notion of separate spheres has been problematised by historians, and rightly so. Nevertheless, as we shall see, the ideals of masculinity and femininity that lay behind the principle of separate spheres, still had powerful relevance and meaning. It was when husbands or wives repeatedly, or conspicuously failed to live up to these ideals that they became vulnerable. This is because the ideals provided the measure by which husbands and wives could refer, either to justify or refute violence in their relationships. Although husbands could argue that it was because their wives had not been silent, chaste and obedient that they deserved chastisement, their wives could also deploy ideas of gender roles and separate spheres to their advantage. Depicting themselves as upholding the ideals of womanhood as wives and mothers, they pointed to occasions when their husbands had not fulfilled their duties, or had interfered and meddled with household management, a sphere where women expected to hold control. Far from depriving women of all authority within marriage, the ideals of femininity could be the source of their strength, and offer opportunities for resistance. As we shall see in Chapter 2, notions of female weakness and fragility were used by some women to draw attention to the wrongs they perceived had been inflicted upon them by their husbands.

Even if ideas about the roles of women and men within marriage were less subject to change than once thought, undoubtedly the context in which marriages were conducted fundamentally altered in the period between the Restoration and the mid-nineteenth century. Industrialization affected the patterns and division of work within the family, and created the potential for wage earning and employment to be conducted away from the home. As the economy restructured, tensions could arise as men and women struggled for survival, which could result in violence. Just as important for many couples was the consumer revolution that flooded the market with new, and better quality goods to buy.[26] Here the difficulties of reconciling the theory of wives' economic dependence upon their husbands, embodied in the common law doctrine of 'coverture', with the practice of everyday living were most acute. Coverture

---

[26] N. McKendrick, J. Brewer and J. H. Plumb, *The Birth of a Consumer Society: Commercialisation in the Eighteenth Century* (London, 1982); the thesis of the consumer revolution is a controversial one, but it is nevertheless a useful shorthand for the economic changes of the eighteenth century, see S. Pennell, 'Consumption and consumerism in early modern England', *Historical Journal* 42, 2 (1999), 549–64.

severely curtailed a woman's property rights, especially her right to manage her lands and receive their rents. Technically, because a wife became a 'feme covert', or one person with her husband, she could not enter into economic contracts in her own name. As we will see, however, not only did married women actively participate in the new consumer economy, they found it to be an arena where they could display through outward visible signs the disorder and unhappiness they were experiencing within their personal relationships.

The environment surrounding the typical family home also changed in this period. With industrialisation came increasing urbanisation. According to some historians a consequence for family life was that it became more private, as urban residence presented more opportunities for anonymity. In towns and cities, according to this line of thinking, neighbours were less likely to intervene or display collective concern at the marital conduct of others. Records of marital violence will be used to test these claims, and will challenge the idea that the change from rural to urban patterns of living brought with it a decline in the importance of community. Indeed, contemporaries were more prone to see the benefits than the disadvantages of marriage in the urban setting. The reaction in this period of some city wives to their husband's threats that they would 'send them into the country', suggests that it was urban life that was believed to give women freedoms and protection from violence, compared to the isolation of country living.[27] To understand the historical roots of our present-day reluctance to intervene in marital violence, we clearly have to look beyond theories of the effects of urbanisation. The final chapter of the book will do this, and offer some new explanations that lie behind the changing responses of others to marital violence.

A key point that will be emphasised throughout this book is the integration of married and family life. Ties between husbands and wives and their families of origin were reinforced, and those between in-laws forged, at times of marital crisis as well as stability. Too often historians forget that marriage marked just one further stage, rather than the endpoint in an ongoing relationship between parents and their adult children. Kinsmen and women, and members of the nuclear family were crucial influences upon the attitudes, decisions and behaviour of married couples. In turn, such was the close and intimate nature of relationships between family members, that the violence of husbands and wives had an impact upon those who witnessed or later learned of its occurrence. Children grew up in an atmosphere fraught with tension, and punctuated with outbursts of violence. For them, learning to cope with, and

---

[27] See, for example, NA, DEL1/361 (1722), f.50v; and LMA, DL/C/179 (1783), f.148v.

accommodate marital violence was a necessity, since while they remained children living under the parental roof there was no escape. The culture in which to place marital violence is a family one.

The historical records of marital violence

One of the most frequent questions that I have been asked while re-searching this book is: where can we find sources of evidence that reveal marital violence in the past? In a way, this is a telling enquiry, because it shows how hidden from modern view marital violence has become. Yet in the period of this study, marital violence was often conducted in front of others, and was the subject of public debate and comment. As well as discussions of this issue that survive in periodicals, newspapers, parliamentary papers, advice and fictional literature, all of which have been used for this book, there are occasional remarks upon instances of marital violence in personal records, such as diaries and autobiographies. But the most detailed and rich documentation of contemporary behaviour, responses and attitudes towards marital violence is contained within court records. The complaints made by wives about marital violence, the responses by husbands, statements by witnesses, and rulings by magistrates and judges were recorded in a wide variety of legal settings. To a certain extent, the type of legal recourse chosen depended upon a couple's wealth, so a range of different court records have been examined to present a balanced picture of marital violence across the social scale. Although there is a geographical concentration of cases in this book from southern England, stories of marital violence from northern counties are examined, since they were heard in the highest courts of appeal for marriage cases, recorded in law reports and justices' note-books, and were retold in national newspapers. The primary sources were deliberately selected for the book so that they gave the fullest possible picture of English marital violence over time, location and social spectrum.

Following marital violence, a wife had three main courses of legal action. She could seek a marriage separation from her husband on the grounds of his cruelty from the church court in her diocese, complain to her local magistrate of her husband's violence, or persuade her friends and family to seek a writ from the Court of King's Bench to question her confinement in her home or other institution. The legal procedures of each will be discussed below. But before we proceed it is vital to acknowledge a number of key limitations of these sources, which have to be taken into account throughout this book as the material they contain is analysed. First, not all couples felt able or willing to involve others in their marital difficulties. The number of husbands and wives living, as one late seventeenth-century minister noted, in 'secret unkindness' with each other, will always remain unknown to us.[28] Second, just as important, and in many cases more important to wives with violent husbands who did seek aid from others, were extra-legal options following marital violence. Other household members, relatives, friends and neighbours were usually the first, and sometimes the only sources of help. This meant that going to the legal authorities was usually a last resort, and a sign that other measures had failed to produce results. Wives were often eager to tell magistrates and the courts that they had tried resolving their marital difficulties in these informal ways. This is fortunate for us as historians because it means that we learn about these alternative methods, but we have to accept that there will have been many instances of marital violence that were never recorded because they did not reach any stage of legal proceedings. Third, it was the chief aim of both magistrates and the personnel in the law courts to reconcile quarrelling couples, not to encourage them to pursue legal action. So important to the stability of society was marriage thought to be, that officials measured the success of their work by the numbers of couples who were persuaded to seek and offer forgiveness for violence, and continue marriage, rather than end it. Hence, although many couples approached the authorities, not all followed through the legal action open to them, and in many cases abandoned it at the early stages.

Fourth, not all couples wanted to continue their relationships, or seek a formal separation following marital violence. The simplest option was to walk out. Husbands seem to have been the more common deserters than wives, and their desertion was often linked to financial difficulties. The records of the poor law can be revealing for these cases.[29] For wives who deserted, economic survival by working outside the traditional family unit was very difficult. Rather than being a permanent solution, running away from violent husbands usually marked the first step for wives who intended to then seek marriage separation. But both marriage partners could launch a suit for 'restitution of conjugal rights' against a spouse who had deserted them. Heard in the church courts, the result of these cases could be that the errant spouse was ordered to return home and resume cohabitation. Forty-five of these cases from the eighteenth-century London consistory (church) court, and the Court of Arches were surveyed for this book. The vast majority of these (thirty-four

---

[28] R. Parkinson (ed.), *The Autobiography of Henry Newcome* 2 vols., (Chetham Society, Manchester, 1852) vol. I, p. 96.
[29] See, for example, Bailey, *Unquiet Lives*, pp. 172–8.

cases) were brought by wives against their husbands, usually to settle disputes about maintenance. Of those brought by husbands against their wives, some resulted in wives claiming that they had been forced to leave because of their husband's violence. Cruelty could be pleaded as a bar to a suit for restitution for conjugal rights, but wives were not always successful in their claims of violence. In 1821 Sarah Barlee failed to convince the Court of Arches of her husband's cruelty when she answered his case for restitution. She was ordered to return to her husband, but refused, upon which she was imprisoned for several years in Ipswich county jail for contempt of court. Despite the many letters that she wrote from jail appealing her case, the authorities would not agree that her husband's violence sanctioned her desertion.[30]

Finally, just as we will never be able to retrieve the full extent of marital violence in the past, so we will never know its true content. Wives and husbands often gave very different accounts of violence in their marriages, and there is no way for us to determine which version of their stories was the closest to the truth. Neither can these records be seen as providing us with direct access to people's voices. When individuals spoke to magistrates or in the courts, their verbal accounts became the written ones upon which historians rely. Lawyers instructed litigants and witnesses what to say, and court officials could alter the language that was spoken as they recorded it.[31] It is how women and men, instructed by their lawyers, told their stories of violence, what they thought would make their stories most persuasive, and why they became involved in legal proceedings at a particular moment in what could be a lifetime of violence, that is really telling for the historian. How witnesses represented their responses to the violence of others can also be revealing. It is upon these perspectives of married life that this book focuses.

Both Rachael Norcott and Mary Veitch accused their husbands of marital violence in the Court of Arches. By doing so they hoped to achieve a decision of marriage separation from bed and board (*a mensa et thoro*), which would allow them to live legally apart from their husbands. Separation could be obtained from the Court of Arches and the

---

[30] E. Foyster, 'At the limits of liberty: married women and confinement in eighteenth-century England', *Continuity and Change* 17, 1 (2002), 51–2; M. Nevill, 'Women and marriage breakdown in England, 1832–57', PhD thesis, University of Essex (1989), pp. 223–34. The fate of Hester Bach in 1775, who also refused to return to her violent husband after she lost a restitution case was as serious, if less dramatic: she was excommunicated, see LPL, CA, Case 347 (1775), D81, f.204.

[31] For a recent and instructive examination of the 'multi-vocal' nature of court records, see, J. Bailey, 'Voices in court: lawyers' or litigants'?', *Historical Research* 74, 186 (2001), 392–408.

lesser church courts if either spouse could prove cruelty and/or adultery. Until the 1857 Divorce Act, which will be discussed at the end of this book, full divorce with the right to remarry was only available by a private act in parliament, and the grounds for this were restricted to those involving adultery. Thus, for women with violent husbands, a marriage separation was the only formal and legally sanctioned way in which they could end cohabitation. Yet, as we shall see, even marriage separation brought significant disadvantages for women. Their husbands retained all income from their real estate, could seize their personal property and return to claim their future earnings, and until 1839, had the right to the custody of their children.

Such was the desperation of many wives who endured violence from their husbands, that they sought marriage separation despite the difficulties they would face even if their cases were successful. Although there was an overall decline in church court business from the Restoration until the mid-nineteenth century, matrimonial cases came to represent an increasing proportion of those that were heard. Stone estimates, for example, that appeals of all types of cases to the Court of Arches declined to around 200 per decade in the eighteenth century, but that matrimonial cases increased from 10 per cent of all suits between the 1660s and 1760s, to nearly 50 per cent of all cases after 1810.[32] The Court of Arches was based in London and heard appeals from decisions made in church courts in the southern dioceses for the province of Canterbury. Appeals from the northern dioceses were heard at York. The Court of Arches also heard cases in the first instance that came to it via letters of request, which was the option chosen by Mary. Rachael's case had already been heard in the London consistory court and this book also draws upon the records of that court. In addition, this book draws upon a number of separation and restitution cases from the Peculiars of the Archbishop of Canterbury, which arose from parishes outside the diocese of Canterbury that came under the Archbishop's immediate jurisdiction. Further appeal from the Court of Arches or York could be made to the High Court of Delegates until 1834, and to the Judicial Committee of the Privy Council from 1834 to 1858. Historians of marriage have made scarce use of the archives of these highest courts of appeal. Upon appeal, all the records produced in the lower courts would be transferred to these courts. This book uses a total of 220 cases for marriage separation or restitution from the London consistory court, the Peculiars of the Archbishop of Canterbury, the Court of

---

[32] Stone, *Road to Divorce*, pp. 33–5.

Arches, the High Court of Delegates and the Judicial Committee of the Privy Council.[33]

The main documents produced and examined by each of these courts were the same. The 'libel' would contain the plaintiff's accusations, or the reasons for appeal, point by point. This could be answered by the defendant, and either party could pose questions to witnesses in the 'interrogatories'. Witness statements were given in 'depositions'. In marriage separation cases parties could also produce an 'allegation of faculties', which was an estimate of the wealth and income of a husband for the calculation of alimony. All of these documents would be given to the judge for him to come to his decision or sentence. A key feature of this procedure was that all parties were examined in private, and it was a legal system based on written not oral evidence. For the frightened and battered wife, this could be appealing. As one witness was told in a nineteenth-century matrimonial case, 'You need not be at all afraid, for you will not have to appear personally in court, but your evidence will all be taken down in writing in a private room'.[34]

The cost of a marriage separation suit depended on the stage a case reached, and a great many never reached the point of calling witnesses, let alone a final sentence. Initiating a case was relatively inexpensive, and was sometimes all that was needed to produce promises of better behaviour from violent husbands.[35] However, costs accumulated from then onwards and were much higher if the case was contested or appealed. One marriage separation case for cruelty cost just £4 4s 0d in 1746, for a case that had lasted a year, but costs were usually much greater.[36] By the mid-nineteenth century, the average cost of a separation was between £120 and £500. In theory, a husband was liable to pay all the costs of the case, whoever initiated it, but in practice this rule might be modified

---

[33] For the Court of Arches see, M. D. Slatter, 'The records of the Court of Arches', *Journal of Ecclesiastical History* 4 (1953), 139–53, and 'The study of the records of the Court of Arches', *Journal of the Society of Archivists* 1 (1955), 29–31; T. E. James, 'The Court of Arches during the 18th century: its matrimonial jurisdiction', *American Journal of Legal History* 5 (1961), 55–66; M. Barber, 'Records of marriage and divorce in Lambeth Palace', *Genealogists' Magazine* 20, 4 (1980), 109–17, and 'Records of the Court of Arches in Lambeth Palace Library', *Ecclesiastical Law Journal* 3 (1993), 10–19; and J. Houston (ed.), *Index of Cases in the Records of the Court of Arches at Lambeth Palace Library 1660–1913* (London, 1972). For the Delegates see, G. I. O. Duncan, *The High Court of Delegates* (Cambridge, 1986).

[34] As cited in, S. M. Waddams, *Sexual Slander in Nineteenth-Century England: Defamation in the Ecclesiastical Courts, 1815–1855* (Toronto, 2000), p. 79; the system could also have its faults, see pp. 80–1.

[35] See, for example, LPL, CA, Case 4282 (1853), H826/5.

[36] Bailey, *Unquiet Lives*, p. 48.

if his wife had substantial separate wealth.[37] The costs of bringing a case meant that litigants in the church courts were overwhelmingly middle class, and sometimes were men and women of gentry or titled rank. A recent survey of the social status of litigants bringing matrimonial business to the eighteenth-century York, Durham and Oxford church courts, for example, estimated that only 15 per cent of the men were from below the middling sort.[38] Cases in the appeal courts of the High Court of Delegates or the Privy Council were even more socially exclusive. Yet there were exceptions. Elizabeth Fawcett was the daughter of a labourer and had worked as a barmaid in the Golden Lion Hotel in Northallerton, Yorkshire, before she married the farmer, John Linton. She answered his restitution case after she had fled from his violence by bringing a suit for separation on the grounds of cruelty to the Privy Council in 1856.[39] Importantly, the witnesses in these cases often represented a much broader social spectrum than the litigants. The views of servants, apprentices, employees and neighbours about marital violence were recorded in this way.

Another aspect of some of the cases that were decided in the church courts is provided by the printed law reports. These have the advantage of recording the sentence as well as a summary of the proceedings of cases, and most significantly, the remarks by judges that can give the reasons for their decisions. Here we see the legal profession's perspective upon the definitions of marital cruelty. Four volumes of law reports, detailing relevant cases from 1754 to 1855 were used for this study. The law reports were based upon just a selection of cases, however, which were those that set new precedents, or could not resolve a particular legal point. A much wider range of legal records needs to be considered alongside these reports to place their findings into perspective.[40]

More attractive than a church court separation to many couples whose differences in marriage had become irreconcilable, was separation by private deed. This was a contract drawn up by lawyers on terms that had been agreed by a husband, wife and her trustees. By its terms a husband would no longer require cohabitation from his wife, or be responsible for

---

[37] S. Wolfram, 'Divorce in England 1700–1857', *Oxford Journal of Legal Studies* 5, 2 (1985), 166; A. Waddilove, *A Digest of Cases Decided in the Court of Arches* (London, 1849), p. 142; and Nevill, 'Women and marriage breakdown', pp. 201–8.

[38] Bailey, *Unquiet Lives*, p. 13 and Appendix 5.

[39] NA, PCAP1/199 (1856), f.113.

[40] The *English Reports: Ecclesiastical, Admiralty, Probate and Divorce* that were used for this book were vols. 161–4 (Edinburgh and London, 1917–21). For discussion of the use of these records by historians see, Hammerton, *Cruelty and Companionship*, pp. 172–3; and S. Staves, *Married Women's Separate Property in England, 1660–1833* (London, 1990), pp. 12–15.

her debts, and in return would pay a maintenance allowance to her.[41] There were several advantages to the private separation deed. As its name suggests, it was considered a more private way of ending a marriage than pursuing the business in the courts. As the heroine's lawyer in one eighteenth-century novel argued, the privacy of the separation deed was preferable to a court case, 'when the affairs of a family are laid open, and every dispute between the husband and the wife exposed', so that 'the whole becomes a public talk, and furnishes a matter of ridicule for the unthinking scoffers of the Age'.[42] The same grounds or standards of proof were not required in order to achieve a private separation deed, and it could be enforced in the Court of Chancery, even though the deeds were never recognised by the church courts. The ease by which they could be obtained meant that in both the eighteenth and nineteenth centuries they were resorted to by both the middle class and the respectable working class.[43] However, like the separations granted by the church courts, private separations did not give the freedom to remarry, and maintenance payments could subsequently be disputed. It was when one of the parties would not agree to their terms, or when a separated couple were reconciled and violence resumed, that we learn of private deeds of separation.[44]

Perhaps the most common course of action after marital violence, and one that could produce a response that was more immediate, enabling couples to continue their relationships rather than end them, was for a wife to approach her local JP or magistrate.[45] Mary Veitch had complained of the treatment by her husband to a magistrate in August 1837, before she began separation proceedings. She received cold comfort from the magistrate, who dismissed her complaint, and appeared to believe her husband's claims that she was 'mad or had been intoxicated'.[46] Other wives were more successful. The chief benefit of this form of recourse was its flexibility. The notebooks of hard-working magistrates record their efforts at arbitration and reconciliation between

---

[41] For one example of a private separation deed that was subsequently disputed see, NA, KB1/27 Part 6, Mich., 33 Geo.3 no.1, affidavit of James Winton (28 Nov. 1792).

[42] E. Haywood, *The History of Miss Betsy Thoughtless* (1751), ed. B. F. Tobin (Oxford, 1997), p. 534.

[43] Staves, *Married Women's Separate Property*, chapter 6; Doggett, *Marriage, Wife-Beating*, pp. 18–22; O. Anderson, 'State, civil society and separation in Victorian marriage', *Past and Present* 163 (1999), 161–201; Bailey, *Unquiet Lives*, pp. 53–4.

[44] See, for example, LPL, CA, Case 9349 (1823), H346/9; and *Westmeath v. Westmeath* (1826), *English Reports* vol. 162, pp. 1006–7.

[45] For helpful outlines of the procedures that could be followed by JPs see, Bailey, *Unquiet Lives*, pp. 38–46; and B. Capp, *When Gossips Meet: Women, Family, and Neighbourhood in Early Modern England* (Oxford, 2003), pp. 110–14.

[46] LPL, CA, Case 9440 (1837), H550/18.

quarrelling couples. The Bedfordshire magistrate, Samuel Whitbread, for example, had various ways of dealing with the complaints made to him by wives who had been abused by their husbands. He ordered a constable to keep an eye over one violent couple, a husband to show remorse at his violent conduct by paying twenty shillings to a local infirmary, and advised another couple to 'part', presumably because he could see no way in which they could live peacefully together.[47] On other occasions, the simple action of issuing a warrant for a husband to appear before a magistrate was enough to make him capitulate. Based in Wiltshire, the magistrate William Hunt excused several violent husbands who promised better future behaviour, and one wife of a labourer was willing to drop her complaint once her husband promised her one shilling a week towards maintenance.[48] As the editors of another magistrate's notebook have remarked, these responses by JPs, meant that 'while many turned to the law, few went to court'.[49] Going to a magistrate to complain of marital violence was certainly a popular response: Portsmouth's JPs recorded 365 complaints of this nature between 1653 and 1781, and by the 1780s and 1790s an estimated one woman a week was appearing before Middlesex JPs accusing her husband of assault.[50]

If wives wanted to prosecute their husbands further then they could swear on oath that they were in danger and request articles of peace. As we shall see, wives did not always have to prove that physical violence had taken place; threats of physical violence, or other forms of violence could be sufficient. If a magistrate agreed with the wife's version of events, the husband would have to enter a recognisance which was a bond binding him to keep the peace (in other words, refrain from being violent to his wife), or obliging him to appear before the next meeting of the court of quarter sessions, and in the meantime keep the peace. A wife could obtain a recognisance from the King's Bench or the Court of Chancery, as well as directly from her magistrate. Her husband had to pay a small fee for the recognisance, and find sureties for the payment of a much larger sum as a forfeit if he did not adhere to its conditions. Without sureties a violent husband could be committed to a house of

---

[47] A. F. Cirket (ed.), *Samuel Whitbread's Notebooks 1810–11, 1813–14*, Bedfordshire Historical Record Society, 150 (Bedford, 1971), pp. 76, 122, 65.

[48] E. Crittall (ed.), *The Justicing Notebook of William Hunt 1744–1749*, Wiltshire Record Society, 37 (Devizes, 1982), pp. 39, 52, 67.

[49] G. Morgan and P. Rushton (eds.), *The Justicing Notebook (1750–64) of Edmund Tew, Rector of Boldon*, Surtees Society, 205 (Woodbridge, 2000), p. 13.

[50] Warner and Lunny, 'Marital violence', 258–76; A. Clark, 'Humanity or justice? Wife-beating and the law in the eighteenth and nineteenth centuries', in C. Smart (ed.), *Regulating Womanhood: Historical Essays on Marriage, Motherhood and Sexuality* (London, 1992), p. 192.

correction, bridewell or gaol.[51] This was a form of prosecution that was relatively cheap (costing as little as a couple of shillings), and could even be achieved on the same day as a violent incident. It often acted as an effective 'wake-up call' for violent men, that penalised any further misconduct. One nineteenth-century wife from Chatham, Kent, for example, recalled that her husband 'did for some time behave better towards her' after she swore the peace against him.[52] To a certain extent this was also a course of action that put wives in control, since they could decide how far they wanted to pursue prosecution. Many wives withdrew their complaints or requested that their husbands were released from custody after recognisances had been issued.[53] This was also largely a woman's legal tool, since it was extremely rare that husbands would attempt to prosecute their wives for violence in this way.[54] Again, it was a strategy that was taken by women in large numbers. Westminster JPs, for example, drew up 176 recognisances after hearing wives' complaints of marital violence in the years 1685 to 1720.[55]

In contrast, only a small proportion of wives who went to their JPs wished to pursue the most severe form of prosecution, which would involve the issue of an indictment, or formal charge, trial of the husband for assault at the next quarter sessions, and a fine or imprisonment if found guilty. In the Essex quarter sessions between 1620 and 1680, of the 579 indictments for assault, not one was for assault between a husband and wife, and in the last third of the eighteenth century, Peter King could only find a 'handful' of these types of cases. Meanwhile, in Bedfordshire between 1750 and 1840, just one-third of all assaults prosecuted by women (committed both outside and within marriage), were brought by indictment.[56] The explanation for the comparative

---

[51] For examples see, CCRO, Ely and South Witchford Division Minute Book (7 January 1797 to 30 December 1802), f.5r; Crittall (ed.), *Justicing Notebook*, p. 41; and R. Paley (ed.), *Justice in Eighteenth-Century Hackney: The Justicing Notebook of Henry Norris and the Hackney Petty Sessions Book*, London Record Society (London, 1991), p. 18.

[52] LPL, CA, Case 821 (1823), D164, f.73.

[53] For examples see, LMA, Edmonton Petty Session Division: Tottenham, Enfield and Wood Green courts, Minute Book, PS.E/E1/1 (5 October 1848 to 4 December 1851), pp. 34–5; Paley (ed.), *Justice in Eighteenth-Century Hackney*, pp. 13, 27.

[54] For a husband who exhibited articles of peace against his wife see, NA, PCAP 3/2 (1834–6), f.186v.

[55] J. Hurl-Eamon, 'Domestic violence prosecuted: women binding over their husbands for assault at Westminster quarter sessions, 1685–1720', *Journal of Family History* 26, 4 (2001), 435–54.

[56] J. A. Sharpe, 'Domestic homicide in early modern England', *Historical Journal* 24, 1 (1981), 31; P. King, 'Punishing assault: the transformation of attitudes in the English courts', *Journal of Interdisciplinary History* 27, 1 (1996), 54; C. Emsley, *Crime and Society in England, 1750–1900* 2nd edition (Harlow, 1996), pp. 44–6; for procedure at quarter sessions see, N. Landau, 'Appearance at the quarter sessions of eighteenth-century Middlesex', *London Journal* 23, 2 (1998), 30–52.

rarity of this kind of case lies first, with its cost. The fees charged for prosecution by indictment could be more than double those charged for a recognisance.[57] Second, from the mid-eighteenth century wives may have been discouraged from prosecuting their husbands in this way, because it was from this period that sentencing for those found guilty of assault became tougher. Those convicted were more likely to be imprisoned than fined, and those who did escape with a fine, faced far higher financial penalties.[58] Few wives and their children could survive for long periods without the economic contribution of their husbands if they were imprisoned. Third, there could be a significant delay before the case was heard at quarter sessions, making other remedies offered by magistrates appear more attractive. But most importantly, as recognised by one defender of women's legal rights, exposure of a violent husband in a public courtroom, and his subsequent punishment, was hardly likely to provoke harmonious marital relations when he returned home. Wives were confronted with the same problem whether husbands had been forced to appear at quarter sessions because of a recognisance or indictment. '"How can I go home to a man that I have sworn the peace against in open court?"' asked Catherine Ettrick after her violent husband was brought before JPs in January 1765.[59] Subsequent violence of returning husbands could sometimes be linked directly to their wives' legal actions. On the very same day that Thomas Knibbs was bound to keep the peace towards his wife, he struck her on the head, and said it was because she had prosecuted him.[60] Thus although going to a magistrate may have been a popular course of action, alerting the authorities to violence in a marriage, and providing them with information that could be useful if a husband's violence worsened in the future, or he deserted his wife, it did not necessarily provide any long-term safeguard for women.

It is probable, as King argues, that the majority of assault cases were dealt with summarily by magistrates, without the need for a trial or jury, in petty sessions.[61] Presided over by at least two JPs, petty sessions dealt with a wide range of minor offences. In central London, increasing demand on magistrates in sessions, from a growing population, led in 1792 to the establishment of police courts. Despite their name, these courts were controlled and administered by magistrates, and not the police force. Each police court was assigned magistrates, who unlike

---

[57] Bailey, *Unquiet Lives*, p. 44.
[58] King, 'Punishing assault', 49–52.
[59] *The Hardships of the English Laws in Relation to Wives* (London, 1735), p. 33; NA, DEL1/598 (1768), Part I, f.476, Part II, ff.1373–82, 2162–3.
[60] LMA, DL/C/183 (1797), f.331v.
[61] King, 'Punishing assault', 46, 53.

their rural counterparts, were salaried. By the 1850s there were thirteen police courts in metropolitan London, manned by stipendiary magistrates who were required to have at least seven years' experience as barristers. Their powers to punish husbands who they believed were guilty of marital violence increased by two important pieces of legislation in 1828 and 1853, which will be discussed fully at the end of this book. These gave magistrates in petty sessions and in the police courts the ability to summarily convict husbands to imprisonment or hefty fines. A summons obtained at a police court cost two shillings and working-class wives made substantial use of these courts to prosecute their husbands. By 1857, more than 99 per cent of common assaults, and all aggravated assaults were tried summarily rather than being committed to trial at quarter sessions or assizes.[62]

For the historian of marital violence, records of assault have the potential to be illuminating, giving a greater perspective on working- and lower middle-class behaviour and attitudes than can be found in the church courts. Furthermore, because assault was an ill-defined offence, encompassing a wide range of behaviours from threats to physical violence that was only just short of murder, it illustrates well the diverse ways in which contemporaries could think about violent behaviour. Clearly, violence was not just understood to be physical in form; an argument that will be developed in Chapter 1. Yet the primary sources that record how magistrates dealt with cases of marital violence also present substantial difficulties for historians.

Recognisances and indictments were usually no more than a folio in length, and only contain brief information about the parties involved and the nature of the offence. Indictments additionally recorded the verdict and punishment. Their language is formulaic and repetitive. A wealth of detail about the history of the marriage before the violent incident, and the violent incident itself, included as a matter of course in most church court cases, is absent from quarter and petty sessions records. Quarter session bundles rarely include husband's defences or answers to their wives complaints, and witnesses were only occasionally examined. The records created by the petty sessions were even more minimal, and their

---

[62] J. S. Davis, 'A poor man's system of justice: the London police courts in the second half of the nineteenth century', *Historical Journal* 27, 2 (1984), 309–35, and 'Prosecutions and their context: the use of the criminal law in later nineteenth-century London', in D. Hay and F. Snyder (eds.), *Policing and Prosecution in Britain 1750–1850* (Oxford, 1989), pp. 399–400, 413, 416–17, 418–19; V. A. C. Gatrell, 'The decline of theft and violence in Victorian and Edwardian England', in V. A. C. Gatrell, B. Lenman and G. Parker (eds.), *Crime and the Law: The Social History of Crime in Western Europe since 1500* (London, 1980), p. 358.

survival is patchy, especially for the period of this study.[63] Much of the important work that magistrates conducted informally in petty sessions and in the police courts, where the poor often sought advice and adjudication in their disputes rather than legal proceedings, was not minuted. The earliest surviving police court register, which recorded its official business, dates from 1877. It was only from 1857 that full information about the numbers of cases tried summarily began to be recorded.[64]

Nevertheless, as well as magistrates' notebooks that record their out of session decisions, this study includes material from quarter and petty sessions held in a number of different places across England. Given the dearth of official records produced by the early police courts themselves, we are extremely fortunate that some of their decisions were reported in newspapers. This book uses records of *The Times* from the early nineteenth century, which contained regular reports on the business of the London police courts, as well as accounts of trials for assault and domestic homicide that were heard in quarter session and assize courts across the nation. *The Times* was written by middle-class male journalists, often with close connections with the legal profession, predominantly for a middle- and upper-class readership. By 1861 *The Times* could boast a readership of 65,000.[65] Improving literacy rates meant that by the end of our period newspapers could be accessed by many members of the working class, but *The Times* was largely perceived as a newspaper for the establishment.

Like the law reports, newspapers contained only a selection of legal cases. Journalists summarised those that would attract public interest, and in the case of marital violence, this could mean those that were particularly bloody, gruesome or sensational. Cases were favoured that had a decisive outcome, and concern at offending readers' sensibilities could mean that the sexual details of incidents of marital violence were left out, even in reports of stories where physical violence had taken a sexual form.[66] The style of reportage was often melodramatic, with journalists casting husbands and wives into ready stereotypes of violent

---

[63] A point confirmed by the investigations of Hammerton, *Cruelty and Companionship*, p. 175; King, 'Punishing assault', 47; and Morgan and Rushton (eds.), *Justicing Notebook*, p. 11; hence the value of Paley (ed.), *Justice in Eighteenth-Century Hackney*, which contains a transcript of the Hackney petty sessions book.

[64] Gatrell, 'The decline of theft and violence', p. 244.

[65] J. Jones, '"She resisted with all her might": sexual violence against women in late nineteenth-century Manchester and the local press', in S. D'Cruze (ed.), *Everyday Violence in Britain, 1850–1950: Gender and Class* (Harlow, 2000), p. 106.

[66] Nevill, 'Women and marriage breakdown', p. 214, footnote 24; Jones, '"She resisted"', p. 104.

villains and tragic victim heroines. Violent husbands in *The Times* were 'rough', 'savage', 'sullen' or 'brutal' looking, to contrast with their wives who were 'decently clad and extremely clean', 'very little', 'pretty and delicate looking'.[67] Physical appearance and demeanour were presented in this newspaper as key indicators of respectability, reputation and corresponding innocence or guilt. As such, as well as providing us with information from cases in the police courts that were otherwise unrecorded, newspaper reports give us insights into the ways in which contemporaries viewed and described each other and their marital conduct. The language, style and content of these reports can tell us much about the cultural assumptions and values of the period. Newspapers shaped as well as reflected public opinion.[68] Since stories of court cases could also record information about magisterial and judicial decision making, occasional instructions by judges to juries, and the immediate reaction of the public inside and outside the courtroom, newspapers can yield data about the legal process that is otherwise missing from the court records themselves.[69] *The Times* also recorded key parliamentary debates, and occasionally editorial comment on these, which has been used for the writing of this book.

We should not see newspapers as simply providing us with a middle-class view on working-class married life. Ordinary people could regard newspapers as a useful resource. We cannot tell how many husbands and wives played to the press in the public gallery to win support, but we do know that their stories could produce a response. As we shall see, editors could receive letters and charitable donations for afflicted couples, provoked by reports of their situation. Husbands also used the provincial newspapers to advertise for the return of their runaway wives, to declare that they would no longer honour their wives' debts, or to present a

---

[67] For examples, see *The Times* (17 May 1831) 4b; (3 September 1836) 5f; (24 September 1836) 6f; (25 August 1838) 7a; and (25 November 1856) 11e; for this style of crime reporting in the press see also, S. D'Cruze, *Crimes of Outrage: Sex, Violence and Victorian Working Women* (London, 1998), chapter 8, and '"A little, decent-looking woman": violence against nineteenth-century working women and the social history of crime', in A-M. Gallagher, C. Lubelska and L. Ryan (eds.), *Re-presenting the Past: Women and History* (London, 2001), pp. 74–7. 'Amusing' stories from the police courts were also retold in forms of popular literature such as, J. Wight, *Mornings at Bow Street: A Selection of the Most Humourous and Entertaining Reports which have Appeared in the Morning Herald* (London, 1824).

[68] See, for example, P. King, 'Newspaper reporting, prosecution practice and perceptions of urban crime: the Colchester crime wave of 1765', *Continuity and Change* 2, 3 (1987), 423–54.

[69] J. Oldham, 'Law reporting in the London newspapers, 1756–1786', *American Journal of Legal History* 31 (1987), 177–206.

version of their marital history.[70] Thus, there was a popular interaction with the press that is sometimes forgotten.

The final legal option of relevance to some women faced with violent husbands was available from the common law court of King's Bench. As well as offering wives some protection from violence, since articles of peace could be obtained from this court, King's Bench dealt with writs of habeas corpus. The habeas corpus writ had been used from at least the fifteenth century to test the legality of imprisonment. The writ was distinct from the better-known Acts of Habeas Corpus which gave automatic rights to prisoners to request courts of law for trial, bail or discharge. A form of the writ, *ad subjiciendum*, was used by the supporters of wives to order husbands, or other private individuals, to bring the woman they were detaining to the King's Bench. The court only issued the writ if affidavits, or sworn statements, proved that confinement was unjust. As with other forms of marital violence, there was much discussion in our period about the right of husbands to confine their wives. Many believed that confinement in the home was justified if a husband could show that it was a form of correction for some wifely misdemeanour. More worryingly, from the eighteenth century, some husbands took their perceived rights to the extreme, and tried to confine their sane wives in private madhouses. Thus writs of habeas corpus from the King's Bench could be directed to the keepers of private madhouses as well as husbands. Cases of disputed child custody were also heard at King's Bench. Sixty-seven cases that related to child or spouse custody survive for the period 1738 to 1800, and provide further evidence of marital violence and conflict.[71]

Drawing upon this wealth of material from a wide range of primary sources, this book starts at the core of the conjugal relationship, and then moves outwards to consider the impact of marital violence upon children, other family members, and the wider community, ending with a discussion of state legislation that penalised marital violence, and regulated divorce. Throughout, it considers the broad spectrum of violence that was both experienced and defined as acceptable or unacceptable by those living in the period between the Restoration and the mid-nineteenth century. It is written from the premise that the knowledge a husband was permitted, in certain circumstances, to be violent to his

---

[70] For examples, see *Fog's Weekly Journal* 29 May 1731, no.134, 24 July 1731, no.142, 15 April 1732, no.180; and *The Bath Journal* 21 March 1747–48, no. 213; see also, Bailey, *Unquiet Lives*, pp. 56–9.

[71] For King's Bench procedure see R. Gude, *The Practice of the Crown Side of the Court of King's Bench* (London, 1828); and Foyster, 'At the limits of liberty', 41–5.

wife affected all marital relationships. For as any modern-day politician knows, the fear of violence can have a powerful impact upon attitudes and behaviour, even if it bears little relation to the likelihood of violence being experienced at first hand. Ideas about violence in marital relationships created the prevailing social atmosphere in which men and women were raised and wed. Thus the study of marital violence is vital if we are to understand the context in which marriages, both harmonious and violent, were being conducted in this period. First, however, we need to return to Rachael and Mary, and examine in detail the types of violence they endured, and how this violence was defined.

1   Rethinking the histories of violence

While both women experienced forms of marital violence, the ways in which Rachael Norcott in 1666 and Mary Veitch in 1837 described what they had endured were very different. According to Rachael's witnesses, her husband knocked her senseless on the head when she was pregnant, threw a large hammer at her leg so that her ankle nearly broke, struck her with a candlestick and was only narrowly prevented from hitting her with a fire fork, threw her on the floor and dragged her by the arms about the house. John Norcott also repeatedly 'scolded and railed' at his wife, calling her a whore, and he refused to support her financially, giving Rachael no money for food or clothes for at least eight or nine months. Rachael's body was testimony to what she had suffered: her ankle had a permanent scar from her husband's attack that was 'somewhat bigger than half a crown', her wound from being hit with the candlestick could still be seen on her temple, and immediately following each violent incident many witnesses could recall seeing blood and then the black and blue signs of bruising.

James Veitch was also accused of failing to provide Mary with money 'to purchase clothing and other necessaries'. He swore and verbally abused her, threw the contents of the slop basin from their tea over her and once struck her on the face. But the cruelty that was alleged in this marriage consisted more of threats than physical blows. James threatened to throw Mary out of his house or to confine her in a madhouse. After her mother's death he kept Mary confined in their home for three weeks, locking the front door. He threatened that he would separate Mary from her elder daughter from her previous marriage and tried to limit the times she could see the child from their own marriage. The servants were told no longer to obey her orders. The distress of this treatment made Mary ill. She trembled and shook in fear at her husband's presence and needed to spend long periods in bed to recover after their quarrels. By the time she brought her case for marriage separation to the church courts her servants, friends and neighbours described her as a person reduced to a state of nervous exhaustion.[1]

This chapter argues that the differences in the way that violence was represented in the Norcott and Veitch marriages were culturally and historically significant. In both cases, Rachael and Mary had gathered sufficient witnesses to support the view that their husband's behaviour was unacceptable, but the definition of what merited intolerable or cruel violence, and how its consequences were manifest were demonstrably different. In Restoration England stories of marital violence told to the church courts, like Rachael's, focused on types of violence and degrees of severity of violence that were far removed from the accounts told by wives like Mary in early Victorian England. Whereas Rachael and her witnesses centred their complaints on physical violence, by the nineteenth century Mary listed a much wider range of abuses. The emphasis had shifted to one that demonstrated how a husband achieved control over his wife through bullying, humiliation and intimidation, rather than just brute physical force. Others who have read through the marital violence cases that reached the courts across this period have observed, although not explained, similar changes. It has been noted that even by the mid-eighteenth century the physical violence alleged in marriage separation suits was not necessarily life threatening, and tended to be less serious than that described in the seventeenth century. Eighteenth-century women were also including threats of violence in their accusations, and were more likely than their predecessors to accuse their husbands of forcefully confining them in their homes. By the later Victorian period greater attention was being paid to the consequences of violence for the women afflicted.[2]

To start to understand the importance of the changes that the Norcott and Veitch cases demonstrate this chapter addresses three key issues. First, it argues that we need to think about how contemporaries defined violence and recognise that definitions extended far beyond the limited parameters of physical violence often chosen by historians. Second, it shows that there were enduring continuities of attitudes towards marital violence, from the seventeenth to the nineteenth centuries. These centred upon the contradiction that while there were circumstances when individuals could be condemned for the exercise of violence in their relationships, there was never a universal or an

---

[1] LPL, CA, Case 6659 (1666), Eee2, ff.94v–99r, 101–102, 123v–124; LPL, CA, Case 9440 (1837), H550/5,18.

[2] Biggs, *The Concept of Matrimonial Cruelty*, p. 22; Stone, *Road to Divorce*, p. 204; Hammerton, *Cruelty and Companionship*, pp. 127, 129; Bailey, *Unquiet Lives*, pp. 114, 124.

agreed view that violence should play no part in marriage. Third, and finally, it will be argued that a vital change occurred during the period of this study that affected contemporary understandings of marital violence. This was the emergence of the belief that certain types of violence and its consequences, as well as responses to violence, were associated with particular social groups. Class became the main interpretative framework through which marital violence was understood and represented. In the process marital violence was rethought and redefined.

Defining violence

When historians have attempted to provide a broad synthesis of levels of violence in past times they have used records of homicide as their measure. In an article which was typically ambitious in its chronological scope, spanning the years 1300 to 1980, Stone argued that English society had seen a decline in interpersonal violence over time, with the most dramatic decline in the homicide rate occurring between the Restoration and the end of the eighteenth century. This period neatly fitted into the time slot he had suggested in previous work for the development of modern personal relationships based on affection and emotional investment. In Stone's interpretation of the evidence, most homicides from the thirteenth to the mid-seventeenth century were committed against non-family members in a social context where tempers were short and relationships were distant, cold and frequently brutal. From 1660, however, the percentage of homicides committed within the family slowly began to increase. Stone posited that this was the result of closer, and hence more emotionally charged relationships, in which 'sexual passion' rather than 'casual brutality' explained fatal assaults.[3] According to Stone's model, the predictions of the seventeenth-century puritan minister, William Gouge, that 'the nearer and dearer any persons be, the more violent will be that hatred which is fastened on them', were fulfilled.[4]

Stone's theory about the decline of violence attracted immediate historical debate.[5] Jim Sharpe concurred that the proportion of homicides that were domestic in the early modern period was smaller than

---

[3] L. Stone, 'Interpersonal violence in English society 1300–1980', *Past and Present* 101 (1983), 22–33.

[4] As cited in, Sharpe, 'Domestic homicide', 35; spellings have been modernised.

[5] J. A. Sharpe, 'Debate. The history of violence in England: some observations', *Past and Present* 108 (1985), 206–15; Stone replied in 'A rejoinder', *Past and Present* 108 (1985), 216–24.

today. But instead of rates of homicide indicating changes in the nature of personal relationships over the early modern period, Sharpe argued that in Essex the percentage of homicides that were domestic remained stable in the period 1560 to 1709, and that the characteristics of violent crime shared many similarities with today.[6]

While both were more cautious in their use and interpretation of court records, John Beattie and James Cockburn have agreed with Stone that there was 'an unmistakable decline' in Surrey, Sussex and Kent homicide indictments between the sixteenth and the end of the eighteenth centuries. But they have also challenged Stone's and Sharpe's findings on the proportion of domestic homicide. Cockburn argues that when Stone and Sharpe looked at past and present statistics on domestic homicide, they were not comparing like with like (for example, excluding figures for infanticide in early modern studies, when these are included in modern categories of domestic homicide), and that when such crimes are taken into account the proportion of domestic homicides remains relatively steady over time. Significantly, for the purposes of our study, Cockburn found that women continued to represent two-thirds of the victims of conjugal homicide from the sixteenth century until the present day.[7] Thus while all historians of violence agreed with Stone that there was a decline in the number of recorded homicides, and that this was particularly marked for the period between the Restoration and the start of the nineteenth century, it took further research for historians to conclude that there was little change over time in the proportion of homicides that were domestic.

Explanations for the decline in the number of recorded homicides tend to follow the line first advanced by the sociologist Norbert Elias, that as society modernised it became more civilised and populated by well mannered citizens who found means other than violence to settle their differences. From the Restoration there was a change of attitudes to violence, Beattie suggests, perhaps triggered by a 'developing civility' and a 'more highly developed politeness of manner'. Evidence for this change of attitudes can be found in the increasing public intolerance for the violence displayed in blood sports, changing views towards the

---

[6] Sharpe, 'Domestic homicide', 29–48.
[7] J. M. Beattie, *Crime and the Courts in England 1660–1800* (Princeton, 1986), pp. 74–112, 135–9; and 'Violence and society in early-modern England', in A. N. Doob and E. L. Greenspan (eds.), *Perspectives in Criminal Law* (Ontario, 1985), pp. 36–60; J. S. Cockburn, 'Patterns of violence in English society: homicide in Kent 1560–1985', *Past and Present* 130 (1991), 70–106; and 'The nature and incidence of crime in England 1559–1625: a preliminary survey', in J. S. Cockburn (ed.), *Crime in England 1550–1800* (London, 1977), pp. 49–71.

practice of duelling, and eventually in the calls for an end to the cruelties of the slave trade and the abolition of capital punishment.[8] Looking at the public violence of London men from the Restoration until 1740, Robert Shoemaker has argued that physical blows were replaced increasingly by verbal insults, marking 'an important stage in the long-term decline of male violence in England'. In turn, as the eighteenth century progressed, there was a decrease in the use of public insult, and a greater intolerance of words that threatened physical violence. Male honour was no longer achieved or defended via the public display of violence.[9] Most recently, Wiener, looking at the historical context of Victorian homicide and rape cases, has pointed out that changes in attitudes towards violence had a gender dimension, for by condemning violence, contemporaries were focusing on behaviour that was overwhelmingly conducted by men. Hence by the nineteenth century, the march of the 'civilising process' was heavily penalising the physically or sexually aggressive male.[10]

But the reliance that historians have placed upon records of homicide in order to think generally about the history of violence has been too great. There are a number of problems with this choice of evidence and the conclusions that have been drawn from its use. First, the records of homicide were seized upon too readily as indicators of levels of violence. Their appeal was perhaps inevitable. Homicide was a criminal offence prosecuted in the courts. It was a crime that was not easily disguised or concealed, and although there was apparent tolerance for other violent activities, this was a serious offence that was universally condemned. Thus homicide was *the* violent crime that was most likely to be reported. But homicide, even Stone admits, was an extremely rare offence. Histories of homicide give us a picture of exceptional degrees of physical violence. People's experience of violence, as some historians have reminded us, was more 'everyday' than this.[11] Women and men were far

---

[8] N. Elias, *The Civilizing Process: The History of Manners* trans. E. Jephcott (Oxford, 1978); Beattie, *Crime and the Courts*, pp. 112, 135–9; D. T. Andrew, 'The code of honour and its critics: the opposition to duelling in England, 1700–1850', *Social History* 5, 3 (1980), 409–34; R. B. Shoemaker, 'The taming of the duel: masculinity, honour and ritual violence in London, 1660–1800', *Historical Journal* 45, 3 (2002), 525–45.

[9] R. B. Shoemaker, 'Reforming male manners: public insult and the decline of violence in London, 1660–1740', in T. Hitchcock and M. Cohen (eds.), *English Masculinities 1660–1800* (Harlow, 1999), pp. 133–50, 'The decline of public insult in London 1660–1800', *Past and Present* 169 (2000), 97–131, and 'Male honour and the decline of public violence in eighteenth-century London', *Social History* 26, 2 (2001), 190–208.

[10] Wiener, 'The Victorian criminalization of men', pp. 197–212, and *Men of Blood*, passim.

[11] See, for example, S. D. Amussen, 'Punishment, discipline, and power: the social meanings of violence in early modern England', *Journal of British Studies* 34 (1995),

more likely to be subject to less severe forms of physical violence, and more frequently through their lifetimes, than ever participate, witness or become the victims of homicide.

Most seriously, the focus on homicide has meant that violence has been defined too narrowly. We are led to believe that violence was only *physical* in its practice and consequences. Indeed, in an otherwise thought provoking article by Susan Amussen on the understandings of violence during the early modern period, there is the bold assertion that 'violence causes physical harm'.[12] This surely oversimplifies the matter, for as this book will show, contemporaries, like us, did not think of violence in such limited terms. Instead, as the stories about both Rachael Norcott and Mary Veitch demonstrate, they recognised that violence could be physical, verbal and sexual in kind, and that the consequences and damage which it could inflict were experienced and exhibited in a variety of ways.

Within marriage forms of physical violence that were short of murder, and the sexual offence of rape, were not defined as crimes in our period. Hence any attempt to write about domestic violence from the perspective of criminal records will give us a seriously restricted view of the place of violence in married life. But those who have looked at other kinds of records to try and uncover the extent of marital violence have also been liable to thinking about violence simply in physical terms. Many historians (myself included) have used labels such as 'wife-beating' and 'wife-battering' to describe what they are researching, believing that terms such as 'domestic' or 'marital' violence are too gender neutral, and act to desensitise us from the brutality of many assaults.[13] But because 'beating' and 'battering' both emphasise physical violence, these terms underestimate the range of violence to which a woman could be subject. As one witness in an early eighteenth-century case of marital violence explained, 'there were several ways of using a wife ill without beating her'.[14]

Of course, there have been historical studies of verbal and sexual violence. In recent years there has been extensive research conducted into the records of verbal abuse that were heard as cases of defamation

33; and S. D'Cruze, (ed.), *Everyday Violence in Britain, 1850–1950: Gender and Class* (Harlow, 2000).

[12] Amussen, 'Punishment, discipline, and power', 2.

[13] See, for example, E. Foyster, 'Male honour, social control and wife beating in late Stuart England', *Transactions of the Royal Historical Society* 6th series, 6, (1996), 215–24.

[14] As cited in, F. Bound, 'An "uncivil" culture: marital violence and domestic politics in York, c.1660–c.1760', in M. Hallett and J. Rendall (eds.), *Eighteenth-Century York: Culture, Space and Society* (York, 2003), p. 53.

and slander, and are found in the archives of the church and secular courts. Our understanding of how contemporaries viewed and interpreted instances of rape has also been advanced. But it is only very rarely that any historian has attempted to integrate these findings into their overall thinking about the meanings of violence in the past.[15] Meanwhile, historians of women's lives who have an interest in their experiences of violence have tended to conduct separate studies into sexual and physical abuse. The classic example is the work by the historian Clark. In two equally groundbreaking books she considered first sexual assault, and then wife beating, but with little discussion of the links between them.[16] Such a division of interests would have been anomalous to many married women living in the early modern period. For as we shall see, women in violent marriages were often subject to a combination of sexual and physical violence. That male abuse of the marriage vows could manifest itself in multiple forms was even recognised to a limited extent by the church courts, which allowed women to sue for separation on the combined as well as separate grounds of adultery and cruelty.

What forms could violence take? Within marriage, violence in all its forms was sexualised. The very context of marital violence was within a sexual relationship. Physical violence often focused upon the genitals, breasts or womb. Frequently, as Rachael Norcott found, violence between couples broke out when they were in bed. Verbal abuse in marriage, as Rachael also experienced, often consisted of sexual insults. Accusations of violence in marriage separation cases that came to the church courts on the combined grounds of adultery and cruelty were concerned largely with the transmission of venereal disease from an adulterous husband to his wife. Physical force was usually involved in sexual violence, and signs of physical injury could be the only evidence

---

[15] For examples of work on defamation see J. A. Sharpe, *Defamation and Sexual Slander in Early Modern England: The Church Courts at York* Borthwick Papers, 58 (York, 1980), M. Ingram, *Church Courts, Sex and Marriage in England, 1570–1640* (Cambridge, 1987), and L. Gowing, *Domestic Dangers: Women, Words, and Sex in Early Modern London* (Oxford, 1996); for examples of work on rape see R. Porter, 'Rape – Does it have a historical meaning?', in S. Tomaselli and R. Porter, (eds.), *Rape: An Historical and Social Enquiry* (Oxford, 1986), pp. 216–79, A. Clark, *Women's Silence Men's Violence: Sexual Assault in England 1770–1845* (London, 1987), G. Walker, 'Rereading rape and sexual violence in early modern England', *Gender and History* 10, 1 (1998), 1–25, and J. D. Gammon, 'Ravishment and ruin: the construction of stories of sexual violence in England, c.1640–1820', PhD thesis, University of Essex (2000); rare exceptions are Beattie, who considers the crimes of rape and attempted rape in his survey of 'Violent offenses' in *Crime and the Courts*, pp. 124–32, and Wiener, *Men of Blood*, chapters 3–4.

[16] Clark, *Women's Silence Men's Violence*; and *The Struggle for the Breeches*.

that sexual assault had taken place. Since unwanted or manipulative sex can be interpreted as 'an additional encroachment on and domination of parts of the body', it can be seen as another form of physical violence. Thus the inter-relationship of these different kinds of violence makes their separate study by historians a dangerous venture.

For some men forms of violence and dominance over women could be sexually arousing. Nevertheless, Randolph Trumbach's claim that 'violence against women was in the eighteenth century a major source of sexual excitement for men', is sensational and unsubstantiated by his evidence. A survey of cases of marital violence used for this book suggests that Trumbach's theory of men's motive for violence is wildly exaggerated.[17] What testimonies of sexual violence in marriage do provide us with is further evidence of the 'substantial gulf between legal and popular understandings of rape'. As Laura Gowing has argued, we need to look further than criminal trials for rape to get an accurate picture of the extent of sexual assault in the past.[18] Just because there was no legal offence of marital rape, does not mean that sexual assault was not experienced, resisted or described in marriage as a violation of a wife's body. Indeed, the etymology of the word 'violence', derived from 'violate', suggests that it had long been associated with the forceful infringement and intrusion of sexual spaces.[19]

We also need to pay more attention to how the operation of violence affected its definition. For example, as we shall see in Chapter 3 on Children and Marital Violence, when women described themselves as the targets of violence, this did not necessarily mean that violence had been inflicted upon them. Instead, violence for women could be defined as something that had been directed towards others – notably, their children. The men who perpetrated this violence could intend it to affect both mother and child. Thus, even without physical or sexual contact with violence, a woman could be harmed by its practice.

Ultimately, studies of violence which take homicide as their starting point give a limited perspective on gender relations. This is because the

[17] Trumbach, *Sex and the Gender Revolution*, p. 325. For a more balanced discussion of sexual violence see, A. Browne, *When Battered Women Kill* (New York, 1987), chapter 6; G. Savage, '"The wilful communication of a loathsome disease": Marital conflict and venereal disease in Victorian England', *Victorian Studies* 34, 1 (1990), 35–54; J. Hearn, 'Men's violence to known women: historical, everyday and theoretical constructions by men', in B. Fawcett, B. Featherstone, J. Hearn and C. Toft (eds.), *Violence and Gender Relations: Theories and Interventions* (London, 1996), pp. 32–3; D'Cruze, *Crimes of Outrage*, pp. 18–20; and S. D'Cruze, 'Introduction. Unguarded passions: violence, history and the everyday', in D'Cruze, (ed.), *Everyday Violence*, p. 17.

[18] L. Gowing, *Common Bodies: Women, Touch and Power in Seventeenth-Century England* (New Haven and London, 2003), chapter 3, especially pp. 90, 101.

[19] Wiener, *Men of Blood*, p. 10.

evidence they yield casts men overwhelmingly into the role of the per-petrators, and women as the 'victims' of violence.[20] Without a doubt, most homicides were committed by men. But, by taking a wider defin-ition of violence, particularly one that includes verbal abuse, we can gain a more accurate and balanced view of the operation of violence within marriages in the past. There was, as we shall see, variation in the ways in which female violence was represented. However, assuming the same definitions of violence as contemporaries allows us to give greater consideration to the part that women played in the violent power struggles of their marriages, and certainly displaces the notion that women were passive victims. Violence was not always simply directed from one person to another; instead, it was a dynamic field of force that could exist between people and within relationships.

In addition, the present study of marital violence will demonstrate that violence affected more individuals than any criminal indictment after a violent incident would seem to imply. Rather than simply involv-ing a perpetrator and victim, marital violence was understood to affect its witnesses, and to have consequences for both family and non-family members. Violence within a marriage bore significance far beyond the conjugal unit, and its effects permeated into society as a whole.

We certainly need to develop a more sophisticated understanding of the relationship between the different forms of violence in the past. Like Francis Place and other early nineteenth-century commentators who looked back upon the eighteenth century as a more brutal and dangerous age, Shoemaker interprets a decline in physical violence on the streets as a measure of progress towards a more civilised age.[21] As such, he creates a scale for assessing the gradations of violence, in which verbal violence is assumed to be less serious, alarming or damaging in its consequences than physical violence. As this chapter will demonstrate, and the ac-counts of Rachael's and Mary's marriages have already started to show, in the domestic context violence appears to have been defined in quite different ways. The forms of violence were not viewed as separate or alternative entities, in which one type of violence could be replaced or substituted by another. Instead violence as it was commonly experienced was described as a continuum, in which its verbal, sexual and physical forms could all merge and be part of an interlocking and devastating whole.[22] The distress of those women who endured verbal abuse from

---

[20] I use the term 'victim' guardedly for reasons that will be explained in the next chapter.

[21] Shoemaker, 'Reforming male manners', 133–150; for the views of Francis Place and others see, Beattie, 'Violence and society', 53–4.

[22] G. Walker, *Crime, Gender and Social Order in Early Modern England* (Cambridge, 2003), p. 23.

their husbands, counters any notion that this was regarded as a more 'respectable', 'genteel', or acceptable means for men to pursue their marital conflicts.

In summary, hitherto historians have defined violence too narrowly, in ways that were alien to those living between the seventeenth and nineteenth centuries. Studying marital violence allows us to widen the parameters of our thinking about violence to include a broader range of behaviour. By looking at evidence of violence in accounts of marital conflict, rather than relying upon the records of criminal proceedings, we can gain a more fully integrated picture of the forms and meanings of violence, and a deeper understanding of the operation of violence in the relationships between women and men. The common characteristics of marital violence, which meant that it was often conducted in front of others, and in both domestic and 'public' spaces, also enables us to question the extent to which we can separate 'public' from 'private' forms of violence. For all the arguments that have been forwarded to explain the apparent decline in the number of reported homicides over time, none explain why civilising or reforming influences upon male behaviour stopped short at the door of the family home. One of the contentions of this book is that the key to understanding the lack of change in the proportion of homicides that were domestic, is found by examining attitudes towards non-lethal forms of domestic violence. Once we recognise the fundamental continuities in attitudes towards marital violence across this period, the statistics on domestic homicide are put into perspective. It is to these continuities that we must now turn.

Defining cruel violence: continuities

Throughout the period from the Restoration to the mid-nineteenth century violence was regarded by many as an acceptable way to resolve disputes and settle the balance of power within marriage. The belief that husbands could legitimately use physical force to correct their wives continued to have a place in popular culture. Nevertheless, this view co-existed with common understandings of the circumstances, levels and types of violence that were always seen as so intolerable that they were cruel. Across the period, there were also appeals to men to exercise self-control in their exercise of marital authority. If we look at legal statements about violence, lay interpretations of violent incidents, and injunctions to men to limit their use of violence, we can learn how and why marital violence was repeatedly defined as cruel.

(1) Marital violence and the law   In the eighteenth century key legal commentators supported the view that husbands had a right to chastise their wives physically. Matthew Bacon's *New Abridgement of the Law*, first published in 1736, and reprinted through seven editions until 1832, stated that:

The husband hath, by law, power and dominion over his wife, and may keep her by force within the bounds of duty, and may beat her, but not in a violent or cruel manner; for, in such case, or if he but threaten to beat her outrageously, or use her barbarously, she may bind him to the peace.[23]

In similar terms, the famous commentator on eighteenth-century law, Sir William Blackstone, wrote that according to tradition, a husband:

might give his wife moderate correction. For as he is to answer for her misbehaviour, the law thought it reasonable to intrust him with this power of restraining her, by domestic chastisement . . . But this power of correction was confined within reasonable bounds.[24]

Although the use of physical correction is condoned, in both these legal texts the writers set limitations upon the extent of physical violence that husbands can inflict upon their wives. It should not be 'outrageous' or 'barbarous', but instead should be confined to correction that is 'reasonable' and in proportion to the wife's 'misbehaviour'. Bacon accepts that a husband may beat his wife, but writes that this should not be in a "violent" way. The use of the word 'violent' in this context may seem strange to us, but as the historian Amussen explains, in this period 'people used the word "violent" when they wished to suggest that behaviour was inappropriate or illegitimate'.[25]

Most importantly, correction could not be 'cruel', for cruel violence merited legal redress. Bacon refers to a woman's right to appeal to the courts after cruel violence, in order to have her husband bound over to keep the peace. Women who were subject to cruel violence from their husbands could also pursue a marriage separation 'from bed and board' (*a mensa et thoro*) from their husbands. In this context, 'cruelty' was a legal category. Since not all violence within marriage was regarded as unacceptable, it became vital for women who wished to pursue these legal options successfully, to draw attention to the forms and occasions of violence that were so excessive or 'unreasonable' that they were cruel.

---

[23] M. Bacon, *A New Abridgment of the Law* 7 vols. (London, 1807 ed.), I, 457, as cited in Doggett, *Marriage, Wife-Beating*, p. 10.
[24] W. Blackstone, *Commentaries on the Laws of England* 4 vols. (Oxford, 1783 ed.), I, 444.
[25] Amussen, 'Punishment', 3.

What at first appeared to many to be the most indisputable way of proving that marital violence had been cruel, was to show that it had been life threatening. If physical violence was such that it endangered 'life, limb or health', then it was thought that the law should be enacted to protect one spouse from the other, and that the duty of both marriage partners to cohabit could be relinquished.[26] Hence women who complained of their husband's violence to magistrates ensured that those they addressed were fully aware of the dangers they faced if intervention did not follow. The JP Henry Norris, for example, recorded the statements of Thomasin Wheeler of Cambridge Heath as she appeared before him on four occasions between 1731 and 1735, each time complaining that her husband had threatened to kill her, or that his violence had been very 'barbarous'.[27] In the church courts, many women who sought marriage separation included statements, supported by their witnesses, arguing that the cruelty of their husbands was such that they could not continue to live in safety with them. One of Rachael Norcott's sisters, for example, stated that John was so cruel that Rachael could not 'live or cohabit with him without manifest danger of her life or limbs or both'. James Veitch was said to be in such a habit of 'constantly swearing at and abusing and threatening' Mary that this 'excited' in her a 'reasonable apprehension of bodily hurt and to the very great and manifest injury of her health'. Other wives said that it was because they feared for their lives that they had been forced to leave their husbands.[28] It is significant that these women were not questioning the right of their husbands to exercise violence against them per se, rather they were disputing the extent or degree of violence to which they had been subject.

Such pleading strategies may have been effective because they did not amount to any challenge to men's authority, and because neither magistrates nor judges wanted the subsequent death of a wife on their consciences. But there is also evidence that by the eighteenth century this tactic was beginning to wear thin. Faced with another wife accusing her husband of cruelty, Norris wearily began to adopt a shorthand for these women's complaints; 'She goes in danger of her life &c from him', he recorded after seeing Sibilla Hunt on 13 October 1735.[29] In the church courts statements about life being endangered by violence became formulaic, and were entered as a matter of course during women's libels.

---

[26] Biggs, *The Concept of Matrimonial Cruelty*, pp. 10, 17.

[27] Paley (ed.), *Justice in Eighteenth-Century Hackney*, pp. 2, 12–13, 21, 26, 27.

[28] LPL, CA, Case 6659 (1666), Eee2, f.95v; LPL, CA, Case 9440 (1837), H550/5; see also, LPL, CA, Case 3789 (1662), Ee1, f.401r; and LPL CA, Case 7022 (1748), D1573, ff.43r,53r.

[29] Paley (ed.), *Justice in Eighteenth-Century Hackney*, p. 30.

Determining whether physical violence was life threatening had become an issue for subjective judgement, and so was no longer a reliable indicator of what was cruel violence.

Perhaps the most frequently repeated statement of what lawyers regarded as cruel violence within marriage was made by Sir William Scott, Lord Stowell, during his judgement on the Evans marriage separation case heard in July 1790. Posing the question 'What is cruelty?', Scott said:

> It is the duty of the Courts, and consequently the inclination of Courts, to keep the rule extremely strict. The causes must be grave and weighty, and such as shew an absolute impossibility that the duties of the married life can be discharged; for the duty of self-preservation must take place before the duties of marriage . . . What merely wounds the mental feelings is in few cases to be admitted where they are not accompanied by bodily injury, either actual or menaced. Mere austerity of temper, petulance of manners, rudeness of language, a want of civil attention and accommodation, even occasional sallies of passion, if they do not threaten bodily harm, do not amount to legal cruelty: they are high moral offences in the marriage-state undoubtedly . . . but still they are not that cruelty against which the law can relieve . . . Still less is it cruelty where it wounds not the natural feelings, but the acquired feelings arising from a particular rank and situation; for the Court has no scale of sensibilities by which it can gauge the quantum of injury done and felt; and, therefore, though the Court will not absolutely exclude considerations of that sort, where they are stated merely as matter of aggravation, yet they cannot constitute cruelty where it would not otherwise have existed.[30]

To reach this definition of cruelty, Scott considered both the type of violent act and its consequences. At first, it appears to confirm the traditional view that cruel violence was something that endangered life. Scott's references to 'bodily injury' and 'bodily harm' suggest that what was important in determining cruelty was evidence of physical violence that caused harm to physical health. Yet in this decision on the Evans case, as John Biggs has recognised, 'the ground was laid for an extension of the definition of cruelty'.[31] This is because Scott's statement, perhaps deliberately, left considerable loopholes which allowed for variation in its future interpretation.

First, bodily injury could be 'actual or menaced'. Threats of violence or a 'reasonable apprehension of bodily hurt' would be sufficient to prove cruelty, in Scott's view, 'because assuredly the Court is not to wait till the hurt is actually done'.[32] This meant that in theory, no physical

[30] *Evans v. Evans* (1790), *English Reports* vol. 161, p. 467.
[31] Biggs, *The Concept of Matrimonial Cruelty*, p. 24.
[32] *Evans v. Evans* (1790), *English Reports* vol. 161, p. 468.

violence needed to have taken place for a woman to accuse her husband of marital cruelty. To determine whether a wife's fears were 'reasonable' subsequent judges asked to be supplied with details of a husband's temper, conduct and general demeanour towards his wife. It was in the recounting of this information that many women provided evidence of violence that had involved economic deprivation, or was verbal or sexual in its nature. Inadvertently, Scott gave couples license to describe the history of their marriages more fully than the courts had previously allowed.

Second, the judgement on the Evans case did recognise that within marital relationships there could be forms of cruelty other than physical violence. Thus Scott listed 'austerity of temper, petulance of manners, rudeness of language', and so on. To Scott these were 'high moral offences' but could only be considered in the context of incidents of threatened or actual physical violence, when they would be regarded by the courts as 'aggravating' circumstances. However, as we shall see, by the mid-nineteenth century this type of evidence alone was sometimes central to accusations of cruelty.

Third, Scott did not rule out the possibility that cruelty to 'mental feelings' could be addressed, since he said that it was 'in few cases to be admitted'. The ambiguity of this statement continued into Scott's discussion of the issue of social status. Scott's reluctance to include the matter of social position within the definition of cruelty seemed to arise from his realisation of the practicable difficulties that the courts would face in assessing the worth of such claims, rather than from any rejection of the idea that the consequences of marital violence, or extent of 'wounded feelings', varied according to class. As a result, 'the Court will not absolutely exclude considerations of that sort, where they are stated merely as matter of aggravation'. In the final section of this chapter we will see why this section of the definition was to become so important.

Perhaps one of the reasons why this judgement was cited so often after 1790 was because it could be all things to all women and men. The ruling on the Evans case was repeated across the period, and as we shall see, was even discussed when MPs came to discuss divorce reform in the mid-nineteenth century. But although the same case continued to be cited, and Scott's words were often quoted, it was used to justify a changing and expanding definition of violence that was cruel. No other judge attempted a definition of cruelty. Dr Lushington, for example, in his ruling on the Neeld separation case in 1831 refused to provide, 'a definition of what is, or what is not, legal cruelty, because I think it exceedingly difficult, and it may be dangerous, for any one to lay down, in terms sufficiently clear and comprehensive, the nature of an offence which might, under different circumstances, assume so many and such varied shapes'.[33] It is little wonder that when Alfred Waddilove came to examine the law on marital cruelty for his nineteenth-century digest of cases, he came to the conclusion that 'it is difficult to lay down, under the infinite variety of possible cases that may come before the Court, any safe definition of cruelty'.[34] By the early nineteenth century, such was the changing and diverse range of complaints that were made under the banner of 'cruel violence', that providing a single legal definition had become an impossibility. To do so would be 'dangerous' or 'unsafe' because this would remove a flexibility of definition which the varied nature of marital violence required.

What we have been dealing with so far is male legal thinking about violence. But outside the legal profession, others reached their own independent definitions of cruelty. Indeed, there is much to suggest that judgements such as that made in the Evans case were simply reflecting and formalising changes in popular attitudes that had begun long before them. As we shall see, lay understandings of cruel violence extended far beyond the narrow definitions of physical violence that damaged 'life, limb or health'. As well as the physical cruelty of punches, blows and beatings, there were accusations of inadequate supply of food or clothing, lack of care during pregnancy or sickness, verbal insults and threats, physical constraint and confinement, and forced or 'unnatural' sexual intercourse.[35] The consequences of such violence were described in ways which demonstrated that danger to health was interpreted to mean harm to mental and sexual health, as well as to physical health or well-being. Evidence was supplied of cuts, bruises, broken bones and of miscarriages, but also of crying, 'low spirits', self-harm, suicide attempts, fits of 'hysteria', and insanity. So in contemporary thinking, the cruel and violent husband need not have been one who had been physically violent to his wife.

In the period from the Restoration until the mid-nineteenth century, not all violence within marriage was regarded as cruel. Unlike the other main offence against the marital vows; adultery, there was no explicit Biblical commandment against violence within marriage. As we have seen, legal arbiters in this period believed that there were circumstances in which a husband could legitimately use physical violence against his wife. But they did not provide a clear definition of when that violence

---

[33] *Neeld v. Neeld* (1831), *English Reports* vol. 162, p. 1443.

[34] Waddilove, *A Digest of Cases*, p. 154.

[35] 'Unnatural' relations were defined at this time as sex that was anal, conducted during a woman's menstruation, or involved flagellation.

amounted to cruelty. Hence violence within marriage was never an absolute and unambiguous moral or legal wrong. This meant that cruelty was always a matter for subjective judgement, and allowed the notions of what constituted cruel violence to change over time, and vary between individuals and social groups.

In practice, before a complaint of violence could reach any legal chamber a significant number of people had to concur that the violence had been cruel. So historians could define cruel violence in this period as violence that provoked a response or intervention by individuals outside the conjugal unit. An overview of the available evidence tells us that in this period a response was most likely when violence amounted to an abuse of authority. That is, when a person in a 'superior' position of power (such as a husband, father or employer) inflicted violence upon an individual in an 'inferior' position (such as a wife, child or employee). Hence violence was generally not labelled as 'cruel' when it was inflicted upon a social equal; in the situation of two male friends fighting, for example. Husbands who faced violence from their wives were in a problematic position if they wanted to voice publicly their objection to such behaviour, precisely because cruel violence was so often formulated as unreasonable behaviour inflicted by a superior upon an inferior. As a recent writer on the issue of 'battered husbands' has noted, 'dependency has been a key notion in identifying victims of family violence. Children, the elderly, and women fit more easily into this category than adult men do'.[36]

Furthermore, such was the acceptance of violence within marriage, that it was rare that a single violent incident would warrant a response. Instead, witness statements reveal that violence within marriage became cruel in what could be a slow and painful cumulative process in which women could sometimes endure years of abuse. What was then the turning point, provoking intervention, and sometimes legal action, rested on a range of factors. Crucially, this is because throughout our period, in both lay and legal terms, the definition of cruel violence was one that was circumstantial and contextual. Just four years after his ruling on the Evans case, Scott was to emphasise the importance of this. For in *D'Aguilar v. D'Aguilar* he stated, 'there may be relative cruelty: and what is tolerable by one may not be by another'.[37] If we now turn to look in detail at the stories of marital violence that were told in our period to officials and in the courts, we will see how Scott had

---

[36] B. Lucal, 'The problem with "battered husbands"', *Deviant Behavior: An Interdisciplinary Journal* 16 (1995), 107; male accusations of violence and cruelty by wives will be fully explored in Chapter 2.

[37] *D'Aguilar v. D'Aguilar* (1794), *English Reports* vol. 162, p. 753.

arrived at this conclusion, and what it meant in practice to women's and men's lives.

(2) Marital violence and economic deprivation There is a growing consensus among historians that if we want to understand marriage in the past, we have to appreciate its economic basis. The importance of economic factors in the decision to get married and in the choice of partner merely marked the start of the material life of any marriage. As one recent historian of marriage has argued, husbands and wives were in a position of co-dependency, in which both were providers and consumers in a family economy. Individual reputation and credit depended upon the ability of both spouses to produce, consume and manage economic resources in an effective and efficient way. Most importantly, contemporaries believed that the distribution of economic resources between wives and husbands reflected the balance of power in marriage, and therefore was a measure of its emotional content and level of harmony.[38]

Thus it should not surprise us that a key similarity of the complaints made by Rachael Norcott and Mary Veitch was their inclusion of accusations of material neglect and deprivation by their husbands. As we shall see, many other wives across the period, and from all social groups, included economic concerns within their accusations of marital violence. The failure of their husbands to share the economic resources of the household in a fair and equitable way was presented as evidence of marital cruelty. Forms of economic deprivation were not types of violence, but to contemporaries, they were what could make other forms of violent behaviour cruel. They exacerbated other forms of violence, and they were a key indicator of the state of relationships within a marriage. The accusations that women made provide us with unique insights into their material worlds. Whether wives could be confident that others would support them in their stories of violence depended, as it will be demonstrated, on the context in which it had taken place, and particularly on the individual and personal circumstances of each wife involved.

Upon marriage, according to the legal doctrine of coverture, all a wife's property became her husband's. In return a husband had a common law duty to provide his wife with the 'necessaries' of life; food, clothing, shelter, and when needed, medical care.[39] The supply of these

---

[38] Bailey, *Unquiet Lives*, chapters 4–5.
[39] Blackstone, *Commentaries* I, 442; Staves, *Married Women's Separate Property*, p. 131; J. Bailey, 'Favoured or oppressed? Married women, property and 'coverture' in England, 1660–1800', *Continuity and Change* 17, 3 (2002), 351–72.

necessaries was so fundamental to the concept of marital union in this period that one of the legal ways of being released from marriage was to seek a separation from 'bed and board'.

Wives who complained of their husband's violence to magistrates frequently remarked upon the failure of their husbands to provide them with necessaries. The Wiltshire magistrate, William Hunt, for example, recorded in his notebook on the 10 September 1746, that he had seen Grace Collings, the wife of a labourer, who charged her husband with 'refusing to maintain her', as well as 'assaulting and beating' her.[40] Sometimes this type of cruelty took a more dramatic form, as was described to the Ely quarter sessions in 1743–44. Witnesses to the marriage of John and Hester Watson related how John had torn his wife's clothes during his violence to her, on one occasion stripped her naked in public, and had thrown her bedding with her out of the house. John's humiliation of his wife by removing her clothing and the focus of his anger on the possessions from their bedchamber demonstrate how forms of economic cruelty and sexual violence could be intricately bound. His determination to destroy his wife's belongings, and rid himself of all that reminded him of her, was accompanied by his threats, repeated on several occasions, 'that he would sell all, and leave her his said wife'.[41] The prospect of a husband deserting his wife would have rung alarm bells for any magistrate, for if there was no husband to supply necessaries, a parish could become liable for their provision. It seems probable, therefore, that when women such as Elizabeth Jackson, married to a labourer, were examined by magistrates, they knew it was important to emphasise the financial repercussions of their husband's violent behaviour. She told them that her husband had,

several times beaten [her] . . . in a very barbarous manner, giving her heavy blows, sometimes with his fist, and one time two or three blows with the wooden end of his hatchet; that he allows her nothing towards maintaining her self and her child by him, which child is not quite seven weeks old, that he hath often said that the Parish shall maintain her without his contributing anything.[42]

The lack of material provision that accompanied the physical violence that Elizabeth suffered was presented as amounting to cruelty, in part, because it was affecting her child as well as herself. Here we begin to see examples of how popular understandings of the concept of cruel violence within marriage were based on an assessment of circumstances. For the complaints of wives like Elizabeth reveal the expectation that

---

[40] Crittall, (ed.), *The Justicing Notebook of William Hunt*, p. 54.
[41] CUL, EDR, Quarter Sessions Files, E47, ff.3,4,6–10; E48.
[42] CUL, EDR, Quarter Sessions Files, E47, f.5.

a man's responsibility to supply necessaries would increase with fatherhood. The cruelty of not fulfilling the marital duty of material provision
was heightened when there were children involved, especially when a
wife had very young children, or a large number of them. As a consequence, magistrates such as Henry Norris were careful to note the detail
which they were given about the children of wives who complained to
them of their husband's violence. For example, Norris saw Hannah
Preston in December 1731 and September 1733. Particularly on the
first occasion her accusations of cruelty centred upon her husband's lack
of maintenance:

Complaint made by Hannah Preston agt: her husband Edward Preston for
Spending his mo: Idly and neglecting to maintain his family, being a wife & 2
Children & threatning his wife.

Norris issued a warrant for Edward Preston to appear before him at the
next petty sessions. By the time Hannah made her next complaint to
Norris in 1733, she had three children, and Norris meticulously
recorded their ages of nine, three, and under one year old. With such a
young family to support, he could not afford to ignore her complaints.[43]

Charges of material deprivation were made in the church courts
during marriage separation cases, as well as in front of magistrates. Some
women in the church courts claimed to have suffered years of physical
hardship. For example, Dorothy Lumley said that in her eight years of
marriage her husband had never bought her any clothes, 'although she
hath for several years last past been in great necessity for the same', and
Mary Luck told the London consistory court in 1803 that her husband
frequently left her without any money for food, and in the winter, would
lock up the coal cellar so that she could not light a fire to keep warm.[44]
Others said that they only survived through begging for material support
from their neighbours, friends and relations.[45] Asking for money to
purchase necessities could strike a raw nerve with men who were aware
that it was their obligation to provide for their families, and could
provoke an angry, violent response.[46] The denial of necessaries was

---

[43] Paley, (ed.), *Justice in Eighteenth-Century Hackney*, pp. 7, 21; the topic of children and
marital violence will be discussed in Chapter 3.

[44] LMA, DL/C, 177 (1774), f.372r; DL/C/187 (1803), f.37v; for similar complaints
about the lack of provision in the English church courts and quarter sessions, see
Bailey, *Unquiet Lives*, pp. 64–7; and for comparison with the situation of wives elsewhere see, J. M. Ferraro, 'The power to decide: battered wives in early modern Venice',
Renaissance Quarterly 68, 3 (1995), 501–6.

[45] See, for example, LPL, CA, Case 7129 (1730), D1610, ff.41v–42r, and NA, DEL1/
285 (1709), f.72r.

[46] See, for example, LMA, DL/C/178, (1777), ff.572r,573r.

represented by women as a form of cruelty that could cause damage to 'life, limb or health' which could be as harmful as physical blows. For instance, Mary Dawson, the wife of a commander of a ship, accused her husband of refusing to supply her with necessaries, said that he had prevented their married daughter from giving her money for food, and had told their butcher not to allow her any more meat. 'By such treatment', she argued, her 'health . . . became much injured'.[47]

Failure to supply necessaries could be central to women's definitions of cruelty, as becomes apparent when we examine their writings and personal testimonies about marriage. This was certainly the case for Elizabeth Freke, a Norfolk gentlewoman, who wrote two versions of her life story, beginning each with her marriage. Elizabeth struggled for years to keep a trust, which she held on behalf of herself and her son, protected from her husband's use. As such, her experiences serve as a good example of the difficulties that wives faced under the legal theory of coverture. Although Freke complained of the 'ill usage' she received from her husband, as far as we can tell, Percy Freke was never physically violent to his wife. Instead, in Elizabeth's eyes, his cruelty was one of abandonment and lack of material provision. Absent for sometimes years at a time while he managed their estates in Ireland, on one occasion she bitterly records, 'Mr Frek thus leaving me to my shiffts without any pitty or comiseration'. The result was that Elizabeth used the first version of her autobiography to let out her initial anger and frustration at her 'unkind husban; [who] never in his life took any care for me or whatt I did'.[48]

Elizabeth's account of her marriage shows that goods meant more to wives than the term 'necessaries' might suggest. The period that this book covers has been identified as one when thanks to industrialisation and commercialisation, there was an increasing range of goods on offer. Research into patterns of consumption is a burgeoning historical field, and there is particularly lively debate about how far goods held different significance for women and men.[49] Many case studies of the

---

[47] LMA, DL/C/182 (1799), f.386r.

[48] R. A. Anselment (ed.), *The Remembrances of Elizabeth Freke, 1671–1714*, Camden Fifth Series, Vol. 18, (Cambridge, 2001), pp. 49, 73, 53; for an account of this marriage see, Fletcher, *Gender, Sex and Subordination*, pp. 163–4.

[49] The literature on the subject of consumption and gender is extensive. Good starting points are L. Weatherill, 'A possession of one's own: women and consumer behavior in England, 1660–1740', *Journal of British Studies* 25 (1986), 131–56; M. Berg, 'Women's consumption and the industrial classes of eighteenth-century England', *Journal of Social History* 30, 2 (1996), 415–34; E. Kowaleski-Wallace, *Consuming Subjects: Women, Shopping, and Business in the Eighteenth Century* (New York, 1997); M. Finn, 'Men's things: masculine possession in the consumer revolution', *Social History* 25, 3 (2000), 133–55; and H. Berry, 'Women, consumption and taste', in H. Barker and E. Chalus (eds.), *Women's History: Britain, 1700–1850* (forthcoming from Routledge).

consumption patterns of individuals based on inventories, wills and personal papers have been written.[50] The perspective we gain from records of marriage breakdown, however, strongly suggests that we should look more closely at these consumers with regard to their personal relationships. For goods assumed an important dynamic of meanings between people and within relationships. Goods 'have a relational value . . . They do not just have a static, narcissistic function, attributing status and identity – they also serve to reinforce social relations'. Objects were used by people to 'mediate their relations with one another' in everyday ways during their lifetimes that research on gift-giving and probate records too easily neglects.[51]

As Amanda Vickery has helpfully reminded us, 'a genuine effort to explore women's relationship with the world of goods must move beyond the moment of purchase – a mere snapshot in the long life of a commodity'.[52] Understanding the history of consumption means examining the uses to which objects were put after they were bought, as well as the motives and processes for their acquisition. For married couples consumption after purchase involved decisions about both the ownership and the management of goods. The conflicts that could subsequently arise reveal that married women derived and invested particular forms of personal and social identity from the possessions that surrounded them, which might bear little relation to their monetary value.

Many wealthy married women were able to gain from their goods a sense of individuality that was independent from their husbands, despite the common law theory of coverture. Women were acutely aware of what in terms of material wealth they brought to their marriages, what was intended to remain their 'separate estate' (specified property preserved in trusts for their 'sole and separate use'), and what they had purchased during the course of their marriages with 'their' earnings. In spite of the theory of property ownership in marriage, wives saw these possessions as

---

[50] See, for example, A. Vickery, 'Women and the world of goods: a Lancashire consumer and her possessions, 1751–81', in J. Brewer and R. Porter (eds.), *Consumption and the World of Goods* (London, 1993), pp. 274–301, and *The Gentleman's Daughter: Women's Lives in Georgian England* (London, 1998), chapter 5; Finn, 'Men's things'; H. Berry, 'Prudent luxury: the metropolitan tastes of Judith Baker, Durham gentlewoman', in R. Sweet and P. Lane (eds.), *Women and Urban Life in Eighteenth-Century England: 'On the Town'* (Aldershot, 2003), pp. 131–56.

[51] S. Cavallo, 'What did women transmit? Ownership and control of household goods and personal effects in early modern Italy', in M. Donald and L. Hurcombe (eds.), *Gender and Material Culture in Historical Perspective* (Basingstoke, 2000), p. 39; T. J. Schlereth, *Cultural History and Material Culture: Everyday Life, Landscapes, Museums* (Charlottesville, 1990), p. 1.

[52] Vickery, 'Women and the world of goods', p. 281.

their own. As Bailey argues, it seems highly unlikely that women were able to 'switch on and off their emotions about possessions according to marital state'.[53] Instead, if marriages failed wives could be anxious to ensure that their property left the marital home with them. The gentlewoman, Catherine Ettrick, for example, claimed that it was 'as an additional cruelty' that her husband refused to return her 'cloths, linen and wearing apparel' after she had fled his house, whereby she was 'greatly distressed'.[54] Lower down the social scale wives took clothing, linen and other household goods that could serve a practical purpose and contribute to financial survival, especially because these goods could be easily pawned. But the inclusion of child-bed linen, and children's linen in the packs carried by wives fleeing from their husbands may suggest that goods could simultaneously hold economic and emotional value.[55] The detailed and lengthy lists that itemise women's possessions, and which were sometimes made in the course of marriage separation disputes, particularly those where the calculation of alimony was in dispute, reveal how down to the last petticoat, women remained cognisant of what they owned in marriage.[56] For historians of gender and consumption, such lists would bear useful comparison with inventories and bequests in wills.

Women could not only be the holders of property within marriage, but they could also expect to play an important role in making decisions about the purchase and use of goods within the family and household economy. Indeed, as Vickery has recognised, wives were usually the 'routine consumers' in marriages, buying the everyday necessities for family use. Many women derived a significant amount of personal pride and satisfaction from this role, and enjoyed being identified as efficient and prudent household managers. 'Nothing can be more galling to a woman of any spirit, than to see herself at the head of a family without sufficient means to support her character, as such, in a handsome manner', declared Eliza Haywood, the author of *The History of Miss Betsy Thoughtless* (1751). Her heroine suffers the cruel indignity of a husband who expects her to fund necessities from her pin money. It seems highly probable that the female readers of this novel would have sympathised with the heroine's fate, for in reality, the insult of being called an inadequate or idle housewife stung deeply. As the period

[53] Bailey, *Unquiet Lives*, p. 98, see also, pp. 99–109.
[54] NA, DEL1/598 (1768), Part I, f.948.
[55] Bailey, *Unquiet Lives*, pp. 102–3.
[56] See, for example, LPL, CA, Case 4177 (1669), Ee3, f.567–571r; LPL, CA, Case 1888, (1676), Ee4, ff.424–427r, 438v–439; and LPL, CA, Case 7022 (1748), G115/50.

progressed, and the Victorian domestic ideal took hold, women's work running the home was given even greater emphasis.[57]

As well as bestowing a sense of self-worth, separate estate gave women a limited degree of authority within marriage. Control over goods within a marriage symbolised power, and if emotional relations between a couple soured, a wife could find her position with regard to goods under threat. This was what the spinster heiress Frances found to her cost when she married the widower Christopher Clarke in 1713. Her husband told her that the friends and relations who were the trustees of her separate estate were 'very rude to him on account of his not being intrusted by her in the managing of her estate and affairs and that he looked like a fool and was pointed and laughed at by everybody on that account'. He asked that he might at least be able to receive the rents from her separate estate, so 'he might thereby gain a credit and reputation and not look so mean and little in the world'. Like other men in his position, when persuasive words failed, he resorted to violence in an attempt to gain more of his wife's estate, and with threats that he would lock her up, and 'tie her to a bed post and was not accountable for so doing'.[58] Here we see how goods assumed meanings within a marital relationship. The control of goods displayed individual status and reputation, but more importantly the affective as well as the material conditions of a marriage. Husbands needed to be seen as the possessors of goods in a marriage, which could put women's separate estate under threat. The ownership, distribution and management of goods in marriage was as much a conspicuous display of mutual trust and respect as it was of material consumption.

Being deprived of goods could be represented not only as causing physical hardship, but also as bearing emotional or psychological costs. There could be no more powerful an emblem of where a wife was held in her husband's affections than how far he allowed her sole charge and responsibility for household possessions. To a wife, her relation to material goods within marriage signalled her status within her husband's eyes. In the courts, economic hardship in marriage was often shown not only as the withdrawal of necessities, but also as the point at which a woman's position as household manager was infringed. For example, Abigail Cockerell declared in 1730 that her husband, 'never gave her one

---

[57] Vickery, *The Gentleman's Daughter*, pp. 166, 130–1; G. Walker, 'Expanding the boundaries of female honour in early modern England', *Transactions of the Royal Historical Society* 6th series, 6, (1996), 235–45; Bailey, *Unquiet Lives*, p. 94; Haywood, *The History of Miss Betsy Thoughtless*, p. 440.

[58] LPL, CA, Case 1893, (1717), D424, ff.48v–49r, 77v–78r; for other examples see, Foyster, 'At the limits of liberty', 47–9.

farthing of money nor suffered her to keep the keys of any thing or to have the direction of any affairs in his family', and instead allowed his sister to take control of the household, and rule over her.[59] Similarly, part of Theodosia Freeman's complaint against her husband was that he 'locked up the meat and provisions for the house from her and commanded the keys to be kept from her'.[60] The household keys were significant indicators of authority, since whoever held them governed access to both household spaces and resources. Without them a woman was powerless. In the mid-nineteenth century, for Mary Ann Turner, 'deprived' by her husband 'of all authority in the house', and 'degraded in the eyes of the servants', this loss of status was made devastatingly clear when her husband told the servants that, 'if she grumbled or made any complaint that they should put her to bed as a child'. Such was the significance of goods to a married woman, that if she was no longer a manager over them within her home, she was devoid of all her identity, even as an adult.[61]

Of course, married women were not just consumers in this economy, and many worked themselves to provide necessaries for their families. These women could present physical violence as something that prevented them from contributing to the household economy, and which as a consequence forced them to become dependent upon others. For example, it was argued that the violence inflicted upon Sarah Chance by her husband, she running a haberdashery shop, 'hath greatly impaired her health and she hath lost the use of her right thumb and a bone in her left hand hath slipped its place and she is thereby rendered incapable of getting a livelihood'.[62] Eleanor Redmain's account of her marriage to a violent and indebted shopkeeper in London, with whom she lived 'in a deplorable and starving condition', reminds us that however poor and wretched circumstances could be within marriage, economic survival outside it was difficult for a woman to achieve if separated from her husband. Eleanor frequently fled to her 'friends' for support. But as we will show in Chapter 4, when we will look at Eleanor's friendships in greater depth, even friends could not provide limitless financial support, and Eleanor was forced to return to her husband.[63] It is impossible for us to know how many other women were like Eleanor and resumed relationships with violent husbands because the fear of poverty was greater than that of blows.

---

[59] LPL, CA, Case 2050, (1730), D431, f.67v–68r.
[60] NA, DEL1/479 (1734), f.183.
[61] LPL, CA, Case 9350, (1853), H824/5.
[62] LMA, DL/C/175 (1767), f.117r.
[63] LPL, CA, Case 7578 (1769), D1727, f.92v.

(3) Marital violence and the life cycle   Across the period, violence that was related to economic resources could be condemned, but there were contexts or circumstances that increased this probability. Here we can see the relative qualities of the concept of marital cruelty. There are many indications that violence of any kind, whether physical, verbal or sexual was more likely to be labelled as unacceptable and cruel within marriage when it was directed against a woman who was pregnant. In the case of pregnancy, contemporary notions of the need for male protection of the physically frail and delicate female seemed to be most clearly demonstrated, and those who did not respect this 'natural' order could provoke outrage. Catherine Jemmat, for example, recalled in her writings how her drunken husband had beaten her when she was pregnant, provoking a 'violent child-bed fever'. The daily 'blows and bruises' that followed were described as so unmanly that they dehumanised her husband; 'I thought I had married a man, I found I had married a monster'.[64]

Women argued that miscarriage could be one of the physical consequences of such violence. As well as the death of the baby, miscarriage also meant that the mother's health was endangered. When contemporaries viewed pregnancy as a sign of domestic harmony, miscarriage within marriage could carry inverse meanings.[65] Sometimes the violence that had been inflicted on the pregnant mother was described as so severe that it was visibly evident on the dead foetus. In June 1775, a fortnight after her husband had beaten her by kneeling on her stomach, and striking her with his fists, Sarah Terry miscarried, and 'the flesh of the said child when born appeared very much bruised, discoloured and quite black'.[66] Such stories are similar to those told in rape cases, when women claimed miscarriage had followed the trauma and physical violence of sexual assault, and that the bruises on their dead babies bore witness to what they had suffered.[67] In a time period when it was understood that miscarriages could be caused by emotional shocks or frights, women were also able to argue that their husband's non-physical violence had led to miscarriage. Elizabeth Jessop, the wife of a surgeon, described her husband as 'very morose in his temper and very covetous', and she blamed this behaviour for her miscarriage. Her midwife was more specific, and said that Elizabeth had miscarried after her husband

---

[64] *The Memoirs of Mrs Catherine Jemmat* (London, 1771), 2nd edition, ii, pp. 55–7.
[65] L. A. Pollock, 'Embarking on a rough passage: the experience of pregnancy in early-modern society', in V. Fildes (ed.), *Women as Mothers in Pre-Industrial England: Essays in Memory of Dorothy McLaren* (London, 1990), p. 40.
[66] LMA, DL/C/179 (1783), f.515v.
[67] Walker, 'Rereading rape', 11; Gammon, 'Ravishment and ruin', 115–16.

had cursed her all night when he did not have a clean shirt to wear in bed. Such cases illustrate how it was thought possible that verbal violence could have physical consequences. But the problem of determining the exact cause of miscarriage meant that violent husbands were sometimes able to deflect the blame away from themselves. Elizabeth's husband and his witnesses, for example, attributed her miscarriage to her previous alarm when she was surprised by a person calling for a coach in a narrow London alley.[68] In cases of marital discord, even the dramatic and involuntary physical trauma of miscarriage could not be relied upon as evidence of marital violence.

However, husbands were expected to make special provisions of care and maintenance for their pregnant wives, and they faced accusations of cruelty when these were not fulfilled. Sometimes these were made in the context of stories of physical violence and neglect to indicate the miserly and spiteful character of the men described. The pregnant Elizabeth Wyatt, 'being in that condition longed for some green peas and intreated and desired the said Thomas [her husband] to buy her a peck which he might have bought for six pence', but he refused. Elizabeth did not blame Thomas for the later miscarriage of the child, but criticised him for not showing more concern for her health afterwards. According to her account, the day following her miscarriage he expected her to resume her normal household duties, would not let anybody 'attend her' or provide 'necessaries', and when she made some chicken broth (a food commonly known for its healing and restorative qualities), he ate most of it. If Thomas had cared for her as he should have done, he would have made arrangements to alleviate his wife from her work, as well as providing her with nourishing food and drink.[69]

When pregnancies did go to full term, middling and upper class women expected to be allowed a period of recovery following their 'confinement' for childbirth, known as their 'lying in'. Historians have debated the extent to which women were permitted an unusual degree of marital and household authority during their lying in, and how far men were excluded from the lying-in chamber.[70] From the records of marriage breakdown it certainly appears that a husband who was physically violent

[68] LPL, CA, Case 5089 (1717), Ee9 12/1,15/1, Eee12, ff.31,47; for early-modern interpretations of miscarriage see, U. Rublack, 'Pregnancy, childbirth and the female body in early modern Germany', *Past and Present* 150 (1996), 84–110.

[69] NA, DEL1/344 (1710), ff.86v–87v,90v; Rublack, 'Pregnancy, childbirth and the female body', 98–9.

[70] See, for example, N. Z. Davis, 'Women on top' in *Society and Culture in Early Modern France* (Stanford, 1975), p. 145; A. Wilson, 'The ceremony of childbirth and its interpretation', in Fildes (ed.), *Women as Mothers*, pp. 68–107, and *The Making of Man-Midwifery: Childbirth in England, 1660–1770* (Cambridge, MA, 1995), pp. 25–30.

to his wife during her period of lying in was open to special condemnation. In 'her weak condition' after the birth of her son, Mary Sherard's husband refused to permit her lying in, but instead pulled and dragged her out of bed and forced her out of her lying-in chamber. The timing of Jarvis Haughton's beating of his wife, 'tho' she had then lain in but about a fortnight' was also deliberately emphasised in his wife's testimony.[71]

It is clear that women believed that they had a right to insist upon material support during and immediately after childbirth, which may have given them more than their average share and control over the distribution of household resources. Preparing for childbirth could involve a considerable monetary outlay for the supply of linens, cloths, and sometimes special furnishings.[72] Resentment was caused if women were denied access to these materials, and could even lead to accusations of life-threatening cruelty. In 1823 Lady Helen Turner only provided a very brief description to the courts of the two occasions in her marriage when her husband had struck her, and instead concentrated the content of her libel against her husband for cruelty upon his behaviour during and following her pregnancies. Such was her shock at her husband's refusal to allow her money for the expenses of her first confinement, that according to her account, 'she suffered great anxiety and distress of mind and her spirits were much depressed'. Her mother, who lived with the couple, also pleaded with Sir Gregory Turner for support during her daughter's confinements, for which she was beaten on the head, and on another occasion, pushed down some stone stairs. Helen alleged that she was so affected by the sight of her husband's violence to her mother, that the first time she had to be treated by a surgeon for 'distress and agitation', and on the second occasion she miscarried. A year later she was pregnant again, and her husband's refusal to pay the rent on their home meant the arrival of officers to force the payment of their arrears. The shock of their visit confined her to bed for several days. By the time she launched her suit for marriage separation she said that her doctors were convinced that her life was in danger, not from her husband's physical violence, but because of her illness that was 'brought on entirely from mental agitation and distress at the neglect and ill treatment of her said husband'.[73]

There is little to suggest that lying-in chambers were 'female spaces' that acted to protect women from male violence. Childbirth and lying in

---

[71] LPL, CA, Case 141 (1706), D32, f.62v–63r; LPL, VH80, (1712), 15/2.
[72] L. A. Pollock, 'Childbearing and female bonding in early modern England', *Social History* 22, 3 (1997), 289–90.
[73] LPL, CA, Case 9349 (1823), H346/9.

could not be times for 'speaking secrets' or 'expressing fears', as some historians have argued, when women found it difficult to enforce men's exclusion from these occasions.[74] Isaac Pewsey may not have entered his wife's chamber after she had given birth in January 1698, but he still managed to abuse her violently by cursing her from the doorway to her room.[75] Nearly 150 years later, the marriage separation case between the Countess and Earl of Dysart provides us with more insights into the use and control of space during childbirth. By this period, despite objections from some medical professionals, the presence of husbands during the birth of their children had become a fairly common practice in upper-class families. Much comment followed the attendance of Prince Albert when Queen Victoria gave birth to her first child in 1841.[76] Following this fashion, Countess Dysart requested her husband to be present as she gave birth, but at the last moment, she was persuaded by her doctor to ask him to leave. The Earl left the room 'in such a manner as to show that he was seriously offended with his wife', and his behaviour on this occasion was later presented by the Countess as evidence of his cruelty. The judge in the Court of Arches would not permit the event to be admitted as an act of cruelty, but he thought that it did bear 'considerable weight' as an explanation for the subsequent discord and violence in the marriage. One of the Earl's letters to his wife, in which he wrote to her that 'the indifference you evinced towards me at that trying hour tended not a little to banish affection from my breast', was cited in the case.[77] As such the story of the Dysart marriage seemed to serve warning to wives of the potential danger of excluding their husbands even from the most intimate of spaces in their lives. Power relations during childbirth and lying in were not subverted to the point that women could control their husband's presence or absence as they wished. Indeed, by the Victorian period, some husbands were regarding their attendance in the delivery room as a right rather than a privilege.

Perhaps some men believed that they had a right to be present at the moment of childbirth because they were bearing its financial costs. For some the monetary burden proved a cause of aggravation. Benjamin

---

[74] Gowing, *Common Bodies*, p. 166.

[75] J. D. Melville, 'The use and organisation of domestic space in late seventeenth-century London', PhD thesis, University of Cambridge (1999), p. 172.

[76] P. Jalland and J. Hooper (eds.), *Women from Birth to Death: The Female Life Cycle in Britain 1830–1914* (Atlantic Highlands, NJ, 1986), pp. 155–64; J. Tosh, *A Man's Place: Masculinity and the Middle-Class Home in Victorian England* (New Haven and London, 1999), pp. 81–2.

[77] *Dysart v. Dysart* (1847), *English Reports* vol. 163, p. 1109.

Brogden, a surgeon and man-midwife, who frequently beat Anne Marie, his wife, became violent after he asked her how much she spent on her 'churching', the religious and social celebration for the birth of a child. 'She telling him how much and that she had also given one shilling to be divided amongst eight or ten poor women that were then there', he called her names, and 'gave her several blows with his fist on her head while the child was at her breast'.[78] According to Mary Rookes, her husband, the Reverend Charles Rookes, was so troubled by the impending cost of children that he did everything he could to try and make her miscarry. He sent her on long walks when she was pregnant, pressed and squeezed her stomach, and asked Mary to request her nurse that if the baby was born dead, to take the body away with her, and so save him the expenses of a funeral. A particularly macabre aspect to his cruelty was Charles' decision, after Mary had taken the advice of two physicians to leave her husband, to send her newspaper cuttings announcing the death of women in childbirth.[79] However disturbing the consequences, these cases do reveal an awareness among husbands that it was their responsibility to maintain their wives through pregnancy and childbirth.

Part of the expense of childbirth could be for medical help from midwives, nurses and occasionally surgeons. Refusal to send for medical help could be presented as cruelty if it could be shown that this put a wife's life in danger. Catherine Ettrick told Durham consistory court that 'being totally ignorant how to manage herself when she was with child', she asked her husband to allow her sister, and then her aunt to visit their isolated farmhouse, but was refused. When her labour pains began her husband would not send for a midwife, saying 'there was no occasion for all that fuss that women made', and eventually her baby was delivered by a washerwoman, as the 'regular midwife' did not arrive until an hour after the birth.[80] Letitia Elizabeth Thompson, described as 'pregnant of her first child and depressed in her spirits in tears', and so perhaps suffering from what we today would label as form of pre-natal depression, was frequently verbally abused by her husband. During her second pregnancy the abuse continued, and her husband would not send for medical help when she became ill, leaving her and her friends fearful that she would go into a premature labour.[81]

---

[78] LMA, DL/C/173, (1758), f.298r; for churching see, D. Cressy, 'Purification, thanksgiving and the churching of women in post-Reformation England', *Past and Present* 141 (1993), 106–14.

[79] LPL, CA, Case 7822, (1839), D1802, ff.6–9.

[80] NA, DEL1/598, (1768), part 1, ff.432–435, 443–444, 447–448.

[81] LPL, CA, Case 9119, (1824), H373/6.

Other women who were affected by life-threatening illnesses that were unrelated to pregnancy also attempted to seek marriage separations on the grounds of their husband's lack of material maintenance. Ann Costellow, wife of William, was ill in the early eighteenth century with a 'cancerous humour in her womb and a leprous humour in her blood', and complained that her illness 'may in great measure be ascribed to the usage of the said William Costellow'. She said that her husband had provided a minimal allowance for her when she stayed in London to see physicians, made her travel back to Chichester when she was not fit, gave her unsuitable food to eat, and declared publicly that he would not pay any of the bills she accumulated for basic food provisions. Their dispute in the church courts centred upon material concerns, William arguing that as the keeper of a goldsmith's shop and malting house he had overreached his means by spending over £80 on doctors, surgeons and nurses for his wife, who was an imprudent household manager, and 'was always careless of her said husband and his affairs'.[82]

Of course, some husbands were reluctant to seek medical help for their wives because they knew that they risked being blamed for their wives' ill health. The wife of a Northamptonshire farmer, for example, lay sick in bed for nearly six weeks after a physically violent attack from her husband. It seems probable that she was not allowed any medical advice during this period because anyone who had seen her bruises and swollen face could have acted as witnesses against her husband. Similarly, Mary Robson believed that in order that her husband's adultery and subsequent infection of her with venereal disease 'should not be publicly known he would not permit her to apply for any medical advice or assistance'. Medical professionals did testify in cases of marital violence, and their involvement will be discussed in Chapter 5.[83]

Historians of medicine have argued that from the early modern period there opened up a 'medical marketplace' with a wide range of practitioners from whom the patient could choose.[84] However, until recently there has been very little consideration of how a woman's marital status could limit her freedoms as a medical consumer: even a monograph that takes part of the church marriage vows as its title, *In Sickness and In Health*, did not problematise the issue of wives as patients.[85] In fact, as a *feme covert*,

---

[82] LPL, CA, Case 2308, (1706), D490, ff.83,95r,98–108r,143r, Ee8, f.143r.

[83] LPL, CA, Case 3059, (1838), H580/5; LPL, VH80, (1803), 57/2.

[84] See, for example, L. McCray Beier, *Sufferers and Healers: The Experience of Illness in Seventeenth-Century England* (London, 1987); and R. Porter and D. Porter, *Patient's Progress: Doctors and Doctoring in Eighteenth-Century England* (Oxford, 1989).

[85] R. Porter and D. Porter, *In Sickness and In Health: The British Experience 1650–1850* (London, 1988).

a married woman was unable to enter into a contract to employ a medical practitioner without her husband's consent. Although medical care was one of the 'necessaries' that a husband was bound to provide for his wife, this obligation did not hold if the husband voiced objection to a particular practitioner. Thus as holders of the household purse, there was potential for husbands to exercise considerable power over their wives in times of illness. They could determine not only whether their wives had medical assistance, but also the type of medical care they received. Wives could be trapped in a three-way medical relationship between themselves, their husbands and their practitioners, which could act to seriously restrict their choices of medical care.[86]

The marriage separation case for cruelty brought by Lady Huntingtower in 1837 demonstrates both how husbands could abuse their position of medical authority over their wives, but also the point at which popular acceptance of this husband's right was breached. Part of Lord Huntingtower's defence against his wife's accusations of cruelty concerning the provision of medical necessaries, was that she should have paid her doctor's bills from her annual separate allowance or estate of £120. But he found it more difficult to answer his wife's allegations that he had refused to allow her laudanum when she was attacked by 'violent spasms' in August 1836. The decision to leave his wife in pain was regarded as intolerable cruelty by some of the servants who acted as witnesses. The couple also disagreed about who should be called to take care of Lady Huntingtower when she was ill. Lord Huntingtower favoured 'the family apothecary', who was, in his opinion, 'a respectable medical practitioner' who lived nearby. But his wife thought the apothecary was 'an ignorant person and knew nothing', and instead wanted treatment from a physician who lived further away. The cost of employing a more distant and perhaps more experienced and socially superior medical practitioner may well have deterred Lord Huntingtower from meeting his wife's wishes. But her lack of confidence in the care proffered by those who he chose to treat her was presented as aggravating her illness, and so as further evidence of his cruelty to her. Commenting on the choice of doctor, one witness critically remarked, 'he treated the whole matter with great indifference and unkindness, he seemed to consider that it was immaterial who attended her'.[87] The suggestion was that simply providing medical care that was convenient and cost

---

[86] C. Crawford, 'Patients' rights and the law of contract in eighteenth-century England', *Social History of Medicine* 13, 3 (2000), 382, 396–401, 409; and L. Wynne Smith, 'Women's health care in England and France (1650–1775)', PhD thesis, University of Essex (2001), chapter 6.

[87] LPL, CA, Case 4915, (1837), H544/6,7,9,12.

effective did not always amount to an adequate supply of 'necessaries'. Rather, husbands were expected in addition to pay attention to the quality of those necessaries, a point to which we shall return later in this chapter.

Women were also bound by their marriage vows to bear with their husbands 'in sickness and in health', and their 'natural' feminine qualities of nurture, gentleness and concern for others were thought to lend themselves towards making them the obvious carers of the sick. Whereas men were expected to provide for the monetary costs of illness in the family, women had the time-consuming task of administering to the practical day-to-day needs of the sick. As we shall see in Chapter 2, women who did not live up to the ideals of their gender faced a difficult task convincing others of the validity of their claims of marital cruelty. This was certainly the case for Dorothy Citty, whose accusations against her husband, Daniel, for cruelty, were heard in the Court of Arches in 1669. Dorothy's charge against her husband was that he had verbally abused her by calling her a witch and a whore, threatened to kill her, and allowed his son from a previous marriage to beat her. But this backfired when Daniel instead accused his wife of cruelty. His witnesses testified that Daniel was nearly blind and 'a very old weak and infirm man . . . and almost helpless'. It was argued that he had only married Dorothy so that she could nurse him, but instead she neglected him, was suspected of trying to poison him with some food she fed him, and 'when he hath been in grief and passion at his wife's unkindness, she hath stood and laughed and mocked at him'. Since she had left him one witness suspected that Daniel would soon become a dependent upon the parish.[88]

In his elderly and frail position, Daniel could accuse his wife of being cruel to him by neglecting her duties, without it reflecting on his authority. No doubt his story of his wife's behaviour would have struck a chord with contemporaries, whose fears about the instability of unequal matches, especially those produced by a significant difference in age between husband and wife, were widely disseminated.[89] Even though Dorothy was not expected to fund the necessaries to care for her husband, her behaviour towards him was seen as harmful by her neighbours, who 'scolded' her for her lack of help. The reaction of her neighbours shows that there was an expectation that both wives and husbands had a duty to support each other in marriage. The form that duty took varied with gender, but if either failed in their duty, there could

[88] LPL, CA, Case 1865, (1669), Eee4, ff.117–118, 202–204, 279v– 280v, 283v–285v.
[89] Capp, *When Gossips Meet*, pp. 77–8.

be repercussions for the parish community, as well as for the couple themselves.

So far we have seen that when women accused their husbands of cruel violence, the evidence that they supplied included, and sometimes centred upon, details of material deprivation. By law, men had an obligation to provide their wives with the necessaries of life. In practice, the quantity and quality of these necessaries was expected to vary over the life cycle. A woman who was pregnant or recovering from childbirth could anticipate different treatment from her husband in this regard. In old age, both wives and husbands were expected to alter their behaviour towards each other. The legal and extra-legal ways in which a woman could respond to a lack of necessaries will be discussed fully in the next chapter.

Too often when historians have considered women's material circumstances in marriage they have become preoccupied with the concept and operation of coverture. This has tended to suggest a static picture of women's position in relation to their husband's material resources, in which their access to and management of goods were settled at entry to marriage, and remained the same until the point of widowhood. But by looking at marriage disputes we can see that the distribution of personal and moveable property (at the very least), was likely to shift between a couple over the course of their marriage. While theoretically men retained ultimate control and ownership of that property, they could face accusations of cruelty if they did not make suitable adjustments to its expenditure over time.

It has also been demonstrated that individual circumstances of age and quality of health were taken into account when contemporaries defined what was cruel violence. While few were prepared to suggest that men should no longer have the right to correct their wives using physical means, that did not mean all forms of violence were condoned. A useful comparison can be made with public attitudes to child discipline today: at the same time that many parents resist losing their right to correct their children by smacking them, cases of child abuse cause outrage. So a lack of consensus about the legitimacy of violence does not mean that it can be exercised with impunity. Physical and verbal violence and neglect of necessary support by both men and women was less likely to be tolerated when a spouse was elderly, sick or dying. Even apparently trivial neglect of necessaries could be treated seriously in these circumstances. Judge Scott made his remark during the *D'Aguilar* case about the relative nature of cruelty after he noted that the wife was over seventy years old, and a witness had deposed that the husband 'took the keys of the closets; deposed her from the management of the family, locked up the tea, cakes, &c'. The deprival of tea and cakes did merit attention, Scott thought, because 'these things would be necessary to persons used to such indulgences, and at such a time of life'.[90] Why 'indulgences' could be regarded as 'necessities' by some is a matter to which we will return at the end of this chapter.

(4) The controls on male violence We need to recognise that throughout the period from 1660 to 1857 there were attempts to regulate male behaviour and limit the occasions of men's violence in marriage. At present, however, there are a series of studies of men and violence, ranging from the sixteenth to the nineteenth centuries, which have been conducted by historians who each claim that it was in 'their' period that the most significant reformation in male behaviour took place. So Amussen says that it was between the sixteenth and seventeenth centuries that new models of masculinity emphasised 'self-restraint and the recourse to law' rather than violence; Hunt argues that early eighteenth-century concepts of civility affected how male violence was viewed; and Shoemaker argues that it was by the end of the eighteenth century that changing ideas of masculinity had led to a decline in the acceptability of public male violence.[91] Both Hammerton and Wiener, focusing on domestic violence, have argued that it was nineteenth-century ideas about masculinity that made all the difference to how male violence was perceived. They argue that male aggressiveness was only seen as a general social problem in this later period, and that a hardening of popular attitudes led to harsher punishments for violent males. Indeed, discussing the mid-Victorian period, Wiener goes as far as to state that 'the violence of husbands against wives was virtually 'discovered' in this era'. But both Hammerton and Wiener have mistaken a rising volume and range of complaints about male violence in marriage during the nineteenth century as marking a change in attitudes.[92] If we step outside the boxes that can confine historians to particular historical periods, we can see the many continuities in ideas about masculinity and violence over time. As it will now be shown, there

[90] *D'Aguilar v. D'Aguilar* (1794), *English Reports* vol. 162, p. 753.
[91] S. D. Amussen, "The part of a Christian man': the cultural politics of manhood in early modern England', in S. D. Amussen and M. A. Kishlansky (eds.), *Political Culture and Cultural Politics in Early Modern England: Essays presented to David Underdown* (Manchester, 1995), p. 220–7; Hunt, 'Wife beating', 25–7; Shoemaker, 'Male honour', 190–208.
[92] Hammerton, *Cruelty and Companionship*, passim; M. J. Wiener, 'Domesticity: a legal discipline for men?', in M. Hewitt (ed.), *An Age of Equipoise? Reassessing Mid-Victorian Britain* (Aldershot, 2000), p. 156, 'The Victorian criminalization of men', 197–212, and *Men of Blood*, passim.

were always voices that condemned male violence in marriage, this was conduct that remained shameful for men, and the lesson that men should learn self-control was as current in the seventeenth as in the nineteenth century. Rather than contrasting 'traditional' and 'reformed' models of masculinity, we should understand that concepts of masculinity were always evolving and being subject to renewed waves of reform and control. Even though the basis for objections to marital violence, and the manner in which they were expressed changed over the period, the message remained the same: violence was always an undesirable, and often an unacceptable way for husbands to manage their married lives.

Condemnation of marital violence can be traced back to at least the start of the seventeenth century. One of the earliest treatises to confront the problem of wife-beating was William Heale's *An Apology for Women*, published in 1609. Heale could find nothing in the law to suggest that a husband had a right to beat his wife, and he ventured that it was unnatural for a man to do so. Men, unlike other animals, argued Heale, had reason, and they should exercise this in their conduct towards their wives. Men's superiority over women was only justified if they used their greater strength with reason. Self-control was essential. Most importantly, marital violence was wrong because it had no scriptural basis. Husbands were directed by the Bible to love and respect their wives. God had created Adam and Eve from the same flesh, and who 'but a frantic, furious, desperate wretch will beat himself?', asked one writer of a conduct manual for married couples. Wife-beating was evidence of such a lack of reason and control that it amounted to madness.[93]

From the outset, however, condemnation of marital violence was not universal. Heale's treatise had been written as a response to a public defence of wife-beating given in 1608 by William Gager. William Whateley, a Puritan preacher and writer of *A Bride Bush*, first published in 1617, agreed that for a man to strike his wife was 'to make an incision into his own flesh', and that correction should never be administered when a man was in a violent passion. The best way to manage wives was 'not to use violence, but skill' of 'mild, gentle and wise proceeding'. But the difficulties of deciding upon the extent of a husband's authority were shown by the fact that by the time the second edition of this work was published two years later, Whateley had changed his mind. He arrived at

---

[93] W. Heale, *An Apology for Women* (Oxford, 1609); W. Gouge, *Of Domesticall Duties* 3rd edition (London, 1634), p. 395. See also, H. Smith, *A Preparative to Marriage* (London, 1591), pp. 72–3; and Foyster, 'Male honour', 215–16, 219–20.

the view, sustained in the third edition, that 'blows' or 'strokes with hand or fist' could be used by husbands when faced with the 'utmost extremities of unwifelike carriage'.[94] One writer in 1650 went even further, composing an entire treatise in defence of a husband's right to beat a disobedient wife. Those clergymen who had ruled against physical correction, he argued, were poorly qualified to give advice, because they were lucky enough to be married to exceptionally obedient wives. Given, as recent research has showed, that Puritan ministers were likely to be married to the daughters of other clergymen, he may well have had a point. But although this author believed that Christ had ordained that husbands could use force to support their patriarchal authority, this was only in cases when husbands were 'godly men' correcting wives who had committed 'high, heady, habitual sins and affronts'.[95] The right to beat was qualified even as it was justified.

In the seventeenth century debates about marital violence focused upon how far it was a spiritual or moral wrong. Different interpretations of the scriptures were used to either condemn or support this aspect of a husband's authority. The argument that it was 'unbecoming the man and the Christian' to be violent to his wife continued well into the nineteenth century and the idea that husbands and wives were one flesh was often repeated.[96] By quoting the words of St Paul, 'No man ever yet hated his own flesh, but nourisheth and cherisheth it, as Christ the Church', ministers were also able to argue that husbands should supply necessaries for their wives, and to suggest that failure in this duty was another form of marital cruelty.[97] Evangelicals at the end of the eighteenth century who were keen to reform family life, such as Hannah More, could simply take up arguments about marital violence where Puritan ministers had left off. But in addition to scriptural arguments against marital violence, what became more important as the period progressed from the Restoration to the nineteenth century, was the

---

[94] W. Whateley, *A Bride Bush* (London, 1623), pp. 99–100, 123–4, 136, 139, 169–73; see also, A. Fletcher, 'The Protestant idea of marriage in early modern England', in A. Fletcher and P. Roberts (eds.), *Religion, Culture and Society in Early Modern Britain: Essays in Honour of Patrick Collinson* (Cambridge, 1994), p. 161–81.

[95] M. A. Vauts, *The Husband's Authority Unvail'd; Wherein it is Moderately Discussed Whether it be Fit or Lawful for a Good Man, to Beat his Bad Wife* (London, 1650), pp. 56, 60, 76–81; J. Eales, 'Gender construction in early modern England and the conduct books of William Whateley (1583–1639)', in R. N. Swanson (ed.), *Gender and Christian Religion* Studies in Church History, Vol. 34 (Woodbridge, 1998), pp. 163–74.

[96] See, for example, D. Crosley, *The Christian Marriage Explained* (London, 1744), p. 45; and W. Giles, *A Treatise on Marriage* (London, 1771), p. 14; the Reverend Henry Young denied that he would ever 'intentionally wound my own flesh' in a letter to his wife about his violence to her in October 1855, see LPL, CA, Case 10404 (1855), H838/2B.

[97] See, for example, M. Mead, *A Discourse on Marriage* (London, 1732), p. 131.

conviction that marital violence was a social wrong. To be violent to one's wife was bad manners. It showed a lack of breeding on the part of the perpetrator, and a failure to be sensitive to the feelings of others, who included not only the wife who was targeted. From the mid-eighteenth century the culture of sensibility added force to the conviction that men should show sensitivity and sympathy towards the company they kept.[98] Marital violence became indecorous, a matter of bad taste, as well as a moral wrong.

Over this period various prescriptive codes of manners, termed successively honour, civility, politeness and etiquette, taught men and women their gender roles and set expectations of behaviour in married life. Although each had different emphases, none had a place for violence in relationships between husbands and wives. Thus even if, as Shoemaker has argued, there was a change during the eighteenth century in ideas about male honour that meant that male *v.* male violence in defence of status and in public was less likely to earn approval, this was not accompanied by an alteration of attitudes about domestic violence.[99] Indeed, it could be posited that as definitions of male honour depended less on public behaviour, conduct at home mattered more. Furthermore, a decline in the importance of public violence as a way to earn and maintain honourable masculinity should not be equated with a decrease in concern for public reputation. Violence was still a measure for assessing men, it was just that in the case of a husband's violence towards his wife, the ability to control and limit the extent of violence was what was important. Codes of manners continued to set exacting standards of conduct for men in domestic life that required public opinion as well as individual conscience to stand in judge.

As a consequence, the reputations of 'public' men were always vulnerable to ruin if an infringement of conduct in their 'private' lives was exposed. A man who was violent to his wife without disciplinary reason, or to excess, was liable to public censure. The scandal that marriage breakdown caused by violence was certainly less scurrilous than that provoked by adultery, but it was damaging nonetheless. As we shall see in Chapter 4, family and social life after marriage separation was difficult. Shame was attached to marital violence, and this was in part because it was an offence that was anti-social, affecting others as well as damaging the marriage itself. Samuel Pepys was 'vexed at my heart to think what I had done' when he gave his wife a black eye in 1664, but

---

[98] G. J. Barker-Benfield, *The Culture of Sensibility: Sex and Society in Eighteenth-Century Britain* (Chicago, 1992), chapter 2.
[99] Shoemaker, 'Male honour', 190–208.

his feelings about the incident extended to more than just personal guilt and remorse. He searched desperately for an excuse that would prevent his wife attending a Christmas party when his shame would be visible to all.[100] When in 1694 a reader wrote to the question and answer periodical, the *Athenian Mercury*, for advice about how a wife should deal with a violent husband, the enquirer was told that 'perhaps the acquainting of her or his friends may not be amiss', because when the husband learned that 'his strict hand will gain him no reputation' he would cease his violence.[101] Across the period, individuals asked violent husbands if they were not ashamed of their actions, crowds jeered and cried 'shame' at notorious wife-beaters, and community rituals brought humiliation and inflicted shame upon these husbands.[102] Occasionally action was taken to exclude a violent man from his community. The elders of Broadmead Baptist church in Bristol expelled one husband from their congregation in 1678 when they heard that he had been 'very much in drink, and very rude, fighting in the street, and that he had given his wife some blows'.[103] In 1672 a Somerset husband denied ever striking his wife, saying that he did 'account it a very unmanly unworthy thing for any gentleman so to do', and when Elizabeth Spinkes brought a cruelty case against her husband in the early eighteenth century, it was alleged that she had tried 'to scandalize [her husband's] good name and reputation and expose him to the world', by telling people that he was violent to her.[104]

Of course, having the reputation of a wife-beater had different repercussions according to social status. For upper- and middle-class men it could mean social and business ostracism, for working-class men the end of vital neighbourhood support in an economy that relied upon mutual trust and aid. But, for their different reasons, husbands from all walks of life feared the label of 'wife-beater'. To take two examples from the nineteenth century: one husband from the upper-middle classes argued that it had been 'to the extreme prejudice of his character' when his neighbours mistook his wife's screams as evidence of his violence, and another husband, this time an unemployed London porter claimed that his wife always carried a bundle of hair in her pocket so that she could accuse him of violence whenever she liked. As a result, his neighbours

---

[100] As cited in Capp, *When Gossips Meet*, p. 104.
[101] *Athenian Mercury* vol. 13, no. 15, q.2 (March 27, 1694); I am grateful to Helen Berry for this reference.
[102] See, for example, LPL, CA, Case 1127 (1663), Eee1, f.63v; LPL, CA, Case 2050 (1730), Ee9, f.186; *The Times* (16 August 1836), 6e; Foyster, 'Male honour', 221–4.
[103] As cited in Amussen, 'Punishment, discipline, and power', 14.
[104] LPL, CA, Case 6244 (1672), Ee4, f.51v; as cited in Hunt, 'Wife beating', 22.

had taken against him, and the common cry was, 'Oh poor woman, what a b – y rogue of a husband she's got'.[105] However improbable the stories they told in their defence, men such as these went to great lengths to avoid the reputation of being violent husbands.

Marital violence invited social condemnation across the class divide. As we will see in Chapter 4, the actions of family, neighbours and friends, as they intervened and tried to defend wives from violence, could speak more than words. But there was also an extended debate in popular literature about the legitimacy of marital violence. In part this was kept alive, as we discussed in the Introduction, by the mythology surrounding figures such as 'Judge Thumb'. Underlying the anti-marital violence message of many popular ballads or songs that circulated through working-class neighbourhoods, however, were serious lessons about the dangers of drink and poverty. Both were shown to wreak havoc upon married life, and to be a cause of violence, in all its forms. But that did not excuse marital violence, or make it any less shameful. A series of ballads by the author Martin Parker printed in the first half of the seventeenth century set the tone for the next two centuries as ballad after ballad taught that only cowards beat their wives, and that violence was an ineffective way of making a bad wife good.[106] As the ballad 'A Word of Advice', printed sometime between the late eighteenth and mid-nineteenth century put it:

> Some men when they're married are spending their lives,
> In drinking and gaming and beating their wives,
> But when that the bloom of their days it is past,
> It only brings shame and sorrow at the last.[107]

Here violence is represented as one more vice of married life, inseparable from others, which leads inevitably to regret and ruin.

Nevertheless, it is important to remember that while there was a long tradition within popular culture of ballads that advised against marital violence, this co-existed with a counter culture that tended to its support. The tone and images that accompanied these ballads suggest that they were intended to be comical. They depict married life as a 'struggle for the breeches', or as a contest between men and women over who

---

[105] LPL, CA, Case 3366 (1811), D757, f.51; *The Times* (25 August 1838), 7a.
[106] M. Parker, 'Well Met, Neighbour!', *Roxburghe* vol. III, pp. 98–103, 'Hold Your Hands, Honest Men!', *Roxburghe* vol. III, pp. 243–8, and 'A He-Devil', in H. E. Rollins (ed.), *A Pepysian Garland: Black Letter Broadside Ballads of the Years 1595–1639* (Cambridge, MA, 1971), pp. 332–6; for later examples of ballads that condemn marital violence, see, for example, 'Worth of a Woman', Madden, vol. 7, 258; 'Good Advice to Bachelors and Maids', Madden, vol. 11, 136; and 'Bourne and his Wife', Madden, vol. 20, 164.
[107] 'A Word of Advice', Madden, vol. 9, 48.

was in command, with violence as likely to originate from the wife as the husband. The continuity of fears about female violence needs explanation, and the next chapter will provide some answers. When wives attempted to gain mastery within marriage, the only solution, argued one ballad was to, 'Bang Her Well, Peter'.[108] Clearly, popular as well as elite opinion was divided about the acceptability of violence in marriage.

Across the period, men were raised in a culture where violence was integral to the process of growing up. Exposure to physical violence began early for men. Learning how to tolerate physical pain, and control the infliction of physical force on others, were essential lessons in the construction of their gender identity. Physical strength was a quality that clearly differentiated men from women, but was also nurtured from boyhood. Educationalists advised parents and schoolmasters to subject boys to regimes of exercise and discipline that would strengthen and harden boys into men. As schoolchildren and as servants or apprentices, boys could endure the physical punishment and humiliation of the birch or whip. From their heroes in popular literature, many boys and young men learned that respect and honour came to those who were courageous and could defend themselves by fighting. As adolescents, periodically men terrorised the streets of urban centres, attacking strangers and young women in an attempt to assert their masculinity. With this upbringing, it is hardly surprising that upon adulthood brawls, fights, boxing matches and duels were common violent ways in which disputes were settled between men.[109]

But in the nineteenth century the ideal of the 'man of dignity', who shunned violence and exercised 'the qualities of reasonableness, forethought, prudence and command over oneself', did not, in fact, represent a 'new man'.[110] Victorian concepts of masculinity reworked old themes to create a masculine ideal that was simply the same model

---

[108] 'Bang Her Well, Peter', Madden, vol. 7, 354 ('bang' meant 'beat' in this period); see also, 'A Wife Well Managed', Madden, vol. 18, 141; and 'Tommy Lamb's Cure for a Drunken Wife', in *Hawky's Garland*, a collection printed chiefly by J. and M. Robertson (Glasgow, 1779–1816).

[109] M. Spufford, *Small Books and Pleasant Histories: Popular Fiction and its Readership in Seventeenth-Century England* (Cambridge, 1981), pp. 225–32; B. Capp, 'English youth groups and 'The Pinder of Wakefield'', in P. Slack (ed.), *Rebellion, Popular Protest and Social Order in Early Modern England* (Cambridge, 1984), pp. 212–18; A. Fletcher, 'Prescription and practice: Protestantism and the upbringing of children 1560–1700', in D. Wood (ed.), *The Church and Childhood* Studies in Church History, 31, (Oxford, 1994), pp. 325–46; Shoemaker, 'Male honour', 199–200.

[110] Wiener, *Men of Blood*, p. 6; James Boswell was striving to be a 'man of dignity' as early as 1763, see P. Carter, 'James Boswell's manliness', in Hitchcock and Cohen (eds.), *English Masculinities*, pp. 116–20.

dressed in a new suit. The virtues of reason and self-control were long essentials in the training of men. 'Teach him to get a mastery over his inclinations, and submit his appetite to reason', John Locke advised in his 1693 treatise on the upbringing of boys.[111] That these qualities, along with physical strength, were what distinguished men from women, was thought important. They enabled men and women to complement each other, and gave men the duty to protect women. 'Your sex wanteth our reason for your conduct, and our strength for your protection', argued one father to his daughter in 1688.[112] The desire to teach men to control their anger, the emotion that could cloud their reason, and make them prone to aggressive and violent behaviour, stemmed back to at least the start of the seventeenth century. As we have seen, Puritan writers such as Whateley, cautioned that husbands should not discipline their wives when they were angry. By the eighteenth century the same lessons in anger control were still being repeated. What had changed by this time was that anger had become an emotion that was more thoroughly associated with men rather than women, and boys and young men had lessons in self-government that were delivered in a more systematic and organised way.[113] Clearly, there needs to be more acknowledgement of these important continuities in ideas about masculinity.[114]

So, in the period from 1660 to 1857, voices from a number of different sources, religious, secular, elite, middling and popular, expressed doubts and sometimes disapproval about the legitimacy of violence in married life. Command over oneself was a skill that adult and married men were expected to acquire. While there was much continuity in attitudes about marital violence, the way that these ideas were transmitted did not stay the same. From the late seventeenth century, for example, the burgeoning middle class, hungry for advice about domestic life, consumed messages about the wrongs of marital violence in new forms of print culture such as the periodical, as well as via the more traditional mediums of sermon and conduct book.

---

[111] J. Locke, *Some Thoughts Concerning Education* (1693), eds. J. W. and J. S. Yolton (Oxford, 1989), p. 255.

[112] The first Marquis of Halifax, as cited in V. Jones (ed.), *Women in the Eighteenth Century: Constructions of Femininity* (London, 1990), p. 18.

[113] E. Foyster, 'Boys will be boys? Manhood and aggression, 1660–1800', in Hitchcock and Cohen (eds.), *English Masculinities*, pp. 151–66, see also, F. Bound, '"An angry and malicious mind"? Narratives of slander at the church courts of York, c.1660–c.1760', *History Workshop Journal* 56 (2003), 73.

[114] John Tosh has identified many important continuities, see 'The old Adam and the new man: emerging themes in the history of English masculinities, 1750–1850', in Hitchcock and Cohen (eds.), *English Masculinities*, pp. 217–38.

In addition, arguments against marital violence were shaped by the changing concerns of the society in which they were expressed. Just as greater emphasis was placed upon the unsociable and insensitive aspects of marital violence as a culture of the ideals of politeness and sensibility came to prevail, so in the nineteenth century they assumed an imperialist tone to reflect the expanding British empire. Hence by 1853 the MP who introduced the Bill to increase the punishment of those found guilty of aggravated assaults, argued that it was a necessary remedy to eradicate 'the evil which . . . constituted such a blot upon our national character', committed by men 'who one blushed to think were Englishmen'. Equally, a member of the House of Lords believed that reform in divorce law was necessary in 'this country, which boasts the most advanced state of civilisation in the world', but where 'the legal position of women has partaken of that situation which it would occupy in the least civilized and most barbarous states'. The treatment of women was considered a measure of civilization and national pride, and a matter where Englishmen needed to prove themselves more advanced and self-disciplined than others, especially those peoples in the empire over which they ruled.[115] Yet even this construction of an historical 'other' had earlier precedents. From at least the seventeenth century the freedom of English wives had been the subject of English pride. According to contemporary propaganda England was a 'land of liberty' in which men had created a 'paradise for women'.[116] By the nineteenth century experiments in social control had extended to legislation to deal with the problem of marital violence, but the historical roots of ideas that led to reform could be found in former periods.

Controls were in place to limit the occasions and extent of marital violence across our period. It was hoped that for the husband who had concern for his reputation these viewpoints and expectations would act to lessen his violent behaviour towards his wife, even if they did not prevent it altogether. But as time progressed, fears were heightened about a particular group of men who were thought to be beyond the reach of these social controls. This group were believed to be prone to particular forms of cruel violence in marriage, and their violence had consequences that were not shared by others. It is to this change in ideas about marital violence that we must now turn.

[115] *Hansard*, vol. 124 (19 March 1853), 1414; vol. 142 (26 June 1856), 1973; for contrasts between England and the empire see, Wiener, *Men of Blood*, pp. 31–4.

[116] Capp, *When Gossips Meet*, pp. 6–7; P. Langford, *Englishness Identified: Manners and Character 1650–1850* (Oxford, 2000), pp. 271–3.

Defining cruel violence by class: change

By the mid-nineteenth century a key change had occurred so that class had become an important determinant for the definition of cruel violence. The types of marital violence that were anticipated in each social group, the impact of this violence upon women, and how wives were expected to respond were all shaped by notions of class difference.

The trigger for change was the idea that marital violence was a social as well as a moral wrong. Rather than seeing marital violence as a breach of moral codes that were applicable to all, it became an offence against manners that could vary with social group. This could create new expectations of behaviour for middle- and upper-class husbands. For example, in the eighteenth century when polite codes of manners placed much importance upon sociability and good conversation, husbands who denied their wives opportunities to mix in their social circle, or who created social embarrassment by verbally abusing their wives, were liable to being accused of marital cruelty. In these social circles, the definition of cruel violence widened as an ever larger range of behaviours came to be labelled as unacceptable.[117] But it also separated middling and elite men from the lower orders by suggesting a false division in the extent and types of marital violence that could be expected from each. If marital violence was a social wrong, thought contemporaries, then only those with no regard for social mores, the rough and idle poor, would resort frequently to its practice. Physical violence, it was assumed, was such a sign of brutish, uncivilized behaviour, that its perpetrators were confined to those social ranks where men were not alert to the sensitivity of others. To put it another way, it was believed that only 'a tenderness of mind produced mild behaviour'.[118] Finally, labelling marital violence as a social offence was significant because it became possible to see this violence as more than simply a sign of the breakdown of a relationship between individuals. Rather, marital violence became regarded as behaviour that was linked to a group instead of disparate married couples, and was a symptom of social disorder that was in urgent need of attention. Thus marital violence was transformed into a matter for social discipline and class control. A new cultural stereotype emerged of the cruel husband. He was working class and subjected his wife to physical

---

[117] E. Foyster, 'Creating a veil of silence? Politeness and marital violence in the English household', *Transactions of the Royal Historical Society* 6th series, 12 (2002), 403–7.
[118] R. McGowen, 'Punishing violence, sentencing crime', in N. Armstrong and L. Tennenhouse (eds.), *The Violence of Representation: Literature and the History of Violence* (London, 1989), p. 146.

and verbal violence that no middle- or upper-class wife could be expected to bear.

What is our evidence for this change? In many ways the seeds for change were found in the relational definition of cruel violence, expressed by Scott in the *D'Aguilar* case: 'there may be relative cruelty: and what is tolerable by one may not be by another'.[119] In practice, as we have seen, people expected husbands and wives to adjust their behaviour relative to a woman's status as a mother, or the health and age of either party. But there also developed the idea that the marital conduct of a husband should relate to his or his wife's wealth. As *The Laws Respecting Women* explained, a husband had a duty to supply his wife with necessaries that were 'suitable to his rank and fortune'.[120] Many individuals assessed what was adequate provision by looking at what in terms of material wealth the wife had brought to the marriage. But wives judged the quality of goods they were given by their husbands according to what they had previously experienced before marriage, or in former marital relationships. Hence a Dorsetshire wife argued that 'the victuals' her husband 'provided for her were of the most inferior kind and by no means suitable to the situation in which she had always lived'.[121] There was also an expectation that goods would be supplied that bore relation to the value of a wife's portion. So David Soux, a Westminster goldsmith could tell the courts that 'notwithstanding' he had only received a £11 portion with his wife, and hence 'no fortune in marriage', he had behaved towards his wife 'as a good and loving husband and maintained her genteely in her apparel and presented her with a gold watch and provided all things decent and fitting for her'.[122]

The new husbands of widows could find themselves criticised if they did not keep their wives in the manner to which they had grown accustomed in their former marriages. Catherine Beverley's two witnesses in 1669, for example, said that her husband, John, had been cruel because he had not treated her in the same way as her previous husband, 'a very rich man', who 'had left her a very good estate'. In contrast, John was 'a Frenchman', used to a 'diet of herbs and other slight eating'. As an

---

[119] *D'Aguilar v. D'Aguilar* (1794), *English Reports* vol. 162, p. 753.
[120] *The Laws Respecting Women* (London, 1777), p. 66, as cited in Bailey, *Unquiet Lives*, p. 62.
[121] LPL, CA, Case 1111, (1805), H50/8.
[122] NA, DEL1/321 (1702), ff.47v,95v–96r; for another example of a husband using a similar defence see, LPL, CA, Case 2050, (1730), D431, f.91r; for the belief that a portion entitled a wife to provision in marriage see also, Bailey, 'Favoured or oppressed?', 361–2.

Englishwoman Catherine was used to eating meat, and 'by this diet of herbs' had been forced to go to her neighbour's house to eat meat, where she complained of 'great hunger'. Her standard of clothing had also declined. Formerly she had been 'a woman of very good quality and fashion', but now her clothes were 'very much worn', and 'very much below her quality and condition'.[123]

Such cases highlight interesting differences between men and women about how they defined their social rank. For husbands, a woman's property and therefore her social rank were subsumed under his within marriage. But those who represented women in cruelty cases suggested that particularly when a woman's social position had been higher than her husband's before marriage, this status, acquired from her parents, or from a previous marriage, was retained throughout her subsequent marriage. Clearly, despite the theory of coverture, upon marriage a woman's identity was not submerged under her husband's.

The most important point to emerge from these cases, however, is that there was a popular belief that it was a woman's status that should determine her treatment within marriage. Women and men shared an understanding of what they were entitled to in marriage, which went beyond the ownership of objects, to the behaviour they were due from their spouse. Crucially, witnesses who saw men being physically violent to their wives also began to use assessments of the women's material worth to explain why they thought such behaviour was cruel. Hence examining a couple's economic status shifted from being a method simply for assessing the adequacy of a husband's provision, to a way of judging all conduct within marriage. John Dorney, a witness in a 1673 marriage separation case, said that despite the wife's scolding, and possibly adulterous conduct, most of his neighbours passed 'their verdict' against her violent husband, because of the good estate she had brought him in marriage. In other cases witnesses were more active and public in their condemnation. One Mrs Newman was present in the Walnut Tree victualling house in Southwark sometime around 1732, and saw Thomas Revell striking his wife with his doubled fist until she was knocked unconscious. She angrily addressed Thomas, saying, 'Thou vile rogue, this woman brought you . . . all that you have, and now to use her so, I don't know but you have murdered her, hanging is too good for you'. While the degree or severity of the physical violence in this case may have provoked a response no matter to whom it was

---

[123] LPL, CA, Case 842, (1669), Eee3, f.544v-547r; E. Foyster, 'Marrying the experienced widow in early modern England: the male perspective', in S. Cavallo and L. Warner (eds.), *Widowhood in Medieval and Early Modern Europe* (Harlow, 1999), pp. 108–24; A. L. Erickson, *Women and Property in Early Modern England* (London, 1993), p. 123.

directed, community knowledge that Thomas' economic status had been enhanced by his marriage to his wife, who had been a widow, increased the sense of outrage when he failed to treat her with respect.[124]

What we see in these cases of marital cruelty is a connection being made between belongings and behaviour. For individuals outside the conjugal unit, the use of material objects within a marriage provided useful and tangible evidence of the quality of relations within it. If a wife was provided with goods that were of a quality that were 'suitable' to her social position, it was assumed that her husband regarded her as worthy of his respect, and would treat her fairly. Married women who subsequently complained of cruel violence shared these assumptions, and made full use of them in their allegations. By proving their social status, which they did by pointing to their position before marriage, they demonstrated their entitlement to a certain standard of behaviour from their husbands. Thus a woman's relationship to material goods was a tool for measuring and maintaining what was regarded as fit and proper conduct by her husband. It set the balance on the scales of power within a relationship, and determined the degree of violence that could acceptably be used within it.

Frequently the meaning of economic provision for wives of the middle and upper classes was assessed by comparison, not with the possessions of their social equals or superiors, but against the goods of those women who worked most closely below them, their servants. Theodosia Freeman in 1734 was said to be so poorly maintained by her husband that she 'wore very ordinary stockings such as the servants usually wear', and had 'linen and hoods' which were 'very mean and far from such as were suitable to a gentlewoman of her rank and fortune'.[125] In the nineteenth century, when a witness for the Countess of Dysart commented upon necessaries, she deposed that 'she sometimes went without what I should consider to be such for a lady; I have known her to be without sugar for tea, or for fruit tart; I have known her to be without wine'. Another said that the Earl of Dysart allowed his wife 'but one candle a night . . . there is scarcely a servant in any family but is allowed more than that'.[126] Here we see the social calibration of consumption; what would have been luxuries for servants, were necessities for a Countess.

As Hammerton has recognised, to be demeaned in front of the servants, or to be treated as a servant was an intolerable form of

---

[124] LPL, CA, Case 1813, (1673), Eee5, f.27v; LPL, CA, Case 7616, (1734), Eee14, f.123r.
[125] NA, DEL1/479 (1734), ff.296–7,303.
[126] *Dysart v. Dysart* (1844), *English Reports* vol. 163, pp. 1110, 1112.

economic cruelty that was unique to those social classes who could afford to employ them. But it was a type of cruelty that had been practised well before it was discussed in the post 1857 Divorce Court that Hammerton has studied. Elite women did not expect to be treated by their husbands in the same way as servants. Just one earlier example is from the eighteenth-century Ettrick marriage dispute. Here it was stated that,

notwithstanding the said Catherine Ettrick was of a very genteel family and had received a good education and had brought him a fortune of £2,000 and upwards yet the said William Ettrick used her as a servant by frequently obliging her to go and sit with the servants in the kitchen not suffering her to sit in the dining room with him . . . and by frequently obliging her to run after his cows and horses in the fields.[127]

For Catherine it was her polite upbringing and training, as well as her material worth that made her husband's behaviour unbearable. Her social status was represented as something that made her undeserving of her fate. As the Ettrick case shows, by the eighteenth century, contemporaries were beginning to use socio-economic status more frequently to mark out the different standards of behaviour that could be labelled as cruel violence in marriage.

A woman's economic position relative to her husband could be expected to govern the quality of her marital relations, but it was also thought to affect her response to violence. The idea developed that the costs of violence bore more heavily upon women used to social privileges. The disparate consequences of economic cruelty were acknowledged by judges such as Dr Lushington, who in 1844 went as far as to pronounce that,

Necessaries and comforts must have some relation to the rank and station of the parties . . . A wife brought up as a gentlewoman would suffer in her health and constitution, nay even her life might be endangered by a mode of living which would be comfortable to a female in a different mode of life.[128]

There was a model of ideal femininity in such statements that was heavily laden with class assumptions. The delicate and frail gentlewoman could not be expected to endure the same material conditions within marriage as the sturdy and hardy working-class woman. We can see from marriage separation cases that from at least the mid-eighteenth century affluent women had been able to benefit from such thinking by

---

[127] Hammerton, 'Victorian marriage', 287–90, and *Cruelty and Companionship*, pp. 92–3, 98, 114–16, 128, 132; NA, DEL1/598 (1768), f.465–7.
[128] *Dysart v. Dysart* (1844), *English Reports* vol. 163, p. 982.

using their social status to appeal against ill-treatment. So Martha Pearse, establishing her social status by declaring herself the daughter of an MP and a navy commissioner, claimed that her husband's threats, verbal and physical violence had led to,

the total destruction of her peace of mind, who being of a weak and tender frame and constitution, and from her cradle till her intermarriage with him most affectionately indulged and caressed by her parents, who were passionately fond of her, was the less able to support herself under so severe and sharp a trial and affliction.[129]

Suffering here is proportional not to the degree of violence inflicted, but to the social status of its victim. Immersed in a new discourse of refinement, the culture of sensibility, the mid-eighteenth-century genteel woman was believed to have more delicate and weaker nerves than men or women from the lower social orders.[130] Thus, as we shall see in the next chapter, she could be represented as more sensitive to the pain of marital violence, in all its forms. For Martha Pearse, softened by the indulgences (both material and emotional) of her social class, marital violence of any type was insupportable, and had both mental and physical effects. Such eighteenth-century cases demonstrate that interest in defining cruelty according to the consequences of violence began well before the 1860s, the date suggested by Hammerton.[131]

By calculating the material wealth of a married woman, and so her social status, contemporaries created indices of tolerance for marital violence. Rather than simply being a useful way for women to claim equitable treatment in marriage, socio-economic status became a method for middling and elite women to demand better conduct from their husbands. Marital conduct was rendered into an indicator of class superiority and difference. This can be seen in changing attitudes towards verbal violence. Women such as Mary Veitch who complained of verbal abuse in the nineteenth century did so in a cultural context which was markedly different from the seventeenth century. In the earlier period, stories of marriage breakdown were full of references to occasions when husbands called their wives whores. John Norcott called Rachael, 'damn'd whore and damn'd jade and threatened he would give her a whore's mark', for example. The term 'whore' was used freely by all social groups, often with little attempt to link the insult with actual behaviour, and neither women nor the justiciary appeared to have had

---

[129] LPL, CA, Case 7022 (1748), D1573, f.43.
[130] Barker-Benfield, *The Culture of Sensibility*, pp. 23–36.
[131] Hammerton, 'Victorian marriage', 274, and *Cruelty and Companionship*, pp. 127, 129.

difficulty in naming the offence.[132] However, during the eighteenth century the manner in which this accusation was made altered. Two cases heard in the London consistory court, both dated 1783, illustrate this point. Jane Prescott, the daughter of a 'respectable clergyman', complained to the court that her husband had used the type of language to her 'as the vilest of men only use to the most abandoned women'. Similarly, Sarah Terry, the daughter of a London silversmith, 'a very respectable citizen', said that her husband had 'daily reviled her' with 'language as the worst of men use to the most abandoned women'.[133]

By the time these two wives came to seek marriage separation, important changes had taken place which gave their accusations of verbal abuse new meanings. The definition of the term 'whore' had altered so that the 'private' whore was distinguished from the 'public' whore or prostitute. Whore was a term of abuse which had become inextricably associated with whom the two wives labelled as 'abandoned women', in other words, the professional prostitute.[134] Furthermore, and significantly, both the prostitutes and the men who used such language ('the vilest of men' or the 'worst of men') were perceived to be from the lower sorts. Patterns of public insult appeared to confirm this view, as by the end of the eighteenth century there had been a significant decline in the social status of those fighting defamation suits for sexual slander in the church courts.[135] Within the marriages of the middling sorts women could not be expected to tolerate the insult of whore because of its new class and sexual meanings. Language that was believed to be part of common parlance in one social class could be represented as verbal violence in another. Hence judges in the church courts condemned men who used the term against their wives. This was even to the point reached in 1823 when James Best, convinced that his wife was adulterous, was still criticised for being cruel by addressing his wife using 'reproofs abounding in epithets always ungrateful to female ears'.[136] Neither the

---

[132] LPL, CA, Case 6659, (1666), Eee2, f.96v; Gowing, *Domestic Dangers*, passim; E. Foyster, *Manhood in Early Modern England: Honour, Sex and Marriage* (Harlow, 1999), pp. 181–2.

[133] LMA, DL/C/179 (1783), f.409v; LMA, DL/C/179 (1783), f.514r.

[134] F. N. Dabhoiwala, 'Prostitution and police in London, c.1660–c.1760', DPhil thesis, University of Oxford (1995), part I.

[135] A. Clark, 'Whores and gossips: Sexual reputation in London 1770–1825', in A. Angerman, G. Binnema, A. Keunen, V. Poels and J. Zirkzee (eds.), *Current Issues in Women's History* (London, 1989), pp. 239–40; P. Morris shows how the polite sensibilities of court officials and government commissioners were offended by the sexual nature of defamation cases brought by the lower orders by this period in, 'Defamation and sexual reputation in Somerset, 1733–1850', PhD thesis, University of Warwick (1985), pp. 13, 233, 236–42, 438–40.

[136] *Best v. Best* (1823) *English Reports* vol. 162, p. 154.

name of whore nor its utterance were fitting for polite society. Thus while James Veitch was said to have 'abused' and sworn at Mary 'with excessive violence' (giving us an example of how behaviour need not have been physical in form to be labelled as violence), the actual words he used were never detailed.[137]

These class-based definitions of violence extended to understandings of physical violence. By the nineteenth century, judges were beginning to interpret Scott's comments about the social factors that could 'aggravate' cruelty, made within his landmark definition, to mean that physical violence within genteel circles should be regarded more seriously than in the lower orders. For Sir John Nicholl, ruling on the *Westmeath* marital dispute in 1827, the physical violence alleged by Lady Westmeath against her husband, was clearly 'aggravated' by the social position held by the couple. He argued that,

A blow between parties in the lower conditions and in the highest stations of life bears a very different aspect. Among the lower classes blows sometimes pass between married couples who, in the main, are very happy and have no desire to part; amidst very coarse habits such incidents occur almost as freely as rude or reproachful words: a word and a blow go together. Still, even among the very lowest classes, there is generally a feeling of something unmanly in striking a woman; but if a gentleman, a person of education . . . uses personal violence to his wife, his equal in rank . . . such conduct in such a person carries with it something so degrading to the husband, and so insulting and mortifying to the wife, as to render the injury itself far more severe and insupportable.[138]

According to Sir John, physical violence within the 'lower classes' occurred more frequently, and did not have the same consequences as violence experienced by members of his own social rank. What was tolerable violence in one social class was cruel in another. In what was to be true to the Victorian fashion for classification, Sir John and his contemporaries tried to separate, categorise and box types of violence into pigeon holes, labelled 'class'.

In the process, forms of violence became associated with different social groups. Physical violence was labelled as the vice of the rough and disorderly poor; mental violence or the torment of words and behaviour intended to be humiliating and degrading, was consigned to the middle and upper classes. This did not mean that the latter forms of violence were viewed as any less harmful to wives. By 1856, as discussions about divorce law reform raged, J. W. Kaye concluded from his study of marital violence:

[137] LPL, CA, Case 9440 (1837), H550/5.
[138] *Westmeath v. Westmeath* (1827) *English Reports* vol. 162, p. 1017.

Men of education and refinement do not strike women; neither do they strike one another. This is not their mode of expressing resentment. They may utter words more cutting than sharp knives; they may do things more stunning in their effects on the victim than the blows of pokers or hammers; they may half kill their wives by process of slow torture – unkindness, infidelity, whatever shape it may assume - society will forgive them. The law, too, has nothing to say to them. They are not guilty of what is recognised as an assault, because they only assail the affections - only lacerate the heart.[139]

The view that physical violence in marriage was a problem for the poor was endorsed by the working class themselves. By the 1830s, working-class radicals were condemning marital violence, seeing it as a symptom of a masculine popular culture of drink and fighting. As we have seen, this disapproval of violence among working people was nothing new, but in the nineteenth century it became politicized. As the Chartists campaigned for an extended franchise, the image of the working man who could not rule his wife without resort to physical violence was deployed by their opponents to argue that such men were not qualified for citizenship. Legislation was passed to punish husbands who were found guilty of physically assaulting their wives. Working-class men, it was argued in parliament, could not be trusted to exercise sufficient self-control in their exercise of violence towards their wives. In turn, the 'respectable' working poor distanced themselves from their 'rude' and 'rough' neighbours who routinely used physical violence against their wives, and instead identified with middle-class ideals of domestic harmony.[140]

So, over the course of 200 years, marital violence was redefined. The cruelty of violence depended upon the social class of the woman it was directed against, as well as her personal circumstances. While continuing to condemn some occasions of marital violence, contemporaries split violence into its different forms, and believed that physical violence and sexual insult was more prevalent in the lower social ranks. Middle- and upper-class couples who did not conform to this pattern of behaviour could expect to be upbraided. Mr and Mrs Waring, for example, whose history of 'gross abuse, coarse language, [and] personal struggles' had caused the 'annoyance and disturbance of the neighbourhood', were scolded by Scott, who ruled over their appeal case for marriage separation in 1813, for conduct that was 'not becoming the decorum of their

---

[139] J. W. Kaye, 'Outrages on women', *North British Review* 25, 49 (1856), 235, as cited in Hammerton, *Cruelty and Companionship*, p. 74.

[140] Clark, *The Struggle for the Breeches*, especially chapters 5, 14, and 'Domesticity and the problem of wifebeating in nineteenth-century Britain: working-class culture, law and politics', in D'Cruze (ed.), *Everyday Violence*, 27–40.

situation in life'.[141] While the Waring marriage shows us that despite common perceptions of violent behaviour, all its forms were found in every social rank, Scott's reaction reveals that the meaning or significance of that violence varied with social position. Violence between Mr and Mrs Waring was shameful in part because of their social class. But sadly there is no evidence that defining certain types of marital violence as socially distasteful acted as a control upon violence. There remained a significant difference between the ideals of conduct in married life and the reality. Middle-class aspirations for companionate marriage, in which violence had little or no part, were never fulfilled.

Conclusion

If we return to the Norcott and Veitch marriages we find that both wives endured violence that was multi-faceted and could not be divided into different components. Clearly violence in marital relationships was not as ordered as nineteenth-century classifications tried to make it. We need to be careful as historians that we do not replicate Victorian attempts to separate physical violence from other forms of marital violence and in this way label it as more serious and worthy of our attention.

We have seen that many people in our period accepted that violence had a place in married relationships. Even as a wider range of male behaviour came to be assessed in marriage separation cases, not all unpleasant or abusive conduct between husbands and wives was treated as violence. 'Cruel' was an adjective that was attached to violence between husband and wife only in certain circumstances. As far as we can tell from the surviving records, no witnesses spoke in defence of John Norcott, but a number spoke for James Veitch. Far from being a cruel man, they described him as a good husband and a kind doctor. So it did not follow that even if a wife brought a separation case for marital cruelty to the courts, that all witnesses would agree that every occasion of violence in that marriage was unwarranted or unacceptable. Continuing toleration for aspects of marital violence may go some way to explain why over time there has been so little change in our most accessible and quantifiable measure of family violence; levels of domestic homicide. Certainly, tolerant attitudes towards marital violence co-existed with the view that in an ideal relationship between husband and wife, violence would be unnecessary. But, in searching for ways to achieve that domestic idyll, condemnation of marital violence did not increase over time.

---

[141] *Waring v. Waring* (1813), *English Reports* vol. 161, p. 700.

What changed was the basis for condemnation and some of the forms in which it was expressed.

In the nineteenth century, Mary's story of violence in her marriage, along with many others told by middling- and upper-class women, exposed the painful truth that social class offered women no protection from marital violence. As we shall see in the next chapter, middle- and upper-class women did not respond silently to violence as their husbands may have wished, and their vociferous complaints meant that the displacement of male violence onto the working classes could never be completed. In these circumstances, it is remarkable that the belief that physical forms of marital violence were more prevalent in working-class marriages proved so stubbornly resilient. As we shall see, the Victorian assignment of different forms of violence to different social groups proved fatal when marital violence became an issue for legislation and attempts at social reform. But trying to define marital violence along class lines did not, as Hunt has claimed for the eighteenth century, and Hammerton for the nineteenth, blind the social elites to the problem of marital violence in their own social ranks.[142] Even if some Victorians were determined to believe that the violence experienced in middle- and upper-class marriages was of a different kind, as Kaye's words show, it could still be regarded as serious, cruel and damaging.

It was because of changes in the ideas about marital violence that Mary was able to use her social status to construct a definition of marital violence that was very different from Rachael's. Mary did not need to accuse her husband of the same degree of physical violence as Rachael, for many of her friends, servants and family to support her view that James Veitch had been a cruel husband. Mary could emphasise other aspects of her husband's behaviour. Threats of physical violence, attempts to stop her socialising in her community by confining her in the house, and the treatment of her children were all submitted as part of her allegation. By listing a wide and detailed range of complaints, Mary's story of her marriage was typical of those made by other women of her class and generation. As we have shown, certain circumstances would always have made marital violence unacceptable, whatever the time period in which women's stories of violence were told. By the nineteenth century, however, as ideas about class became more important to definitions of cruel violence, the conduct of James Veitch was more likely to be regarded as intolerable for Mary because it was unsuitable for a couple in their social position. In this context, even though Rachael

[142] Hunt, 'Wife beating', 24–8; Hammerton, *Cruelty and Companionship*, p. 73.

and Mary both endured physical blows, verbal insults and forms of economic deprivation from their husbands, this behaviour would have been interpreted differently. However, as the next chapter will show, the decision about whether violence in marriage was cruel was not made until the behaviour of both the wife and the husband had been taken into account. Women who were the targets of violence had to meet the expectations of their gender and class roles before their complaints would meet sympathetic ears. Their conduct prior to, during, and after violence came under close and critical scrutiny.

2   Resisting violence

Rachael Norcott first fled from her husband John's violence in 1664, when she sought refuge with one of her sisters. John found her there, and facing criticism for his behaviour from Rachael's family and friends, dramatically wished, 'that his tongue might rot out if ever he abused her again'. Such words appear to have persuaded Rachael to return to her husband, for she was to endure another two years of violence before she began separation proceedings.[1]

Asking why women remain with violent men is a question that is frequently asked today, but this is in a society where divorce is widely available. During the period of this study, divorce was not possible on the grounds of violence, and there were many economic and social factors that acted to dissuade women from pursuing a marriage separation on the basis of cruelty. Thus, even if their personal safety was at risk, some women calculated that it was not in their best interests to leave. From the Restoration to the mid-nineteenth century, a more relevant enquiry was not why women stayed with violent husbands, but how women learnt to cope with their violent partners. Thus on 12 March 1789 one London debating society considered the motion, put forward by 'a young lady', whether 'a Lady that is married to a tyrannical husband be more likely to promote her own happiness by a spirited opposition, or a patient submission to his temper and conduct?'[2] As this chapter will show, there was considerable pressure upon women to show 'patient submission' to their violent husbands. Yet, as we shall see, for women who stayed with their violent husbands, 'patient submission' was not necessarily incompatible with 'spirited opposition'. While women were eager to demonstrate that they had conformed to their ideal gender

---

[1] LPL, CA, Case 6659 (1666), Eee2, f.95.
[2] D. T. Andrew (ed.), *London Debating Societies, 1776–1799* London Record Society (London, 1994), p. 252; the debate had been provoked by the publication of the *Trial of Lady Strathmore*, who had been imprisoned in Streatlam Castle, County Durham, and then accused of adultery by her husband, Andrew Robinson Bowes. See, Foyster, 'At the limits of liberty', 44.

roles, which emphasized patience and obedience, they were also able to achieve a measure of opposition and resistance to male violence that did not compromise their femininity. Middle- and upper-class wives were aided in part by changing notions of the acceptability of certain types of male violence, as outlined in the previous chapter, but they also found new ways to respond to male violence as ideas of femininity developed. So, as this chapter will demonstrate, the options for response to violence open to Mary Veitch in the early nineteenth century were very different from those available in the 1660s to Rachael Norcott.

When forms of marital violence were widely tolerated, and not all violence was regarded as 'cruel', women could be expected to accommodate violent behaviour within their relationships and daily lives. But being forced to live with violence never implied passivity on the part of women, for women themselves could use forms of violence as tools of empowerment as well as resistance. As we shall see, women's resistance was not always displayed in forms that were direct, immediate or overt. Although our evidence is weighted towards occasions when women openly resisted their husband's dominance, we gain occasional glimpses, especially by reading women's private papers, of how wives challenged their husbands in less obviously confrontational ways. Wives who refused to communicate, perform housework, or manage servants and children were all resisting the subjugation that their husband's violence aimed to achieve.

This chapter will first examine various forms of prescriptive literature to show what were thought the ideal ways for a wife to respond to marital violence. These responses were ideal for men because they did not challenge their authority, and they will be compared with the practice of women's behaviour. We will go on to show how conforming to these ideal patterns could have serious consequences for women's mental well-being. For internalising the messages of prescriptive literature along with the harm that marital violence could inflict left mental as well as physical damage. Other wives met violence with violence, and this chapter will consider the different forms that female and male violence could take within marriage. A key distinction between the violence of wives and husbands, as we will see, was whether it could be presented as a just response to provocation by the other spouse. In the final section of this chapter the new options for resisting marital violence that developed during the eighteenth century for middle- and upper-class wives will be outlined. Overall this chapter seeks to demonstrate how the effects of marital violence upon women's and men's bodies and minds were understood, and how the range of responses to this violence was shaped by gender, class and historical period.

Responding wisely: didactic advice

Guidance for wives who faced violence from their husbands in our period was available at all social levels. Prescriptive literature taught wives the importance of obedience and submission, even to husbands who were violent and cruel. Yet by comparing prescription with practice, we can see how for wives who adhered to the gender roles that were dictated, there was still room for resistance. Indeed, prescriptive codes for gender roles contained the very seeds of resistance. For women, it was believed, had a strength of character through their feminine virtues of modesty, piety and chastity, which could overcome their weakness, and be a positive force within marriage. Used strategically, as we will see, wives could deploy these feminine virtues to draw attention to the cruelty of their husband's violence. Ideals of femininity were also adopted by women and developed as sources of personal defence, enabling them to cope with and explain male violence in an ongoing relationship.

Those in the lowest social ranks could learn about how to manage marriage from hearing and singing popular ballads. Some ballads, such as 'The Brother's Advice to his Sister, After Marriage', from a collection dated c.1780–1820 gave generic advice to a wife, teaching her to bear with her husband's faults, and if her husband reprimanded her, to 'love him ne'er the less'.[3] Other ballads were more specific about what to do in the case of marital violence. While the 'Worth of a Woman' advised men not to beat their wives, the companion ballad, 'Worth of a Husband' told wives that,

> . . . if he shou'd have bang'd your hide, you must not take it amiss,
> But take him round the neck and give to him a kiss,
> And if he gets drunk at night, and beat you as a warning,
> You must give him a pint of stout the first thing in the morning.[4]

Impractical as this advice was, its sentiments were repeated in the prescriptive literature produced for the more literate middling and upper social ranks. According to Hannah Woolley, a wife's duty was to please and placate her more irascible husband. A wife with her husband should,

Be quiet, pleasant, and peaceable with him, and be not angry, when he is so; but endeavour to pacify him with sweet and winning expressions; and if casually you should provoke him to a passion, be not long ere you show some regret, which

---

[3] 'The Brother's Advice to his Sister, After Marriage', Bell Collection.
[4] 'Worth of a Woman' and 'Worth of a Husband', Madden vol. 7, 258 and 257. These ballads are also printed in vol. 8, 1434 and 1432.

may argue how much you are displeased with your self for so doing; nay bear his anger patiently, though without a cause.[5]

Bearing patiently with a husband's faults might bring about an improvement in his behaviour, thought Lady Sarah Pennington, but it was also the only way for a wife to achieve 'any tolerable degree of ease', and preserve a 'tranquillity of mind, under so disagreeable a connection'.[6]

While teaching women the virtues of silence and obedience was nothing new, in the eighteenth and early nineteenth centuries there developed the notion that it was within women's innate nature to pacify and civilize men. 'Women were formed to temper mankind, and soothe them into tenderness and compassion, not to set an edge upon their minds', wrote the *Spectator* in 1711.[7] Femininity was constructed in such a way as to place a new moral responsibility upon wives to reform their husband's behaviour through their own example. Qualities such as patience, mildness, gentleness and the desire to please others were labelled as feminine and were valued because of what they could offer men. 'We are made of differing tempers, that our defects may the better be mutually supplied', thought the first Marquis of Halifax.[8] For the writer of one conduct book, one of the 'advantages of female society' for men was its 'delicacy . . . which serves well to check the boisterous, to tame the brutal, and to embolden the timid'. Thus in this period gender was constructed in complementary as well as relational terms.[9] As the Reverend Wilkes explained, the burden fell upon women to amend the conduct of men,

In the occurrences of matrimonial life, it is a rule proper to be observed – to preserve always a disposition to be pleased. An ill-managing man is often brought to see his errors, and to reclaim, by the mild advises of his wife, and her obliging condescensions to humour him. By her gentleness, and sweet temper, he is prevailed on to inspect into himself, and to remove every imperfection that is displeasing to her . . . Meekness and complacency, are the only weapons wherewith to combat an irregular husband. The engaging softness of a wife, when prudently managed, subdues all the natural and legal authority of any reasonable man. Her looks have more power than his laws, and a few sweet words, from her, can soften all his fury.[10]

[5] H. Woolley, *The Gentlewoman's Companion; Or, a Guide to the Female Sex* (London, 1675), p. 106.

[6] S. Pennington, *A Mother's Advice to her Absent Daughters*, 8th edition (London, 1817), pp. 72, 74.

[7] D. F. Bond (ed.), *The Spectator*, 5 vols. (Oxford, 1965) 1, 242 (5 May 1711).

[8] As cited in Jones, (ed.), *Women in the Eighteenth Century*, p. 18.

[9] *The Young Man's Own Book. A Manual of Politeness, Intellectual Improvement, and Moral Deportment* (London, 1833), p. 89; Fletcher, *Gender, Sex and Subordination*, chapter 19.

[10] W. Wilkes, *A Letter of Genteel and Moral Advice to a Young Lady* 8th edition (London, 1766), p. 195.

The stress upon female submission, patience and forbearance was as current at the end of our period as at its start. The publications of Sarah Stickney Ellis on women as wives, mothers and daughters, for example, widely publicised these as important values for the Victorian domestic idyll.[11]

Such was thought to be the influence of women upon men's behaviour, that wives were encouraged to examine their own conduct if their husbands were violent. A culture of female self-blame was engendered. This was further promoted by the publication of works by writers such as the evangelical Hannah More. Her *Cheap Repository of Moral and Religious Tracts* was produced at the end of the eighteenth century as a reaction against the proliferation of popular ballads and chapbooks, which as we shall see, did not always advise married couples to resolve their disputes in ways approved by upright Christians. More's tracts were widely distributed to the poor. One tells the fictional story of Sarah Smithwaite and her husband Richard, a mason. Initially their marriage is a success, but after two years their relationship turns sour, and matters come to a head when Richard nearly strikes Sarah in anger. But instead of this tract focusing on the dangers and wrongs of male violence, its chief message is how a wife can turn a good man bad. Hence the title of the tract is 'The Wife Reformed', and it is Sarah who is taught how gadding and idle gossiping meant that she neglected her home and family, allowing the alehouse and alcohol to become more attractive alternatives for Richard than the fireside comforts of their home. By scolding her husband, and arguing with him Sarah raises Richard's passions with almost devastating results. It is left to the village curate to point out the error of her ways and bring about her reform.[12]

Let's turn from prescription to practice. There is evidence that some women played at least lip service to the advice they received about marital violence. When wives accused their husbands of violence they were careful to represent themselves as living up to the ideals for their gender. Thus Rachael Norcott's witnesses said that she was 'a modest and civil woman and of a good, sober and honest life and conversation . . . of a mild and sweet nature and disposition'.[13] Other women emphasised

---

[11] See, for example, S. Ellis, *The Wives of England, their Relative Duties, Domestic Influence, and Social Obligations* (London, 1843), chapters 4 and 7; and Davidoff and Hall, *Family Fortunes*, pp. 180–5.

[12] [H. More], 'The Wife Reformed' in *Cheap Repository of Moral and Religious Tracts* (London, 1797), pp. 1–16; for historical context see, S. Pedersen, 'Hannah More meets Simple Simon: Tracts, chapbooks, and popular culture in late eighteenth-century England', *Journal of British Studies* 25 (1986), 84–113.

[13] LPL, CA, Case 6659 (1666), Eee2, f.96r.

that they had been careful household managers. Mabell Whitmore, for example, said in 1752 that she was,

> a person of a modest sober virtuous life and conversation of a quiet meek mild and affable temper and disposition and hath always behaved herself as a loving kind affectionate and dutiful wife . . . and as a frugal faithful and industrious manager of . . . [her husband's] estate and affairs.[14]

This veritable roll call of ideal feminine qualities was necessary if a woman expected her complaints about her husband to be taken seriously. As will be shown later in this chapter, when the issue of provocation is discussed, it was important that women portrayed themselves in this way to avoid being thought of as culpable for the violence they had endured. Other historians have demonstrated that when women were the targets of physical or sexual violence, their reputations (or in nineteenth-century parlance, respectability and character), would be assessed before they could be classified as 'victims'.[15] It was very difficult for a woman to be a victim unless she had conformed to her ideal gender role. As the judge ruled in the Taylor separation case in 1755,

> I was of opinion a wife was not entitled to a divorce for cruelty, unless it appeared that she was a person of good temper, and had always behaved well and dutifully to her husband, which the appellant had not done.[16]

As we will see, these attitudes would only begin to change in the nineteenth century.

The idea that wives could be at fault if marriages were violent was so deeply ingrained that when their husbands became aggressive some wives took it upon themselves to search for explanations. During the Restoration, Mary Rich, Countess of Warwick, believed that her husband's bad temper and abuse of her during his long illness was a judgement from God, and a punishment for marrying against her father's wishes. In her diary she took entire responsibility for marital quarrels, in one instance reproaching herself for being 'too earnest and too passionate' with her husband.[17] Her example shows us that wifely obedience could be accepted uncritically in marriage, and in this context how a husband's violence was an additional rather than a primary source of his wife's low self-esteem.

---

[14] NA, DEL1/559 (1752), f.266r.
[15] See, for example, Clark, *Women's Silence Men's Violence*, pp. 10, 56–7, 73–4; and C. A. Conley, *The Unwritten Law: Criminal Justice in Victorian Kent* (Oxford, 1991), pp. 73–9.
[16] *Taylor v. Taylor* (1755), as cited in Biggs, *The Concept of Matrimonial Cruelty*, p. 145.
[17] As cited in, A. Kugler, 'Constructing wifely identity: prescription and practice in the life of Lady Sarah Cowper', *Journal of British Studies* 40 (2001), 319.

Other wives used ideas about their gender roles to more strategic effect. Many who turned to the courts for relief were keen to emphasise that they had patiently endured lengthy periods of violence before they took this course of action. Theodosia Freeman, for example, ended her accusations of cruelty against her husband with the statement that,

she hath long patiently borne this outrageous and cruel treatment and twice has returned to live with him again in hopes that . . . he would in time become sensible of the wickedness and injustice thereof and that her patience and submission might prevail over his cruel disposition and soften him into better and gentler usage.[18]

Such forbearance could win admiration from witnesses. So a servant in the Norcott household said that he had 'often wondered' how Rachael 'could bear' her husband 'with such patience'.[19] Wives could also attempt to conceal their husband's physical violence by attributing their injuries to other causes. When a witness asked Ann Boteler why her face was bruised, Ann told her that she had fallen over a stile, even though Ann's husband, Sir Oliver later confessed to have hit her.[20] Occasionally women displayed a forgiveness that could result in them withdrawing their complaints and ending legal proceedings against their husbands. Although forgiveness was a key Christian virtue, which both men and women were expected to exercise, as we shall see, women's supposed greater religiosity meant that in practice there could be more pressure on them to pardon marital wrongs. The results could be tragic. In the mid-nineteenth century, Georgiana Pipkin twice withdrew her complaint against her husband for assault from Edmonton petty sessions in Middlesex. But a week after her second complaint she was held in custody for attempting to poison herself.[21] Her repeated efforts to control her husband's violence appear to have left her in such despair that she attempted suicide.

There is no doubt that for those trying to help women who were being subjected to violence from their husbands, the decision to be reconciled and return to the marital home could be very frustrating. Mary Haggitt, the wife of an Anglican minister, expressed her 'astonishment' when a female parishioner whom she had accompanied to a magistrate to complain of marital violence appeared from his office 'arm-in-arm' with the

[18] NA, DEL 1/479 (1734), f.206–207.
[19] LPL, CA, Case 6659 (1666), Eee2 f.124r; for other examples of witnesses praising the patience of wives see, LPL, CA, Case 2391 (1667), Eee2, ff.291v,296r; and NA, DEL 1/559 (1752), ff.347r,393v.
[20] LPL, CA, Case 1041 (1672), Eee4 f.851r.
[21] LMA, Edmonton Petty Session Division: Tottenham, Enfield and Wood Green, PS.E/E1/1, pp. 96, 285, 287.

husband and returned home with him. Mary considered that the wife 'had almost lost all claim on her interference, for being so foolish as to go back to him', and believed that it was because the wife was 'so passionately fond' of her husband that she could not see sense.[22] However, significantly, Mary was persuaded to help the wife again when she was in distress. Most of Mary's contemporaries would have viewed the wife's decision to return in a favourable light. In the courts, judges were reluctant to apply the strict letter of the law which saw reconciliation as evidence of condoning violence, but instead regarded the return of a wife after violence as 'even praiseworthy'.[23] Indeed, as we have seen, the authorities believed that their first aim should be to encourage couples to resume peaceful cohabitation. Overall what this means is that although women may have been persuaded to return to violent husbands for some of the same emotional reasons as today, due to affection and/or fear, the reaction to this decision from outside the conjugal unit tended to be different. Such was the strength of the ideals of femininity which emphasised patience and self-sacrifice, that women who continued or resumed relations with violent husbands were generally viewed sympathetically rather than critically. Here is a key change in the meanings attached to women's behaviour between the period of this book and the present. The discourses of femininity were so different in the past, that staying with violent men could be regarded as a positive virtue.

So far we have considered the impact of general advice for women in violent marriages. But there were specific notions about women, their bodies and sex that affected the ways in which they were expected to respond to sexual violence. These were subject to change. Whereas in the seventeenth century women could be viewed as sexually voracious, by the start of the nineteenth century many thought of women as sexually passive. Sexual innocence as well as chastity became valued for women.[24] In this context some wives claimed to have been ignorant of the cause of their illnesses when they became sick from venereal disease transmitted to them by their husbands. Anne More argued that soon after her marriage her husband gave her VD, which she had for several years 'in a miserable condition not being sensible what it was'.[25] Certain wives, no doubt, played upon notions of their sexual innocence in an attempt to enhance the sense of injustice and outrage at their

---

[22] NA, PCAP 3/2 (1834–36), f.214r.

[23] *Westmeath v. Westmeath* (1826) *English Reports*, vol. 162, p. 1030.

[24] For a summary of the extensive literature on these changes in sexual attitudes, see, Shoemaker, *Gender in English Society*, pp. 59–67.

[25] NA, DEL1/356 (1720), f.120; for a similar case see also, NA, PCAP 3/1 (1834), f.214v.

husband's cruelty. So the wife of a gunsmith alleged that when she became ill from VD ten days after her marriage, she remained innocent of its cause as even the medical practitioner who treated her would not tell her the name of her illness. In her affidavit she also accused her husband of using sexual insults against her, but said that this was in such 'obscene and gross language', that 'it is utterly impossible without the greatest violation of decency for this Deponent in any manner to recite inasmuch as this Deponent could not even report the same to her said mother'.[26] While keeping her reputation for female sexual modesty and delicacy intact, this ploy encouraged the reader to imagine exactly what *was* said. From these cases we can see plainly that even if wives delayed making sexual accusations against their husbands, and were reticent when they did so, the pressure upon women to be sexually innocent did not render them passive when that innocence had been offended. Despite the lack of development in legal thinking about the issue of sexual violence within marriage, (there was no concept of marital rape in English law until 1991), women made accusations of sexual cruelty against their husbands in the context of marriage separation suits.

However, it is also apparent that sexual naiveté was not always affected by wives to win sympathy from the courts. At a time when some women claimed that they did not realise that they had been raped until they were informed by their doctors, it is convincing that sexual innocence could be genuine.[27] In a tragic case heard in 1803, Elizabeth Skurray, a woman of 'irreproachable manners', said that three of her children had died from VD after her adulterous husband had infected her when she was pregnant, arguing that due to her 'inexperience' she was unaware of the cause of their deaths until the start of the case.[28] It seems certain that Elizabeth would have acted to protect both herself and her babies if she had known the true nature of her illness. Keeping women sexually innocent may have acted as a shield for the sexual infidelities of men, but there could also be a heavy price to pay.

Much evidence suggests that female patience and tolerance of men's behaviour, whether practised intentionally or not, rarely reformed violent husbands. There were other ways in which women could gain inner strength within ongoing violent relationships, and maintain society's approval. Writing was a strategy that was shared by some women who faced marital cruelty, who possibly found it a cathartic process, as well as

---

[26] NA, KB1/30 part 3, East.39, Geo.3, no.1, affidavit of Ann Palmer Rea (6 April 1799).
[27] Clark, *Women's Silence Men's Violence*, pp. 64–5.
[28] LMA, DL/C/187 (1803), f.337–338v.

a vital one of self-definition and preservation. Elizabeth Shackleton, for example, who has been the focus of influential work by Vickery, vented her annoyance at her violent and drunken second husband by writing extensively in her diary. Such diary writing did not outwardly challenge men's behaviour, but because it allowed women to express their feelings, it may have served as a private act of resistance.[29]

This was certainly the case for another eighteenth-century genteel wife, Lady Sarah Cowper. From July 1700 she kept a diary in which she recorded her struggles with a difficult husband. Her writings are particularly exciting for the historian because they reveal her responses to a wide range of prescriptive literature that she read during her lifetime. Here we have evidence of one woman's reading habits, and how the ideals for marriage that were contained within what she read, were appropriated and applied in ways that suited her particular circumstances. In other words, we have a case study of how prescription was shaped and altered in practice. Despite the fact that the key message of what Lady Sarah read was the importance of wifely submission, she used her readings to resist total deference to her husband, justify her position, and confirm her belief that the wrongs her husband had done were undeserved. Lady Sarah's interpretations of what she read convinced her that if her husband failed in his marital roles and duties, she no longer owed him hers. This was not just an intellectual exercise expressed in angry and frequent writing, but had a direct impact upon Lady Sarah's behaviour. Infuriated by her husband's interference in domestic and household management, which she believed was her right to control, Lady Sarah decided, 'I will resign the whole to the Managment of Sir W and resolve to live quiet in my Chamber'. This 'experiment' in resistance worked, although it took Sir William several months before he asked Lady Sarah to resume her household duties in return for his better behaviour. As the historian Anne Kugler has concluded, this refusal to do housekeeping was 'action in a passive sense', allowing Lady Sarah to withdraw from feminine duties without direct confrontation. It forced her husband to recognise his dependence upon his wife, and confirmed the importance of feminine skills and qualities to marital harmony. This was an effective strategy that may well have been pursued by other wives.[30]

---

[29] Vickery, *The Gentleman's Daughter*, pp. 214–22. For other examples of Englishwomen who wrote of marital cruelty see, Anselment, (ed.), *The Remembrances of Elizabeth Freke*, and *The Memoirs of Mrs Catherine Jemmat* Vols. 1 and 2.

[30] Kugler, 'Constructing wifely identity', 291–323.

Lady Sarah found some refuge from her marriage troubles in her religious beliefs. In a period when many couples had their marriages solemnised in church, and church leaders preached and wrote extensively about the nature of marriage, religion seemed to offer an obvious source of solace and support. Catholic women could turn to Saint Rita of Cascia, a saint of suffering and the battered wife, whose cult survived the Counter-Reformation and by the twentieth century in Italy, became more popular than that of the Virgin Mary.[31] In Protestant areas, church ministers and their wives, (as we will see further in Chapter 5), could provide practical support. Women also found within their own spiritual beliefs a means of comfort, personal empowerment, and a way of finding an explanation for their experiences. As Bernard Capp has argued, attending religious services and sermons offered women an important social outlet, and for wives who were in unsatisfactory marriages, religion might 'fill the emotional vacuum'.[32] A good example of this is Abigail Abbot Bailey, an eighteenth-century woman living in New England, whose husband was physically violent to her soon after their wedding, and after twenty-one years of marriage, committed incest with their sixteen-year-old daughter. As a Congregationalist, Abigail found strength in her deeply held religious beliefs, recording her prayers and developing relationship with God in her diaries, and later in her memoirs. It was from the church community that Abigail found assistance when she finally decided to seek a divorce.[33]

Abigail won support from her friends and neighbours not only for her patient endurance, but also because for years she had responded to male violence in an appropriately 'feminine' way. Piety was popularly regarded as a female virtue, and women were believed to have a greater propensity to religious conviction than men. The association of women with piety was so significant that in marital disputes it was only wives, never husbands, who were accused of neglecting their faith. Women often began their accusations against their husbands with claims of their piety, as well as other female qualities, but their words and charges of cruelty could also be discredited if their husbands could prove a lack of religious faith and practice. So John Deye, answering an accusation of marital violence, argued in 1703 that his wife 'never would take the sacrament saying her father never did it and cared not to go to church'.[34]

[31] O. Hufton, *The Prospect before Her: A History of Women in Western Europe Volume One 1500–1800* (London, 1995), p. 363.
[32] Capp, *When Gossips Meet*, p. 362.
[33] A. Taves, (ed.), *Religion and Domestic Violence in Early New England: The Memoirs of Abigail Abbot Bailey* (Bloomington, 1989).
[34] NA, DEL1/330 (1703), f.111v.

This statement came in the midst of a more general accusation of wifely disobedience, and it is clear that others associated an irreverence for God with a disregard for husbandly authority. For example, when Samuel Cockerell was asked to respond to his wife's libel of cruelty, he claimed that she, 'to his great trouble would seldom go to church and had very little sense of religion or of her duty to him as a wife'.[35] We can set this link between piety and wifely duty in context if we remember that church ministers frequently cited Paul's demand, 'Wives, submit yourselves unto your husbands, as unto the Lord', and that the promise to obey was part of a woman's vows in the Anglican wedding service.[36] Hence, it was important if a wife, subject to her husband's violence, was to win sympathy for her case, to preserve at least an outward appearance of religious devotion.

Yet that same devotion could also be a source of aggravation to violent men. Sir Oliver Boteler, in what was an exceptionally violent marriage, was said to have often taken 'offence at his said Lady for her piety and devotion', and declared that 'he hated a wife that said her prayers, and threatened to damn her body and soul, and frequently disturbed and forced her from her closet when he knew she was at prayers'.[37] Such behaviour was described by witnesses who spoke in support of Lady Ann's accusations of cruelty, but it shows how women's resort to spiritualism could be deeply threatening. Husbands such as Sir Oliver perceived God as an alternative and competitive source of authority for their wives, rather than as one that supported their earthly superiority over women. Fears about how religious belief could detract from a wife's reverence for her husband were expressed nearly two centuries later in Anne Brontë's *The Tenant of Wildfell Hall* (1848). Helen Huntingdon's brutal husband, Arthur, tells her,

you are too religious. Now I like a woman to be religious, and I think your piety one of your greatest charms, but then, like all other good things, it may be carried too far. To my thinking, a woman's religion ought not to lessen her devotion to her earthly lord.[38]

Whether in fiction or reality, these husbands enacted the troubling scenario anticipated by Puritan conduct book writers, who debated the casuistical question of whom a wife should obey if her husband ordered

---

[35] LPL, CA, Case 2050 (1730), D431, f.100r.
[36] Ephesians chapter 5, verse 22. For example, this was quoted in Gouge, *Of Domestical Duties*, p. 15.
[37] LPL, CA, Case 1041 (1672), Eee4, f.858v; this case is further discussed in Foyster, 'Male honour', 217–24. Stone gives his version of the story of the Boteler marriage in his, *Uncertain Unions and Broken Lives*, pp. 299–303.
[38] A. Brontë, *The Tenant of Wildfell Hall* (1848) ed. (Harmondsworth, 1994), p. 166.

her to do something that was against God's word.[39] While the Puritans argued that God should always be the greater authority, some husbands tested the extent of their wives' piety by becoming violent when they prepared to leave the home for church services, or by physically trying to prevent their wives from attending church.[40] In Lady Ann's case, Sir Oliver intruded into her closet, which was intended as a space for private reflection and prayer. Husbands could interpret literally the Biblical teaching that a husband should rule over his wife as Christ did over the Church, and require their wives to mimic supplicatory ecclesiastical rituals. So on one occasion when Sir Oliver found his wife praying in her closet he 'made her kneel down by his bedside' and 'forced her to bow and incline herself with her face to the floor', telling her 'I will have or will make you as submissive as my spaniel'. Other husbands made their wives kneel before them, sometimes for hours at a time, but few linked this behaviour so blatantly to religious worship as Sir Oliver. He was known to make 'himself sport' by making Ann say the Lord's Prayer while she knelt to him, laughing and insulting her while she did so.[41]

In summary, religious devotion was an approved way of coping with marital violence that enabled some women to gain a measure of self-esteem and personal strength. That religious devotions were an irritant to some violent men is an indication of the power that individual believers could gain from their faith to resist harm and personal injury. It was religious thinkers, particularly those inspired by the Puritans or Evangelicals, who wrote much of the available prescriptive literature about marriage. The existence of advice within a range of prescriptive sources about how wives should deal with violent husbands not only suggests that this was thought of as an area of potential contention within marital relationships, but also that women could not be guaranteed to respond in appropriate ways. Wives were taught the virtues of patience and kindness, even in the face of extreme violence, but these were not passive qualities. Nor were these qualities expected to be gender specific, even if they were more usually related to women. For husbands could be advised to be patient with the faults that would inevitably arise from relationships with the 'weaker vessels' who were their wives.[42] But, far from indicating some kind of parity of expectations within marriage, this advice derived from the belief that husbands

---

[39] See, for example, Gouge, *Of Domestical Duties*, pp. 329–31.
[40] See, for example, NA, DEL1/344 (1710), f.95.
[41] LPL, CA, Case 1041 (1672), Eee4, ff.856v,859v; for other examples of husbands who made their wives kneel to them, see LMA, DL/C/179 (1783), f.410v, and LPL, CA, Case 3059 (1838), H580/5.
[42] See, for example, Gouge, *Of Domestical Duties*, pp. 398–9.

had a God-given as well as natural superiority over their wives. While prescriptive literature written from both a godly and secular perspective shared the assumption that it was the gender characteristics of men (their passions and tendency to anger) that were most likely to result in violence within marital relationships, it was also believed that women had the feminine qualities that could be deployed to allow them to defuse occasions of difficulty and tension, and hence successfully avoid becoming the targets of male violence. As we shall see, the notion that women were in part to blame for men's conduct could be as destructive to women's sense of well-being as any violence they could experience.

Mental responses

It is clear that contemporaries recognised that marital violence could have emotional consequences and cause psychological as well as physical harm to its targets. Some women responded to violence by internalising both its damaging effects and the ideal conduct for their gender to such an extent that it became a destructive pathology. The feelings of fear, humiliation and inadequacy that marital violence could provoke, combined with those of shame at the failure to prevent or reform men's behaviour. Of course, the majority of records that we are left with do not allow us direct access to the language that women may have used to express their feelings and subjective experiences, so we cannot be confident that they would have understood their lives in these ways, or attributed their behaviour to the same causes.[43] Certainly in a period before the development of modern psychiatry, there was little thought about how to treat women affected mentally by marital violence. But through women's actions, their mediated words in the courtroom, and the descriptions of others we can begin to learn about how women responded at a particular emotional level to the violence of their husbands.

As the previous chapter showed, if wives were subject to violence that endangered 'life, limb or health' they were thought to merit legal protection. Even if marriage separation or divorce were not permitted for mental cruelty alone, that did not prevent women making complaints about how their mental as well as physical health had been affected by marital violence. Here we see evidence of the courts documenting the consequences of marital violence long before Hammerton has argued they became interested in such issues.[44] Sarah Terry, for example,

---

[43] Anne Laurence has recognised this problem for historians in 'Women's psychological disorders in seventeenth-century Britain', in A. Angerman et al. (eds.), *Current Issues in Women's History* (London, 1989), p. 203.

[44] Hammerton, *Cruelty and Companionship*, pp. 127–9.

argued in 1783 that due to her husband's verbal and physical violence, 'her health and spirits became greatly impaired and she grew weak in body and more and more dejected in mind in so much that her extreme misery became apparent to every person who had an opportunity of seeing and conversing with her'. In a period when medical and popular understandings of the body meant that physical and mental health were closely related, the costs of violence upon Sarah were displayed and witnessed through both physical appearance and conversation. She was only twenty-two years old, 'yet her constitution is so much impaired by the said cruelties that it is not probable she can ever recover her former good state of health'.[45] By presenting herself both physically and mentally as one of the 'weaker sex', Sarah could demonstrate her inability to sustain ill-treatment.

Some women were open about how close they had come to being driven insane by their husband's treatment. Martha Pearse claimed that her husband's behaviour had endangered her life and had led to 'the total destruction of her peace of mind', but was incensed when her husband threatened to treat her as if she was mad, and confine her in a madhouse.[46] Other witnesses to violent marriages saw a clear link between what a wife had endured and her subsequent mental health. A cousin to Elizabeth Corne described to the King's Bench in 1773 how Elizabeth's husband had treated her 'with great brutality and often beat and abused her', and said that it was from this 'ill usage' that she became 'disordered in her senses and suffered to run the streets'. Alice Shepheard, 'having been unhappy in the marriage state went out of her mind' in about 1770. She was sent by her friends to the house of a Chelsea widow who made it 'her business to take care of lunatics'. By 1775 Alice had 'retrieved her senses', but her husband refused to pay the fees he owed for her board, meaning that she continued to be confined. It was popularly thought that her husband wanted to keep her confined 'in hopes it will shorten her days', because he feared that if she was released she would tell her relations in Ireland of the 'severe and cruel treatment she has met with from her husband'.[47]

---

[45] LMA, DL/C/179 (1783), f.518v; for another example of a wife who claimed that violence had taken a toll on her mental as well as physical health see, LMA, DL/C/179 (1780), f.235v.

[46] LPL, CA, Case 7022 (1748), D1573, ff.43r,52v–53r,70v,79–80r.

[47] NA KB1/19/2 Hil.13, Geo.3, no.1 and 2, affdts. of Edward Gates (29 January 1773) and James Tappenden (3 February 1773); NA, KB1/20/6 Trin.15, Geo.3, no.2, affdt. of Edmund Kelly (26 June 1775).

We also learn of the mental effects of violence upon women from people outside the family unit who dealt with the consequences. The casebooks of the astrologer-physician Richard Napier for the years 1598 to 1632 reveal that he saw 135 individuals who were suffering mental problems caused by marital quarrels. Eighty-four per cent of these cases were brought by married women who complained of mental anxiety after forms of economic cruelty as well as physical, verbal and sexual violence.[48] Some were able to profit by offering cures for wives with difficult husbands. Peter Banks in the 1670s sold magical remedies in Newcastle that were said to make even the most cruel husband loving. One desperate and suggestible wife bought a year's happiness with her husband for 10s. and two new shirts.[49] Other wives were less easily comforted. A century later Dr George Young, based in Edinburgh, treated with opium a 'gentlewoman who lost the use of her reason on a sudden, by the barbarous treatment of her husband'.[50] As public institutions for the care of the insane were built, their nineteenth-century casebooks record a steady intake of female patients admitted after 'ill treatment' by their husbands. Of patients admitted between July 1834 and November 1852 in which a cause was noted in the West Riding Pauper Lunatic Asylum, for example, 12 per cent were said to arise from problems with relationships with the other sex.[51] Such causes of insanity could specifically be related to women. In the early years after the opening of the Dundee and Glasgow Asylums, marital problems as a cause of mental illnesses were only attributed to women in the admission records.[52]

We should not assume, however, that increasing familiarity with, or recognition of marital violence as a cause of insanity, led to sympathetic or effective treatment. Opium may have offered a new way to ease the discomfort of physical violence and numb painful memories, but it did not deal with the root cause of mental illness. It was prescribed to help women endure and continue to live with violent partners. As Roy Porter recognised, doctors were far more concerned to restore the family status quo than confront the perpetrators of their patient's illnesses. He recounts the horrific treatment administered in the mid-eighteenth

---

[48] M. Macdonald, *Mystical Bedlam: Madness, Anxiety and Healing in Seventeenth-Century England* (Cambridge, 1991), pp. 99–103.

[49] Capp, *When Gossips Meet*, p. 85.

[50] As cited in A. Ingram, *The Madhouse of Language: Writing and Reading Madness in the Eighteenth Century* (London, 1991), p. 37.

[51] M. Levine-Clark, 'Dysfunctional domesticity: female insanity and family relationships among the West Riding poor in the mid-nineteenth century', *Journal of Family History* 25, 3 (2000), 350.

[52] R. A. Houston, 'Madness and gender in the long eighteenth century', *Social History* 27, 3 (2002), 320.

century by the doctor Patrick Blair on a woman who was mentally disturbed and refusing to have sexual relations with her husband. On three occasions Blair ordered the wife to be blindfolded, stripped and tied to a chair while jets of cold water were released on her for increasing periods of time, while he demanded to know whether she would submit to her husband. When he was about to begin the treatment for a fourth time, 'being terrified', the wife 'kneeled submissively', promised to 'become a loving obedient and dutiful wife', and went that night to bed with her husband 'with great cheerfulness'.[53] This unfortunate wife was probably from the middling or upper social ranks to merit such individual attention from a physician, but lower down the social scale women could also face prejudice and a lack of pity when they claimed illness from marital violence. The case notes for Mary Ann Wilson, admitted to the West Riding Pauper Lunatic Asylum, for example, recorded that she 'says she has been much beaten by her husband, but there are no marks of injury', and for another wife that, 'her mind chiefly dwells upon imaginary ill treatment of her husband, whom she charges with cruelty of her'.[54]

It is difficult to believe that women could have avoided being harmed by a culture that placed so much pressure upon them to cope with violent men, and emphasised the importance of them conducting self-analysis and critique if their husband's violence persisted. Self-blame could lead to shame when men were violent. Mabell Whitmore was said to have kept to her room after one beating from her husband, 'being ashamed to appear and be publicly seen with such a bruised face'.[55] While this behaviour could be interpreted as a desire to protect her husband's reputation as well as her own, it is clear that for other women their unhappiness became so unbearable that they committed acts of self-harm or suicide. Marriage breakdown was one of the main reasons that contemporaries gave for suicidal thoughts or actions. Elizabeth Jessop in 1717 was said to have threatened to kill herself and would take scissors and razors to bed with her to use for this end, and Maria Pulteney would talk 'idly and extravagantly' of her intentions to drown herself or slit her throat. But when suicide was a crime and widely regarded as a sign of insanity, we learn of Elizabeth's and Maria's suicide

[53] As cited in R. Porter, 'Madness and the family before Freud: the view of the mad-doctors', *Journal of Family History* 23, 2 (1998), 163–4; spellings have been modernised.

[54] As cited in Levine-Clark, 'Dysfunctional domesticity', 354. The tendency not to believe these women's claims may have been exacerbated in this period by the scepticism that had come to surround married women and illness, and which will be fully explained towards the end of this chapter.

[55] NA, DEL1/559 (1752), f.444v.

threats from their husbands who used them as evidence against claims of marital violence. According to Elizabeth's husband, her suicide threats were made in the context of other behaviour that indicated her mental instability. Dressed only in her shift she would go down to the river at night and 'talked to the moon', and sit in the house 'on the floor stark naked with her shift pulled up to her arms'. The husbands of both Elizabeth and Maria blamed their wives' drunkenness, not their violence, for their condition. Rather than being indicative of desperation in the face of marital violence, evidence of self-inflicted injuries could be used to detract attention away from husbands. So the husband of Elizabeth Jessop argued that if his wife had marks of injury it was from her violence, not his. In her 'crazed and distracted condition', he said, she sometimes 'pulled off her own hair and beat herself', wounding herself with some scissors, and then telling others that he had done it.[56]

No doubt, some wives like Elizabeth and Maria did attempt to drown their sorrows in drink. By wasting household resources on alcohol, and acting in unseemly ways when they were drunk this was hardly an ideal feminine way to respond to marital violence. But it is noticeable that when couples complained of the drinking habits of their partners, husbands and wives were depicted as behaving in very different ways. Men's drinking took place outside the home and was represented as a sociable activity involving jovial fellowship with other men. There was a culture of male drinking in alehouses, taverns or pubs that 'probably helped to reinforce a sense of male dominance or an atmosphere of patriarchy under siege'.[57] By contrast, women drank alone and in the home. Mary Ann Turner, for example, was described by her husband as a solitary and unhappy woman, drinking gin in bed with swollen eyes from 'fits of crying', and a bruised body from her stumbling around drunk, instead of from any mistreatment by him.[58] Drinking for women in these circumstances provided none of the contentment it provided for men. For such women drinking offered little comfort or reassurance, but was undertaken to numb the senses and mental anguish of their married lives.

---

[56] LPL, CA, Case 5089 (1717), Ee9, f.12/1–4; LPL, CA, Case 7469 (1739), Ee10, f.66; M. MacDonald and T. R. Murphy, *Sleepless Souls: Suicide in Early Modern England* (Oxford, 1990), pp. 262–3; O. Anderson, *Suicide in Victorian and Edwardian England* (Oxford, 1987), pp. 121, 129, 135. For other examples of husbands claiming that injuries were self-inflicted see, LPL, CA, Case 3366 (1811), D757 f.52, and LPL, CA, Case 4282 (1853), H826/6.

[57] Abrams, 'Companionship and conflict', pp. 113–14; see also, Clark, *Struggle for the Breeches*, chapter 3; and A. L. Martin, *Alcohol, Sex, and Gender in Late Medieval and Early Modern Europe* (Basingstoke, 2001).

[58] LPL, CA, Case 9350 (1853), H824/7.

We can surmise that many women's mental responses to marital cruelty remained hidden from the view of both contemporaries and historians. When misery and harm were manifest it was in the more extreme reactions of mental illness, self-harm or even suicide. But here the difficulties of linking cause and effect meant that husbands could avoid responsibility for their wives' behaviour. The 'battered wife syndrome', where women who stay with their violent partners are regarded as suffering from a kind of mental impairment that explains their reluctance to leave, has proved a recent and controversial way of looking at how women respond to marital violence. But cases of marriage breakdown in the past clearly illustrate that pointing the finger of blame back at the target of violence, rather than at its perpetrator is by no means a modern-day phenomenon.

Violent responses

To date we have a very partial historical understanding of women's violence within marriage. This is despite the fact that evidence of marital violence gives us an excellent opportunity to compare and contrast female and male violence. It is all too easy to focus on the fictional and humorous portrayals of wife violence found in the numerous ballads and types of popular literature of the period, or on the sensational accounts of wife violence that became lethal, than analyse the more mundane realities of female violence. As we shall see, there were significant differences in the practice of female and male violence, and in our period attitudes were to change towards the acceptability of some types of female violence, as they did with male violence. If we extend our definition of violence beyond one narrowly based on physical meanings, we can also see how women could use forms of violence as tools of negotiation within their marriages. Evidence of women's violence in marriage proves that there were occasions when wives belied the stereotype of feminine passivity. However, it will be demonstrated that throughout our period all forms of female violence remained problematic as a response strategy to male violence.

It is clear from accounts of marriage breakdown that some relationships could literally be battlegrounds for power, in which women as well as men could resort to forms of physical violence to assert dominance. There were cases when women's violence reached such an extent that husbands had their violent wives bound over to keep the peace.[59] In the

---

[59] For examples see, NA, PCAP 3/2 (1834–6), f.186v; Capp, *When Gossips Meet*, p. 120; and Bailey, *Unquiet Lives*, p. 129.

church courts, information about the violence of wives was usually only disclosed in the answers given by husbands and their witnesses to cruelty accusations. In her work on the northern church courts, Bailey has also found that details of female violence were chiefly related as 'secondary complaints' by men after primary allegations of cruelty or adultery had been made.[60] I have come across only one case of marriage separation for cruelty that was initiated by a husband against his wife. Joseph Kirkman was a harpsichord-maker who in the early nineteenth century successfully argued that the physical and verbal violence of his wife was such that he should no longer have to live with her. Even in this rare case, however, the violence may not have been all one way, since Joseph's wife accused him of beating her.[61] Claims of the violence of wives could also be made as responses to suits of restitution of conjugal rights. James Fisher, a hairdresser and wigmaker, answered his wife's restitution case by accusing her of adultery and cruelty. He said he was in danger of his life 'owing to the brutal and savage disposition' of Arabella, his wife, who on one occasion had held a knife over his head and sworn that she would kill him. Arabella was found guilty of adultery and cruelty, although it is interesting that the statement that said she had committed acts of cruelty was later crossed out.[62]

Such was the importance of husbandly authority that normally no self-respecting man would admit that his wife had been violent to him unless he could show that he had regained control in the struggle that followed. So Thomas Stoddard in 1684 said that he gave his wife one blow with his whip that 'did her no harm' after she threatened him with a fire-fork and Samuel Cockerell in 1730 gave his wife 'two or three slaps in the face' after she had 'assaulted' him and pulled off his wig. Pulling wigs, hair, beards or moustaches and using household implements to inflict injury were common forms of female violence.[63] Thus the portrayal of women hitting their husbands with pokers, fire shovels, ladles, rolling pins, pots and pans in popular literature may well have been a reflection of actual practice.[64] Whereas generally men could rely solely

---

[60] Bailey, *Unquiet Lives*, pp. 129–30.
[61] LMA, DL/C/186 (1806), f.734–750, *Kirkman v. Kirkman* (1807), *English Reports*, vol. 161, pp. 598–600.
[62] LMA, DL/C/179 (1782) f.192–216.
[63] LPL, CA, Case 8770 (1684), Ee6, f.11r; LPL, CA, Case 2050 (1730), D431 f.101v–102r; for similar examples of accusations of wife violence see, LPL, CA, Case 1127 (1663), Eee1, f.79r; LPL, CA, Case 2477 (1692), Ee7, f.128v; and LPL, CA, Case 4915 (1837), H544/6.
[64] For examples see, 'The Drunken Husband', Madden vol. 9, 80; 'A Man that is Married', Baring-Gould vol. 4, 346; and 'A New Song called the Fire Shovel', Bell Collection.

upon the physical strength of their kicks and punches, women enhanced the impact of their blows with the use of domestic tools that were ready to hand. As Hammerton has noted, attacking a husband's hair or moustache was 'physical resistance which was humiliating rather than violent'. It was the indignity of such offences that really hurt.[65] Sometimes husbands claimed that their wives had directly challenged them to a fight. For example, after an argument in bed over his treatment of a servant, according to John Head his wife had said, 'By God come out and see which is the best man'. Getting out of bed his wife pressed her fingers against his windpipe until she almost strangled him. After all this provocation, John argued, it was 'absolutely necessary' for him to 'use some force to free himself from her which he accordingly did by gently throwing her on the floor'. Such a 'gentle' application of force was supposedly repeated after his wife 'flew' at him again, at which he 'lay her on the floor'.[66]

What we are gaining from these types of cases is a perspective of female violence from the husband's viewpoint. Women's violence is described as wild, passionate and even life threatening, to contrast with the restrained and reasoned response of male violence. To maintain a reputation for manliness, a husband who claimed that his wife had been violent towards him was likely to represent her violence as extreme or excessive. Thus it is possible that less severe violence was not reported, and hence that in the domestic context the 'dark figure' of unrecorded female violence was even greater than male violence. The prevailing popular view of husbands who said they were subject to violence from their wives certainly was far from sympathetic. In one ballad, for example, a wife confidently pronounces,

> When a woman beats her husband he poor fool complains.
> The world will laugh and say 'tis right that she should do't again.[67]

The popular response could be a 'charivari', which as we will see in Chapter 4, was a loud mocking demonstration designed to shame the husband into regaining control. Evidence that communities had developed such rituals shows a recognition, sometimes absent today, that men could be subject to violence by their wives.[68]

---

[65] Hammerton, 'Victorian marriage', 227, and *Cruelty and Companionship*, p. 112.
[66] LPL, CA, Case 4407 (1737), D997, f.53–4.
[67] 'A New Song Called the Fire Shovel', Bell Collection.
[68] For the problems of identifying the 'battered husband' today, see for example, M. J. George, 'Riding the donkey backwards: men as the unacceptable victims of marital violence', *Journal of Men's Studies* 3, 2 (1994), 137–59; T. Newburn and E. A. Stanko, 'When men are victims: the failure of victimology', in T. Newburn and E. A. Stanko,

In marriage separation cases female violence provokes male violence in the accounts we have, and not vice versa. It is men not women who use violence as self-defence. In the courtroom, men used evidence of their wives' violence to discredit their stories and showed how male violence was used in the last resort as a corrective to female disobedience. Thus male violence could be represented as legitimate in a way that was impossible for female violence. As Garthine Walker writes, 'Men's domestic violence was perceived as an extension of their nature and expected role; women's marital violence was a manifestation of *un*naturalness'.[69]

Women's violence had a dangerous and deadly potential. Across the period everyday violent tussles between wives and husbands could be laughed away in popular songs from ballads to the music hall, but female violence also had a strength that could be dismissed less easily. When female violence was directed against men it subverted a political and gender order that rested on patriarchal ideals. Female violence was so powerful that it could turn the world upside down. A husband who was married to a violent wife lost his claim to manhood, and could be portrayed as a cuckold, confined to the home doing the household chores, while his wife wore the breeches and governed him and all around him. Thus a violent wife not only subverted her own gender identity, but also threatened her husband's masculinity by exposing him as impotent and helpless. In law, the different meanings and significance of female and male violence in marriage were demonstrated in our period by the penalties for killing a spouse. A husband who killed his wife could be found guilty of murder, but until 1828 a wife who killed her husband could be charged with petty treason. The punishment of burning for those convicted of petty treason ceased after 1790, but anxieties about husband murder meant that petty treason remained an offence for longer.[70]

Fears about murderous wives were current in fiction and reality from the seventeenth through to the nineteenth centuries. The story of Arden of Faversham, which was based on real events that took place in 1551, and told of Alice's murder of her husband for her lover Mosby, so fascinated contemporaries that it formed the basis of both a play and subsequent ballads that entertained audiences for the next century.[71]

(eds.), *Just Boys Doing Business? Men, Masculinities and Crime* (London, 1994), pp. 153–65, and Lucal, 'The problem with 'battered husbands'', 95–112.

[69] Walker, *Crime, Gender and Social Order*, p. 140.

[70] M. J. Wiener, 'Alice Arden to Bill Sikes: Changing nightmares of intimate violence in England, 1558–1869', *Journal of British Studies* 40 (2001), 194.

[71] *Arden of Faversham* (London, c.1591); for a ballad see, for example, 'Mistress Arden of Faversham' (1633), *Roxburghe*, vol. VII, Part I–II, pp. 49–53. For seventeenth-century

Although poison had long been a weapon of choice by murderous wives, by the nineteenth century concerns had reached fever pitch. In this context, a husband such as Lord Huntingtower, who countered claims of marital violence by accusing his wife of threatening to poison him, knew that he would touch a raw nerve of fear and sympathy.[72] Press interest in murder trials that followed death by poison, and the easy purchase and widespread use of arsenic in household goods generated popular pressure for its sales to be regulated. In 1851 an Arsenic Act was passed, which forced buyers of arsenic to sign a register, and sellers to mix arsenic with indigo or soot so that its presence in food would be more noticeable. It is significant that murder by poison was always a form of lethal violence associated with women. Women certainly had the means to carry out this crime since they spent so much time in the household and were responsible for preparing food. Yet the labelling of murder by poison as a female activity also tells us about popular perceptions of the nature of female violence. This was violence that did not rely upon physical strength or direct confrontation, but instead depended upon trickery and stealth, a rejection of the female gender role of caregiver, and a fundamental betrayal of trust. Rather than spontaneous violence, the purchase and preparation of poisonous victuals required planning and premeditation. As Frances Dolan has explained, murder by poison was a 'violation of domesticity', in which 'the dependent who should share the bed and table, and solace and nurture her husband's body, abuses intimacy to invade and destroy that body'.[73] So disturbing was the notion of the woman who killed using poison as her method, that it belied the reality that it was men who were more likely to be accused of marital homicide than women, and that husbands could be as capable as their wives of deploying poison to murderous ends.[74]

---

interest in spousal homicide see, J. Wiltenburg, *Disorderly Women and Female Power in the Street Literature of Early Modern England and Germany* (Charlottesville,1992), pp. 214–23.

[72] LPL, CA, Case 4915 (1837), H544/10.

[73] F. E. Dolan, *Dangerous Familiars: Representations of Domestic Crime in England, 1550–1700* (Ithaca, 1994), p. 30; for nineteenth-century anxiety about poisons see, G. Robb, 'Circe in crinoline: domestic poisonings in Victorian England', *Journal of Family History* 22, 2 (1997), 176–90, and P. W. J. Bartrip, 'How green was my valance?: Environmental arsenic poisoning and the Victorian domestic ideal', *English Historical Review* 109 (1994), 891–913.

[74] For comparative prosecution rates for spousal homicide see, for example, Sharpe, 'Domestic homicide', 37–8. For examples of husbands who were accused of using poison to murder their wives, see, D. Turner, *Fashioning Adultery: Gender, Sex and Civility in England* (Cambridge, 2002), pp. 124–5.

It is certainly the case that over our period public attention shifted from a limited focus on the murderess to wider anxieties about male as well as female violence. Hence, as Wiener has explained, the popular figure in the nightmare of domestic violence changed between the Elizabethan and Victorian periods from Alice Arden to Bill Sikes.[75] Significantly, however, Bill Sikes in Charles Dickens's *Oliver Twist* (1838) was not married to Nancy, the woman he murdered. Dickens was writing within a culture where the seduction-and-betrayal theme had caught hold of the popular imagination, and it was the man who seduced a young, unmarried woman, and then murdered her, who caused the greatest horror. At least until the end of our period it was the seducer killer, not the wife murderer who alarmed the Victorians.[76] So, although there were changes in popular fears about violence between the sexes, this did not necessarily reflect an alteration in how non-fatal violence within marriage was understood.

Furthermore, there was sustained public interest in determining why women killed. While adultery was the most common motive given for murder, marital violence was also considered. 'The Laird of Waristoun' was a popular Scottish ballad that was published after Jean Livingston was executed in 1600 for ordering the murder of her husband. As well as warning against arranged marriages and unequal matches, the ballad story recounts how Jean was driven to her scheme of murder after suffering six years of violence from her husband.[77] When Mary Hobry (or Aubry) murdered her husband in 1688, at least four accounts of the murder were published. In these it is made clear that Mary turned to murder after a history of violence from her husband. In *A Hellish Murder* (1688), which was one version of events, for example, Mary is described as being subject to a savage beating and attempted rape by her husband on the night of the killing.[78] In the eighteenth century, Wiener notes a new level of sympathy for murderous women in the press coverage of their cases. In popular culture Alice Arden was now portrayed as a victim of an arranged marriage, and motivated by the sentiment of love she held for Mosby.[79] But when murder followed marital violence this creation of the female murderer as a victim of her circumstances was

---

[75] Wiener, 'Alice Arden to Bill Sikes', 184–212, and *Men of Blood*, chapter 4.

[76] Wiener, *Men of Blood*, pp. 134–44.

[77] K. M. Brown, 'The laird, his daughter, her husband and the minister: unravelling a popular ballad', in R. Mason and N. Macdougall (eds.), *People and Power in Scotland: Essays in Honour of T. C. Smout* (Edinburgh, 1992), pp. 104–25.

[78] Dolan, *Dangerous Familiars*, pp. 34–5; Amussen, 'Being stirred to much unquietness', 76.

[79] Wiener, 'Alice Arden to Bill Sikes', 191–8.

intended to indicate the horrific consequences of the abuses of husbandly authority. It was a measure of the disruption of male violence and its unacceptability within marriage that it could drive women to behaviour that was so contrary to their natural feminine traits. Women's violence may have undermined the patriarchal order, but it was depicted as emerging from a domestic context that had already been destabilised by male conduct.

Female victimisation by men, however, did not lessen the heinous nature of their subsequent lethal crimes. Popular representations of the female murderess were moral tales that did not question her final fate on the scaffold, even if they accepted that male violence had led her there. So the pamphlet account of the case of Sarah Elston who stabbed her husband with some scissors in September 1677, explained that she had not intended to kill him, but 'only thought to do him some slight mischief in revenge of his cruelty in beating her'. Nevertheless, the pamphlet was entitled *A Warning for Bad Wives*, and instructed other wives with violent husbands 'to avoid their fury, by going out of the way for the present . . . rather than stay bandying of words, or teasing them with reproachful language; which she admitted had often been her own fault'.[80] Thus Sarah was made to assume responsibility for her husband's violence as well as her own.

The recognition that a husband's cruelty could explain a wife's murderous actions also did not necessarily translate into any legal justification for her behaviour that might warrant some mercy. In the seventeenth century none of the murderous wives described above, and depicted in popular literature, escaped the gallows. Anne Williams was tried by the Old Bailey for petty treason in 1747. She was accused of causing her husband's death by stabbing him with a knife in his side. Like a number of other women who faced the same charges, Anne said that she had endured a history of violence from her husband. On the day of the murder she claimed that her husband, Thomas, began 'as usual in striking and beating me'. A fruit seller who worked in the same market as Anne supported her account and testified:

I seldom saw her in the market scarce a month together, but I saw her with black eyes, and her face bruised some way or another . . . the Woman used to take care to get an honest livelihood. I believe she was very badly used.

Anne was found guilty, but of the lesser charge of manslaughter. Rather than assume that the jury reached this verdict because of their sympathy for her plight as a battered woman, it is equally possible that the jury

---

[80] As cited in Capp, *When Gossips Meet*, p. 88.

were convinced by Anne's story that Thomas fell upon the knife in the course of his violent struggle with her, or that she escaped being punished as a wife for petty treason because she declared that she had never married Thomas. Given that today lawyers can find it difficult to convince juries of the validity of marital violence as a defence for husband killing, it seems likely that it was one of the latter reasons. The circumstances of female violence could be considered by the courts, but it is not clear if and when these became mitigating factors.[81]

So male violence did not excuse female violence, or act as an identifiable legal provocation to killing. Arguments about provocation that made violence just, appear to have been more successfully deployed by husbands rather than wives, although as we shall see, even men faced difficulties using this as a defence by the end of our period. As historians of rape have recognised, the cultural constructions of femininity that emphasised physical weakness and suffering made physical resistance and self-defence problematic for women, even when they faced extreme danger of a physical or sexual kind.[82] Thus women were severely restricted in their use of physical violence, even when it was in retaliation. Women were expected to be the victims, not the perpetrators of marital violence, and this made reciprocating violence, let alone initiating it, difficult. Arguably, it was not until Thomas Hardy's *Tess of the d'Urbervilles* (1894) that a woman could assert revenge for domestic violence by murdering her tormentor, and retain sufficient sympathy for her position so that her punishment by hanging could be portrayed as unjust.[83]

Physical violence was not the only violent way that women could respond to male cruelty in marriage. If we widen our lens beyond physical violence we can see that women in the past could be violent to men in ways that were not physical, and the injuries they inflicted were not always visible for the eye to see. At the start of our period women were thought to have a natural propensity for verbal violence. Scolds may have only come to the notice of the authorities when they became a public nuisance, but their scolding often began at home. Hen-pecked husbands complained that they had been verbally abused and insulted by their wives. John Deye told the High Court of Delegates in 1703 that his wife's 'turbulent, scolding, brawling' nature meant that 'no quiet' for 'herself, neighbours or family could be had'. As a result John argued

---

[81] The Proceedings of the Old Bailey (http://www.oldbaileyonline.org), Ref: t17470909–21.
[82] Walker, 'Rereading rape', 9–10.
[83] V. B. Morris, *Double Jeopardy: Women Who Kill in Victorian Fiction* (Lexington, Kentucky, 1990), chapter 7.

that he could find no peace, for his house was 'more like a Bridewell, or the worst of places than home'.[84] In their verbal abuse wives could exploit their husband's sensitivity about their social position and family honour. A student at Lincoln's Inn in 1662, for example, said that he was 'provoked' to slap his wife on her face after some 'hot and angry words' between him and his wife, when she called him a 'beggar, and said he was no Gent . . . and did speak scornfully and contemptuously of this Respondent's kindred'.[85] Through their words women could threaten physical forms of violence. Awareness of their comparative lack of physical strength may have encouraged women to engage in this type of 'fantasy aggression' more frequently than their husbands. Women could also use words as a defence tactic against their husband's violence. As we will see in Chapter Four, wives told their friends of the violence they were suffering in the hope that neighbourhood disapproval would act as a control upon their husband's behaviour. That men could label such talk as 'gossip', in an attempt to diminish its value, was evidence in itself of their fear of the power of female speech. These fears could have consequences for married relationships. In Dickens' *The Old Curiosity Shop* (1840–1), when the violent Mr Quilp discovers his wife holding a tea party for her friends, and overhears them discussing 'the propensity of mankind to tyrannise over the weaker sex', he punishes her by keeping her waiting on him all night while he calmly smokes his pipe.[86]

Words were not the only weapons that wives could find in their mouths. Screaming and crying could draw attention to marital problems and condemn a man to as much scorn as any words. Spitting was thought highly offensive. When the tutor John Ryves married his widowed mistress she gave him the 'greatest affront a Gentleman could receive' by allegedly spitting on his hand and face some thirty times. She also told him that 'she had done him the honour to raise him off the dunghill to her bed and said she was convinced his . . . mother was a vile whore'. The absence of words could be equally as damaging to men's self-esteem as their utterance. John lived to regret allowing his marriage service to proceed after his wife refused to include the word 'obey' in her wedding vows, for she had often told him since that 'as she did not promise to obey she was not bound and therefore would not'.[87]

---

[84] NA, DEL1/330 (1703), ff.106v–107v, 113r.

[85] LPL, CA, Case 5830 (1662), Ee1, f.234v.

[86] Foyster, *Manhood in Early Modern England*, pp. 58–65; Capp, *When Gossips Meet*, pp. 105–6; C. Dickens, *The Old Curiosity Shop* (1840–1), (London, 2000), pp. 36–46.

[87] LMA, DL/C/172 (1752), ff.214r, 222r, 224v; for other examples of this practice see, J. R. Gillis, *For Better, For Worse: British Marriages, 1600 to the Present* (Oxford, 1985), pp. 151–2.

We have seen in the previous chapter how over our time period attitudes changed towards men who directed verbal abuse at their wives, especially when it had a sexual content. From the eighteenth century we can also detect changing views of female verbal violence. Being verbally aggressive and showing frustration in marital life by using angry words became increasingly problematic for women on two grounds. First, as ideals of femininity were reconfigured in the eighteenth century, in terms of anger, women came to be seen as less passionate than men. This contrasted with the situation in the late sixteenth and early seventeenth centuries when anger was a passion associated with women because of their lesser powers of reason. Hence the minister John Downame in 1609 thought that anger in 'domestical matters' was peculiarly 'the fault of women, or at least a womanish fault'.[88] A century later, the *Spectator* thought anger was a 'male vice', which was 'altogether repugnant to the Softness' which was so 'endearing' and 'natural' to the 'Fair Sex'.[89] It was so against a woman's nature to be angry, that 'sweetness of temper' was labelled as 'most ornamental' to the female sex in George Chapman's 1773 *Treatise on Education*.[90] Women were expected to use their 'natural' qualities of feminine persuasion and win their husband's favour through gentle remonstrance rather than critical upbraiding.

Second, by the eighteenth century, whereas for men only certain types of angry language had become linked with the working classes, for middle- and upper-class women, raising their voices and using any form of angry words was socially unacceptable. Angry voices could now only be expected to be heard from a certain class of woman. As one mid-eighteenth-century writer explained, it was 'a Fishwoman at Billingsgate' who was most likely to display an angry spirit.[91] It was 'below a gentlewoman' to argue, thought the *Tatler*, and 'absolutely intolerable' in 'a lady of genteel education', wrote another.[92] Using verbal violence, whether or not it was retaliatory, was a difficult option for a wife in the eighteenth and nineteenth centuries if she did not want to lose her social respectability. A woman who did direct angry words

---

[88] J. Downame, *A Treatise of Anger* (London, 1609), pp. 28–9; see also, G. Kennedy, *Just Anger: Representing Women's Anger in Early Modern England* (Carbondale and Edwardsville, 2000), chapter 1.

[89] 'Male and female roles', *Spectator* Number 57 (5 May 1711), as cited in A. Ross, (ed.), *Selections from The Tatler and The Spectator* (Harmondsworth, 1982), p. 252.

[90] G. Chapman, *A Treatise on Education* (Edinburgh, 1773), p. 98.

[91] W. Webster, *A Casuistical Essay on Anger and Forgiveness* (London, 1750), p. 17.

[92] As cited in F. A. Childs, 'Prescriptions for manners in English courtesy literature, 1690–1760, and their social implications', DPhil thesis, University of Oxford (1984), p. 249; for further discussion of the cultural constructions of anger in this period see, Foyster, 'Boys will be boys?', 151–66.

towards her husband also risked being discredited by him in any subsequent legal action for cruelty. As we shall see, in defining a wife's angry words as nagging or scolding, it could be argued that she had provoked her husband to physical violence.

Some women found that there were ways of both conforming to their gender and class ideals and expressing hurt and injury after male violence. The alternative to angry words, silence, could be effectively deployed. As Peter Burke has recognised, 'keeping silent is itself an act of communication . . . Silence – accompanied by the appropriate gestures or facial expressions – may be warm or cold, intimate or exclusive, polite or aggressive'.[93] In this way, words were not needed when Mary Strudwick wore 'a cloth hanging over her eyes' to hide the bruises caused by her husband's violence, or when Anne Marie Brogden wore gloves for several days to hide 'from her acquaintance' the evidence of her husband's beatings.[94] For covering up cuts and bruises were powerful, non-verbal ways of signalling to others that violence had been committed, which could attract attention rather than deflect it (why was Mary hiding her eyes, why was Anne Marie wearing gloves all the time?). Wearing the early-modern equivalents of dark glasses allowed these women to send messages about what they had suffered without compromising their femininity or social position.

Other wives remained more assertive and were not hesitant in rebuking their husbands if they did not perform what they perceived were men's marital responsibilities. As Ellen Ross has shown, at the end of the nineteenth century working-class women, more concerned with economic survival than any conformity to polite sensibilities, could subject their husbands to 'fierce questions and taunts', as well as physical attack if they did not hand over their wages at the end of each working week.[95] In the sphere of family finance, and as the managers, if not the owners, of the household budget, women had the potential to exert considerable power over their husbands. Causing harm to a spouse through the use of economic goods was possible for women as well as men. Pawning goods became an essential part of the working-class domestic economy, but in popular literature it was portrayed as an activity that wives could use to punish errant and violent husbands. For example, a ballad that was printed a number of times in the nineteenth century presented a wife with 'an excellent plan / If you wish to reform a drunken man'. It

[93] P. Burke, *The Art of Conversation* (Oxford, 1993), pp. 123–4.
[94] NA, DEL1/361 (1722), f.106r; LMA, DL/C/173 (1758), f.297r.
[95] Ross, 'Fierce questions and taunts', 582; see also A. August, *Poor Women's Lives: Gender, Work, and Poverty in Late-Victorian London* (London, 1999), pp. 131–3.

told the story of a wife 'plagued' with a drunken husband who reduced him to begging her for forgiveness. She achieved this by first pawning the bed, then all his clothes, and finally by beating him with a fire-poker and dirty rag.[96]

Further up the social scale, the historian Margot Finn has shown how some wives were able to exploit one of the legal qualifications of coverture and use the 'law of necessaries' to gain advantage over their husbands in unhappy marriages. Chapter 1 demonstrated that men could exercise a form of economic cruelty towards their wives by withholding goods that were regarded as life's necessaries. But husbands had a duty to provide their wives with these necessaries, and wives had a legal right to make contracts with vendors for these goods. Wives pledged their husband's credit when they purchased necessaries, making husbands legally responsible for their payment. If a wife was forced to separate from her husband because of her adultery she could no longer pledge her husband's credit, but importantly, a wife who had fled from a violent husband could continue to rely upon him for the payment of necessaries. Wives used the law of necessaries as a bargaining tool during separation proceedings to achieve better terms. For example, during the lengthy legal battle over accusations of cruelty and adultery between the Westmeaths in the early nineteenth century, Lady Westmeath managed to have her husband imprisoned in the King's Bench after he did not pay for her necessaries of food, clothing, household goods and rent.[97]

Thus the law of necessaries could be deployed to dramatic effect. But the results for wives were not guaranteed. Bailey has found that in the eighteenth century, the courts did not always settle these cases in the wife's favour.[98] It seems probable that the likelihood of success was increased when a marriage relationship had already broken down. As a mechanism for negotiation in the daily struggles between wives and husbands its potential was more limited. This is because wives could only pledge their husbands' credit for goods that were deemed 'suitable' to their social position. The legal question of what was a necessary and what a luxury in a marriage was debated in a cultural context of increasing anxiety about the dangers of material consumption. When women were identified as the shoppers most subject to excess and desire, it became relatively straightforward for husbands to counter their wives'

---

[96] 'The Drunken Husband', Madden versions printed in vol. 9, 80; vol. 10, 374; vol. 18, 744. The version in vol. 18 was printed by John Harkness, Preston, who was active between c.1838–80.

[97] M. Finn, 'Women, consumption and coverture in England, c.1760–1860', *Historical Journal* 39, 3 (1996), 703–14.

[98] Bailey, *Unquiet Lives*, pp. 67–8.

accusations of violence with claims of unrestrained expenditure and waste. So when Elizabeth Idelle said that her husband had not given her any money to 'buy and provide her necessaries', he said that she had kept him at great expense, and reduced the value of his estate due to her 'extravagances and evil management'.[99] Whether Elizabeth had deliberately driven her husband into debt in revenge for his bad treatment, or if she had engaged in what modern-day psychologists might recognise as 'comfort buying' to ease her unhappiness, we will never know. What such cases do provide us with is further confirmation that in marriage goods assumed a meaning that was beyond their material value and practical function.

Like men, married women could engage in forms of economic cruelty, and physical and verbal violence, even if they assumed very different patterns. But whereas women could use sexual insult, particularly that of 'cuckold' against their husbands, sexual violence that employed the use of physical force was unknown. Some women were courageous enough to refuse sexual relations with their husbands, and there was some contemporary discussion about whether this was a wife's right when her husband had been adulterous or had contracted venereal disease. For example, in the 1690s the *Athenian Mercury* told one wife of an adulterous and infected husband that, 'if you'd take our advice, he shou'd keep a long *Lent* first, before you again trusted him'.[100] However, if a wife could exact revenge in an unhappy marriage by taking the sexual initiative herself was another issue. The debate in 1778 run by one London society over the question, 'Whether any degree of ill-treatment from a husband to a wife, can justify the latter in defiling the marriage bed?', remained unresolved and the meeting had to be adjourned.[101] It seems highly unlikely that faced with a violent partner many wives would have had either the physical or emotional strength to use sex or abstain from it as a bargaining tool to gain better treatment. The fact that moralists gave individuals in marriage equal and reciprocal sexual duties and rights was cold comfort to wives who did not have the means to resist forced or unwelcome sexual relations.[102] The portrayal of wives in

---

[99] NA, DEL1/285 (1709), ff.72r,82r; M. Berg and E. Eger, 'The rise and fall of the luxury debates', in M. Berg and E. Eger (eds.), *Luxury in the Eighteenth Century: Debates, Desires and Delectable Goods* (London, 2003), pp. 7–27.

[100] As cited in H. Berry, *Gender, Society and Print Culture in Late-Stuart England: The Cultural World of the Athenian Mercury* (Aldershot, 2003), p. 202; the italics are in the original.

[101] Andrew (ed.), *London Debating Societies*, p. 44.

[102] For the views of early-modern moralists about marital sex see, M. R. Sommerville, *Sex and Subjection: Attitudes to Women in Early-Modern Society* (London, 1995), pp. 132–4.

popular ballads rejecting their husbands sexually by kicking them out of the marital bed, was pure fantasy.[103]

In summary, wives could be violent to their husbands in a number of different ways, although some forms of violence were likely to have been deployed more frequently than others. Like male violence, women's violence could involve an integration or combination of all its components. Since accounts of female violence were so often related by men, it is difficult to know how women themselves experienced or explained their use of violence. It would be mistaken to assume that all violent wives were victims of male violence, for such was the nature of marital quarrels that it was not always clear whether female or male violence was mutual or defensive. Views towards female violence changed over our period, and by the mid-nineteenth century, vocalising discontent in marriage through verbal insult was socially unacceptable for elite women. As we shall see, they found new ways of signalling abuse. The question of whether a wife could defend herself and not be seen as acting provocatively is one to which we will now turn.

Provocative responses

It was because the main defence to male violence in marriage was that it had been provoked by wifely insubordination and disobedience, that we learn about female violence. Husbands claimed to have been provoked to violence by the physical and verbal violence of their wives. Other more trivial complaints, such as poor dress, cooking and hospitality were presented as sources of aggravation. In turn, wives and their witnesses took care to declare that they had done nothing to provoke their husbands. For example, the cook in the Veitch household declared, 'I never knew Mrs Veitch to give her said husband any provocation whatsoever, but unprovoked he used to put himself into the most violent passions'.[104] The assumption was that if a husband could not present his violence as a form of chastisement, then it was unacceptable. Thus cruel violence was unprovoked violence. But the concept of provocation could only be deployed effectively as a defence for male violence while husbands were thought to have a right to chastise their wives using physical means. As it will be demonstrated, once physical violence was questioned as a legitimate form of correction in marital relations, even a wife who behaved provocatively could be represented as undeserving

---

[103] See, for example, 'My Wife will be my Master', *Roxburghe* vol. 7i, pp. 188–9, and 'The Jolly Widdower: Or, A Warning for Batchelors', *Pepys* vol. 4, p. 102.

[104] LPL, CA, Case 9440 (1837), H550/18.

of violence from her husband. By the end of our period providing evidence of provocation to the courts became less reliable as a defence strategy for men.

Some historians have argued that in the nineteenth century increasing unwillingness to accept arguments of provocation from violent men is evidence of a new and progressively mounting intolerance for domestic violence.[105] But it is crucial in this context to distinguish between judicial and popular attitudes. As we shall see, although judicial responses to male violence did change, and became more critical of the defence of provocation, generally these diverged from the popular view, which held fast to the idea that a husband had a right to correct his wife using physical violence. These two viewpoints coexisted, and it was when they clashed in the courtroom that their differences became most clear. It is also important to recognise why nineteenth-century magistrates and judges were less likely to accept the provocation defence than their predecessors. This was not a matter of rising condemnation for marital violence. As the previous chapter showed, there were always circumstances when marital violence was seen as unacceptable. Rather, the opportunities for men to successfully plead provocation were narrowed in the nineteenth century, as a sector of the ruling elite (the judiciary), attempted to intervene and control male violence. Significantly, they were most persistent in their efforts, but also met with the greatest resistance, in the police courts that dealt with the working class. Marital violence in this period was not seen as a new problem, but the debates about the validity of the provocation defence did give a basis to try new solutions.

The idea of provocation was best known in the criminal courts where it could be used to reduce a charge of murder to manslaughter. In cases when husbands had killed their wives, they could be convicted only of manslaughter or even be acquitted if they could prove that their wives had provoked them, usually by their habitual drunkenness, infidelity, or both. In the early part of our period ideas of male honour and manhood were so dependent upon the sexual control of women that a special rule of provocation was developed for a man who killed upon the discovery of his adulterous wife. Whereas a wife who killed her husband after the provocation of his adultery could be guilty of petty treason, a husband who killed an unfaithful wife could successfully plead manslaughter. Men who became violent in such circumstances could expect leniency.

---

[105] M. J. Wiener, 'The sad story of George Hall: adultery, murder and the politics of mercy in mid-Victorian England', *Social History* 24, 2 (1999), 174–95, and *Men of Blood*, chapters 5–6.

In the mid-eighteenth century, when a London corkcutter found his wife in bed with her lover, and killed the lover, he was convicted of manslaughter and ordered to be burnt 'gently' in the hand, 'because there could be no greater provocation'.[106]

But by the Victorian period judicial attitudes towards male violence had shifted to such an extent that reprieve for men who killed their adulterous wives was less assured. The historian Wiener recounts the case of George Hall, a working-class man, convicted for the murder of his wife in 1864. Despite the provocation given by Hall's wife of desertion and suspected adultery, it took considerable popular support for Hall, demonstrated by petitions containing nearly 70,000 signatures, and last minute intervention by the Home Secretary, for him to escape the gallows.[107] Judicial opinion now held that men should master their passions and their anger, even when faced with great provocation. As one judge ruled in a 1837 murder case, 'though the law condescends to human frailty, it will not indulge in human ferocity. It considers man to be a rational being, and requires that he should exercise a reasonable control over his passions'.[108] New understandings of male anger had developed in the law. In the courts in the seventeenth and eighteenth centuries wifely provocation was represented as the trigger for righteous anger and outrage in husbands that could give a moral justification for their violent actions. The man who killed his adulterous wife could be regarded as administering a kind of retributive justice. By the nineteenth century, provocative behaviour was seen as leading to anger that was a loss of self-control, and could only serve as an excuse for violence. Temporarily, an angry man in this state was not responsible for his actions.[109]

The mental state of the defendant, as well as the conduct of the victim became the focus of attention. So when a group of medical practitioners reviewed the case of George Hall they concluded that, 'the terrible wrong [of a wife's desertion and adultery] . . . inflicted on the prisoner would have produced even in an educated mind the most intense anguish, and must have had on a mind, which appears to have been at no time well balanced or strong a still more agonizing effect'.[110] In their

---

[106] As cited in Beattie, *Crime and the Courts*, p. 95. The legal debates during murder trials in America followed a similar line of thinking, see, S. T. Moore, '"Justifiable provocation": Violence against women in Essex County, New York, 1799–1860', *Journal of Social History* 35, 4 (2002), 889–96.

[107] Wiener, 'The sad story of George Hall', 174–95.

[108] *R. v. Kirkham* (1837), as cited in J. Horder, *Provocation and Responsibility* (Oxford, 1992), p. 98.

[109] Horder, *Provocation and Responsibility*, chapters 2 and 5.

[110] As cited in Wiener, 'The sad story', 181.

assessment of the case, manly self-control became a matter determined by social class, with the working-class husband deemed weaker willed than his social superior. Violent acts committed by working-class men upon their wives were causing such concern that the issue of provocation was less likely to be allowed for consideration. Neighbours and relatives of the wife of a former Spitalfields weaver offered explanations for her brutal murder by her husband in September 1855, but the deputy coroner would not accept these as grounds for provocation. 'Neither drunkenness nor jealousy', he said, 'was a sufficient excuse for the committal of such a crime as this, and it would be for the jury to consider what state of mind the prisoner was in when he committed this act . . . If they were satisfied it was a premeditated act they would, of course, return a verdict of murder'. The weaver was found guilty and hanged.[111] Subsequent husbands whose lack of self-control meant that their passions overcame their powers of reason could be treated as mad. The defence of insanity began to overtake that of provocation as modern psychiatry and legal medicine developed.[112] Significantly, regarding the wife murderer as insane was only possible when responding to provocation with lethal violence was seen as an irrational rather than a partially justifiable act.

The defence of provocation also began to lose its strength when it was used by husbands accused of non-lethal violence against their wives. There had always been the concept that physical correction should be in proportion to a wife's offence. So the author of *The Lawes Resolution of Women's Rights* argued in 1631 that a husband could only exercise 'reasonable correction' of his wife, and in the eighteenth century Blackstone thought that a husband's 'power of correction' should be 'confined within reasonable bounds'.[113] 'Reasonable' physical chastisement was defined in practice as an appropriate response to wifely disobedience. When a witness to John Robinson's beating of his wife in 1696 told him, 'that he was a very ill man to beat his wife at that rate', as Amussen has recognised, it was the rate that was the problem, not the fact that he was being violent.[114] In his famous ruling on the Evans marriage separation case in 1790, Scott noted that while some behaviour by

---

[111] *The Times* (21 September, 1855) 4f.
[112] R. Smith, 'The boundary between insanity and criminal responsibility in nineteenth-century England', in A. Scull, (ed.), *Madhouses, Mad-Doctors, and Madmen: The Social History of Psychiatry in the Victorian Era* (London, 1981), pp. 363–84.
[113] T. E., *The Lawes Resolution of Women's Rights* (London, 1631), as cited in Amussen, "Being stirred to much unquietness", 71; Blackstone, *Commentaries on the Laws*, vol. I, p. 444; Foyster, 'Male honour', 215–24.
[114] As cited in Amussen, "Being stirred to much unquietness", 78.

a wife merited correction, there were types of violent response that were so excessive that no provocation could justify them. If the allegations made against Mr Evans were true, thought Scott,

> they are of that nature and species, that they cannot be justified by any misconduct on the part of Mrs Evans; for though misconduct may authorise a husband in restraining a wife of her personal liberty, yet no misconduct of hers could authorise him in occasioning a premature delivery, or refusing her the use of common air.[115]

Scott created a scale that matched provocation with just retaliation. He applied this scale in two other landmark cases, *Holden v. Holden* (1810), and *Waring v. Waring* (1813). Yet his deliberations on these cases showed an uneasy recognition that husbands could not always be trusted to respond to provocation in such a measured way. Scott advised Mrs Waring that 'by provocations' she may 'have brought upon herself the ill-treatment complained of', and told her to look to amend her own conduct before she complained of her husband's. But he added hastily, 'I do not mean by this that every slight failure of duty, on the part of the wife, is to be visited by intemperate violence on the part of the husband'.[116] Scott was also to concede that, 'it is not necessary that the conduct of the wife should be entirely without blame' for a court to find a husband guilty of cruelty.[117] His judgements, though, still displayed an acceptance of violence in certain circumstances, which let husbands continue to present arguments of provocation to the courts. In Scotland, the defence of provocation was only successful in one separation case heard between 1714 and 1830, but in England and Wales it was not until *Kelly v. Kelly* (1869–70), that the behaviour of a wife was dismissed as a relevant factor in the judgement of marital cruelty.[118] In response to Kelly's claims that his wife frequently lost her temper, the appeal judges answered that 'a wife does not lose her title to the protection of this court merely because she has proved unable to bear with perfect patience and unfailing propriety of conduct the ill-usage of her husband'.[119] The premium upon female patience had at last been questioned.

Earlier in the nineteenth century, and in the courts that tended to hear cases brought by women of lower social status, judgements could bear similarities to Scott's rulings. Mr Ballantine was one magistrate in the London police courts who dealt with Thomas Sinnock, a lighterman and

---

[115] *Evans v. Evans* (1790), *English Reports* vol. 161, p. 471.
[116] *Waring v. Waring* (1813), *English Reports* vol. 161, pp. 699–700.
[117] *Holden v. Holden* (1810), *English Reports* vol. 161, p. 616.
[118] Leneman, "A tyrant and tormentor", 48–9.
[119] As cited in Hammerton, 'Victorian marriage', 288.

bargemaster accused of beating and kicking his wife in October 1832. When Sinnock argued that he 'ought to beat' his wife when she was disobedient, Ballantine immediately replied 'but not in that brutal manner', and asked how the wife had been insubordinate. Like Scott, Ballantine believed that while there were some degrees of violence that were always unmerited, that did not remove a husband's right to correct his wife. Ballantine did not miss the opportunity to advise the aggrieved woman that, 'as a good wife, you should obey your husband, who is the master of his own house'. By refusing to pass judgement on the assault until the wife had seen to the removal of a young sailor who lodged in their house, and whose presence supposedly had provoked Sinnock to anger, Ballantine and his fellow magistrate condoned his violence.[120]

But the judgements made in other police courts show that Ballantine's views were out of step with his contemporaries. Control of working-class violence had become such an issue for middle-class magistrates that they could display little tolerance for considerations of provocation. When a gunmaker was accused of beating his wife and stabbing her with a knife in October 1824 he said that he had been provoked to such behaviour by his wife's drunkenness, neglect of their children, and avoidance of her household duties. On the evening the stabbing occurred, 'when he came home to dinner, he found the whole place in confusion – the bed even unmade, the rooms uncleaned – no dinner ready – and his wife in a state of intoxication'. The magistrate would hear none of it, and ruled 'no conduct on the part of any woman could warrant such a desperate outrage'.[121] Other magistrates were more explicit in their refusal to permit provocation as a defence for marital violence. When one husband in Bow Street magistrate's court argued that he had given his wife a black eye and had intended to break her arm because of her 'provoking tongue', the magistrate angrily interrupted:

Hold your tongue, Sir, and don't insult the ears of those about you, by setting up the provocation of a woman's tongue in justification of such an outrage as you say you contemplated upon your poor wife. Go and hide your head in prison, and don't expose yourself further.[122]

Arguments about provocation could be roundly dismissed. In 1836 'a respectable tradesman' tried to suggest that it was the 'extraordinary aggravation' of his wife remonstrating with him for spending so much time away from their family home, that was responsible for his violence

[120] *The Times* (13 October 1832) 4a.
[121] *The Times* (8 October 1824) 3d.
[122] *The Times* (13 October 1825) 3b.

to her. But the simple statement by the magistrate, 'Still she is your wife, and nothing could justify your striking her', put an end to such a claim.[123]

Further up the social scale, the recognition that physical violence by husbands against their wives could be viewed by judges as unacceptable, whatever the circumstances, led some men to reassess the way in which they presented their defence. Whereas early in the eighteenth century a husband such as Jacob Bor was quite open about how he gave his wife 'moderate correction' after she 'provoked' him by her drunkenness and 'bad and unmannerly language', men 100 years later were less likely to assert their rights of chastisement to the church courts.[124] Some submitted straightforward denials of violence, rather than become embroiled in complex and sometimes lengthy debates about provocation.[125] Others argued that their wives had deliberately tried to provoke them to physical violence, knowing that this type of male behaviour was likely to be condemned. So Morgan George Crofton said that his wife knew that he was 'hasty of temper', and planned to 'irritate' him until, 'he should commit some violence in momentary anger in consequence of which she might be enabled to effectuate a separation from him'.[126] Similarly, James Best argued in 1823 that once he decided that 'it was the intention' of his wife 'to provoke him to commit some act of violence towards her of which she might take advantage', he tried whenever possible to avoid her company.[127] While it seems highly unlikely that any wife married to a bad tempered husband would risk serious harm in order to have grounds for separation, what these cases do reveal is that husbands were well aware of the expectation that they should be restrained in their behaviour towards their wives.

What we see during the period of this study is the limited extent to which the legal establishment could shape a popular culture where for so long violence had a place in married life. Whereas the opportunities to advance arguments of provocation may have narrowed in middle- and upper-class circles, nevertheless, judges and magistrates found that they shared a residual reluctance to surrender completely a husband's rights of chastisement over his wife. Meanwhile, prosecutions for assault in the early to mid nineteenth-century police courts show middle-class

---

[123] *The Times* (26 October 1836) 6f.

[124] NA, DEL1/364 (1721), f.78v.

[125] See, for example, LPL, CA, Case 3926 (1846), H736/7, and LPL, CA, Case 4282 (1853), H826/6.

[126] LPL, CA, Case 2412 (1818), H277/10.

[127] LPL, CA, Case 821 (1823), D164, f.115; *Best v. Best* (1823), *English Reports* vol. 162, pp. 145–58.

magistrates imposing standards of marital conduct upon a working-class populace that was far from compliant. Taking a moral stance on marital violence and declaring that it was never legitimate, flew in the face of the popular view that husbands had a right to correct their wives when provoked. Of course, the idea of provocation as a popular defence for male violence has never been entirely abandoned. Women can still be represented as somehow asking for violence, particularly rape, by their behaviour or dress. In our period consideration of the conduct of a wife who alleged violence by her husband continued to be important. The responses by wives to violence could be used as evidence against them, and in this way women were held partly responsible for their fate. But as Linda Gordon has recognised, 'to focus on women's "provocations", and to examine men's grievances against their wives . . . is to uncover the evidence of women's resistance'.[128] By bringing cases of marital violence to magistrates and to the courts, wives provoked male behaviour of another kind. They stimulated discussion about men's rights over their wives and debate over how far chastisement needed to be of a physical nature.

Nervous responses

Rachael Norcott and Mary Veitch were separated not only by nearly two hundred years of history, but also by the responses that were available to them when they suffered marital violence. They shared some of the same consequences of violence: both displayed bruising to witnesses in and outside their households. But when Mary wanted others to know of her anger, pain and unhappiness with her husband she also adopted a pattern of behaviour that would have been considered highly unusual and understood in different ways during Rachael's lifetime. Mary took to her bed. This was not because she needed a period of recovery from any physical injuries that she had received. It was to draw attention to violence. Mary's health, according to her daughter, was affected in very particular ways by her mistreatment. 'She was scarcely ever well by reason of Dr. Veitch's treatment of her – Her illness was nervousness occasioned by his constant ill-treatment'. This nervous illness reached such a point that it could be triggered by the mere presence of James Veitch:

---

[128] L. Gordon, *Heroes of their Own Lives: The Politics and History of Family Violence* (London, 1989), p. 286.

His very knock at the street door used to put her in an agitation; and when he entered the room she became immediately so nervous that her hand trembled so that she could not hold anything.

It was when Mary could endure her nervous illness no longer that she was forced to leave her husband. 'Her reason for quitting', it was said, 'was that she was worn out and that her health had given way under his system of constant ill-usage of her'.[129]

Mary's nervous illness was a new form of protest and a way of responding to marital violence that had developed in the eighteenth century. New medical theories of the body emerged, which focused upon the nervous system rather than humoural imbalance as the cause of ill-health. In the mid-eighteenth century these combined with a culture of sensibility that enhanced the importance of sentiment and feeling. The result was that nervous illness became all the vogue. Importantly, nervousness assumed both gender and class meanings. Women were thought to have more sensitive, delicate or weaker nerves than men. The social elite convinced themselves that a greater susceptibility to nervous illness was a sign of refinement and class superiority. The soothing treatments and calming atmosphere advertised by fashionable spa and seaside towns for the sufferers of nervous ailments, helped to sustain the belief that there was something rather special about suffering from these complaints.[130] This allowed women such as Mary to react to marital violence in nervous ways that confirmed or even enhanced their femininity and social status. A new way of responding to marital unhappiness had evolved that matched the criterion for the ideal woman.

Nervous illness was described by wives in the marital disputes of the eighteenth and nineteenth centuries in a variety of ways. Sometimes the women afflicted were described like Mary to be suffering from general complaints such as shaking, or 'agitated nerves' and 'nervous afflictions'. Other descriptions were more detailed. Wives were said to be affected by 'fits', 'freaks', 'vapours', a 'want of appetite and spirits', crying and 'deep melancholy', as a result of their husband's treatment.[131] Women could be afflicted by a single, or a combination of these disorders. Mary Viscountess Coke, for example, who had been confined in her husband's Norfolk house, was alleged to be suffering from a long list of nervous illnesses;

---

[129] LPL, CA, Case 9440 (1837), H550/18.
[130] G. S. Rousseau, 'Towards a semiotics of the nerve: the social history of language in a new key', in P. Burke and R. Porter (eds.), *Language, Self and Society* (Oxford, 1991), pp. 214–75; J. Oppenheim, *'Shattered Nerves': Doctors, Patients, and Depression in Victorian England* (Oxford, 1991), pp. 3–15; Barker-Benfield, *The Culture of Sensibility.*
[131] See, for example, LPL, CA, Case 3366 (1811), D757, ff.25,29,37,182, and LPL, CA, Case 3926 (1846), H736/6,7.

'hysteric fits', cold hands and arms, 'her pulse extremely languid, her appetite very little, her sleep little, a frequent nervous cough'.[132]

The most dramatic of nervous incidents was the fit that was labelled as 'hysterical'. Wives were reported as having hysterical fits after physical and verbal violence, and in response to domestic confinement. But as I have shown elsewhere, hysteria also allowed women a vehicle of expression after sexual violence. It was only when Sophia Roper fell into hysterics in August 1817 that her parents could confront her husband about his sexual cruelties towards her. Screaming and shaking, flinging limbs one direction and another, and resisting anyone who tried to hold them still, during a fit of hysteria women could use their voices and bodies in a manner that usually the restrictive standards for female conduct made impossible. Nervous illnesses gained women an indulgence or privileged position to temporarily behave in ways that would otherwise be seen as unacceptable. A hysterical fit brought sexual violence out into the open, and created a point of crisis that demanded a response.[133]

For some women there is no doubt that nervous illnesses offered an outlet for frustration and hurt, and an opportunity to provide others with evidence of violence, which could eventually enable them to obtain separation from their husbands. But whilst nervous responses did help these individuals, a number of issues meant that nervousness did not become a general solution for all women facing marital violence.

A key problem with responding nervously to marital violence was that nobody was certain what caused these illnesses, in particular, hysteria. Medical practitioners could not agree. While Thomas Willis and Thomas Sydenham had introduced the idea that fits of hysteria had a neurological cause, older ideas concerned with the uterus proved stubbornly resilient. If there was doubt amongst medics about hysteria, this left lay people free to interpret nervous illnesses as they wished. To wives and their supporters, violence was the source of the emotional shocks or crises that triggered women's fits of hysteria or nervous illness. But husbands could as easily argue that it was women's own anger or their drunkenness that had tipped the balance towards hysteria. So Lord Huntingtower said in 1837 that nothing should be inferred from an occasion when his wife fainted, since 'his said wife whenever even slightly irritated or provoked was in the habit of going into hysterics or fainting from the violence of her own temper and passions'.[134] Almost a century earlier, the Reverend Charles Pulteney denied that he had driven

[132] LPL, CA, Case 2068 (1750), D435, f.138v.
[133] Foyster, 'Creating a veil of silence?', 408–14.
[134] LPL, CA, Case 4915 (1837) H544/6.

his wife to 'vapours', 'hysterics' or a 'deep melancholy', but argued that all of these afflictions had been caused by his wife's heavy drinking. Similarly, John Head said that it was because his wife had sat up all night drinking that she suffered from 'hysteric or other disorders', adding with sarcasm, 'if any such she had'.[135] By dismissing nervous illnesses as expressions of marital discontent, men could deprive women of their agency, and attempt to force them into a position of passive subjection. Without a clear link between violence and nervous illness, the strength of this response was seriously diminished.

Furthermore, although contemporaries recognised that wives could endure terrible violence from their husbands, and genuinely suffer ill-health as a result, there was always an underlying suspicion that women could sham illness. Nervous illnesses were thought particularly prone to affectation. Even in the early novels of sensibility, women's ability to practise what Henry Fielding called 'the arts of counterfeiting illness' were satirised. People joked about how women pretended to be ill so that their husbands were duped into supporting all-expenses-paid trips to spa towns.[136] Husbands believed that wives could have control over their nerves, so that all it took was a measure of willpower for women to avoid nervous fits. Hence, in his description of one domestic incident, John Marsh complimented his wife by recording how she was 'not fine Lady enough to increase our confusion by falling into fits', bearing news of a fire in their laundry with 'great composure'.[137] By the time Jane Austen's novel, *Pride and Prejudice* (1813) was published, readers could be assured of sympathising with Mr Bennett, whose wife often used her nerves to get her own way. 'You delight in vexing me', she accused him, and 'have no compassion for my poor nerves'. 'I have high respect for your nerves', he replied, 'They are my old friends. I have heard you mention them with consideration these twenty years at least'.[138]

If and when nervous illnesses were affected, they surely must have begun to lose their appeal within fashionable circles once they were adopted by the lower social orders. Whereas in the eighteenth century, nervousness and hysteria were illnesses of the polite and genteel, during the nineteenth century a much wider section of the population was said to be suffering from these disorders. Hospital and Poor Law records

---

[135] LPL, CA, Case 7468 (1739), Ee10, f.66; LPL, CA, Case 4407 (1737), D997, f.46v–47r.

[136] Barker-Benfield, *The Culture of Sensibility*, pp. 29–34.

[137] John Marsh, 'History of my Private Life', xv (1 January 1793), pp. 67–9, Unpublished manuscript, HM54457, Huntington Library, San Marino, California; I am grateful to Helen Berry for this reference.

[138] As cited in Oppenheim, *'Shattered Nerves'*, p. 209.

reveal that the working classes could be labelled as suffering from hysteria.[139] In the nineteenth-century criminal courts fainting had become a routine part of the female defence, no matter what the social class of those accused.[140] Without their social exclusiveness nervous illnesses lost their special qualities.

In the period of this study wives who exhibited nervous illnesses avoided being cast into a permanent bed-ridden sick role. The wives who confronted marital violence with nervous illnesses intended them to act as escape routes from marriage, rather than as a reason for long-term recovery within the marital home. Thus they saw nervousness as a key for release from marriage, and not, as some historians have argued for the later Victorian period, as just a way of being allowed to temporarily opt out of marital roles.[141] However, women could never escape from the fact that nervous illnesses were always 'borderline mental states', which had close associations with insanity.[142] Mary Veitch had good reason to be concerned when her husband threatened to 'lock her up in a madhouse', not only because he was a physician whose word might have carried some weight in these matters, but also because as the following case study shows, these were threats that were sometimes carried out.[143]

Like other genteel wives who faced sexual violence, Frances Fletcher responded to her husband's 'vile and unmanly practices' of masturbation and flagellation, as well as verbal and physical violence, with hysteria. She 'lived in continual terror from such the ill usage of her said husband and the same prayed very much on her spirits and injured her health and at several times brought on hysteric fits'. Such a 'nervous affliction' reduced her 'to a state of great debility'. But to her horror, Frances' husband decided to represent his wife as insane so that he could have her confined. She was sent from their London home to Southampton where she was cared for by a woman who usually 'guarded' the insane, and on her return her husband summoned several eminent mad-doctors to rule upon her condition. Her claims of marital violence in the separation case

[139] R. Porter, 'The body and the mind, the doctor and the patient: negotiating hysteria', in S. Gilman, H. King, R. Porter, G. S. Rousseau and E. Showalter, *Hysteria beyond Freud* (Berkeley, 1993), pp. 227–8.
[140] Wiener, 'Alice Arden to Bill Sikes', 197.
[141] See, for example, C. Smith-Rosenberg, 'The hysterical woman: sex roles and role conflict in 19th century America', *Social Research* 39 (1972), 652–78; and E. Showalter, *The Female Malady: Women, Madness, and English Culture, 1830–1980* (London, 1987).
[142] Oppenheim, *'Shattered Nerves'*, p. 6.
[143] LPL, CA, Case 9440 (1837), H550/5.

she brought against her husband in 1811 were overlooked, while lengthy evidence was submitted and debated regarding her sanity.[144]

In this case, reacting to violence with hysteria was fatal, for Frances switched attention from her husband's behaviour to her own. Her hysteria had become another mechanism that her husband could use to control and dominate her, and her illness was seen as a demonstration of female weakness and dependency. Her story shows how what was an enabling tool for some women could become a form of subjection for others. Nervous illnesses and hysteria had become more popular responses to marital violence in the eighteenth and nineteenth centuries. But whether they were real or feigned, 'natural' and unavoidable reactions, or part of a calculated strategy to attract notice, they were undoubtedly risky forms of resistance. There was always the danger that signs of nervous illness would be interpreted as symptoms of madness, and that male medical interventions rather than legal solutions were offered as the cure.

Conclusion

This chapter has shown that there were many 'healthier' ways of responding to marital violence than nervous illness. Women's responses could assume multiple forms. They could exhibit considerable fortitude and willpower to shape the circumstances of their marital lives. We have seen that ideas of gender and class shaped expectations of how women should behave, but that many wives could not or would not conform to these ideals. When faced with violence some women simply did whatever they could to survive, regardless of social conventions. This could include retaliatory violence. Marriage separation cases provide important evidence of the range and nature of women's violent behaviour, and of contemporary recognition that this could be produced, although never justified, by a husband's violence. Potentially more successful were the methods of protest that confirmed women's femininity and social status. Evidence of unprovoked violence that had been met with patience, silence, sexual innocence or nervous illness was difficult for men to defend and was met with sympathy. We should not forget, however, the many women who responded to male violence not through active resistance, but by internalising its negative and destructive elements. For these women, the pain of violence could endure long after it had been inflicted.

[144] LPL, CA, Case 3366 (1811), D757.

As Chapters 3 and 4 will show, women who faced violence were not alone. Responding to violence was often a collective family, household or neighbourhood matter. The effectiveness of a woman's initial response to violence was in some ways measured by how far she was able to gather support from those who lived and worked around her. They might then act as witnesses in subsequent legal proceedings. Going to court was often a final resort for women with violent husbands, but of course, it was in itself an act of resistance. How women's stories of violence were heard in the courts was partly dependent, as we have seen, upon the extent to which they had lived up to the ideals for their gender and class. Many of those ideals were closely tied to the assumption that a wife was also a mother, and it is to the arguments about how marital violence had an impact upon parenting and childhood that we now turn.

3   Children and marital violence

Today, when marriages break down and there are children from that marriage, issues of childcare, welfare, maintenance and custody are considered of paramount importance. Long and bitter disputes over child custody and access arrangements have become a standard feature of modern divorce proceedings. In our 'child-centred' culture, protecting children from violence, and removing them from homes where they could be at risk from physical and/or sexual abuse is a major concern. A wide range of professionals, from social workers to police officers are trained to minimise the harm that can be inflicted upon children who endure violence, directly or indirectly, from their parents. It is highly unusual, especially in cases of divorce due to marital violence, for mothers not to gain custody of their children.

The situation could not be more different from that experienced during the period from the Restoration until the mid-nineteenth century, as represented by the Norcott and Veitch marriages. There were children living in both households. In the case of the Norcott children, harm was inflicted upon them from their father even as they lay in their mother's womb. We know that Rachael Norcott had been pregnant on two occasions when her husband, John, struck her. She was 'big with child' when he hit her so hard on the head that she was knocked senseless to the floor, and six or seven years later, a midwife was present in the household when Rachael had to be treated for injuries that her husband had inflicted. Later, experiencing corporal punishment as children, the Norcott children could share with their mother in the physical pain she suffered from John. On one occasion when Rachael tried to 'pacify' John as he was disciplining 'one of his sons', he turned his violence upon her. In both the Norcott and the Veitch families children were witnesses to their parents' quarrels. Mary Veitch already had one daughter, Louisa, from her previous marriage when she married James. She bore two children with James, but by the time she brought her separation case in 1837, only one child, a daughter aged 10, was still living. Louisa was often present when her stepfather verbally abused her mother, and it was

Louisa's courtship with a man that did not meet with James' approval that was the occasion of some of his most violent quarrels with her mother. But in the legal separation proceedings brought by Rachael and Mary the issue of child protection or custody does not merit a single mention. In this apparently 'adult-centred' culture, the concerns of the parents were all that were important. In this period, there was nothing to be discussed about childcare arrangements following separation, since even if Rachael and Mary were successful in proving their cases, the law declared that all children should be in the custody of their fathers. A man whose violence had been declared so cruel that his wife no longer had to reside with him, still had the absolute right as a father to the custody of his children.[1]

Nevertheless, there were key changes in the ways in which children were described in the stories of marriage breakdown in the Norcott and Veitch families. The position of Rachael Norcott's children formed only part of the narrative of her abuse. They simply provided the context in which she was physically harmed; the suffering that her children may have endured was presented by witnesses as only incidental to the more important issue of conjugal violence. In contrast, Mary Veitch's children were central to her claims of marital cruelty. For Mary Veitch, it was her husband's threats to separate her from Louisa, his refusal to let their own daughter return home from boarding school to see her, and instructions to her headmistress not to admit Mary to the school, which were as harmful to her as any physical violence. Collectively this type of behaviour amounted to a form of mental cruelty that Mary's delicate health could not sustain. Without these accusations concerning their children, Mary had little case to bring against her husband. The testimony of the nineteen-year-old Louisa, who had been just six years old when her mother married James Veitch, was the first and most important of a long list of statements taken from witnesses who spoke for Mary.

We can begin to understand why the accounts of children in the Norcott and Veitch marriages were so dissimilar once we appreciate that by the nineteenth century there had been significant changes in the concepts of childhood and parenthood. This chapter will look at these. It will consider the position of children in their parents' quarrels, and debate whether contemporaries were aware of how witnessing marital violence could affect children. Children's strategies for coping with living in violent families will be discussed, and their accounts of what they saw and experienced will be analysed by looking at their statements in court,

---

[1] LPL, CA, Case 6659 (1666), Eee2, ff.95–99r, 101r-102; LPL, CA, Case 9440 (1837), H550/5,9,18; Peter Earle also notes the absence of consideration of children in marriage separation cases in *The Making of the English Middle Class*, p. 234.

and later writings that reflected upon their childhood. Throughout the chapter, the inter-relationship and inter-dependency between children and their parents will be discussed. As Bailey has observed, too often histories of childhood are discussed 'separately from marriage, as if the relationship between spouses was isolated from that between them and their children'.[2] This chapter will reintegrate the stories of children and married adults into new histories of the family. Parenting shaped married life. It will be argued that the increasing emphasis upon the role of wives as mothers was vitally important to women who faced marital violence, for it gave women such as Mary Veitch new ways to challenge their husband's conduct. In this changed cultural environment, a man who was violent to his wife, who was also a mother, could be subject to double condemnation. Finally, this chapter will consider the issue of the law on child custody. Two years after the Veitch marriage dispute was heard, the first Infant Custody Act was passed. By giving mothers of children under the age of seven the ability to claim the custody of their children, this Act was a radical departure from the previous legal position of near automatic custody of all children to their fathers, and it began a process of giving mothers increased rights over their children that has continued until today. But it will be argued that far from indicating new concerns for children's care, legislative change came about to protect the interests of adults rather than children. It is the contention of this chapter that in the period of this study, children were the neglected victims of the violence between their parents.

Before we proceed, it is necessary to include a note about definitions. Useful work has been conducted on establishing differences in this period between 'childhood' and 'youth'.[3] The latter category was applied to older children, particularly teenagers. There is no doubt that contemporaries did regard youth as a period of new and different opportunities for young people. Serving as apprentices or domestic servants, adolescents could observe the marriages of their employers as well as their parents. Older children often provide us with the most articulate records of their experiences. However, in the context of marital discord, there is little evidence that adults varied their conduct according to the age of their children. Therefore, in this chapter, the term 'children' will include all young people under the age of twenty-one and will be applied to those individuals who were economically dependent, usually upon their parents.

[2] Bailey, *Unquiet Lives*, p. 27.
[3] See, for example, I. K. Ben-Amos, *Adolescence and Youth in Early Modern England* (London, 1994), and P. Griffiths, *Youth and Authority: Formative Experiences in England 1560–1640* (Oxford, 1996).

Children in history

Childhood has a history. That has been the conclusion of historians working on this theme since the 1962 publication in English of the groundbreaking work by Phillipe Ariès on children. Rather than childhood being a constant, 'natural' phenomenon, historians have shown that ideas about children have changed over time, and are cultural constructions. They have varied, not only according to historical period, but also due to the age, gender and social class of the child. Ariès initiated a controversial debate by suggesting that until the seventeenth century there was no concept of childhood. Children, he argued, were simply seen as mini adults, who did not merit any separate or different treatment. Other historians have contributed to the debate by suggesting that in the seventeenth century, moralists, particularly the Puritans, developed new ideas about children that defined them as distinct from adults. The Puritans regarded children as innately sinful, and thought that it was the duty of every Christian parent to train their children towards godly lives through education and strict discipline. In contrast, John Locke's *Some Thoughts Concerning Education* (1693) was far more secular in tone, and marked a turning point in thinking about children. For Locke, each child was an individual, with different temperaments and abilities. The role of the parent in educating the child was crucial since in terms of a child's thinking, she or he was a *tabula rasa* or blank slate, ready to be shaped and formed. It was nurture, not nature, that was important. 'Nine parts of ten are what they are, good or evil, useful or not, by their education', he wrote. By teaching children to develop their capacity for reason, Locke believed that they would learn the difference between right and wrong. Locke still saw children as inferior forms of adults, they were like 'weak people under a natural infirmity', but Jean-Jacques Rousseau in the mid-eighteenth century believed that children were born innocent, and it was this innocence that made them different from their parents. According to Rousseau, children had distinct sensitivities, and naturally tended towards good rather than harmful behaviour. Romantic writers of the late eighteenth and early nineteenth centuries developed these ideas even further by suggesting that the innocence of childhood was a state of being to which all adults yearned to return, and that it was children who could teach adults valuable lessons of truth and virtue, rather than vice versa.[4]

[4] P. Ariès, *Centuries of Childhood* (London, 1962); Locke, *Some Thoughts Concerning Education*, pp. 83, 141. For introductions to the history of childhood see, H. Cunningham, *Children and Childhood in Western Society since 1500* (London, 1995), and C. Heywood, *A History of Childhood* (Oxford, 2001).

Historians have disagreed about the influence of these changing ideas about childhood, but it is significant that their arguments have focused upon what impact they had on the nature of the parent-child relationship. It is what these ideas about childhood meant in terms of demands upon parents that has been seen as important. How children were viewed is thought to have determined the role that parents took in their children's lives, whether as harsh disciplinarians, thoughtful educators, or respectful nurturers of childhood innocence. The emotional content of the parent-child relationship has been measured chiefly by looking at how adults felt about their children, with little thought given to whether children's views of their elders altered over time.[5]

As the history of childhood has emerged as the history of parenting, so consideration has been given to how the role of parents has changed over time. There is consensus that parenting was always gendered, with distinct duties for mothers and fathers. Importantly for this study, from the mid-eighteenth century, there is evidence of increasing attention being paid to defining motherhood. Mothering assumed a new importance as women were portrayed in both secular and spiritual texts as the guardians of family morality and social stability. Rising expectations of mothers to care for their children led to criticism of the practices of swaddling and wetnurses, and eventually of women who worked long hours outside the family home. The mounting responsibilities upon mothers to be the full-time nurturers and moral instructors of their children were theoretically made possible by the middle-class ideal of domesticity, in which women confined to the 'private' sphere of the home were supposedly left with plenty of opportunity to spend 'quality time' with their children. To be a mother it was no longer simply enough to bear children, a woman had to demonstrate her ability to raise her children as well. As Judith Schneid Lewis writes, motherhood 'had once been an ascribed function. It was becoming an achieved status'.[6] Such was the valorisation of motherhood that the category of woman could become indistinguishable from mother. 'Womanliness', thought the nineteenth-century poet Robert Browning, 'means only motherhood; All love begins and ends there'.[7]

---

[5] For opposing views in the debate over changing parental affection towards children see, Stone, *The Family, Sex and Marriage*; and L. A. Pollock, *Forgotten Children: Parent–Child Relations from 1500 to 1900* (Cambridge, 1983).

[6] J. S. Lewis, *In the Family Way: Childbearing in the British Aristocracy, 1760–1860* (New Brunswick, NJ, 1986), p. 62.

[7] As cited in E. J. Yeo, 'The creation of 'motherhood' and women's responses in Britain and France, 1750–1914', *Women's History Review* 8, 2 (1999), 202.

Gender is considered a relational category by historians; changes in ideas about one sex inevitably lead to changes about the other. The issue of parenting provides an ideal example of this in practice. As motherhood was placed on a high pedestal, so fathers had to reconsider their roles. It remains the case that far less scholarly attention has been paid to fathers compared to mothers in history, and that, in particular, working-class fatherhood has been neglected.[8] Nevertheless, pioneering work on middle-class fatherhood in the Victorian period suggests that the importance attached to the moral authority of the mother left fathers in a difficult and often ambiguous position. There is little doubt that most men were proud to become fathers, and that being a father could enhance a man's masculinity by proving virility and contributing to social reputation. Men were eager to share in the experience of becoming a parent. As we have seen in Chapter 1, during the nineteenth century, some fathers wished to be present at the birth of their children, and by this time the man midwife was securely established. Many men also welcomed the opportunities that fatherhood could bring. As workplaces for most men became separated from the home, the domestic sphere was popularly regarded as the one space where a man could be himself, and escape from the pressures of life outside. There was a new recognition that home could be 'a man's place'. Family life and children could be sources of joy, leisure and rejuvenation. Yet there were also contradictory demands on men that could bear heavily on their abilities as fathers. The expectation that men should be the material providers and disciplinarians in the household continued. This placed competing claims upon men's time, and rested uneasily with the notion that fathers should be loving and benevolent carers. John Tosh has argued that four patterns of fatherhood were the result; the tyrannical, absent, distant or intimate father.[9] As we shall see, the records of marriage breakdown provide most evidence of the tyrannical father. Arguably, it was because mothers were given so much responsibility for the moral education and training of children, that some men compensated by inflating their remaining roles of strict authority and discipline.

Over the period of this study what changed about ideas of childhood and parenting was not so much what children were thought to require

---

[8] For an exception see, L. Abrams, '"There was nobody like my daddy": Fathers, the family and the marginalisation of men in modern Scotland', *The Scottish Historical Review* 78, 2 (1999), 219–42.

[9] J. Tosh, 'Authority and nurture in middle-class fatherhood: the case of early and mid-Victorian England', *Gender and History* 8, 1 (1996), 48–64, and *A Man's Place*, chapter 4.

for a good upbringing, as what was most important. As the scales tipped towards nurture and moral inculcation, so attention shifted to mothers who were thought most suited to the task. But what did this shifting focus in parenting mean to children's lives? As Hugh Cunningham has noted in his review of the historiography on this subject, it has been all too easy to study the history of childhood, or ideas *about* children, and altogether miss the history *of* children.[10] Children's voices and the records of their experiences can be difficult to retrieve. Many accounts of childhood were written retrospectively. This is where records of marriage breakdown, which note, often incidentally, the position, activities and responses of children to the world around them can be so valuable. Occasionally, we can also try to recover and interpret children's voices. They give us a unique view of family life through children's eyes. If Cunningham is correct, and 'more, perhaps, than any other branch of history, the history of childhood has been shaped by the concerns of the world in which its historians live', then it is surprising that given our present-day anxieties about child abuse, divorce and lone parenting, that this type of study has not been attempted before.[11]

Finding the children in marital violence

Childhood experiences of parental violence that occurred when children were babies or very young, were often told by their mothers. Women widely believed that their husbands were violent to their children as an indirect way of harming them. Mary Sherard thought in 1706 that her husband often called their baby a bastard, knocked it out of her arms, and threatened to dash out its brains, because she 'loved the said child'. Ann Marie Brogden was even more explicit. She said that her husband knew all too well that 'she was very fond of their child and that any ill treatment of the child would greatly affect and hurt her'.[12]

Mothers like Mary Veitch who were denied access to their children were viewed sympathetically by the courts. In the earlier ruling on the *Evans v. Evans* case, Scott had admitted that it was within a father's rights to prevent a mother access to her children, 'yet I should deem it a most improper exercise of marital power, very disgraceful to the person who practised it, and a most wanton and unnecessary outrage upon

---

[10] Cunningham, *Children and Childhood*, pp. 1–3.
[11] H. Cunningham, 'Histories of childhood', *American Historical Review* 103 (1998), 1195.
[12] LPL, CA, Case 141 (1706), D32, f.63–64r; LMA, DL/C/173 (1758), f.300r. See also, LPL, CA, Case 1041 (1672), Ee3, f.740r, Eee4, f.860r. Randolph Trumbach tells the story of the Brogden marriage in, *Sex and the Gender Revolution*, pp. 338–40.

the feelings of a mother'.[13] It was this sensitivity to motherly feelings that raised the question of whether violence to a child in the presence of its mother constituted cruelty that could be submitted as evidence in marriage separation cases. In his judgement in *Bramwell v. Bramwell*, Dr Lushington decided that such evidence could be admitted, but was uncertain whether this alone would be sufficient to prove marital cruelty.[14] Nevertheless, the number of cases in which women provided details of how the violence of their husbands had affected them as mothers, shows that they regarded child and marital violence as closely related.

Nothing could gain greater sympathy for a woman than a husband who prevented her from fulfilling her maternal duty of feeding her baby. One nineteenth-century mother described her anguish when her husband 'locked her up from her infant at the time the child which she suckled was crying for the breast and kept her confined upwards of an hour taunting her at the distress she showed on hearing the cries of her said infant'. Given the increasing attention being paid at this time to the moral virtues and medical benefits of breast-feeding, a husband who did not let his wife nurse their child was depriving her of the most fundamental of her roles as a mother.[15]

As they grew older, children like Rachael Norcott's son, could find that incidents that began as occasions of dispute about their discipline, could escalate into full-scale violent arguments between their parents. A 'slight altercation' between the parents of one daughter about whether she could stay up late in 1846, for example, allegedly resulted in the mother being subject to a beating from the father, which only ended when her mother fell into a fit of hysteria.[16] Parents were popularly believed to have a right to chastise their children using physical means, but they did not always agree upon the extent to which that right should be exercised. When Francis Jessop began 'correcting' his son by striking him in the chest, Francis's wife, Elizabeth, 'desired him rather whip his son than strike him in that manner'. In the early eighteenth century when this incident occurred, it was the severity of the punishment that was at issue not the principle. Such a reaction corresponds

---

[13] *Evans v. Evans* (1790) *English Reports* vol. 161, p. 497.

[14] *Bramwell v. Bramwell* (1831) *English Reports* vol. 162, p. 1292; Biggs, *The Concept of Matrimonial Cruelty*, pp. 155–6.

[15] LPL, CA, Case 9119 (1824), H373/6; for other examples of mothers who were abused when they were breast-feeding see, LMA, DL/C/173 (1758), f.298r, and LMA, DL/C/175 (1767), f.116r. For changing attitudes towards breast-feeding see, R. Perry, 'Colonizing the breast: sexuality and maternity in eighteenth-century England', *Journal of the History of Sexuality* 2, 2 (1991), 204–34.

[16] LPL, CA, Case 3926 (1846), H736/6,7.

with similar thinking at this time about wifely correction, which was outlined in the previous chapter. Physical chastisement by men of their subordinates in their households could be legitimate if it had been provoked or deserved, and if it was carried out with a degree of self-control. When it came to the disciplining of children, it appears that physical correction was mainly administered by fathers, and that mothers could act as the arbiters that justice was done.

Parents who did not agree, and were frequently quarrelling could send contradictory messages to their children. On another occasion when the Jessops fell out, it was over their son's conduct towards them. Apparently Elizabeth reminded their son that he should show his respect for his parents by taking off his hat when he greeted them. But the child's father, Francis, 'bid him keep it on and cock [it] up' whenever he saw his mother.[17] As we shall see, fathers who encouraged their children to show such disrespect could sometimes also induce them to direct physical violence towards their mothers. These violent men saw their children as offering another way for them to undermine their wives. It left children with an impossible conflict of loyalties.

Thus harm to children often formed part of the pattern of violence to women in marriage. Threats or actual violence to children could be an additional tool of cruelty that husbands used against their wives. Given that modern-day studies have shown that there is a high correlation between child and wife abuse, it seems likely that many of the children of women who complained of violence had themselves experienced the wrath of their fathers.[18] Since parental quarrels could be triggered by disputes over them, children may have worried that they had provoked violence. But when their fathers were drunk or prone to violent anger, even the slightest aggravation could lead to the most extreme fits of rage. Returning home in the early hours of the morning, one Cambridgeshire farmer dragged his wife out of bed and began pinching her hard. Hearing their parents, the children started crying, to which he cursed, 'Damn the children. I will kill them. I will whip their skins over their ears if they do not hold their tongues'.[19] Evidence of these types of outbursts, as will be discussed later in this chapter, could be used by wives as indicators of how far husbands had lost control of their authority. For the children involved, such experiences must have been terrifying. The question of

---

[17] LPL, CA, Case 5089 (1717), Ee9, f.15/3.
[18] See, for example, M. Hester, C. Pearson and N. Harwin, *Making an Impact: Children and Domestic Violence: A Reader* (London, 2000), chapter 2.
[19] CUL, EDR, Quarter Sessions Files, E49, Examination of Mary Harford (24 December 1754).

how far contemporaries understood these psychological consequences is one to which we will now turn.

Young and impressionable minds?

Often the only voices that we hear of very young children who lived in violent homes are their cries. When the Reverend John Jenkins tried to beat his wife and swore he would kill her in front of their three- or four-year-old son in July 1771, the child was said to be 'much terrified and crying' at the behaviour of his father. In another example, a child of a similar age was being held in its mother's arms when his father bolted the parlour door and threatened to hit his mother with his fists. The child was so frightened, and screamed 'in such a manner' that the mother thought 'the child would have gone into fits'.[20]

Such occasions demonstrate, unsurprisingly, that seeing the violence of their parents could be deeply upsetting for children. Furthermore, children did not always have to be present during their parents' violent quarrels to be aware of them. Children overheard disputes, and a hostile atmosphere between parents could speak more than words. Even though children could themselves be subject to harsh regimes of corporal punishment in the home, school or workplace, this by no means desensitised them to violent behaviour. The entire length of childhood could be lived in the shadow of parental conflict. As one sixteen-year-old sadly told the courts, 'so long as he can remember anything his said Father and Mother have lived unhappily together'.[21] But to what extent was parental disagreement and violence thought to have a long-term as well as immediate impact upon children? If childhood was understood as a time of socialisation when the child could be moulded under adult supervision, and/or a period of innocence free from worldly concerns, what were thought the consequences of marital violence for childhood development?

Parents were advised that childhood was a formative time when children could be influenced by the adults who surrounded them. Writers of conduct books about family life taught parents that great care should be taken in the employment of domestic servants, as children were prone to imitate and repeat what they saw and heard in their company. Parents were told to be guarded in their speech in front of children.[22] 'Children should not', William Fleetwood taught,

---

[20] LMA, DL/C/177 (1773), f.306r; LMA, DL/C/173 (1758), f.299v.
[21] LMA, DL/C/289 (1806), f.207r.
[22] See, for example, J. Dod and R. Cleaver, *A Godly Forme of Householde Governement* (London, 1630), Q4; Locke, *Some Thoughts*, pp. 127, 133–4.

be so much as witnesses of anything indecently said or done by parents: All the domestic differences, the idle and unseemly quarrels and debates, the simple and unkind words and actions, that much too commonly pass betwixt parents, should be concealed and hidden from children: For they observe and treasure up these evil follies, and, secretly at least, side with the one, and learn to hate or despise the other, or entertain too soon, a mean opinion of them both; which undermines all manner of esteem and dutiful observance.[23]

It is revealing what this passage tells us about why parents were instructed to avoid making their children the observers of their disputes. If quarrels took place in front of children, then Fleetwood believed that parenting would become difficult, because children would be less obedient and have diminished respect for one or both parents. The consequences were thought of entirely in terms of what they would mean for the parents. No consideration was given to the effects upon children outside the parent-child relationship.

Parents do seem to have been aware of the advice to be wary of their angry speech in front of their children. In answer to a long list of complaints of marital violence, one of the few matters that William Ettrick would admit to was that, 'in their mutual altercation before their children expressions were sometimes dropped by both of them which were not altogether proper for them to hear'.[24] In the mid-nineteenth century, Elizabeth Young, seeing her husband's mood and predicting that there were 'likely to be high words which I did not wish the children to hear', supervised their removal from the dining room where they were seated.[25]

But there is little evidence that this sensitivity to the effects of verbal violence upon children extended to concern about the longer term impact of witnessing physical violence. When Scott ruled in 1794 that seeing marital violence at nine years old would 'make an indelible impression on the mind and memory of a child', he was thinking only about the reliability of children's testimony in a court of law, not how far these experiences would affect the subsequent behaviour and personality of children.[26] Contemporaries were certainly interested in trying to determine the roots of violent behaviour, and in the seventeenth and early eighteenth centuries many criminal biographies and forms of popular literature that told tales of murder and violence looked back to childhood for explanations. However, the source of violence was usually traced to the decisions or conduct of the individual in childhood,

---

[23] W. Fleetwood, *The Relative Duties of Parents and Children* (London, 1705), p. 12.
[24] NA, DEL 1/598 (1765), f.1040–1041.
[25] LPL, CA, Case 10404 (1855), H838/5, f.38.
[26] *D'Aguilar v. D'Aguilar* (1794) *English Reports*, vol. 162, p. 751.

rather than to the influence of the adults or environment in which the child was raised. A single occasion of childhood wilful disobedience or immorality could be depicted in these texts as a life-changing point of no return, which had spiralled out of control to inevitable sin and crime in adult life.[27] The failure to overcome the evil of crime was often shown as occurring despite the best efforts of parents and other adults to provide moral guidance. The Biblical notion that the sins of the father would be visited on his children was rarely realised in this type of literature.[28] At least until the eighteenth century, the violent criminal was either born or self-made, not brutalized by an upbringing with parental violence.

There appears to have been a transition in these ideas during the eighteenth century. The life histories of criminals began to pay more attention to childhood, and in particular, to the consequences of severing the parent-child bond. But disruption in parent-child relationships was generally imagined in this literature as a consequence of poverty or death, not parental divorce or separation.[29] By the nineteenth century, there are signs that violence was beginning to be understood as a 'learned' response. When investigations began into juvenile delinquency in the early nineteenth century, 'the improper conduct of parents' was accounted to be one of the main causes of children's offences.[30] The feminists, Harriet Taylor and John Stuart Mill, writing in 1850, bemoaned the 'demoralizing effect' for children of being raised in violent households. Think, they said, of

the children born and bred in this moral atmosphere – with the unchecked indulgence of the most odious passions, the tyranny of physical force in its coarsest manifestations, constantly exhibited as the most familiar facts of their daily life – can it be wondered if they grow up without any of the ideas and feelings which it is the purpose of moral education to infuse, without any sense of justice or affection, any conception of self-restraint – incapable in their turn of governing their children by any other means than blows?[31]

[27] C. B. Herrup, 'Law and morality in seventeenth-century England', *Past and Present* 106 (1985), 109–10; P. Lake, 'Deeds against nature: cheap print, Protestantism and murder in early seventeenth-century England', in K. Sharpe and P. Lake (eds.), *Culture and Politics in Early Stuart England* (Basingstoke, 1994), pp. 265–6.

[28] L. B. Faller, *Turned to Account: The Forms and Functions of Criminal Biography in Late Seventeenth- and Early Eighteenth-Century England* (Cambridge, 1987), pp. 29, 32–4, 56–63.

[29] I. K. Ben-Amos, 'Reciprocal bonding: parents and their offspring in early modern England', *Journal of Family History* 25, 3 (2000), 304.

[30] H. Shore, 'Home, play and street life: causes of, and explanations for, juvenile crime in the early nineteenth century', in A. Fletcher and S. Hussey (eds.), *Childhood in Question: Children, Parents and the State* (Manchester, 1999), pp. 96–114.

[31] H. Taylor and J. S. Mill, 'The Case of Anne Bird', *Morning Chronicle* (13 March 1850), in A. P. Robson and J. M. Robson (eds.), *Sexual Equality: Writings by John Stuart Mill, Harriet Taylor Mill, and Helen Taylor* (Toronto, 1994), p. 70.

The problem of both this writing and the enquiries into juvenile delinquency was that conclusions about working-class family life were being drawn by middle-class observers. In line with changing thinking about physical violence, outlined in Chapter 1, the middle class were all too ready to condemn working-class parents for social disorder. This was not accompanied by a willingness to accept that all parents, of whatever social background, had the potential to influence their children's behaviour in negative ways. Nor is there evidence that working-class parents themselves thought about their conduct in this manner.

Across our period, children were believed to have impressionable minds in so far as it was understood that the decisions that adults took about their care could affect their mental well-being. So one motive that was widely ascribed to childhood suicide was the fear of punishment from an adult.[32] The Quaker, William Thompson, warned parents that 'like commonly begets its like', when he discussed the faults of those who corrected their children when they were angry. 'Passion in parents', he warned, 'is apt either to generate the same in their children; or else to render them dumpish, and melancholick'.[33] In the same vein, *The Times* in September 1836 ran a story about the 'fatal effects of terrifying children', which related how a 'little girl' of six or seven years old had been made an 'idiot' after she had been locked in a dark cellar all night as a punishment.[34] Thus contemporaries understood that direct cruelty to children could produce traumatic results. But the idea that behaviour conducted between adults could constitute indirect cruelty and be harmful to children was not current at this time.

From the Restoration to the Victorian age, parents were thought responsible for children's welfare primarily in terms of their physical and spiritual needs. Parents, and often those who employed children as apprentices or servants, were expected to feed, clothe and sometimes provide housing for children. These were the basic necessities of life that a husband was also bound to supply for his wife. In addition, adults had a duty to provide a good moral example to children. So, when one nineteenth-century writer concluded that marriage separation was sometimes in the best interest of children, he considered the damage done to 'young and impressionable minds' of living with parents who were in 'perpetual dissensions and unchristian hatred'. It was the thought that such parents would not provide a model of Christian

---

[32] T. R. Murphy, '"Woful childe of parents rage": Suicide of children and adolescents in early modern England, 1505–1710', *The Sixteenth Century Journal* 17, 3 (1986), 265–8; MacDonald and Murphy, *Sleepless Souls*, pp. 251–6; and Anderson, *Suicide*, pp. 180–2.

[33] W. Thompson, *The Care of Parents is a Happiness to Children: Or, The Duty of Parents to their Children, and of Children to their Parents* (London, 1710), p. 11.

[34] *The Times* (21 September 1836) 3c.

marriage that most troubled him. Similarly, the views held by Taylor and Mill, outlined above, were affected by their concern that a lack of attention to the moral education of children would have a long-term detrimental impact upon the wider social order.[35]

Little consideration was given to the emotional needs of children. Like their mothers, while they may have suffered psychological harm due to family violence, there was very limited knowledge about how to deal with the consequences of such harm. 'The most striking feature' about the ages of patients suffering from mental problems who visited the physician Richard Napier in the seventeenth century, was that there were so few children.[36] Child health was defined primarily as physical health. Whereas paediatrics emerged as a form of medicine in the Victorian era, child psychiatry would be delayed for much longer.[37] That the impact of the adult world upon children was conceived only in physical terms is shown by the early-modern belief that the curses of adults could deform babies as they lay in the womb.[38] While adults were thought to have the potential to harm children's bodies, their power to affect children's minds in negative ways appears not to have been acknowledged.

Without a full understanding of how children's psychological development could be affected by being witnesses to adult violence, there was little reason for parents to adjust their behaviour so that physical violence did not take place in their presence. We are left with only rare examples of when children were removed from these scenes of conflict, and these can be difficult to interpret. Hester Watson told Ely Quarter Sessions in March 1743 that she had been beaten by her husband, 'after he had first ordered his son John Watson junior to go out of the house and to shut . . . the door', and in York, John Doughty 'turned a little girl' out of the room before punching his wife on the face and chest in 1837.[39] Louisa said that she was ordered out of the room when her stepfather, James Veitch, argued with her mother. She noted that this was something, 'which he always did when he began to quarrel with my

[35] [Edwin Hill Handley], 'Custody of Infants Bill', *The British and Foreign Review* 7 (July, 1838), 315.

[36] MacDonald, *Mystical Bedlam*, pp. 42–3.

[37] M. Pelling, 'Child health as a social value in early modern England', *Social History of Medicine*, 1 (1988), 135–64; A. Digby, *Making a Medical Living: Doctors and Patients in the English Market for Medicine* (Cambridge, 1994), pp. 279–90.

[38] E. Foyster, 'Silent witnesses? Children and the breakdown of domestic and social order in early modern England', in A. Fletcher and S. Hussey (eds.), *Childhood in Question: Children, Parents and the State* (Manchester, 1999), p. 67.

[39] CUL, EDR, Quarter Sessions Files, E48 (bound in Roll for April 1748); York Minster Archives, Petty Sessions records of the JPs for the Liberty of St. Peter, York, F2/3/2/71.

Mother'.[40] Given that, as we shall see, children could act as witnesses in the courts, it may be that they were ordered away as a defence strategy so that these men could be violent with impunity, rather than out of any desire to protect childhood innocence. Of course, in the heat of anger, few men would have stopped to give thought to any children who were present. But it is telling that this was not made more of an issue in the courts. As later discussion in this chapter will show, while physical violence by fathers to children could be used by women in a bid for marriage separation, the notion that men could be labelled as poor fathers and condemned in their use of marital violence because it had been conducted in front of children, seems not to have been entertained.

Perhaps we should not be too hasty in our criticism of our predecessors, given that in today's society debates continue about the impact of children being exposed to violence in the media, such as on television, cinema and the Internet. Before 1960 most textbooks on child development had no mention of parental violence, and psychologists have yet to demonstrate conclusively that witnessing violence in childhood is a predictor for the child victim to become the perpetrator of violence in later life. As feminists have pointed out, 'the oft stated view that battered children become spouse batterers in adulthood ignores the fact that few women batter their husbands'.[41] Rather than teaching children that conflicts could be resolved through violence, seeing their parents behave in this way may have had the opposite effect and given children an aversion towards relationships that tended towards discord. This seems to have been the case for Dudley Ryder, who kept a diary as a young law student living with his parents in the early eighteenth century. It gives us rare insights into how the parental relationship was viewed from the child's perspective. There is nothing to suggest that Dudley's father was physically violent towards his mother, but Dudley certainly learnt lessons from his parents about adult relationships that shaped his intentions for the future. He recorded one Sunday in 1715:

Concerned to see my mother so peevish and fretful, continually saying some ill-natured thing or other to my father or the maid. I will endeavour if possible not to have a fretful uneasy wife. How easy it is to observe the faults my mother is guilty of in contradicting another, though I am too apt to be guilty of the same kind of peevishness myself. I have too much of her temper, but I am resolved to endeavour to quell at its first rise every secret resentment and uneasiness that comes upon me.[42]

[40] LPL, CA, Case 9440 (1837), H550/18.
[41] K. Yllö and M. Bograd, 'Foreword', in K. Yllö and M. Bograd (eds.), *Feminist Perspectives on Wife Abuse* (London, 1988), p. 7.
[42] W. Matthews (ed.), *The Diary of Dudley Ryder 1715–1716* (London, 1939), p. 38.

While vowing to take care to avoid marrying 'a fretful uneasy wife', Dudley's experiences of observing his parents interact had also taught him that it took two people to make a quarrel, and hence he determined to keep his own irritability in check. Living in his parents' household had impressed upon him the importance of compromise and even temper to marital harmony. Like so many of us today, he intended to conduct his own adult relationships differently from his parents, believing that this would bring him happiness. Other children, as we shall now see, also made adjustments to cope with growing up admidst parental discord.

Children's strategies

Historians are beginning to recognise that children had agency, in other words, they had some ability to shape their own lives. 'Child-rearing was not just something done to a child', writes the historian Linda Pollock, 'he or she participated in the process'. Although children's choices and decisions were limited by the adults that lived and worked with them, this did not render them into passive individuals. Within the boundaries set by adults, children could exercise considerable influence upon their own lives and even those of their parents.[43]

The eighteenth- or early nineteenth-century ballad, 'The Cruel Cooper of Ratcliff' told the tale of a son's relationship with the cooper, his violent father. His father often beat his mother, and one day, 'with grief of heart';

> The youth with tears did take his mother's part,
> Cries he, Father, I'm afraid you will
> With kicks and cuffs my tender mother kill.
> Hearing these words he then his son did beat,
> And that night turn'd him into the street.[44]

Taking an active role in their parents' quarrels was not an easy decision to take, for as this ballad shows, the penalties for children could be severe. Yet it is clear from evidence of actual marriages, that many children felt compelled to do more than simply be the onlookers to adult relationships.

Many took practical steps to help their mothers. It was only after the daughter of Sarah and Thomas Chance had fetched two of their

---

[43] L. Pollock, 'Parent-child relations', in D. I. Kertzer and M. Barbagli (eds.), *The History of the European Family* Vol. 1: *Family Life in Early Modern Times 1500–1789* (London, 2001), p. 220; see also, Heywood, *A History of Childhood*, p. 4.

[44] 'The Cruel Cooper of Ratcliff' Part I, Baring-Gould.

neighbours that Thomas stopped beating his wife.[45] Children could serve as useful messengers. The children of George Wilkinson were sent to meet his wife on her way home from church in 1851 to warn her that George had threatened to 'break his wife's back when she returned home'.[46] Intervention by other children brought them into the centre stage of violent disputes. John Harbin's two sons joined two servants and a neighbour who were trying to prevent him striking his wife in 1668, and one of the children attracted more attention to the scene by shouting out, 'Oh Lord you will kill my Mother'![47] Even very young children were thought capable of expressing their disdain at family violence. One servant in the Dysart household found their two- or three-year-old child in the same room as where the Countess had been attacked by the Earl. 'Though so young', the servant remembered how he was 'stamping his little foot in indignation against his father, and using words which I cannot remember'.[48] Three teenage children testified on the cruelty of their stepfather, Joseph Turner, when he was accused of violence towards their mother in 1853. One daughter was making gingerbread to take back to her boarding school when her mother rushed screaming into the room, pursued by her stepfather. She tried to stop her stepfather hitting her mother again, only to be violently pushed away.[49]

Children were not always put at a disadvantage by the violence of their elders. Simon Forman, who became an apprentice to a hosier in the second half of the sixteenth century when he was about fourteen years old, found that the marital violence between his master and mistress provided him with an opportunity to become a confidant and trusted male companion for his master. 'Often times' he saw his master and mistress quarrel, and he thought that twice his master nearly killed his mistress by throwing a pair of tailor's shears at her. Far from being disturbed by these events, Simon, who disliked his mistress, remembered with relish, the 'many times' that he and his master would 'one complain to another of his mistress and her pride'.[50]

Like Turner's stepchildren, other children took the step of giving formal witness statements to the courts about what they had seen and heard. Whether or not they had freely chosen to do so is unclear, but as

---

[45] LMA, DL/C/175 (1767), f.115r.
[46] LPL, CA, Case 9986 (1851), H792/2.
[47] LPL, CA, Case 4163 (1669), Eee4, f.82.
[48] *Dysart v. Dysart* (1847) vol. 163, p. 1113; in this case the judge said that he was 'not disposed to attach much importance to what the child may have said or done'.
[49] LPL, CA, Case 9350 (1853), H824/5,15.
[50] J. O. Halliwell (ed.), *The Autobiography and Personal Diary of Dr Simon Forman* (London, 1849), p. 10.

legal bystander witnesses, children, especially those who were under the age of twelve, were problematic on three counts. First, there was the issue of whether children could accurately remember what had occurred. Second, it was thought that the children of the parties fighting separation suits were too closely related to give impartial testimony. Finally, lawyers disagreed about what age a child would understand the meaning of an oath, and therefore the difference between truth and lies. It is noticeable that none of these reasons touched upon the consequences for the child of giving testimony. Rather, they focused only upon what child statements meant for adult concerns. As a result of objections to children's testimony, according to legal theory, no child under the age of fourteen could act as a witness in the church courts, and no child could testify on behalf of a parent.[51]

But in practice, children did give witness statements about the marriages of their parents, although stepchildren were the majority of these child witnesses. Children's testimony was also heard in other church court business, most notably during slander cases.[52] Changing legal opinion was reflected in a test case of 1839, when a father challenged his wife's decision to allow their children to testify in a cruelty suit against him. Despite the fact that the oldest child was ten years old when the alleged violence took place, the judge ruled that children were 'legal and competent witnesses for or against father or mother', although involving children in these cases was 'a measure which, if possible, ought to be avoided'. Unfortunately, further explanation as to why courts should refrain from taking child testimony was not provided. However, one suspects that the issue was again one concerned with the reliability of child testimony, rather than with any discomfort at the notion of children talking about their parents' marriages. For the same test case also raised questions about the accuracy of a statement given by a seventy-year-old man. The politics of age, in which the words of the very young and elderly were under equal scrutiny, seems to have been at play here.[53]

---

[51] J. Prentiss Bishop, *Commentaries on the Law of Marriage and Divorce* (Boston and London, 1852), p. 330; C. Donahue, 'Proof by witnesses in the church courts of medieval England: an imperfect reception of the learned law', in M. S. Arnold, T. A. Green, S. A. Scully and S. D. White (eds.), *On the Laws and Customs of England* (Chapel Hill, 1981), p. 130; Gowing, *Domestic Dangers*, pp. 50–1. For judges expressing concerns about child testimony on these grounds, and occasionally dismissing it as a result see, *Oliver v. Oliver* (1801), *English Reports* vol. 161, p. 583; and *Saunders v. Saunders* (1847), *English Reports* vol. 163, p. 1135.

[52] Morris, 'Defamation and sexual reputation in Somerset', pp. 356, 362–4; Waddams, *Sexual Slander in Nineteeth-Century England*, p. 92.

[53] *Lockwood v. Lockwood* (1839) *English Reports*, vol. 163, p. 412–13. In Scotland teenage children also testified during the marriage separation cases brought by their parents, see

Children could be proud of their good memories, and ready to challenge the notion that they were less reliable witnesses. Aged six when her mother married James Veitch, Louisa told the Court of Arches that, 'though I was quite a child at the time I perfectly recollect the circumstance of my said mother's marriage to James Veitch'. Having no memories of her own father, Louisa nevertheless was certain that James's behaviour, 'was not that of a kind husband towards a wife'.[54] As Louisa's words show, giving statements to the courts gave children unique opportunities to pass judgement upon the behaviour of their elders. In a period when silence was a virtue considered especially important for children, and they were expected to be seen but not heard, cases of marriage breakdown provided children with one opportunity to tell their own family stories.

However, we do need to be very cautious when using these records. As Ludmilla Jordanova has warned, we are unlikely to find an 'autonomous, authentic voice of children' in the past, because children's language and attitudes were learned from adults.[55] As with all witnesses who gave statements to the courts, children's words were shaped by conventions to fit a particular legal agenda. Children's stories would have been structured and organised into narratives that were intelligible to adults by the clerk who recorded them. We are left with their reported speech. In addition, when children testified about their parents, their duty of loyalty to each parent required them to display a lack of predisposition towards one party or the other. Hence when the sixteen-year-old Joseph Kirkman testified in a cruelty suit brought by his father against his mother, he was praised for speaking, 'with a very credible degree of impartiality respecting his mother's conduct', for although he gave details of his mother's insults towards his father, he also bore testimony, 'to her extreme kindness to her children'. By avoiding accusations of bias, Joseph showed that a cruel spouse need not have been a cruel parent.[56] But for others, satisfying the requirements of the law, and presenting statements that they knew might lead to the break-up of the family home, must have led to agonising dilemmas of conscience. When a mayor of Bristol was issued with a writ of habeas corpus questioning the confinement of

Leneman, "A tyrant and tormentor", 45. For the meanings that were attached to age, see, K. Thomas, 'Age and authority in early modern England', *Proceedings of the British Academy* 62 (1976), 205–48.
[54] LPL, CA, Case 9440 (1837), H550/18.
[55] L. Jordanova, 'New worlds for children in the eighteenth century: problems of historical interpretation', *History of the Human Sciences* 3 (1990), 78–9.
[56] *Kirkman v. Kirkman* (1807) *English Reports* vol. 161, p. 599–600; for another marriage case in which a child was commended for her lack of partiality see, Nevill, 'Women and marriage breakdown', pp. 142.

his wife in their home, three of his sons spoke in his defence and justified her treatment on the grounds of her indecent behaviour and occasions of temporary insanity. The eldest son remarked that,

> however painful it may be to this deponent's feelings to bear testimony to the inconsistency and indelicacy of a parent's conduct, still he feels it his duty so to do, not only to prevent his mother from disposing of her fortunes amongst such persons as are highly unworthy of it . . . but as well to screen the character of this deponent's father from reproach and contempt, to which the character of a cruel husband is deservedly exposed.

To give evidence, this son had to decide which story of marriage was most convincing; his mother's account of wrongful confinement and cruelty, or his father's of necessary confinement in the face of financial and social ruin. But as a witness who was a child of the parties involved, he could not make that judgement upon his elders without couching it in remorseful terms.[57]

Of course, when violence by their fathers was alleged, children were aware that if they testified for their mothers, and a marriage separation resulted, they were likely to end up in the custody of their fathers. In these circumstances, children may have calculated that it was not in their own interests to be too critical of their father's conduct. Unsurprisingly, children were often frightened of their violent fathers. Francis Mead, the fourteen-year-old son of a shoemaker, was said to 'give his evidence with great reluctance and considerable fear of his father's displeasure', when his father was tried for the murder of his mother in 1853. That his father was violent to both his children and his wife became clear from the statements given by other witnesses, who explained that they did not intervene when they heard violence occurring in the Mead household, because they assumed that it was 'only' Francis being beaten by his father. In fact, Francis was witnessing his father beating his mother to death, an event that despite his pleading with his father, he was powerless to prevent. The words his mother was alleged to have said to his father as she lay dying; 'take care of my children, and don't beat Frank', completed the evidence of a case which through the accounts of witnesses had been presented as much as a family tragedy as a marital one. Francis's father was found guilty of manslaughter, and 'so strong was the feeling against the wretched prisoner' that 'yells and hootings of upwards of 300 persons' greeted him as he left for Newgate.

---

[57] NA, KB1/26 part 1, Hil.29, Geo.3, no.2, affidavit of Robert Cann Edgar (24 January 1789); punctuation has been added for ease of comprehension.

Nevertheless, nothing further was reported about the fate of Francis, who effectively was left orphaned by his parent's violence.[58]

Given the mounting importance attached to childhood innocence, by the nineteenth century it was very difficult for a child to give statements about issues of sexual violence without being discredited. When Harriet Stone accused her husband of 'acts of a most revolting and disgusting description, in the presence of his child, as well as his wife', the judge in the case angrily dismissed the evidence of a witness who based her statement on what the child, the Stone's six-year-old daughter, had told her. Solely to base such serious allegations on the evidence of a child was seen as 'monstrous'.[59] As historians working on child sexual abuse in the eighteenth and nineteenth centuries have recognised, even when they had been harmed by sex, it was seen as inappropriate for children, especially girls, to talk explicitly about it. Doing so invited questions about their own sexual reputations, and subsequently challenges to their accusations of abuse by adults. Children had not learned to be guarded in their speech about sex, and to contemporaries their explicit and frank language could be so shocking that it distracted attention from the alleged offence.[60] In contrast, evidence from legal cases of child rape in the seventeenth century suggest that the courts were less insistent upon reticence about sexual abuse from child victims and witnesses.[61] Children were silenced as our period progressed.

In marriage separation cases the issue of children who had witnessed adult sexual violence was complicated by court procedure. In the criminal courts, where children appeared in person on the witness stand, contemporaries made assessments about a child's evidence from their appearance and behaviour. But in the church courts, witness statements were simply taken in writing. In a ruling on a marital dispute in which a father was accused of acquiescing in the sexual abuse of his child, one judge explained why he found the child's statement problematic;

[58] *The Times* (9 June 1853) 6f.

[59] NA, PCAP 3/12 (1846–7), ff.427v, 430r.

[60] J. Gammon, "A denial of innocence': female juvenile victims of rape and the English legal system in the eighteenth century', in Fletcher and Hussey (eds.), *Childhood in Question*, pp. 74–95; L. A. Jackson, 'The child's word in court: cases of sexual abuse in London, 1870–1914', in M. L. Arnot and C. Usborne (eds.), *Gender and Crime in Modern Europe* (London, 1999), pp. 223–30, and *Child Sexual Abuse in Victorian England* (London, 2000), chapter 5; and Clark, *Women's Silence Men's Violence*, p. 55.

[61] M. Ingram, 'Child sexual abuse in early modern England', in M. J. Braddick and J. Walter (eds.), *Negotiating Power in Early Modern Society: Order, Hierarchy and Subordination in Britain and Ireland* (Cambridge, 2001), p. 81.

It is not very easy to say what degree of credit can be given to so young a witness, not produced or examined in Court; for when a witness of such tender years gives evidence, the conduct and demeanour is all in all; it is impossible to judge from a written deposition only.

Nevertheless, in this case a judgement was made, and the charges were dismissed, partly because of factors relating to the child's age. It was thought that 'she has sworn rather too confidently to matters occurring when she was only six'.[62] Even in a written statement it appears that a child could appear too knowledgeable and 'confident' in their memory of sexual abuse.

In summary, there were occasions when children's actions or words were decisive in determining the fate of adult relationships. But their ability to talk about what their parents' lives meant for them was seriously limited. Throughout our period, children were taught not to speak of family affairs outside the home, or repeat what they had heard between their parents.[63] Although they were permitted to testify in the courts, this was in a context that was strictly controlled by adults, and the weight accorded to their words was never equal to their elders. As a result, most children who witnessed the violence of their parents kept quiet. Standard statements given at the opening of marriage separation suits required the parties to state how many children they had. These reveal the many children who were born into violent families, but who never gave testimony in the courts. Given the adult attitudes towards children that we have discussed, it is unlikely that many were shielded from seeing or hearing their parents' quarrels. But we cannot tell the suffering that children endured as a result, for even when they reached adulthood, children avoided speaking critically of their parents. In diaries, and even more so in the autobiographies written during our period, commentary upon the nature of relationships between the writer's parents was extremely rare. It was only at the start of the twentieth century that autobiographers began to make more candid remarks about childhood spent with violent parents.[64] From the Restoration until the mid-nineteenth century, the duty to respect parents and protect them

---

[62] *Chesnutt v. Chesnutt* (1854), *English Reports* vol. 164, p. 118.

[63] See, for example, P. Sylvestre du Four, *Moral Instructions for Youth: Or, A Father's Advice to a Son* (London, 1742), pp. 73–4; *The Accomplished Youth: Containing a Familiar View of the True Principles of Morality and Politeness* (London, 1811); and *The Polite Present, Or the Child's Manual of Good Manners* (Glasgow, 1833), pp. 23, 31.

[64] J. Burnett (ed.), *Destiny Obscure: Autobiographies of Childhood, Education and Family from the 1820s to the 1920s* (London, 1982), p. 230; Hammerton, *Cruelty and Companionship*, pp. 134–49.

from negative discussion outside the family often denied children the opportunity to express their feelings about their experiences.

We have much evidence of children's resilience and determination to cope while their parents remained together. If childhood was thought of as a time of innocence, then surely knowledge of parental violence brought about its premature ending. Thus violence could shift the boundaries between childhood and adulthood. A reversal of roles could occur, in which children became responsible for the needs of their parents, rather than vice versa. But as with the story of Francis Mead, whose father murdered his mother, we know little about the position of children after violence had run its course. In post-separation families, how did former interparental conflict affect subsequent parent-child relationships? What kind of childhood did girls and boys experience with fathers who had separated from their mothers on the basis of their violence?[65] Given the nature of our sources, these are questions that historians may not be able to ever fully answer.

Parents' strategies

Dependency, both emotional and economic is often seen as a condition of childhood. But as this section will show, in the context of marriage breakdown, children and their parents were often in a position of co-dependency. Parents could use their children to fight their battles, and they could rely upon them for emotional support. In turn, shared experiences of family tension and conflict could serve to either strengthen or loosen the bond between parent and child. Marital violence frequently had an impact upon parenting, but it was also the ties of affection, obligation and duty towards children that could persuade parents to remain within unhappy marriages.

When Fleetwood and other conduct book writers warned parents of the 'fearful case' of those who made their children pawns in their marital disputes, they highlighted a situation that was all too common. For Fleetwood, 'children are the pledges of mutual love, and the cement of affection; the use of them is, naturally to make up differences', but evidence suggests that children were often deployed to fuel disputes and drive parents further apart.[66] Just as some violent men could seek

[65] These questions were inspired by listening to a paper on modern-day childhood by Christien Brinkgreve, 'Understanding post-divorce family relationships', delivered at the Fifth European Social Science History Conference, Berlin, March 2004, and I am grateful to her for discussing this research with me.

[66] Fleetwood, *The Relative Duties*, pp. 13–14; see also, J. Nelson, *An Essay on the Government of Children* (London, 1756), p. 172.

to demean their wives by depriving them of their position as mistresses of the household, as we saw in Chapter 1, so also wives claimed that their husbands were cruel because they did not allow them to function as mothers. Frances Fletcher complained that her husband, 'not content with wounding and distressing' her feelings, 'forbade her . . . without any just cause . . . to give any orders respecting her children'. As a wealthy woman, many of the mundane tasks of motherhood were performed by others, but Joseph Fletcher could still inflict damage upon his wife's identity, status and authority as a mother by removing her power as a decision-maker in their children's lives.[67]

A few fathers involved their children more directly in family violence by encouraging or ordering them to join in with the abuse of their mothers. Elizabeth Boteler, aged seven or eight years old was seen by several witnesses 'with tears in her eyes' striking her pregnant mother on the stomach and boxing her on the ear after she was ordered to do so by her father, Oliver. He reportedly said that 'he would never endure her' if she did not follow his commands and wished that she told her mother 'that she did not love her'. Elizabeth's younger brother, aged just three years old, did not escape from such treatment, and was ordered to tell his mother that he hated her, with the threat of whipping if he said he loved her. Both children were forced to spit at their mother.[68] For women this could be the hardest form of cruelty to bear. Martha Pearse suffered verbal and physical violence from her husband, insults from his relations, confinement in her home, and treatment as a madwoman. But she said that 'what cut the deepest and affected her spirits beyond imagination', was to be, 'continually reviled by her own child, who was trained up in constant disobedience to her and daily taught, directed and compelled by her said husband. . . to taunt at and insult her'.[69]

It was not unusual for comments to be made about the parenting abilities of a marital partner during marriage separation cases. Often this simply became one parent's word against the other. Elizabeth Ann Heathcote said that her husband, 'for the purpose of annoying' her, 'was in the habit of treating his children (when he did take notice of them, which was but seldom) with great harshness'. Her bitterness was matched by her husband, who claimed that to vex him, Elizabeth was particularly severe when disciplining their son, Frederick, 'whom she

---

[67] LPL, CA, Case 3366 (1811), D757, f.40.
[68] LPL, CA, Case 1041 (1672), Eee4, ff.853r,858r,863v,867; for other examples of children who were forced by their fathers to abuse their mothers see, LPL, CA, Case 9240 (1699), Eee8, f.635v; and NA, DEL 1/598 (1765), Part One, f.488.
[69] LPL, CA, Case 7022 (1748), D1573, f.84r; punctuation has been inserted for ease of comprehension.

supposed to be his favourite'. Their children were used to express mutual hatred and discontent.[70] It is of interest that contemporaries thought it was relevant to include details of parent-child relationships in what were disputes about marriage. Since it was assumed that young children would be in the custody of their fathers following marriage break-up, the question of their care was not the issue. Instead, providing evidence of how an adult had behaved as a parent was regarded as indicative of their attitudes and conduct in other personal relationships.

Inconsistencies of behaviour were not unknown, and as noted in the Kirkman marriage discussed above, violence in parenting and marriage did not always run in tandem. But when so much about the parent-child relationship was conducted in front of others, whether they be other family members, servants, employees or friends, the conduct of parents towards their children provided a useful guide to the likely temperament and demeanour of adults in the intimate and sometimes more private aspects of the marital relationship. Thus the parent-child relationship served as the public face of family life. Isabella Foster, a witness in a cruelty suit brought in 1855, remarked of the husband, 'I have seen him so indifferent to his own children that he seemed wanting in affection to them, and I think when that is the case, a person cannot be said to be of an affectionate disposition'.[71] Good parenting was seen as such an essential measure of character that it was the foundation against which other personal relationships could be assessed.

Both men and women were scrutinised according to their parenting, and some anticipated this by including statements about how they had been good fathers or mothers as well as marriage partners in their submissions to the courts.[72] However, if there were any failings in parental duty, it was mothers who were subjected to the most severe criticism. Godfrey Lee said in 1700 that he had been forced to send his children away when they were very young because of his wife's 'unnatural hatred and great cruelty to them', and as evidence of her cruel nature John Ryves recalled how his wife in her former marriage had put the hand of her five-year-old daughter in a pan of red hot coals as punishment 'for some childish fault'.[73] Women's reputation was so inseparable from their role as mothers, that even when they fled from violent men, their loss of rights of custody over their children did not mean the cessation of their motherly duties. Mary Strudwick was

---

[70] NA, PCAP 3/1 (1834), ff.211v, 216v.
[71] LPL, CA, Case 10404 (1855), H838/5, f.111.
[72] See, for example, LPL, VH80/22/16 (1723); and LMA, DL/C/182 (1793), f.404r.
[73] LPL, CA, Case 5587 (1700), Ee8, f.192r; LMA, DL/C/172 (1752), f.212v.

accused of being an uncaring mother because she had not enquired after her children's health or visited them at the nurse's house where they lived, even though it was the violence of her husband that had driven her from her children and their family home in Hatton Garden.[74] Occasionally mothers overcame considerable difficulties to maintain communication with their children after marriage separation. Lady Sarah Pennington's husband was allegedly so angry at his inability to lay his hands on her inherited property, that he made accusations about her conduct (probably concerning her chastity), and forced her to accept a private separation. Concerned to tell her children that 'you have still an affectionate mother, who is anxious for your welfare, and desirous of giving you some advice with regard to your conduct in life', Sarah published a book of instructions for them in 1762.[75]

The knowledge that they would lose access to their young children if they left their husbands dissuaded or at least delayed women's decision to quit violent marriages. When Catherine Ettrick told one witness about life with her violent husband, she said that she 'often bore with his ill usage upon the account of the children'.[76] It was in part because she had, 'a very tender regard and affection for her infant son', that Anne Marie Brogden tried to live with her husband's brutality.[77] 'Being very unhappy upon being obliged to leave her children', Sarah Chance asked her husband if she could return home, even though she had been whipped and struck by him and his mistress who shared their house.[78] Husbands could use the threat of keeping the children as a way of enhancing their power over their wives. It was because John Geils repeatedly told his wife that, 'he would have the children' whenever she attempted to talk to him about separation, that she remained with him for so long.[79]

Today, even in a divorcing society, we hear of parents who stay together in unhappy marriages, 'for the sake of the children'. The belief that children benefit more from being raised in a family with two parents to care for them, than by one parent who has been separated, has a long history. It was not always women who endured disagreeable partners for their children. Joseph Kirkman, who was one of the few husbands

---

[74] NA, DEL 1/361 (1722), f.238v–239r.
[75] Pennington, *A Mother's Advice*, p. 10; see also, T. Bowers, *The Politics of Motherhood: British Writing and Culture, 1680–1760* (Cambridge, 1996), p. 32.
[76] NA, DEL1/598 (1768), Part I, f.828.
[77] LMA, DL/C/173 (1758), f.301r; for a similar example see, Ben-Amos, 'Reciprocal bonding', 296.
[78] LMA, DL/C/175 (1767), f.115v.
[79] NA, PCAP 3/12 (1846–7), ff.394r, 396r.

who brought a cruelty case against his wife, admitted to a servant that, 'he would not live with his said w[ife] but for the sake of his children'. With eight children he may well have wondered how he could manage without her.[80] Certainly, it is possible that when marital relationships failed, parents became more dependent upon the affection and attention they could receive from their children than their marriage partners. According to Mary Wollstonecraft, 'the most neglected wives make the best mothers'.[81] When husbands lacked the ability to satisfy the emotional needs of their wives, children filled the vacuum. Thus children may have acted as ties to the family, which made leaving even violent marriages much more difficult.

At the same time as motherhood became regarded as an increasingly important badge of status for women, it continued to be associated with suffering. Whereas women had long been admired for enduring the pain of childbirth, they were now expected to endure the longer term trials of child rearing. Mothering was intended to be about giving (birth, nourishment, nurture), not receiving. If motherhood could be imagined as a prolonged self-sacrifice, then in the context of marriage breakdown, women were thought naturally prone to put their children before themselves.[82]

Mothers who did otherwise inspired shock and horror. When Sophia Sellers, the wife of a labourer from Barking was charged with attempted suicide before a police court in 1831, she explained that she had tried to drown herself, 'on account of the ill-usage she received from her husband'. It was because she had two children that the magistrate who examined her, and the reporter for *The Times*, who later told the story of her case, were appalled by her actions. Having explained that there were ways that she could have obtained protection from her husband's violence, her examination focused entirely upon her failure as a mother. 'Her loss would have been a severe calamity to her children', preached the magistrate, 'who could not help the faults of their father'. Asking her, 'if she was not fond of her children?', and her replying that she was, the magistrate speculated upon what could have happened after her death. 'Suppose your husband ill-used your children, or permitted them to be ill-used after they had lost your protection, what a cruel act it would have been on your part to deprive those dear children of the assistance it is in your power to afford them', he said.[83] This mother

---

[80] LMA, DL/C/289 (1806), f.201v.
[81] As cited in Lewis, *In the Family Way*, p. 69.
[82] Lewis, *In the Family Way*, pp. 57–9.
[83] *The Times* (18 June 1831) 6e.

was expected to be a living sacrifice for her children, enduring the violence of her husband because without her it would be directed to them. Her duty was to protect her children by suffering for them, and to assume responsibility for the 'faults' of their father, because neither he nor they could. In this family where male violence was experienced, it was assumed best for the children if the mother remained present. It highlights the inconsistency of views that were held about who should care for children if marriages became violent. For as we shall now see, the law regarding child custody meant that if a violent marriage ended through separation rather than suicide or death, until 1839, mothers had no rights to prevent their children from living with their violent fathers.

Child custody

The 1839 Custody of Infants Act marked an important first step in giving mothers rights over their children after marriage separation or divorce. The Act allowed mothers to petition the Court of Chancery for custody of their children up to the age of seven, and for periodic access to children who were seven years and older. The Act had been pioneered by Caroline Norton, an upper-middle-class woman whose husband, George, had deprived her of access to their three children. She had experienced physical violence from George and he had ensured that their marriage was discussed in newspaper gossip columns after he accused her of adultery with Lord Melbourne, who was prime minister when George sued him for 'criminal conversation'.[84] George had so little proof of his wife's adultery with Melbourne that the case was immediately dismissed, but after their separation (which was never legally sanctioned) he refused to let Caroline see their children, including their youngest son who subsequently died aged eight, and he continued to claim her earnings from her literary career. Caroline discovered that George was acting within the law, and that in cases of marriage breakdown, no matter who was at fault, husbands nearly always gained the custody of their children. Appalled by her lack of rights over her children and property, Caroline began a campaign to raise public awareness and bring about legislative change. She wrote pamphlets, including an open letter to the Queen in which she appealed to their shared interests as women, and sought help from her political friends such as Serjeant-at-Law Thomas Talfourd and Lord Lyndhurst, who introduced the Bill

---

[84] For an explanation of this legal action see, S. Staves, 'Money for honour: damages for criminal conversation', *Studies in Eighteenth Century Culture* 11 (1982), 279–97.

that became the Act of 1839. She later commented upon the 1857 Divorce Act.[85]

There is no doubt that the 1839 Act was a significant improvement in women's rights, which was, as we shall see, the logical outcome of changing ideas about motherhood. Yet Caroline Norton was a suitable figurehead for this legislation because in her anti-feminism and unwillingness to confront many of the realities of women's and children's lives who endured marital violence, she represented the conservatism of her age. Her descriptions of her marriage betrayed the prejudices of her class, which labelled physical violence as a vice of the poor:

We had been married but a few weeks when I found that a part of my lot was that which generally belongs to a lower sphere – and that, when angry, Mr Norton resorted to personal violence.[86]

There were many limitations and weaknesses to the 1839 Act, and scarce attention to the needs of children. In many ways, the 1839 Act was a missed opportunity that could only be remedied by later legislation.

What was the situation with regard to child custody prior to 1839? Although the church courts had no jurisdiction over child custody, from their records we do occasionally learn of how couples managed the issue of childcare following marital violence. In part this was because in calculating alimony, the church courts needed to know who was bearing the costs of child maintenance. Especially when couples had very young children, it appears that even before the 1839 Act mothers could gain their custody without apparent objection.[87] Private separation deeds often gave mothers the custody of children, although the 1820 Westmeath case showed that such agreements gave women no long-term security, as fathers could subsequently win back their children if quarrels resurfaced.[88] Other women, like Ann Sparkes in 1811, took their children

---

[85] Much has been written about Caroline Norton. For a biographical introduction see, M. Forster, *Significant Sisters: The Grassroots of Active Feminism 1839–1939* (London, 1984), chapter 1. Norton's writings on child custody include, *The Separation of Mother and Child by the Law of 'Custody of Infants' Considered* (London, 1838), and *A Plain Letter to the Lord Chancellor on the Infant Custody Bill* (London, 1839). Her pamphlet addressed to Queen Victoria was entitled, *A Letter to the Queen on Lord Chancellor Cranworth's Marriage and Divorce Bill* (London, 1855), in J. O. Hoge and J. Marcus, *Selected Writings of Caroline Norton* (New York, 1978).

[86] C. Norton, *English Laws for Women in the Nineteenth Century* (London, 1854), in Hoge and Marcus, *Selected Writings of Caroline Norton*, pp. 31–2.

[87] See, for example, LMA, DL/C/177 (1773), f.306v; and LPL, CA, Case 2412 (1818), H277/9.

[88] Staves, *Married Women's Separate Property*, pp. 163–4, 177. The story of the Westmeath marriage and the lengthy battles over child custody that followed is told in Stone, *Uncertain Unions and Broken Lives*, chapter 12.

with them when they fled, only to have their children then snatched back from them.[89] When children were already in their father's custody at the time that separation cases were heard in the church courts, men such as John Deye in 1703 made statements that they were 'willing to take care of their said children'.[90] To show how reasonable they were to their wives, husbands could outline how they had allowed their wives access to their children while they were in their custody. David Soux boasted that he had never been violent to his wife when she had visited their children, and Sir James Ashe said that his wife could visit their children whenever she wished, although he would not permit them to visit her, for fear that she would not allow them to return.[91]

Before the 1839 Act, it was in the common law courts, most notably the King's Bench, that parents could challenge child custody. The judges of King's Bench stuck rigidly to the rule that fathers had the right to the custody of their children, and it was because their decisions became increasingly controversial that popular pressure mounted for legislative change. Parents who disputed child custody could attempt to obtain a writ of habeas corpus from the King's Bench in which the party holding the child would be forced to come to court and justify their custody. Statements given in these cases, and the rulings upon them give us important insights into contemporary attitudes towards parenting and childhood in families post separation or divorce.

Mary Hargreave, her brother-in-law, and four of her children were forced to appear in the King's Bench in 1792–3 in response to a writ of habeas corpus that had been issued by her husband, George. Mary had fled from her husband in Lancashire to her sister's house in London after years of violence that had been brought on by her husband's insanity, which became worse when he drank heavily. Periods of confinement in a private madhouse had not helped, and alarmed by reports that two young men sharing the Hargreave name had died 'raving mad' in nearby Preston, Mary felt she had no option but to leave in order to preserve the safety of herself and her children. George was persuaded that a private separation would be 'most conducive to their mutual happiness'. But arguing that his insanity was not hereditary but temporary and caused only by his excessive drinking, George, his relatives and friends then fought to get his children back. First, they claimed that Mary was inadequate as a mother. She was said to ill-treat the children by disciplining them severely. In contrast, George was described as a kind and

---

[89] LPL, CA, Case 8572 (1811), H164/6.
[90] NA, DEL 1/330 (1703), f.143v.
[91] NA, DELl 1/321 (1702), f.97r; NA, DEL 1/329 (1708), f.160.

indulgent father, who nevertheless held authority over his children. His sister commented that 'tho' greatly indulged by him', his children 'always appeared to be under such government that a word from him would at any time bring them to obedience'. He was said to have taken 'great pains and delight in teaching his children to read and giving them other instructions as a kind parent'. Second, as if she was a token, it was agreed that the custody of the youngest child, a daughter, would be given to Mary because she had 'discovered a strong partiality' towards this child. The other children, it was argued, should be returned to their father, where 'they will be in perfect security and enjoy many blessings and advantages which could not be expected to be derived from their mother'.

In response, Mary portrayed another picture of how parenting had been conducted in their household. She said that she had only given her children 'gentle and moderate correction' to teach them important lessons such as telling the truth. Her mother concurred, and said that she never saw her daughter correct her grandchildren 'with anything except a little rod over their hands and arms'. Taking advice from her friends, Mary had been told that following her separation from her husband 'it were better that he should have the boys than the girls', but she remained convinced that, 'it would be a great misfortune to any of her children who should be intrusted to his care'. The belief that extra effort should be made to keep the girls in their mother's care persisted, with their grandmother declaring that, 'the said George Hargreave is highly improper to be the instructor of young minds but more particularly of girls whose morals would be corrupted by their father's accustomed bad language'.[92]

Frustratingly, the outcome of this dispute is unknown, and the meaning of the words written on the outside of one affidavit, '3 May Special Rule agreed on' is unclear. But what it shows is how far parenting at this time and in this legal context was regarded as involving only the education and disciplining of children. The inculcation of moral standards was clearly thought crucial to good parenting. All children were to be taught the value of truth, and girls in particular, sexual morality and decency. There is little said in the Hargreave case about other aspects of children's welfare; who washed, dressed and fed these children on a day-to-day basis? What input did love or affection have in making a good

---

[92] NA, KB 1/27 Part 5, Mich.,33 Geo.3 no.2, affidavits of George Edward and Elizabeth Ellinthorpe (5 November 1792), Alice Hargreave, Oliver Hargreave and George Hargreave (7 November 1792); KB1/28 Part 2 East., 33 Geo.3 no.2, affidavits of Mary Hart (16 April 1793), and Mary Hargreave (20 April 1793).

parent? Apart from learning from Mary that the children were frightened by their father when he was violent, we do not know about how the children themselves regarded their parents. The writ of habeas corpus ordered the children to appear before King's Bench, but there are no affidavits to suggest that they ever spoke formally to the court. Instead we see how children could be regarded and treated differently according to age and gender. The youngest child was offered to the mother, while the older children and the boys were thought more capable of living with their violent father and resisting his bad influence. In this way the case anticipated the provisions of the 1839 Act that deemed mothers the more suitable parent for younger children.

Most notably, none of those who gave testimony in this case thought George Hargreave's marital violence relevant to his abilities as a father. If anyone was portrayed as presenting a physical danger to the Hargreave children, it was their mother by her correction of them. The idea that a home where a mother had been forced to flee in fear of her life from a drunken and deranged man might not be the best location for the upbringing of children was not raised. This seems to be in keeping with other cases of the time. It was only in *Blisset's Case* (1774) that Lord Mansfield, chief justice of the Court of King's Bench, refused to give the father custody of a child after he had heard of his violence against the mother and the child, and of the father's bankruptcy. Even in this case, the court balked at returning the child to its mother, and instead ruled that it should be sent to a boarding school, an easy option that was taken on other occasions.[93] Certainly, the Court of Chancery could intervene if it was proved that a parent was abusing their children directly.[94] But when Lord Ellenborough succeeded Mansfield in 1802 a stricter rule was pursued with regard to decisions of custody. This became most notorious in the case of *Rex v. De Manneville* (1804). Mrs de Manneville, who had separated from her violent husband, a Frenchman, applied to the King's Bench for a writ of habeas corpus after he had 'seized and violently torn' her child from her, supposedly as she was breast-feeding. As Ellenborough found that he could not charge the father with depriving his child of sustenance, since he had supplied a wetnurse for his child, he upheld the right of the father to the custody of his child. Again

---

[93] W. Forsyth, *A Treatise on the Law Relating to the Custody of Infants, in Cases of Difference between Parents or Guardians* (London, 1850), p. 64; M. L. Shanley, *Feminism, Marriage, and the Law in Victorian England, 1850–1895* (London, 1989), p. 133. For a case when the King's Bench enforced the father's request that his children should be sent to boarding school rather than live with his estranged wife see, NA, KB1/28 Part 6, Hil., 35 Geo.3 no.1, affidavit of Richard Hodges (5 February 1795).

[94] Forsyth, *A Treatise on the Law Relating to the Custody of Infants*, pp. 13, 52.

the potential for ill-treatment of the child by his violent father was not discussed. The sentimental potential of this story of maternal anguish, coupled with its appeal to anti-French feeling was long lasting. As one campaigner for change in the law of child custody later wrote:

This is a very strong case. Here is an Englishwoman possessed of property, married to a needy French emigrant, whose only complaint against his wife appears to have been her reluctance to will away that property in his favour. The circumstances under which the child was taken were most gross, and such as would seem the act of a savage rather than one educated in a civilized country. The child itself was only a few months old; unweaned, and utterly dependant on the mother; but because as Lord Ellenborough observed, 'there was no pretence it had been *injured* by want of nurture' . . . . he was held not to have abused his 'right', but to have the same claim to the custody of his child as any other man.[95]

With patriarchy and the paternal right being upheld in such dramatic circumstances, how can we explain the change of thinking that gave rise to the Custody of Infants Act of 1839? There certainly had not been an alteration of attitudes towards violent men and their abilities as fathers. Even though Norton herself had experienced violence from her husband, she paid more attention in her writings to the plight of the mother whose husband was adulterous. Concern about how the morals of children could be 'contaminated' by living in a household where a father lived in open adultery with his lover, and revulsion at the idea of the children of an 'innocent' woman being raised by an adulteress, was what most troubled both her and her supporters.[96]

During a period when contemporaries did not fully understand how marital violence could be indirectly harmful to children, it is perhaps not surprising that there was so little concern about leaving children in the custody of violent men. It was assumed that once a man had been separated from his wife his violence would cease. Alarmingly, there continued to be a reluctance to accept the relationship between marital violence and child abuse. As late as the 1880s a judge ruled that five children should be in the custody of a father who had been separated from their mother on the grounds of marital violence since:

---

[95] *Observations on the Natural Claim of the Mother to the Custody of her Infant Children, as Affected by the Common Law Right of the Father* (London, 1837), pp. 9–10; the emphasis is in the original. For discussion of the significance of this case see also, D. C. Wright, '*De Manneville v. De Manneville*: Rethinking the birth of custody law under patriarchy', *Law and History Review* 17, 2 (1999), 247–307.

[96] *Observations on the Natural Claim*, pp. 2, 15; Stone, *Road to Divorce*, pp. 177–8.

we have no reason to dread injury to the health or morals of the child. To leave his wife with the defender were to subject him to an influence exciting and tempting him to violence towards her. To leave his little child in his house is, or may well be, to introduce a soothing influence to cheer the darkness and mitigate the bitterness of his lot, and bring out the better part of his nature.[97]

Here it is the child's role to inspire improved behaviour from his parent. Such a view was woefully naive, and shows that men could still challenge and obtain the custody of their children, no matter how violent their conduct.

Changes in attitudes towards marital violence and children do not provide an explanation for the 1839 Act. We need instead to set it in the context of other early nineteenth-century ideas about gender and family roles. By the time the Bill on child custody was introduced, the middle classes had placed motherhood on a high moral pedestal, but there was concern that they had set an ideal that was out of the reach of most mothers. As a consequence, much effort was expended on trying to remove the obstacles that could prevent women fulfilling their most natural role. Those fighting for factory and mine reform, for example, argued that these were workplaces that separated mothers from their childcare duties. Thus the Factory and Mine Acts that were introduced in the 1840s, and limited women's working hours and occupations, were measures that were introduced in part to reinstate women's position in the home. In the meantime, the Poor Law Amendment Act (1834) was much criticised for separating families in the workhouses. It also created an inconsistency of women's rights to child custody. Under the new poor law, mothers of illegitimate children were made responsible for their maintenance, while all women who were married surrendered their children's custody to their husbands. The institution of marriage looked very unappealing on these grounds. To argue for the importance of women spending time at home with their young children, and then deprive them of their ability to fulfil this function if they bore legitimate children, and had no responsibility for the marriage break-up, seemed grossly unfair. As Norton noted:

It is apparently very easy to feel great humanity for one set of mothers and not for another; to abhor the unnatural separation of near relatives when it is expedient to raise a cry against the working of the New Poor Law, and to defend that unnatural separation when it is expedient to oppose the Infant Custody Bill.

[97] As cited in D. C. Wright, 'On judicial agency and the best interests test', *Law and History Review* 17, 2 (1999), 323.

Women of Norton's social rank, who were not expected to work, were left with 'no other real and fit occupation *but* the education of her children', she argued, which made separating the mother from her children that much more of a hardship.[98]

Those who fought for legislative reform were able to use contemporary notions of motherhood and fatherhood to their advantage. As the virtue of breast-feeding continued to be extolled, it was thought unnatural to deprive a baby from its mother. Pregnancy, the pain of childbirth, and breast-feeding, it was argued, created a tie between mother and child that should not be broken. 'Does *nature* say that the woman, who endures for nearly a year a tedious suffering, ending in an agony which perils her life, has no claim to the children she bears?', Norton wrote. A father, in contrast, 'who has slept while she watched; whose knowledge of her sufferings is confined to the intelligence that he is a father; and whose love is *at best* but a reflected shadow of that which fills her heart', should not have custody of his children, for 'the voice of nature cries out against the inhuman cruelty of such a separation'.[99] In practice, as Norton noted, 'the father's custody is seldom or ever *real*, as the child, though nominally in its father's possession . . . is almost always of necessity confided to a third party'.[100] In a world where life was ideally divided between the separate spheres of home and work, men could be portrayed as simply too busy to be troubled with fatherhood. According to this pattern of parenting, motherhood was active, time-consuming and even life-giving, whereas fatherhood was represented simply as a matter of ownership and status, with encumbered tasks that easily could be delegated to others. In debates over child custody, it was mothers who could be portrayed as coping best with lone parenting. As a result, Norton and others argued that fathers were not deserving of the custody of their young children if marriage separation occurred, and that women could ably perform their motherly duties even if they were prevented from doing those assigned to wives. Following this line of thinking, a good mother need not be a wife.

It is interesting that opponents to the Bill on child custody did not counter the negative picture that Norton and her supporters portrayed of fatherhood. Instead, they were more concerned that the Bill would lead to a rush of cases brought by women seeking separation on trivial grounds, since they naively believed that if women had child custody, there would be less to persuade them to make difficult marriages

---

[98] Norton, *A Plain Letter*, p. 118.
[99] Norton, *The Separation of Mother and Child*, pp. 9–10.
[100] Norton, *A Plain Letter*, p. 53; see also, *Observations on the Natural Claim*, pp. 51–2.

work.[101] This view may explain why the Bill was rejected in the House of Lords when it was first introduced in 1837.

Even with this delay, when the Bill eventually became law in 1839, for a number of reasons it could only be seen as a limited achievement for women. First, there was no intention that this Act should give 'rights' to mothers that placed them on an equal platform with men. Norton herself was vehemently against what she described as the 'wild and stupid theories' of feminists, and believed in 'the natural superiority of man'. The double sexual standard was maintained, whereby a mother who had committed adultery still lost all claim to child custody. Women were not represented, even by those who advocated legal change, as gaining any new powers by the Act. Instead, the change in the law was simply intended to ensure that parliament fulfilled its role of protecting women.[102]

Second, in the debates that preceded the Act, men's roles as fathers were constructed in restrictive ways, but so also were women's as mothers. Full-time maternal care and nurturing, especially of younger children, was depicted as so 'natural' to women that it left little room for mothers to pursue lives that were in any way independent from their children. What was best for the child was assumed to be best for the mother. Certainly, the lives of women and children were intertwined; they often shared in the experience of domestic violence, for example. But conflating mother's interests with their children denied them a separate identity and status, even as women who were no longer tied to the marital union. So although women obtained the ability to challenge paternal rights in 1839, their duties as mothers still bound them to a traditional role in the family that was positioned securely within the confines of the home.

Third, it was no accident that mothers were only given the means to dispute the custody of children who were under the age of seven. For, although the separation of a child from its mother during infancy was regarded as 'dangerous and unnatural', this was because babies required their mother's milk, and young children the attention of their mothers to the numerous 'petty cares which surround the cradle'. In contemporary thinking, the far more important aspects of childcare could not begin until a child had begun to exercise reason, which was around the age of seven. This was the age at which many children were sent away to

---

[101] See, for example, the debates on the Bill that were reported in *The Times* (15 February 1838) 3b and (24 May 1838) 4c; and [Handley], 'Custody of Infants Bill', 276–82.

[102] Norton, *English Laws for Women*, pp. 2, 15, 168, 171; see also Norton, *A Letter to the Queen*, p. 98.

school, and when boys were separated from the feminising influence of their mothers. Even those who campaigned for change in the law of child custody argued that it was only when children reached the age of seven that the most significant impact of parenting would be felt:

No one will say that a child of seven years of age has formed *opinions*, the father can instil what opinions he pleases. The *disposition* of the child *is* probably formed, the guidance of which would probably, under the father's roof, have been left to a servant, instead of the tender and watchful care of a mother; but all the rest is still in the father's power.[103]

In this model of child development, mothers through their breast milk and 'tender care' can influence a child's temperament, but fathers teach their children the views and values that will determine how they apply themselves in adult life. Both parents were seen as influential, but one suspects that it was chiefly the father's role that children would have remembered.

Fourth, this was legislation that had been framed by the middle classes, and as such it was of little relevance to those in the lower social ranks. Children were a considerable economic burden that few fathers in the working classes were willing to fight to retain. Finding the resources to dispute custody in Chancery was simply not an option for most parents. Informal living arrangements were made, but working-class children could be deserted or abandoned by one or both of their parents if marriages broke down.[104] For the remaining parent, economic survival was their main concern, and to those who had to support them, they posed a considerable burden to the poor rate. Even if a woman was left with her children, until the Married Women's Property Act was passed in 1870, a separated but still married mother was vulnerable to her husband, who could at any time return and seize earnings or property from her and their children.

Finally, the 1839 Act was concerned chiefly with adult authority and responsibilities, not children's needs or welfare. Mothers did not gain the ability to care for very young children because violent or adulterous fathers were thought unsuitable. It was not until the 1857 Divorce Act, when the judges of the new Divorce Court were given discretionary powers to determine child custody as they deemed 'just and proper', that discussions began in earnest about what might be in the best interest of children. It was in this court that evidence was submitted concerning the strength of parental affection for children. But the common law

[103] *Observations on the Natural Claim of the Mother*, pp. 52, 68.
[104] See, for example, A. Levene, 'The origins of the children of the London Foundling Hospital, 1741–1760: a reconsideration', *Continuity and Change* 18, 2 (2003), 222–7.

courts still upheld the rights of fathers and it took more legislative change, in the form of the Custody of Infant Acts of 1873 and 1886 for women to gain the custody of older children, even if they had been proved guilty of adultery, and for mothers to gain equal right to name testamentary guardians in the case of their death. Children had to wait until 1925 for the 'best interests test' to become the main criterion for determining their custody.[105] The idea that children might have 'rights' when their parents separated or divorced was unheard of in our period.[106]

Children shared much in common with their mothers in our period and contemporaries often treated them alike. Within the family, children and their mothers held subordinate positions to their fathers or husbands. The male head of the family had powers of correction over both his children and his wife. Thanks to the property laws, theoretically at least, wives were as economically dependent upon their husbands as their children. Women could be admired for their child-like qualities, especially sexual innocence. As a consequence of these similarities, reforms concerning children and women frequently went hand-in-hand. We have discussed the legislative change regarding working hours and practices, and we have seen how the first Infant Custody Act of 1839 assumed that children's interests were the same as their mothers. Later legislation dealing with the issue of marital violence more directly, most notably the 1853 Act for the Better Prevention and Punishment of Aggravated Assaults upon Women and Children, also dealt with children's and women's welfare together. This was a trend that would continue into the twentieth century.[107] But of course, the needs of children and adult women were very different, and the result could be legislation that satisfied neither.

Children and women were treated collectively because men believed that patriarchal power over women rested upon a father's absolute control of his children. The valorisation of motherhood in the eighteenth and early nineteenth century fitted uncomfortably with the patriarchal ideal because it gave women authority in the domestic sphere. Nevertheless, it took until 1839 for women to be given formal but limited recognition of their role as mothers. For the fear was that in relinquishing some power as fathers, men risked losing their overall position of authority in the family. The courts were reluctant to make the connection

---

[105] Shanley, *Feminism, Marriage and the Law*, chapter 5; Anderson, 'State, civil society and separation', 191–4; Wright, 'On judicial agency', 319–24.

[106] Treatises such as Elizabeth Dawburn's, *The Rights of Infants* (Wisbech, 1805), were actually concerned with the importance of mothers breast-feeding.

[107] For this pattern in America, see, Gordon, *Heroes of Their Own Lives*.

between cruelty to children and to mothers because to do so was to demonstrate that an unfit father was also an unfit husband. As far as contemporaries were concerned, the issue of child custody was about far more than children's lives. The fundamental issues of the gender hierarchy and appropriate gender roles in the family were at stake. The result was that child custody disputes often became sites for gender conflict between adults, and children themselves were all but forgotten.

Conclusion

Parents from the mid-seventeenth through to the mid-nineteenth centuries shared with us in the affection they felt for their children. Although lawyers and legislators could neglect the affairs of children, there is no evidence to suggest that parents were less loving towards their children in the past. Then, as now, mothers could remain in unhappy marriages for the sake of their children. Of course, not all women who experienced violence from their husbands had children, and some were past childbearing age when they first experienced marital violence. But violence to women was often closely associated with motherhood, and frequently began in pregnancy. Children were considered in the court cases relating to marriage breakdown more frequently by the nineteenth century, and women were able to use their position as mothers in their pleas for legal intervention or separation, but there is no evidence that this was of benefit to the children themselves. Changing ideas about childhood and parenting do not indicate any linear progress or improvement in the treatment of children.

Marital violence is a multiple victim activity: it affects more than just the person to whom the violence is directed. As we will see in the next chapter, marital violence had an impact on other family members, friends and neighbours, as well as children. Assault and marriage separation cases certainly shattered the illusion that the home was a safe haven for either women or children. Children were not helpless for they developed coping strategies when they encountered marital violence, but it is difficult to tell how effective these were, and what damage this type of violence inflicted. Time and again in this chapter we have had to confront either the crying or the silences of children. For most children, it seems, the sight of parental violence produced a response that words could not express.

4   Beyond conjugal ties and spaces

This chapter, and the one that follows, argues against the idea that over the course of our period marital violence was increasingly conducted in private. It will be shown that although violence between husbands and wives often occurred in domestic locations, this did not make it any less of a public activity. Marital violence could not be confined to conjugal ties and spaces, but instead could affect all those with whom a couple came into contact, spilling out into places of social as well as familial interaction. Violence was the mechanism by which family matters became community concerns. Indeed, by its very practice marital violence broke down any distinction that could be made between 'private' and 'public' behaviour, for it knew no boundaries.

My argument differs significantly from that advanced by other historians, who have concluded that it was the growing privatization of marital violence which explains why it became a problem that few people outside the conjugal unit were prepared to confront. It was over the course of the period chosen for this book that this important change is thought to have occurred. From an event witnessed by many, marital violence became shrouded with secrecy. What had been behaviour that attracted the attention, intervention and regulation of others, changed to conduct popularly viewed as the business of only the couple themselves. In the process, it is argued that the response of those who lived and worked around a couple enduring marital violence became one that we might recognise today.

Between the Restoration and the nineteenth century, a combination of social, cultural and economic forces are believed to have contributed to these changes. Early writers of the history of the family thought that as family structure altered from one described as 'open lineage' in form to a 'closed nuclear' one, the importance of kinship ties diminished, leaving women with a smaller network of support when marriages broke down.[1]

---

[1] For this model of family development see, Stone, *The Family, Sex and Marriage*, chapters 3–4.

Changes in family structure were believed to be accompanied by new attitudes towards personal relationships. While the premium upon affectionate or companionate relations between husband and wife may have been raised, historians assumed that the development of an ideal of 'individualism' was at the price of 'community'.[2] In this context, the fate of every married woman was her own, and the relationships in her neighbour's house were of little consequence to her. Meanwhile, the expanding population gravitated towards towns and cities where neighbours were increasingly strangers.[3] As the conjugal unit became more introspective, the desire for privacy increased. Houses of the wealthy were designed to frustrate the prying eyes of those outside, and within households, by the late eighteenth century, domestic servants lived and worked at a physical distance from their employers. Thus, a wife who was being subject to violence from her husband, could feel alone even within a household occupied by many.[4] The middle-class ideal of 'separate spheres', which designated the domestic realm a private female space, and the world outside the home as the public arena for men, could leave women as prisoners in their own homes.[5] The final nail in the coffin of support for the woman married to a violent husband is believed to have been produced in the eighteenth century by changes in codes of manners for those who aspired to social refinement and gentility. For the middle classes, civil, and later, polite codes of manners made marital violence so shameful that it became 'unspeakable', and as Hunt has argued, 'it is very difficult to intervene in the unspeakable'. The result of 'the cult of civility' was to 'create that veil of silence around respectable families that has proved such an obstacle to dealing with domestic violence right up to the present day'.[6]

So, according to historians, we should expect to find that a key difference between the violence in the Norcott marriage during the 1660s, and in the Veitch marriage that began in 1824, would be who else was involved. Coming from similarly 'respectable' families, was

---

[2] A. Macfarlane, *The Origins of English Individualism: The Family, Property and Social Transition* (Oxford, 1978), p. 5; K. Thomas, *Religion and the Decline of Magic: Studies in Popular Beliefs in Sixteenth- and Seventeenth-Century England* (London, 1971), pp. 555, 561.

[3] P. Burke, 'Some reflections on the pre-industrial city', *Urban History Yearbook* (1975), 19; Shoemaker, 'The decline of public insult', 101,126, and *The London Mob: Violence and Disorder in Eighteenth-Century England* (London, 2004), p. 296.

[4] P. Ariès, 'Introduction', in P. Ariès, G. Duby, and R. Chartier (eds.), *A History of Private Life* vol. 3, trans. A. Goldhammer (London, 1989), pp. 1–2; Stone, *Family, Sex and Marriage*, pp. 253–5, and *Road to Divorce*, pp. 212, 229; and Amussen, "Being stirred to much unquietness", 81–4.

[5] Davidoff and Hall, *Family Fortunes*.

[6] Hunt, 'Wife beating, domesticity and women's independence', 23–8.

Mary Veitch more isolated than Rachael Norcott? Did the importance of the nuclear family, individualism, privacy and good manners prevent others from knowing about and intervening in the Veitch marriage? Far from it. If anything, Mary was able to call upon a wider circle of support than Rachael. The evidence given by witnesses in the Veitch marriage extended to over two hundred and eighteen folios, whereas Rachael called just six witnesses. While acting as a witness in legal separation proceedings could be viewed as the most formal type of intervention, it is clear from witness statements that both Mary Veitch and Rachael Norcott had been affected by the words, actions and responses of their families, neighbours, friends and servants throughout the course of their violent marriages.

They had relied upon a broadly similar range of support. Rachael's two sisters spoke in her defence and described how, since she had fled from her husband, Rachael had lived with her brother. As we have seen in the previous chapter, Mary's first witness was her daughter from her first marriage. As well as family members, the violence, or its consequences in the Norcott and Veitch households, was witnessed by servants. John Payne served in the Norcott household for six months, and recalled how on one occasion a visiting master and his apprentice had kept watch over John Norcott 'for fear' that he 'should do some mischief' to his wife. Numerous servants were living in the Veitch household and testified in the subsequent court case. They did not need to be present in the same rooms as their master and mistress to know that all was not well. The cook, Sarah Matthews, for example, became aware of the marital discord of her employers in part because of their repeated quarrels and changing directions to her about where they should take breakfast. Sarah reported in all seriousness that she believed that the health of her genteel mistress had been affected as a result. 'I consider that Mrs Veitch's indisposition must have been aggravated by her having to take the breakfast upstairs herself', she said, 'for she used to have to go to bed again after she had done so'.

Friends who lived outside the household also became involved. Anne Hand, a neighbour living in Richmond, concurred that the cause of Mary's 'nervousness' was her husband's treatment. The experiences of the Veitch and Hand families shows that instead of creating a culture of embarrassment or denial of marital violence, the desire to display good manners provided new opportunities for detecting and reacting to abuse. It was at no less a polite occasion than a tea party, held by Anne and her husband, and attended by Mary and James Veitch, that Anne first became aware of what her neighbour was suffering. She noted that Mary 'appeared to be in a state of terror and alarm the whole evening; she was hardly able to speak'. It was her lack of participation in this occasion of respectable sociability, and non-engagement in polite conversation that triggered alarm bells. Just two nights later, Mary came to the Hand's house, 'crying and sobbing most piteously', and it took Anne an hour of careful consolation before the risk of Mary going into 'hysterics' had been overcome. No sense of polite decorum prevented Mary from showing her neighbour a bruise that she said had been caused by her husband, or Anne and her husband visiting James separately to 'expostulate' with him about his behaviour, and to determine whether Mary could safely return.[7]

Examining the marriages of Rachael Norcott and Mary Veitch allows us to question the assumptions that historians have made about the involvement of individuals other than the couple themselves in marital violence. Certainly, marital violence was conducted as a 'public' activity in the seventeenth century, but it was one that did not become more 'private' by the nineteenth century. The variety of those who became aware of circumstances in the Norcott and Veitch marriages was typical of cases taken from across the period. Given this, it is surprising that so few historians who have studied marital violence have broken away from the pattern of looking at it simply in terms of the violence of husband versus wife, or perpetrator versus victim. Many more individuals were involved. In contrast to today's thinking, in the mind-set of those living in the period of this book, becoming involved in the marriages of others was not always seen as intrusive, but was an expected part of everyday social interaction. Of course marriage signified a special partnership between two people, but it did not separate them from the involvement of others.

If the change in our current responses to the marital violence of others cannot be found within theories about the privatisation of family life, neither can satisfaction from the many explanations for that change. Historians of the family continue to debate the importance of kinship ties, and this chapter begins by contributing new material to show how wider family members, from the seventeenth to the nineteenth century, persisted in offering advice and practical support when marriages broke down.[8] Meanwhile, early modern historians have shown that the

---

[7] LPL, CA, Case 6659 (1666), Eee2, ff.94v–102, 123v–124; LPL, CA, Case 9440 (1837), H550/18.

[8] For a sample of the debates on kinship see, M. Chaytor, 'Household and kinship in Ryton in the late sixteenth and early seventeenth centuries', *History Workshop Journal* 10 (1980), 25–60; K. Wrightson, 'Household and kinship in sixteenth-century England', *History Workshop Journal* 12 (1981), 151–8; D. Cressy, 'Kinship and kin interaction in early modern England', *Past and Present* 113 (1986), 38–69; W. Coster, *Baptism and Spiritual Kinship in Early Modern England* (Aldershot, 2002).

yearning for privacy in the eighteenth century was nothing new, and that for most married couples private spaces were difficult to achieve or maintain.[9] Certainly the notion that women should remain within the 'private' sphere of the home has been exposed as an ideal that rarely became reality.[10] As we shall see, homes could not be private spaces while servants were ubiquitous, and changes in the architecture and room usage of homes cannot be linked in any simplistic way to a growing demand for privacy from the eyes and ears of household employees.[11] Nor were towns and cities full of strangers; instead they were populated by residents who found stability by forming social and economic ties with their neighbours. It remained in everyone's interest to know their neighbours, even if definitions of 'community' altered over time.[12] Finally, while codes of manners changed over the period, they silenced neither wives who were subject to violence from their husbands, nor civil or polite society from acting to voice objection to such conduct.[13] As the next chapter will suggest, the key to understanding community responses to marital violence lies not with any fundamental alteration in the way that family life was conducted, but with the emergence and development of the professions.

This chapter starts by examining the relationships that families and kin formed with wives who had violent husbands, and then looks at the role of servants within violent marital disputes. We then step outside the household to investigate how friends and neighbours became involved. Both individual and group activity and responses will be investigated. Two overall themes will recur in this chapter. The first is that not all intervention by others was beneficial to women in violent marriages. It is a mistake to think that the past was a golden age for women because more people appear to have been aware of, and prepared to take action in, cases of marital violence. Rather, as we shall see, some who became

---

[9] L. A. Pollock, 'Living on the stage of the world: the concept of privacy among the elite of early modern England', in A. Wilson (ed.), *Rethinking Social History* (Manchester, 1993), pp. 78–96; and Melville, 'The use and organisation of domestic space', especially chapter 3.

[10] See, for example, Vickery, 'Golden age to separate spheres?', 383–414.

[11] T. Meldrum, *Domestic Service and Gender 1660–1750: Life and Work in the London Household* (Harlow, 2000), pp. 76–83; P. M. Humfrey, "I saw, through a large chink in the partition . . .' What the servants knew', in V. Frith (ed.), *Women and History: Voices of Early Modern England* (Toronto, 1995), pp. 51–80.

[12] See, for example, J. Boulton, *Neighbourhood and Society: A London Suburb in the Seventeenth Century* (Cambridge, 1987), chapters 8–9; P. Earle, *A City Full of People: Men and Women of London 1650–1750* (London, 1994), pp. 171–8; and A. Shepard and P. Withington (eds.), *Communities in Early Modern England: Networks, Place, Rhetoric* (Manchester, 2000).

[13] Foyster, 'Creating a veil of silence?'.

involved condoned the use of violence, would not support wives who fled from violent husbands, and even caused further violence by their words or deeds. Second, it will be demonstrated how violence led to the adjustment and realignment of personal relationships. Aside from the obvious fact that marital violence was about the relationship of wife and husband, this form of violence and its aftermath produced new family and household structures and definitions, formed friendships and enmities, and challenged neighbours to rethink the membership and identity of their communities.

Relative values

It was only logical that wives who had been subject to marital violence should turn to their parents for help when they so often shared the same living spaces. While households containing multiple generations of the same family were rarely permanent living arrangements, it is clear from marriage separation cases that there were points in the family life cycle when married couples and their parents were co-resident. Living with parents was not unusual for a short period immediately following marriage. Women often invited their mothers to stay or returned to their mother's home when they were expecting their first children, and widowed parents could come and live with their married children during old age. It was at these times that parents could learn about and witness at first hand the nature of the relationship between their children and marriage partners. In 1707 it was because they were living in her parents' house following their marriage, that Anne Strengthfield's father was able to intervene when her husband tried to draw his sword against her; while she was staying in their house, Lady Turner's mother in 1820 saw how her son-in-law mistreated her daughter during her pregnancies; it was when she became a widow that Mary's mother came to live with her and James Veitch. Parenting, in terms of nurture and responsibility for care, clearly did not end with the marriage of children.[14]

It is apparent from many of the responses of parents to knowledge of their children's violent marriages, that it was more than their physical proximity to their offspring that drove them to become involved. The strength of the emotional ties between parents and their children is shown by the anger and hurt they expressed to the violent partners of

---

[14] LPL, VH80/13/1 (1708); LPL, CA, Case 9349 (1823), H346/9; LPL, CA, Case 9440 (1837), H550/18; E. Foyster, 'Parenting was for life, not just for childhood: the role of parents in the married lives of their children in early modern England', *History* 86 (2001), 313–27.

their children. In August 1716 George Healy asked his son-in-law, 'if he was not ashamed to use his wife in that manner', after he had struck his daughter with such force on the mouth that she almost bit through her lip, and the sixty-four-year-old mother of Marianna Greenway remarked upon how 'distressing' it was to be in her daughter's company when she and her husband visited the couple, because her son-in-law was so cruel to their daughter. 'He made us uncomfortable by finding fault and quarrelling with her', she said, and 'we thought that probably our presence might make matters worse for we could not sit by and see our daughter to be badly treated without interfering'.[15] Mary Fawcett, the wife of a Northallerton labourer, stated in her daughter's marriage separation case for cruelty that 'my daughter was very unwilling to complain and did not wish to make us unhappy by reciting her troubles'.[16] Sensitivity to the violence that was inflicted upon loved ones reached tragic proportions in the Daine family. According to Solomon Daine, a Kent yeoman, the return of his only child, Hannah, to his home following the break-up of her marriage, brought such 'great grief and concern' to his wife, that it was 'the sole and only cause' of his wife 'going mad'. His wife, and Hannah's mother, was so disturbed by Hannah's accounts of her unhappy marriage, and upset when Hannah subsequently became sick from venereal disease transmitted by Hannah's husband, that she 'was gone distracted out of her senses with the thoughts of it and was forced to be tied in her bed'. Meanwhile Solomon 'was afraid' that 'being under so great a concern' at this sad state of affairs 'it would have the same effect on him'. The consequences of marital violence were spreading through Hannah's family, and, like the disease that her husband had given her, she had no easy means of putting an end to the suffering.[17]

However, just like their daughters, parents were rarely the passive victims of marital violence. As George Healy's words showed, they could scold their son-in-laws, or follow the Reverend Richard Walter's example, who lectured his daughter and son-in-law at dinner about 'the deserts of a man who used his wife ill'.[18] It could be the family of a husband, as well as that of his wife, who could intervene to condemn his behaviour.[19] As we shall see in this chapter, intervention during

---

[15] NA, DEL1/368 (1721), f.69v–70r; LPL, CA, Case 3926 (1846), Eee42, f.146–147.
[16] NA, PCAP 1/199 (1856), f.114.
[17] NA, KB 1/6, part 1, Mich 12, Geo II, no.1, Affdt. of Solomon Daine (25 November 1738).
[18] LMA, DL/C/179 (1783), f.410v.
[19] See, for example, NA, DEL1/368 (1721), f.119v–121v; and LPL, CA, Case 10404 (1855), H838/2, 3.

heated and violent quarrels was always risky, and parents and other family members had no special immunity from being targeted themselves by angry husbands.[20] However, parents could also retaliate with violence. This could take extreme forms. When the physician Alexander George Sinclair came to try and persuade his wife to leave her parents' house in Stroud, Kent, where she had fled from his cruelty, her parents beat him up, and in a rough form of popular justice, subjected him to a ducking in the River Medway until he nearly drowned. After Alexander had his father-in-law arrested for assault, his wife's mother declared that she would rather murder her daughter than see her return to him.[21]

There were, of course, less dramatic forms of action. The parents of a woman had a powerful sanction that they could use while their son-in-law remained dependent upon them for the payment of his wife's portion or dowry. Parents withheld or delayed payment if they were dissatisfied with the treatment of their daughters. In a marriage separation case brought on the grounds of adultery and cruelty in 1693, for example, it was revealed that a father had stopped paying his daughter's portion once he discovered that her husband had been infected by venereal disease from a suspected adulterous affair. A cook-maid remembered overhearing the father list the items he had already given his son-in-law, telling him 'that if he had behaved himself to his daughter as he ought to have done he would have made it up a considerable fortune'.[22] Financial penalties could also be wielded later in life. The grandfather of Elizabeth Corne, hearing that her husband neglected to provide for her, and often beat her, changed his will so that she would be paid £100 a year in quarterly payments, which would be 'for her sole and separate use and benefit', and so not subject to her husband's 'intermeddling'.[23] Such cases should warn us against placing too much emphasis upon the importance of independence as the 'central characteristic of manhood in early modern England'.[24] Even when they were married, and had established their own households, adult men could remain dependent upon the good nature of their wife's relations. As Barry Reay has recognised from his study of nineteenth-century

---

[20] For examples of parents or kin also being attacked by husbands see, NA, DEL1/598 Part I, f.429–430; and LPL, CA, Case 9349 (1823), H346/9. See also, J. S. Adler, '"My mother-in-law is to blame, but I'll walk on her neck yet": Homicide in late nineteenth-century Chicago', *Journal of Social History* 31, 2 (1997), 263.

[21] NA, KB1/27, part 2, Mich 32, Geo III, no.1, Affdt of Alexander George Sinclair (7 November 1791).

[22] LPL, CA, Case 1055 (1693), Eee7, f.691v.

[23] NA, KB1/19, part 2, Hil 13, Geo III, no.1, Affdt. of Edward Gates (29 January 1773); for a similar example see, Bailey, *Unquiet Lives*, p. 34.

[24] Amussen, "The part of a Christian man", p. 214.

records, 'couples formed new "independent" households but most did so amid a community of kin'.[25] Marriage was no splendid isolation.

Parents were not reluctant to declare what they perceived to be their rights over their children. It seems that many believed that they only gave their daughters in trust upon marriage, and that if husbands treated them cruelly, they relinquished their position of authority over their wives. These beliefs were expressed, tested and disputed in the Court of King's Bench, which dealt with writs of habeas corpus that could arise after a wife sought refuge from her husband with her parents. There were numerous cases when wives returned home to their families of origin after marital violence, but since a husband had 'a right to the custody of his wife; and whoever detains her from him, violates that right', as Lord Mansfield put it, those who offered refuge could have a writ of habeas corpus directed against them. Nevertheless, there were cases when the judges of King's Bench were reluctant to return a wife to her husband if evidence could be produced that she had been subjected to 'unreasonable cruelty' from him. Thus, in 1766 Abraham Gregory was unsuccessful in his use of a writ of habeas corpus, which was directed to the mother and uncle of his wife, from whom she had sought shelter, because it was found that his wife had been 'very ill used' by him.[26] Parents could respond to writs of habeas corpus by arguing in defence of their custody of daughters. Robert Wheeler, for example, a gunmaker from Birmingham, believed that for his daughter 'the house of her parent is the natural and most proper place' for her 'to resort to for safety and protection'.[27] Put this way, returning to the family home was a 'natural' response after unnatural treatment. The popularity of the parental home as a place of refuge throughout this period suggests that, even though marriage could mean movement to a new household established by their husbands, women never completely broke their ties with the home where they had been raised.

Given that they were often instrumental in marriage formation, it is not surprising that parents and other family members could play an important part in taking the steps to either arrange legal protection for women subject to marital violence, or to begin separation proceedings

---

[25] B. Reay, 'Kinship and the neighbourhood in nineteenth-century rural England: the myth of the autonomous nuclear family', *Journal of Family History* 21, 1 (1996), 99.

[26] For examples of wives who sought refuge with one or both parents when they fled from violent husbands see, NA, DEL1/321 (1702), ff.41v, 43v; LMA, DL/C/177 (1775), f.699r; LMA, DL/C/187 (1803), f.39r; and NA, PCAP 1/199 (1856), f.58. For an outline of the custody rights of parents and husbands over women see Foyster, 'At the limits of liberty'.

[27] NA, KB1/30, part 3, East 39, Geo III, no.1, Affdt. of Robert Wheeler (9 April 1799).

between the couple. It was on the advice of her solicitor that Elizabeth Heathcote fled to her father's house in January 1827. When her husband followed her, and tried to kill her by beating her with a stick, her father had him arrested for assault, and bound over to keep the peace.[28] Before they would let her return home to her husband, Anne Henshall's parents made her husband sign a confession that they had written, admitting he had tried to poison her, and promising that he would never make such an attempt again.[29]

Faced with irreconcilable marriage breakdown, a judicial separation required the support of witnesses, and few women could afford to proceed without the backing of their families. Hence Anne Marie Brogden said that she had endured nearly four years of violence from her husband before she initiated separation proceedings because she was reluctant to tell her mother of what she was suffering. This was because she had married without the consent of her mother and relations, 'and having greatly disobliged them was loath to complain to them'. Such was the importance of kin in married life, that, if they were not involved at the start of marriage negotiations, their support could not be guaranteed for its duration. Anne's decision to marry against the wishes of her family had isolated her from them, leaving her to bear the consequences on her own.[30] Her case contrasts with that of Mary Pindar, whose financially advantageous marriage in 1708 at the age of fifteen was contrived by her parents. Mary's husband became violent to her within a year of their marriage, and she remained with him for ten years before launching a marriage separation suit. However, perhaps because they had been so vital in its arrangement, Mary's parents frequently offered her refuge in their house, challenged their son-in-law about his behaviour, and along with Mary's brother were alleged to be the main reason why she eventually left him.[31] So, if parents and other relatives were involved at the outset, then they could be prepared to share the responsibility if relationships fell apart.

Such was the part that parents could play in their children's married lives, that husbands could blame them for provoking their violence or, as in the Pindar marriage, encouraging marriage separation. Henry Strudwick attributed his marriage breakdown in 1722 entirely to his

---

[28] NA, PCAP 3/1 (1834), f.213.
[29] As cited in J. Bailey, 'Breaking the conjugal vows: marriage and marriage breakdown in the north of England, 1660–1800', PhD thesis, University of Durham (1999), p. 19.
[30] LMA, DL/C/173 (1758), ff.296r, 301r.
[31] NA, DEL1/368 (1721), ff.58v–70r, 78v–84r, 145, 269v–280r. In early modern Venice parents acted in similar ways to protect their daughters from marital violence, and file for separation, see, Ferraro, 'The power to decide', 502–4, 505, 507, 509.

widowed mother-in-law, who he said had withheld payment of his wife's inheritance and portion, and had used all means possible 'to alienate his said wife's affections from him'. During one quarrel, he reported that his wife had threatened to return to her mother whom she believed would 'not only receive her kindly but reward her with her whole estate for so doing'. According to Henry, it was his wife's mother, not him, who kept her living 'under the greatest awe and fear'.[32] Strudwick's mother-in-law was represented as detracting and diminishing his authority as a husband, and evidence from records of working-class marriages in the mid- to late nineteenth century shows that women's parents could continue to be seen in this way.[33] It was in part because of the 'apprehension' of her husband's 'violent resentment of any interference' of her mother or any other member of her family, that Frances Geils told her mother 'to leave her alone to deal as she could' with her husband.[34] In this light, parents could be regarded as having the potential to aggravate rather than ameliorate differences between married couples. At least initially, Frances chose to face her husband on her own, believing it to be her best strategy.

It is clear that some husbands were jealous and suspicious of the emotional ties between wives and their families. William Hanham, for example, thought that his wife's sister had exercised 'an undue and improper influence' over his wife, and that she had tried to 'weaken' his wife's 'affection' for him. Believing that she was a rival to his attentions, he refused to let the sister visit, and forbade his wife the use of the carriage in an effort to try and stop her travelling to see her sister. By the time his wife brought the separation case against him, her sister was dead, but this did not prevent one of William's witnesses defending his behaviour by suggesting that the relationship between Hanham's wife and her sister was anything but 'ordinary'. In an attempt to discredit her case, she was described as speaking of her sister 'in terms which were romantic and full of enthusiasms: declaring that she was an angel', and worse, that she had stated, 'her preference for her sister to her husband'.[35] Although a judge ruled subsequently in 1831 that depriving a wife of the company of her family did not constitute a 'substantive act

---

[32] NA, DEL1/361 (1722), ff.81–100v, 225v–240v; for other examples of disputes between husbands and their mother-in-laws, see, M. R. Hunt, 'Wives and marital "rights" in the Court of Exchequer in the early eighteenth century', in P. Griffiths and M. S. R. Jenner (eds.), *Londinopolis: Essays in the Cultural and Social History of Early Modern London* (Manchester, 2000), pp. 108–9, 115.

[33] Conley, *The Unwritten Law*, p. 80; and D'Cruze, *Crimes of Outrage*, pp. 67–8.

[34] NA, PCAP 3/12 (1846–7), f.394r.

[35] LPL, VH80/81 (1825), 4, 6, 11.

of cruelty', it was an acknowledgement of the influence of parents and kin that some husbands tried to isolate their wives from their support, and that some, like William Hanham, even went as far as to question the nature of their relationship.[36]

For parents, the balance between taking an interest in their children's marriages, and being labelled as interfering was a difficult one to achieve. This was not just a matter for interpretation by the couple themselves. Judicial statements reflected an inconsistency of opinion. It was declared in 1847 by the judge in a separation case to be 'infinitely to her credit' that Mrs Saunders had given refuge to her daughter-in-law, who was escaping from the violence of her son.[37] Yet in 1832 the magistrate at Hatton Garden police court, hearing a case of assault by an Islington milkman on his wife, scolded the father who said that he 'felt it my duty to interfere for the protection of my daughter'. He 'had no right to interfere between man and wife', the magistrate announced.[38] But although they risked criticism, it is clear that many parents felt compelled to intervene, especially when they perceived that their children's lives were in danger.

It was not only husbands who could find their parents-in-law troublesome. A number of wives shared Eleanor Naylor's experience, whose husband replaced her position in the household with his mother, telling Eleanor that 'she was no longer Mistress of his house'.[39] Others were horrified to find that rather than condemning the husband's behaviour, his relations joined him in being violent.[40] Both husbands and wives were highly sensitive to any slight on their family's good name. Robert Bendish, a merchant from the City of London, defended his violence to his wife by declaring that in 1673, when his wife called 'his sisters whores and said that his family was a base, mean and beggarly family', he had been 'highly provoked'. In 1783 Jane Prescott added her husband's insistence that she called her father and mother 'the most shocking of names', to her catalogue of complaints against her husband that she said amounted to marital cruelty.[41] Clearly parents and other family members had a value to these couples that was of more than just practical significance.

---

[36] *Neeld v. Neeld* (1831), *English Reports*, vol. 162, pp. 1442–6.

[37] *Saunders v. Saunders* (1847), *English Reports* vol. 163, p. 1136.

[38] *The Times* (18 July 1832) 6d–e.

[39] LPL, CA, Case 6548 (1777), D1471, f.186v; for other examples see NA, DEL1/344 (1710), f.88v, and LPL, CA, Case 5932 (1849), H765/7.

[40] See, for example, LPL, CA, Case 4177 (1669), Ee3, f.615r; LPL, CA, Case 10060 (1673), Eee5, ff.200, 209v; NA, DEL1/551 (1749), f.62–65.

[41] LPL, Case 757 (1673), Ee4, f.59v; LMA, DL/C/179 (1783), ff.409v, 417v.

Yet, in return, parental and other kin support could not always be relied upon when women decided to seek marriage separation. The uncle of Elizabeth Bound, for example, believed that the judges of the Court of Arches should encourage his niece to return and 'live quietly' with her husband, rather than grant her a separation on the grounds of her husband's adultery and cruelty. More than a century later, Lady Westmeath's mother went even further to prevent her daughter's separation, and stood as a witness for her son-in-law, Lord Westmeath. We can only explain such behaviour by understanding first, that marital disputes were shameful to both married parties and their families, no matter who was the instigator, and second that in this period there was no place for the separated wife in family life. Hence Elizabeth Bound's uncle said that a reconciliation would prevent, 'the disreputation to their family, which otherwise would necessarily follow', and the judge in the Westmeath case concluded that it was because Lady Westmeath's mother was 'so averse to publicity, and to the affair becoming "town talk"', that she had done everything she could to avoid a separation case being brought.[42]

Of course, we cannot tell from marriage separation cases how women were treated by their families if they were able to achieve separation, for the court records fall silent after a judgement had been reached. As a result, attempts by historians to examine the family lives of couples after marriage breakdown have tended to concentrate upon the fate of wives who were deserted by their husbands.[43] To find out about how couples fared after legal separation we have to turn to other sources. Eliza Haywood's *The History of Miss Betsy Thoughtless* (1751), and Anne Brontë's *The Tenant of Wildfell Hall* (1848), were both unusual novels of their time, because they discussed the subject of a wife who was unhappily married. Yet this subject matter was clearly a pertinent one: Haywood's novel had gone through ten editions by 1800.[44] In her novel, the orphaned Betsy Thoughtless is married to the brutish Mr Munden. Betsy takes Lady Trusty, who she regards as 'a second mother', into her confidence, and tells her of her marital woes. But alarmed as she is about how Betsy is being treated, Lady Trusty counsels against separation. 'Consider how odd a figure a woman makes, who

---

[42] LPL, CA, Case 1055 (1693), Eee7, f.662; *Westmeath v. Westmeath* (1827), *English Reports* vol. 162, p. 1014–15. In Scotland women could also be persuaded by their relatives to return to violent husbands, see Leneman, 'A tyrant and tormentor', 46.

[43] Bailey, *Unquiet Lives*, chapter 8.

[44] N. Tadmor, *Family and Friends in Eighteenth-Century England: Household, Kinship, and Patronage* (Cambridge, 2001), p. 15.

lives apart from her husband', she remarks. In words that would be similar to those used in the Westmeath case, Lady Trusty warns that,

the whole affair, perhaps with large additions to it, will soon become the talk of the town, – every one will be descanting upon it, and how much soever Mr Munden may be in fault, you cannot hope to escape your share in the censure.

Blameless as she is, Lady Trusty explains that Betsy cannot hope to emerge from a marriage separation without it also tainting her reputation. Furthermore, in a society before easy access to divorce, a marriage break-up was bound to provoke scandal and gossip. Perhaps Haywood was writing from experience, for all that is known about this author's personal life is the fact that she was married and had separated from her husband.[45]

It was Brontë who explored more fully the life of a wife who lived apart from her husband. Helen Huntingdon is depicted as struggling for a long period of time to keep her unhappiness with her drunken and lecherous husband, Arthur, a secret from her brother, uncle, aunt, and best friend. When she suggests a private separation to her husband, he will hear nothing of it; 'he was not going to be the talk of all the old gossips in the neighbourhood; he would not have it said that he was such a brute his wife could not live with him'. Unable to agree upon a separation, Helen feels she has no option but to take matters into her own hands. Disguised as a widow, Helen leaves her husband, taking their young son with her, and sets up home in another part of the country, working as an artist to make her living.[46]

As a bold attempt to describe the fate of a separated wife, Brontë's story is a commentary upon attitudes towards such women in the mid-nineteenth century. Condemnation of marital violence is shown to have negative as well as positive consequences for women. Concerned about how others will view them, men such as Arthur do all they can to prevent others discovering their violence, and hence refuse formal separation. Although she is by no means the guilty party in their marriage breakdown, Helen finds it necessary to assume the role of a widow to try to avoid the gossip that would otherwise arise from her unusual marital status. Even then, she cannot escape suspicion, and becomes subject to slander among her neighbours about her sexual conduct. The ways in which members of communities viewed separated women will be discussed later in this chapter. In terms of family life, like the figure of the

---

[45] Haywood, *The History of Miss Betsy Thoughtless*, pp. ix, 452, 469; for commentary on this novel see also, C. Flint, *Family Fictions: Narrative and Domestic Relations in Britain, 1688–1798* (Stanford, 1998), pp. 234–41, and Tadmor, *Family and Friends*, passim.

[46] Brontë, *The Tenant of Wildfell Hall*, p. 249.

widow or spinster, the separated wife did not fit into any ideal structure or pattern. Economic survival was similarly difficult; only in fiction could a woman make a living from her painting. Even if they had achieved a judicial separation, and had been awarded alimony, evidence from the church courts shows that payments were frequently irregular or stopped altogether. Unlike the widow or spinster, the woman who was separated from her husband never represented more than a tiny minority of the population, and, most importantly, had no past or future prospects that could position her within the familial and social hierarchy. As one early seventeenth-century writer explained to a wife contemplating separation from her husband, although the separated wife had to 'live alone like a widow', her life was 'worse than a widow: for those may marry again, but so could not you'.[47] In this context, it is telling that neither Haywood nor Brontë were able to effect a complete separation of their heroines from their husbands. Both Betsy Thoughtless and Helen Huntingdon return to nurse and be reconciled with their dying husbands, and afterwards, despite their previous experience of married life, they proceed to marry the book's hero. Ultimately, it seems that for both novelists, satisfying their readers' need for sentiment, rather than presenting a radical alternative to married life, was too tempting an opportunity to miss.

In summary, we have seen how from the perspective of married couples, parents could play an important part both provoking and dealing with the consequences of violence. Although in the early modern period around 50 per cent of women's fathers had died by the time they married, new husbands could find their mothers-in-law determined to defend their daughter's best interests. From the mid-seventeenth century, rising life expectancy for those of middling social status meant that an increasing number of parents had the potential to exert a 'stifling effect on the next generation'.[48] While their parents were alive, there were few who could escape from their control. There is no doubt that the presence of parents could act to curb and keep a check upon the violence of husbands. Mary Veitch's mother had moved into her home when she became a widow. But when she died, Mary's husband with foreboding announced, as her daughter recalled, that 'now . . . she was dead and had left him unrestrained control over everything, (which was the lease),

---

[47] R. Snawsel, *A Looking-Glasse for Married Folkes* (London, 1631), ed., Amsterdam, 1975, p. 78.

[48] Erickson, *Women and Property*, pp. 93, 96; P. Sharpe, 'Dealing with love: the ambiguous independence of the single woman in early modern England', *Gender and History* 11, 2 (1999), 227.

that he might use us both as badly as he chose'.[49] Even without parents, however, women still had a wealth of family and kin to whom they could turn. Others stepped into the breach: sisters, brothers, uncles, aunts, even grandparents. It may be because her parents were dead, for example, that Rachael Norcott turned to both her sisters for help.[50]

Violent marriages exposed the different meanings that people attached to the notion of 'family' in this period. Husbands could expect the family life of their wives to shift to them upon marriage. Even before their union bore any children, they alone wished to represent a wife's new family. Their definitions of family could thus be very narrowly self-focused. But tensions could arise because women frequently regarded families in other ways. Husbands were seen as additional members, not substitutes to pre-existing family structures and ties. For women, families included a widespread network of kin.[51] They expected the emotional attachments and commitments that they had formed in child-hood and youth to last a lifetime. In return, families could show a loyalty to their younger generation long after they had left home or had got married. In this sense, the longevity of relationship ties within the family were reciprocal.[52] Families did not have to reside in the same households to retain their identity, unity and strength. Parents retained a belief that their daughters were part of 'their' family, belonging to them. This meant that violence against a woman could be seen as an attack or affront to her family, as well as herself. Hence a violent husband was accountable to both his wife and her family, and this in part explains why so many family members became involved during occasions of marital violence. However, while most parents and other kin were ready to offer help, protection and temporary shelter to wives in their family, many hesitated before supporting the permanent separation of these women from their husbands. Just as individuals were not expected to make marriages without the approval of their families, so ending marriage also had to be a collective decision, for both could have repercussions for future family life. But whereas the formation of marriage held the possibility of bringing benefits to other family members, the ending of marriage bore advantage only to the couple themselves. The prospect of a separated wife returning to live permanently with her family of birth was for most families, financially unsustainable, but for even middling

---

[49] LPL, CA, Case 9440 (1837), H550/18.

[50] LPL, CA, Case 6659 (1666), Eee2, ff.94v–96r, 101r–102v.

[51] An idea also suggested by D'Cruze, 'A little, decent-looking woman', p. 79.

[52] Ben-Amos, 'Reciprocal bonding', 291–312, and 'Gifts and favors: informal support in early modern England', *Journal of Modern History* 72 (2000), 295–338.

and upper class families, the idea was an anathema. There had developed no definition of family life in which the separated wife had a social role, even in fiction.

Violent households

The historian who has done most in recent years to encourage us to reconsider the concept of family in our period is Naomi Tadmor. According to Tadmor, when people living in the eighteenth century referred to their family, they could include members of their household who were unrelated by marriage or blood. The idea of the 'household-family' was present in the writing of diarists as well as in fictional literature.[53] But this concept does not appear to have been expressed in the records of the courts that dealt with marriage breakdown. While we will see that household residents such as servants and apprentices could become intimately involved in the marital lives of their employers, their conduct in these affairs did not merit in their employer's words, membership of a 'household-family'. So although working alongside a family where there was marital violence inevitably meant coming into contact with the conflict between a couple, shared and privileged knowledge of family violence did not lead to any fundamental change in the way that household employees were viewed. They continued to be defined and described differently from family and kin. Hence our evidence allows us to question how far Tadmor's thesis has validity outside the realm of introspective or fictional literature. There is no doubt, however, that marital violence unsettled the balance of power and authority in the household. The end result could be the break-up of households and the termination of employment, as well as marital relationships.

Given that family homes were places of work for much of our period, and that even members of the lower middle class could expect to employ one or two household servants, violence within a marriage could not be kept a secret for long. The importance of servants as witnesses to adultery is now well established.[54] All forms of marital violence were witnessed by servants, and even sexual violence could become apparent to female servants as they washed and dressed their mistresses, and became aware of changed bodily functions and cycles through the laundry of clothes and bed linen. But it was because marital violence

---

[53] Tadmor, *Family and Friends*, chapters 1–2.
[54] See, for example, Gowing, *Domestic Dangers*, pp. 191–2, 246–8; and Turner, *Fashioning Adultery*, chapter 5.

was so often conducted in front of them, that it could not be ignored. The immediate and direct response of servants or other household employees could prevent or lessen the impact of violence. It was as a result of the intervention of one of Rachael Norcott's maidservants, for example, that her husband was stopped from striking her with a fire fork.[55] Servants also offered protection to wives with violent husbands by allowing them to sleep in their beds.[56] It was the talk of servants that could raise the alarm in the wider community. Despite instructions by conduct book writers to keep silent about the affairs of the households in which they worked, most servants could not resist gossiping about the marriages of their employers. The consequences could be dramatic, as demonstrated by a 1630 'riding', or loud public demonstration, which occurred when a maidservant told others of 'some difference' between her master and mistress. As we shall see below, this type of event could be triggered by marital violence instigated by husband or wife, but the result was the same. It brought marital violence to public notice and condemnation.[57]

Like family members, servants could find that intervening in violent marriages carried risks to their personal safety. When in October 1769, the Reverend John Jenkins locked all the doors of his house and started to beat his wife with a stick in front of the servants, one who tried to help his mistress was struck on the arm.[58] Servants employed in the household of John Harcourt told the magistrate, Richard Wyatt, in September 1774, that he had threatened that if anybody, 'gave assistance to his mistress he would run him through the body' with his knife.[59] Servants could, of course, be dismissed in a way that family members could not. When Mary Perkins and her fellow servant threatened to tell others that it was their master, not mistress, who had struck the first blow in a violent quarrel, they were both turned out of the house. Permitted to return, the two servants then found themselves used as a bargaining tool by their master. No doubt suspicious of their loyalty to him, he refused to sleep with his wife until she agreed to fire them both.[60]

But, as the master of Mary Perkins found when she testified against him in his marriage separation case, knowledge of marital violence gave

[55] LPL, CA, Case 6659 (1666), Eee2, f.97v–98r.
[56] See, for example, NA, DEL1/321 (1702), f.41r; for other examples of servants acting to protect their mistresses from violence see, Meldrum, *Domestic Service*, pp. 93–6.
[57] Griffiths, *Youth and Authority*, p. 171; Meldrum, *Domestic Service*, p. 50.
[58] LMA, DL/C/177 (1773), f.305r.
[59] E. Silverthorne (ed.), *Deposition Book of Richard Wyatt, JP, 1767–1776* Surrey Record Society, 30 (Guildford, 1978), p. 47.
[60] LPL, CA, Case 1049 (1716), Eee11, f.201r.

servants a position of power over their employers that the servants could relish. It was because marital violence was so frowned upon, that if they were witnesses to it, servants had the unusual opportunity of being the judges of the behaviour of their masters, rather than vice versa. Most left it until they were in the safety of the courtroom before they would openly condemn their employer's violence. Lady Huntingtower's maidservant declared to the Court of Arches, for example,

> if I had known before I entered Lady Huntingtower's service that she and Lord Huntingtower had not lived happily together, or that there was a chance of what afterwards occurred, or anything like it, no money should have induced me to enter it.[61]

But some were far bolder. George Whitmore was stunned when one of his servants, Ann Davis, not only prevented him from hurting his wife with a penknife, but, 'upbraiding' him, told him 'that he had best take care that his said wife came to no harm for that if she did that knife should appear in judgement against him if it was twenty years after'. It was reported that at this George was 'quite thunderstruck and so much confounded that he had not one word to say for himself'.[62] His violence to his wife had so undermined his position as head of his household, that his servants had become the voice of domestic order and morality.

As the new guardians of respectable domesticity, female servants pondered how they would have coped with being married to such violent husbands. The nurse who attended George Whitmore's wife, Mabell, after childbirth declared that, 'she would not have lived her life to have underwent such cruelties', and agreed with the Whitmore's washer-woman, who 'wondered how she could live so long with him'.[63] Some drew comparisons between the social status of themselves and their mistresses. Mary Veitch's cook believed that Dr Veitch, 'was a very violent man, I have a good spirit myself', she said, 'but I used always to be afraid of him'.[64] If a spirited working woman was intimidated by her master, how could her genteel and more sensitive mistress be expected to manage?

Believing that their servants and female apprentices were likely to be sympathetic, many wives took deliberate steps to show them their injuries.[65] Knowing that their servants could act as witnesses in courts of law against them, husbands tried in vain to prevent servants learning of their

---

[61] LPL, CA, Case 4915 (1837), H544/9.
[62] NA, DEL 1/559 (1752), f.457r–458r.
[63] NA, DEL 1/559 (1752), ff.346v, 354r.
[64] LPL, CA, Case 9440 (1837), H550/18.
[65] See, for example, LPL, CA, Case 4834 (1669), Eee3, f.237v.

violence. It was because Samuel Freeman told his wife's maidservant that, 'she had nothing to do betwixt man and wife', that she only saw the bruises and blood that were the consequences of his violence, rather than the blows that produced them.[66] Others went to greater lengths to hide their violence from their household. After Sir Cuthbert Shafto had dashed his wife's head against a marble slab, he burnt her bloody clothes, 'lest the servants should perceive the same'.[67] The role reversal of master and servant that began with marital violence, was completed once masters such as Shafto started acting surreptitiously even within their own homes.

Living and working in an atmosphere of marital violence was wearying and depressing. For young apprentices and servants, witnessing the marital violence of their employers could be very difficult. The nineteen-year-old apprentice, Joseph Willis, admitted that for the past three-and-a-half years he had been 'made very unhappy by the frequent wrangles and disputes' that occurred between his master and mistress.[68] Servants in the Prescott household in the early 1780s agreed that there was no 'peace or happiness' to be had while their master was so violent to his wife. They complained that 'they could get no sleep at nights' because of 'cries' of their mistress when she was being beaten. It was because of 'the constant noise and confusion' in the house, that a number of servants decided to quit.[69] The basis of their decision appears to have been a common one. The historian Tim Meldrum has found that the most common reason that London servants gave for their departure from their places was their employers' marital breakdown. In a period when there was a greater demand for servants than supply, servants could afford to take the moral high ground, because they knew that they could always find work in more congenial surroundings.[70]

Marital violence by their employers gave servants unique forms of authority, and numerous opportunities to act in non-servile ways. However, the families who employed them, and the courts who listened to their stories, rarely forgot the lowly social status of servants. Like children, the reliability of the words of servants could be questioned and doubted. Judge Scott regretted that in cases of marital discord, 'friends, dependants, and servants alone can speak', believing that, 'they must have some bias, and the Court must be on its guard against it'.

---

[66] NA, DEL 1/479 (1734), f.254–256.
[67] NA, DEL 1/678 (1800), f.230.
[68] NA, KB1/19 Part 1, East., 14 Geo.3 no. 2, affidavit of Joseph Willis (12 May 1774).
[69] LMA, DL/C/179 (1783), f.425r, DL/C/282 (1783), ff.308, 311, 332.
[70] Meldrum, *Domestic Service*, pp. 60, 121–2; see also, Bailey, 'Breaking the conjugal vows', p. 112.

The 'bias' of servants who were 'females', Scott explained, was that they 'naturally range themselves on the side of their own sex'. Servants, it was thought, knew little of the 'cause or commencement' of marital quarrels, and were prone to 'colour' their descriptions of what they did see or hear.[71] Reliant as they were upon the testimony of servants, this was a society that was reluctant to acknowledge that working-class people were often the watchmen and women of middle- and upper-class marriages.

The politics of household service were highlighted by marital violence for it could provoke new struggles for power within the household.[72] Since violence could lead to marriage separation and the disbandment of households, it could put the livelihoods of household employees at stake. Thus it was more than a principled opposition to violence that could motivate servants and other household employees to become involved. But the politics of the household were also complicated by the fact that violence within the home could have multiple perpetrators and targets. It needs to be remembered that this was a society that gave women as managers of households the authority to correct their servants and children physically. Wives could themselves have a history of being violent to members of their household and family, which could affect their position if they became the target of marital violence. Hannah Menham, for example, had already been brought twice before the JP, Edmund Tew, for assaulting her maidservants, before she then accused her husband of violence in March 1760.[73] Therefore, there was no necessary alliance between servants and their mistresses. As Scott recognised, servants would 'judge and speak according to their own supposed injuries'.[74] Household employees could be ready to condemn female as well as male violence. Hence when William Heathcote was accused of marital cruelty, he responded with the counter-claim that it was his wife who was violent and cruel, especially to their children. It was her violence, not his, he said, which had led to their servants giving 'warning to quit their places'.[75]

---

[71] *Waring v. Waring* (1813), *English Reports* vol. 161, p. 700; *Best v. Best* (1823), *English Reports* vol. 162, p. 149; *D'Aguilar v. D'Aguilar* (1794), *English Reports* vol. 162, p. 753; *Westmeath v. Westmeath* (1826), vol. 162, p. 1017; and *Dysart v. Dysart* (1847), *English Reports* vol. 163, p. 1105.

[72] For the politics of service see, K. Wrightson, 'The politics of the parish in early modern England', in P. Griffiths, A. Fox, and S. Hindle (eds.), *The Experience of Authority in Early Modern England* (Basingstoke, 1996), p. 17, and Capp, *When Gossips Meet*, chapter 4.

[73] Morgan and Rushton (eds.), *Justicing Notebook*, pp. 97, 103, 118.

[74] *Waring v. Waring* (1813), *English Reports* vol. 161, p. 700.

[75] NA, PCAP 3/1 (1834), f.217r.

It should also be recognised that servants and household employees could develop opinions, and conduct their own relationships in ways that supported rather than rejected marital violence. Henry Dean, a servant in the Dysart household, was said to so look up to his master, that he boasted to others, 'that if he had such a wife' as his mistress, he would 'do to her' what his master had only threatened to do.[76] Harriet Hanham objected to staying in Knowle House, Surrey, without her husband, because it meant living close to their gamekeeper, who had 'behaved in a brutal manner to his wife'.[77] So the family lives and violent experiences of household employees shaped not only the ways in which they responded to the violence of their employers, but could also affect how their employers related to them. In the violent household, complex patterns of relationships based on the differing age, gender, social and marital status of its inhabitants, as well as the many levels of authority, responsibility and duty that structured domestic arrangements, produced responses to marital violence that were varied and far from predictable.

Friends

Marital violence could form, cement and test friendship. In a period before the existence of professional counselling services, women turned to those who lived around them for consolation, advice and support. Revealing and sharing intimate knowledge of a marital relationship with others could be a way of gaining friends. As Meldrum comments, it would not be surprising, given that mistresses who were subject to marital violence could share sleeping spaces with their maidservants, if this contributed to friendship between mistress and maid.[78] Marital violence also tried existing friendships. The practical and financial support that friends offered could be of as much value as the emotional comfort they provided. Thus it was reported by one of Rachael Norcott's sisters that in the eight or nine months that her husband had refused to provide maintenance for her, Rachael had depended on her 'friends', who, 'out of charity', had helped to support her.[79] Despite their importance to her survival, Rachael's 'friends' remained nameless, and could have been drawn from a range of different personal networks. For in this

---

[76] *Oliver v. Oliver* (1801), *English Reports* vol. 161, p. 583.
[77] LPL, VH80/81/4 (1825).
[78] Meldrum, *Domestic Service*, p. 94.
[79] LPL, CA, Case 6659 (1666), Eee2, f.95v.

period the term 'friend' referred to a wide number of people who could
be kin, business partners, political allies, and even marriage partners.[80]

A case study of the friendships of Eleanor Redmain, who brought a
marriage separation case for cruelty to the Court of Arches in 1769, gives
us the opportunity to learn more fully what role friends could play when
marital relationships were in crisis. Eleanor married Roger in 1758, and
they lived in London where they kept a cheesemonger's shop. Roger
abused Eleanor verbally and physically, threatening to kill her, knocking
and kicking her, and pressing so hard against her chest that 'blood came
from her mouth and nose'. To escape from such savage treatment the
first place Eleanor fled to was the house of Mary Cooke, 'who had before
been her servant', where she stayed for two days. Eleanor then went to a
Mr Gee, who gave her refuge for two weeks, and at her encouragement,
'remonstrated' with Roger about his behaviour. Finding that her
husband was unapologetic, but that Mr Gee was not willing to house
her anymore, Eleanor was 'constrained by necessity to return again' to
her husband. He then beat her daily. Their business took a turn for the
worse, and Roger was imprisoned in the Fleet for debt. Refusing to
support her any longer, and 'being destitute', Eleanor then went to a
Mrs Sherron 'who had known her since childhood', where she lived
upon her charity for three months. As she found with Mr Gee, the
financial support of her friends could not last indefinitely, and once
again Eleanor was forced to return to her husband, this time joining
him in the King's Bench prison, where he had been transferred. After he
had forced her to pawn her clothes for his relief, Roger refused to have
anything more to do with Eleanor, so she 'applied to Mrs Harvey her
relation', and lodged in Holborn. Deciding that she could not 'subsist on
the charity of her friends' any longer, she became a servant in Romford,
Essex. Eleanor would not leave her position until Roger promised, on his
release from prison, to treat her kindly. It was 'by the charitable assistance of her friends' that they furnished a house, and with the loans of
money made by 'her friends' that they were able to set up a poulterer
shop. But Roger returned to his old ways, beating Eleanor when she was
unable to persuade her friends to lend them more money, and squan-
dering what they had on drink and gambling. Finding herself, 'in a
deplorable and starving condition', Eleanor applied to Thomas Bidwell,
who had been a friend to both of them, for a position. With his help,
Eleanor got employment in a milliner's shop, where she also lived, and
was able to earn enough to support herself and her husband. Roger
visited Eleanor one day in the shop, and went into a fit of rage when

---

[80] Tadmor, *Family and Friends*, chapter 5.

Bidwell refused to allow Eleanor to return to live with him, unless that was what she wanted. The fear and upset provoked by this incident left Eleanor, who was heavily pregnant, to suffer an agonising three weeks of labour, a premature birth, and the loss of her baby within the first month of its life. It was at this point that Eleanor exhibited articles of peace against her husband, and then sued him for cruelty in the church courts.[81]

During the eleven years of violence that she suffered from her husband, we know from Eleanor's account that she sought the help of at least five different friends. Of those she defined as the 'friends' who gave her 'charitable assistance', she included a servant, a family friend, and a 'relation'. Friends had been made through family and household connections, and Eleanor had both male and female friends to whom she could turn. Her friendships were expected to stand the test of time, hence one of Eleanor's friends dated back to her childhood. She was careful to distinguish between 'her' friends, and, for reasons that will become clear below, those like Bidwell, whom she had made with her husband. Friends served a variety of functions in this violent marriage. They offered refuge and maintenance, listened to Eleanor's stories of cruelty, and showed their trust in them by challenging her husband about his conduct, and trying to negotiate the terms by which she would return. Eleanor's friends invested money and effort in the Redmain marriage not only when she was forced to live apart from her husband, but also in her attempts to rebuild the marriage. They gave finance and found employment opportunities for Eleanor, presumably in the hope that they would give the marriage a more stable foundation.

The part that Eleanor's friends played in her marriage was similar to other women's experiences at this time.[82] During a woman's life cycle, friendships were remembered and revived, and, like other relationships, they could be based upon the exchange of both affection and finance or property. Eleanor was unlikely to have forgotten to repay what her friends had given her; evidence from women's wills shows that friends were often the beneficiaries of the most personal items that a woman owned.[83] Like their connections with their families, women's friendships endured and survived for a lifetime.

Of course, what Eleanor's friends failed to do was to prevent her husband's violence. Other wives believed that friends could serve this

---

[81] LPL, CA, Case 7578 (1769), D1727, f.76v–133r.
[82] For further examples see, LMA, DL/C/175 (1767), f.184v; LMA, DL/C/181 (1790), f.381r; and LMA, DL/C/184 (1794), f.527r; and Capp, *When Gossips Meet*, pp. 105–7.
[83] Berg, 'Women's consumption', 421, 423.

purpose, and that they could rely upon their friends for protection. It was at the 'request' of Elizabeth Blakemore that her neighbour, Ann Amies, was 'almost daily' at her house in Staffordshire, and frequently stayed the night, as Elizabeth hoped that this would stop her husband's violence.[84] Thus violence in marriage could give another meaning to the notion of a female companion. After her husband threatened to kill her with a knife in November 1797, Mary Biggs thought, 'it dangerous to remain in the house with her said husband without some friend', and so invited a Miss Catherine Ross to come and live with her. Catherine's own lack of marital experience, clearly did not deter Mary from believing that her presence would be helpful.[85]

It was in recognition of the strength and power of women's friendships, that husbands attempted to denigrate them. Fear that friends could rival and threaten their position of authority over women, meant that female friends of wives were often labelled as 'gossips'. Gossip was talk of marital affairs that men thought was inappropriate, critical and time wasting. A popular culture of ballads and stories that mocked female talk as mere gossip had long existed, and continued to flourish in this period.[86] A result could be that women such as Elizabeth Jessop were forced to deny that they had ever talked to others about their treatment by their husbands, arguing that they had instead borne cruelties alone and with a patient resignation.[87]

But jealousy of women's friendships could also have more serious consequences. Roger Redmain was so angered by Thomas Bidwell's interference in his marriage that he sued him in two courts of law for debt, and argued that he was 'the supporter and encourager' of Eleanor's separation case against him. He went even further and accused his wife of adultery with Thomas, bringing a successful action for 'criminal conversation' against Thomas in the Court of Common Pleas. Whereas Eleanor denied ever committing adultery with Thomas, arguing that she, 'always considered him in the light of a father and protector', her husband could not tolerate her dependency upon another man. In his eyes, the basis of such a friendship had to be sex. That of all her friends Eleanor chose to remain the longest with a male friend opened her to accusations of misconduct that detracted from her husband's violence. The result of the criminal conversation case showed how difficult it was

---

[84] LPL, CA, Case 946 (1720), Eee12, f.84.

[85] LMA, DL/C/182 (1798), f.171r.

[86] See, for example, Foyster, *Manhood in Early Modern England*, pp. 58–65; 'Faults on both sides', Madden vol. 8, 256; and 'A man that is married', Baring-Gould vol. 4., 346.

[87] LPL, CA, Case 5089 (1717), Ee9, 15/5.

for a married woman to resort to the help of another man without raising suspicion.[88]

Aware of how women's friends could challenge their position and question their right to use violence against their wives, some husbands attempted to confine their wives within their homes. Domestic confinement aimed to isolate a wife from support by restricting the number of friends or family with whom she had contact. Hence Elizabeth Jessop countered her husband's accusations of gossip by stating that it had not been 'in her power' to tell others about her husband's violence. This was because he had not allowed her any visitors, or for her to visit others, 'for some years' before she left him.[89] Lawyers argued that husbands had a right to confine their wives in their homes, when their wives' behaviour had been 'gross' or 'extravagant'. But in a period when social visits and paying hospitality were such important markers of polite (and hence elite) status, husbands could find that domestic confinement could backfire. Their attempts to socially isolate their wives could be used as evidence of cruelty in marriage separation suits, and friends could challenge confinement by directing writs of habeas corpus against them. The domestic confinement of wives was more likely to be condemned than condoned. For example, Elizabeth Heathcote could expect sympathy when she related that after her marriage in 1820 her husband kept her in confinement, refusing to allow her 'to receive any visitors at the house, or to visit any of the neighbouring families, and would not permit her to go to the parish church, in order to prevent her from becoming acquainted with the neighbouring families'. A servant in the Dysart household added to her mistress's accusations of marital cruelty by claiming that the earl, 'did debar Lady Dysart of society; I heard him tell her ladyship that he would not have a pack of people coming there after her', ordering that all visitors should be told that his wife was 'not at home', if they called.[90]

Most husbands did all they could to avoid being accused of such behaviour. Richard Alchorn, for example, rigorously denied ever locking or restraining his wife in their chamber after she had called him names and 'bid him kiss her breech' in front of his mother-in-law. At a time when there was considerable national pride in the freedoms afforded to

---

[88] LPL, CA, Case 7578 (1769), D1727, ff.142v–150, 190–193r, 244–250r, 271v–272r.
[89] LPL, CA, Case 5089 (1717), Ee9, 15/5.
[90] NA, PCAP, 3/1 (1834), f.213v; *Dysart v. Dysart* (1847), *English Reports*, vol. 163, p. 1118; for domestic confinement see, Foyster, 'At the limits of liberty', and 'Creating a veil of silence?'; for the importance of visits and hospitality see, S. E. Whyman, *Sociability and Power in Late-Stuart England: The Cultural World of the Verneys 1660–1720* (Oxford, 1999), chapter 4, and Vickery, *Gentleman's Daughter*, chapter 6.

English women, it was damaging to a man's reputation to be seen to be limiting his wife's liberties.[91] The majority of husbands who relied upon the labour of their wives could not afford to confine their wives for any period of time anyway. When marriages broke down, wives from the middling ranks of society, such as Elizabeth Heathcote, claimed a right to make friends, and women like Lady Dysart fought to keep them. It is no wonder that friendships were so closely guarded when friends could be such a vital part of the network of support for the wife in a violent marriage.

Violence and the community

As evidence of how violence became privatised over the eighteenth century, Shoemaker has argued that in London a profound change occurred in the relationship between the individual and the community. London life was not anonymous, he admits, but by the end of the eighteenth century people 'did not know their neighbours or take an interest in their activities as much as they had used to'. Domestic violence was pushed behind closed doors.[92] This section contends that in London, and elsewhere, there is little proof of a decline in the willingness of communities to intervene in marital violence. Indeed there is far more material to demonstrate that in our period repeated attempts to expose and shame men who were violent to their wives meant that marital violence had no hiding place.

Intervention in marital violence did not always have to be invited, and those who became involved were not necessarily the family or friends of the married couple. Instead, Restoration to Victorian society was one in which neighbours played an active part observing and regulating each other's marriages, and one where even strangers to a married couple could become embroiled in their violent quarrels. As we shall see, intervention was usually individual and spontaneous, but could become a group activity that was semi-organised. An occasion of marital violence was a time when neighbours made judgements that could determine the nature of a couple's future social interaction, as well as their marital relations. It sometimes marked the moment when mere neighbours became friends. But it could also lead to a social distancing between a married couple and their neighbours. While few people wished to include husbands who were violent to their wives within their communities, they could also be reluctant to support women who had

---

[91] LPL, VH80/1/7 (1686); Langford, *Englishness Identified*, pp. 271–3.
[92] Shoemaker, *The London Mob*, p. 296, and 'The decline of public insult', 98, 126.

separated from their husbands on this basis. Violent men could be expelled from communities, but this still left little place for the women who had been their targets. If communities were neighbourhoods with a shared identity and values, they were not places that readily harboured and tolerated either the perpetrators or victims of marital violence over the long term.

Neighbours (defined here as those who lived in close physical proximity to a married couple) were often described as intervening when husbands were violent to their wives. Elizabeth Ball told the Court of Arches in 1663 that her mother used to go and knock on the door of John Bradley's house in Westminster, and 'call upon him to forbear beating his wife', whenever she heard her cries. John threatened this neighbour, but she escaped lightly compared to another, who was struck by him 'for interposing'.[93]

The reputation of a couple in their community could be crucial in determining how their neighbours responded if they experienced marriage difficulties. Numerous neighbours spoke for Mary Holford when she brought a case for marital cruelty against her husband, Thomas, in 1690. The fact that she had always behaved 'civilly' amongst her neighbours in Lindfield, Sussex, was contrasted with the uncivil conduct of her husband, who was described as being violent and bad tempered with his neighbours as well as his wife. Marital violence had bound Mary closer to her neighbours, whereas it had alienated her husband from them. 'If it was not for the kindness of her friends', said one female neighbour about Mary, she 'would have been in great need since she left her husband'. Disapproval of marital violence united Mary's neighbours into a moral community that offered emotional as well as practical support.[94]

The history of Thomas Holford's behaviour towards his neighbours condemned him in their eyes when his wife accused him of violence. Similarly, it was when Nathan Fernandez was 'unable to bring forward a single person to say anything in his favour', after he was charged with assaulting his wife in 1856, that the magistrate in the Thames police court concluded that Nathan was deserving of a punishment of six months hard labour in the House of Correction. Even by this late date, judgement by community reputation was still important.[95] Marital violence could be seen as extension of other forms of disorder: it was not surprising to learn that a man had been violent to his wife when he

---

[93] LPL, CA, Case 1127 (1663), Eee1, ff.56v, 62v.
[94] LPL, CA, Case 4688 (1690), Eee7, f.110v–128r.
[95] *The Times* (30 January 1856) 11d.

already had a reputation of being a difficult neighbour. Nearly 38 percent of violent husbands in Portsmouth between 1696 and 1781 had also
been reported to the town's magistrates for assaulting a non-family
member. Demonstrably, and in practice, there could be no clear division
between public and private life.[96] Furthermore, in a period when scolds
were defined as women who had caused problems for their neighbours as
well as their husbands, women's violence could be subject to the same
kinds of collective scrutiny. It was because Margaret Granfield was
'a very contentious and troublesome woman', who had assaulted parish
officers in Rettendon in 1646, that her neighbours concluded that she
controlled her husband and 'ruled the roost' in her household.[97]

It was in part because marital violence so often took place outside the
home that it was difficult for others to avoid. Women could be subject to
violence from their husbands in drinking places, streets, alleys and
backyards, markets and shops. Popular condemnation of marital violence meant that when it was conducted so blatantly, it could attract the
attention of crowds, rather than just individuals. When Thomas Bates, a
firesmith, started beating his wife in a public house near St Paul's in
London, and then dragged her along a street, striking her as he went
along, 'a great mob or tumult' gathered around them.[98] More than a
hundred years later, marital violence could still draw a crowd. In July
1851 while they were visiting London from their home in Deal, Kent,
George Wilkinson abused his wife, and held up his stick to threaten her
in the High Road near Kennington church. Even though they were
probably strangers to most of those living nearby, a crowd of people
came to the scene.[99]

Many members of crowds were more than onlookers to violence. They
could voice their disapproval, such as 'several persons' who gathered
beneath the window of Emily Jane Hart's house in the mid-nineteenth
century, and cried 'shame' at her husband who was beating her
within.[100] Outrage at marital violence could also develop into more
organised displays and protests, known as charivaris, ridings or rough
music. These loud, mocking rituals were intended to shame individuals
who had offended community norms, and were forms of popular justice.

---

[96] Warner and Lunny, 'Marital violence in a martial town', 264.
[97] As cited in J. A. Sharpe, *Crime in Seventeenth-Century England: A County Study* (Cambridge, 1983), p. 120, spellings have been modernised; for scolds see, M. Ingram,
'"Scolding women cucked or washed": a crisis of gender relations in early modern
England?', in J. Kermode and G. Walker (eds.), *Women, Crime and the Courts in Early
Modern England* (London, 1994), pp. 48–80.
[98] LPL, VH80/31/12 (1743).
[99] LPL, CA, Case 9986 (1851), H792/2.
[100] LPL, CA, Case 4282 (1853), H826/5.

E. P. Thompson's original suggestion that evidence of a change in the targets of charivaris, from the termagant wife in the seventeenth century to the violent husband in the nineteenth century, demonstrated a shift of attitudes towards marital violence, has rightly been questioned.[101] Instead, across the period, both violent husbands and wives were subject to charivaris. For example, in 1667 a notorious wife-beater, William Bullocke, was forced to take shelter 'to avoid the fury of the people' in Bristol when they pelted him with dirt as he walked through the streets.[102] William's fate was similar to that of Patrick Kirby, 'a ruffianly-looking Irishman', who nearly two hundred years later, charged with assaulting his wife, was 'followed by a crowd of at least 200 persons, who pelted him with mud, and yelled at him in the most discordant manner', as he was taken to the Marylebone police courts in 1836.[103] The law in these cases acted as a supplement, rather than an alternative to community forms of punishment. So it was when a violent husband from Islington in 1748 was being transported from a JP to prison that he was subjected to a charivari of 'peltings, hissings and blows of two thirds of the women in the town'.[104] Charivaris were also enacted when wifely violence was the issue. In 1827 it was reported that a cotton spinner from Hyde had tried to stop a riding in which a crowd sang a mocking rhyme that drew attention to the root of his shame;

> Tink of a kettle, tank of a pan,
> This brassy faced woman has beaten her man,
> Neither with sword, dagger or knife
> But with an old shuttle she'd have taken his life.[105]

Significantly, not all husband- or wife-beaters were targeted by charivari. Hence historians should be hesitant about using the evidence of charivari to prove any general or universal popular condemnation of marital violence.[106] Of course, charivaris did not happen every day, and it appears that they were provoked by a particular set of circumstances. Marital violence needed to be widely known, repeated over a period of time, or have reached extreme levels. It helped if the offender was also an unpopular member of a neighbourhood, and bore the appearance of a wife-beater, as was suggested by the 'ruffianly-looking'

---

[101] E. P. Thompson, *Customs in Common* (London, 1991), chapter 8; for commentary upon Thompson's thesis see, Hammerton, *Cruelty and Companionship*, pp. 15–21.
[102] LPL, CA, Case 1432 (1667), Eee2, f.538–40; for discussion of this case see, Foyster, 'Male honour, social control and wife beating', 222–3.
[103] *The Times* (16 August 1836) 6e.
[104] *The Bath Journal* (11 July 1748).
[105] As cited in, Clark, *The Struggle for the Breeches*, p. 84.
[106] Hammerton, *Cruelty and Companionship*, pp. 18–19.

Patrick Kirby. All these particulars were met in the case of Mary and James Page in 1824. James was infamously violent to his wife. Mary had a 'spotless character' in the village of Cheesehill, near Winchester, but James, who worked as a bargeman, was known to ill-treat his wife, and attracted a crowd on one occasion when he beat her at a public fair. Mary showed others a 'large knotty faggot stick', which she claimed her husband used to hit her, and was forced to call a surgeon when James beat her while she was pregnant. On 16 October 1824, after just eight months of marriage, James hit her so severely on the head that she gave birth to a still-born child, and Mary died less than two weeks later. As the *Hampshire Telegraph* reported,

When the corpse was removed from the house in which the unfortunate woman died, the utmost confusion took place: a mob of women assembled round the cart, and with every mark of anger and disgust, protested against the removal of the body, of which they openly declared James Page, her late husband, to be the murderer![107]

The pressure for justice to be done came too late for Mary Page. We are left with the question of why neighbours delayed intervening in such cases, even though they clearly disapproved of marital violence? We have to turn to other cases for answers. First, there is the straightforward explanation that violent husbands could make violent and threatening neighbours. Some were simply too afraid to take steps to interfere in their neighbours' marital quarrels. The numerous occasions when the violence of husbands turned to others was enough to demonstrate the physical dangers of intervention.

Second, intervention was not always forthcoming if a husband could represent his violence as legitimate correction. An alewife in 1752 described how a crowd of over a hundred people gathered outside her establishment when George Whitmore was beating his wife inside. She believed that they would, 'certainly have rescued Mrs Whitmore out of the clutches of her husband . . . but that as it was the case of a man and his wife and he had given out she had robbed him they all forbore to intermeddle hoping he would take her home with him quietly'.[108] Although George Whitmore's behaviour was enough to cause a disturbance, his pretence that his wife had done him wrong, meant that nobody would prevent him from exercising his right to correct his wife. Instead they just hoped the problem would go away.

Tragically, for women such as Mary Page, at a time when men were popularly believed to have a right to beat their wives, even if there was

---

[107] As reported in *The Times* (8 November 1824) 3 d–e.
[108] NA, DEL1/559 (1752), f.590v–591r.

pressure on husbands to find other means to correct their wives and settle their disputes, the price could be toleration of marital violence. Richard Donellan and his wife were known to live 'very unhappily together' in Brompton, Kent, but in September 1818 when a neighbour heard the noise of a person being strangled, and a child crying out, "Oh! What are you going to do with mammy?", nobody took any notice because, 'occurrences of this kind . . . were so common'. The strangled body of Richard's wife was later found dumped in a well.[109] Similar apathy in 1855 affected the neighbours of a wife from Spitalfields who was known to be 'constantly quarrelling' with her husband. Both parties in this case were renowned for their 'brutal violence towards each other', so that when one neighbour, the labourer John Davis, heard the wife cry in the night, he did not get up 'because it was a frequent practice for the deceased to cry 'Murder' when having a row with her husband'.[110] Fatefully, this wife had cried wolf once too often.

However, while the conduct of neighbours could act to condone marital violence, they were normally not willing to be so acquiescent if they thought that violence had reached a lethal potential. Elizabeth Shott reported in 1663 that her husband, who was a constable, refused to respond to a neighbour's request to go and 'part' John and Cecily Bradley, who were fighting, 'because they were man and wife'.[111] Over a century-and-a-half later a Stockport watchman was tempted to behave in the same way when he believed that the noise and shrieks he had detected were simply 'somebody beating a woman'. But as he was leaving the scene he heard a cry of 'murder', which persuaded him to investigate further. Thus even tolerance of marital violence had its limits.[112] As Scott proudly asserted in his judgement on one 1801 London case of alleged marital violence, 'every body knows that, in this great town, a prompt assistance would be given to a wife calling upon their humanity for protection from a husband's attempt to murder'.[113]

While a wife could expect this minimum level of support, we have seen that in practice many received far more. The kindness of strangers is worth noting. In the space of two weeks in 1856, *The Times* recorded the charity of two anonymous donors to four wives whose cases of assault by their husbands had been formerly reported in the newspaper. 'F. H. S.', for example, gave five shillings' worth of stamps 'for the use of Ann Reid, the poor woman who was so brutally ill-treated by her

[109] *The Times* (13 March 1823) 3c.
[110] *The Times* (21 September 1855) 4f.
[111] LPL, CA, Case 1127 (1663), Eee1, f.80v.
[112] *The Times* (9 August 1832) 4d.
[113] *Oliver v. Oliver* (1801), *English Reports* vol. 161, p. 585.

husband'. The other donor gave generous cash gifts.[114] Clearly, instances of marital violence could produce pity and empathy on the part
of others; during the same year the story of Matilda Fernandez's sufferings at the hands of her husband, for example, was said to have 'excited
great commiseration in a crowded court'.[115]

But it often took more than sympathy and altruism for the neighbours
of wives subject to violence to intervene. As we have seen, violent
husbands frequently made poor neighbours, and the disorder caused
by marital violence spilled out beyond the boundaries of the household.
The mere noise of marital violence could be sufficiently aggravating to
motivate action against it. In the sixteenth century, a London bye-law
had forbidden wife-beating after 9 pm because its noise disturbed inhabitants. That steps could be taken to restrict marital violence, because it
was defined as disturbing the public peace, shows that it was recognised
as an act that had consequences for more than simply the married
couple. A 'respectable' neighbourhood was one where relations between
husbands and wives were quiet and orderly. In addition, throughout the
period of this book, ideals of 'good neighbourliness' encouraged others
to make a stand against excessive marital violence. In so doing, members
of a community established and reinforced limits of acceptable behaviour for their own personal relationships as well as other married
couples. Thus, as Bernard Capp observed astutely, 'compassion and
self-interest pulled in the same direction'.[116]

The motivation to become involved in the personal lives of others
could cease at the point of marriage separation. We have already seen
how separated women had no easy position to assume in family life. In
practice, separated wives and husbands could form new households
that were structured differently from those inhabited by nuclear families.
We know that separated women sometimes joined the households of
widowed parents, and that their husbands could appoint female servants
or relatives as 'surrogate' wives who would carry out the female tasks of
household management and childcare for them. Economic survival was
possible under these conditions.[117] But for women, marriage separation
could also mean social ostracism. As Wollstonecraft explained in her
unfinished novel, *The Wrongs of Woman: Or, Maria* (1798):

---

[114] *The Times* (23 January 1856) 11f; (25 January 1856) 9e; (5 February 1856) 9f.
[115] *The Times* (30 January 1856) 11d.
[116] Capp, *When Gossips Meet*, pp. 106, 107; S. Mendelson and P. Crawford, *Women in Early Modern England* (Oxford, 1998), p. 128. For the origins of the ideal of 'neigh-bourliness', see, K. Wrightson, *Earthly Necessities: Economic Lives in Early Modern Britain* (London, 2000), p. 75.
[117] Bailey, *Unquiet Lives*, pp. 179–80.

The situation of a woman separated from her husband, is undoubtedly very different from that of a man who has left his wife. He, with lordly dignity, has shaken off a clog; and the allowing her food and raiment, is thought sufficient to secure his reputation from taint. And, should she have been inconsiderate, he will be celebrated for his generosity and forbearance. Such is the respect paid to the master-key of property! A woman, on the contrary, resigning what is termed her natural protector (though he never was so, but in name) is despised and shunned, for asserting the independence of mind distinctive of a rational being, and spurning at slavery.[118]

Limited evidence suggests that Wollstonecraft's depiction of life after separation was not exaggerated. When reform in the law on divorce was debated in parliament during 1856, Lord Lyndhurst argued that there was an urgent need to address the position of the separated wife. From the moment that a legal separation was granted, he said,

the wife is almost in a state of outlawry. She may not enter into a contract, or, if she does, she has no means of enforcing it. The law, so far from protecting, oppresses her. She is homeless, helpless, hopeless, and almost wholly destitute of civil rights.[119]

Lyndhurst had probably been influenced by his friend, Caroline Norton, who wrote with experience about 'the unnatural position of a separated wife'. While her campaigns for divorce reform focused upon the child custody and property rights of separated women, her descriptions of her own life story included accounts of suffering on a more personal level. In these writings the loneliness and misery of her position is acute:

My husband is welcome to the triumph of knowing, that, through the long years of our separation . . . I wavered and wept . . . that there have been hundreds of dreary evenings, and hopeless mornings, when even his home seemed to me better than no home.

Even for the strident Norton, a house was only a home when it was inhabited by a married couple. Her social interaction with others had been affected by her marriage break-up, and left her in the unenviable category of the 'separated wife':

it is impossible to have felt more keenly than I did, the confused degradation of that position; not in the society where I am received (least there, because there my story was best known), but in other classes, which I have said I do not less respect.[120]

---

[118] M. Wollstonecraft, *The Wrongs of Woman: Or, Maria* (1798), ed. G. Kelly (Oxford, 1998), pp. 157–8.
[119] *Hansard*, vol. 141 (20 May 1856), 410.
[120] Norton, *English Laws for Women*, p. 140.

Norton cared about how she was regarded by individuals in classes other than her own, perhaps because as a separated woman she feared that she would not be afforded the degree of deference and consideration that a married woman could normally expect from those beneath her on the social scale. She assumed that familiarity with her circumstances would bring understanding and sympathy from members of her own social set. But this could not be taken for granted. Elizabeth Shackleton, an eighteenth-century gentleman's daughter, was deeply unhappy in her marriage to her second husband, who was violent and drunken. However, this did not make her anymore sympathetic towards an old friend, Mrs Knowles, who separated from 'her Drunken Hog' of a husband because of his cruelty in 1779. According to Vickery, the historian who has studied Elizabeth's diaries and letters, Elizabeth treated Mrs Knowles 'as an outlaw', suggesting that she saw marriage separation as 'social suicide'. For Elizabeth, marriage breakdown so unsettled and dislocated her relationship with Mrs Knowles, that continuing this friendship on the same basis was an impossibility.[121] Much of this chapter has shown how wives who were subject to violence from their husbands were not alone: they were surrounded by family, servants, friends and neighbours who listened to their woes and helped to ease their pain when they could. Instead, evidence suggests that loneliness could be the fate of the wife who no longer lived with her violent and cruel husband, and that it could be other women who were the agents of social ostracism.

The position of the separated husband was very different from that of his wife. Although the reputation of being a violent man within marriage was personally disadvantageous, the subsequent social status of a man whose marriage had broken down on this basis appears to have been little affected. Knowing that his sister, Dame Margaret, was unhappily married to Sir Thomas Elmes, partly because of Sir Thomas' violence to her, did not prevent Sir Ralph Verney from inviting his brother-in-law to a family gathering at his house in 1653. It was Sir Thomas' decision to excuse himself from this social circle. Replying to Sir Ralph's invitation, Sir Thomas wrote, 'Your sister and myself do live so unlovingly together that I have no heart to come to her friends; neither do I like to have my friends come to me, lest they should take notice of her unkindness to me'. The couple would eventually separate, but Sir Thomas' social isolation seems to have been entirely voluntary and self-imposed.[122] In this context, husbands such as Gwynn Vaughan,

---

[121] Vickery, *The Gentleman's Daughter*, p. 76.
[122] As cited in, J. T. Cliffe, *The World of the Country House in Seventeenth-Century England* (London, 1999), p. 77; spellings have been modernised.

who responded to his wife's request for separation in 1777 by telling her that, 'she might go if she would that his character was established and that she was the party who would suffer not he', were justly confident of their position.[123] Indeed, the damage of marriage separation to violent husbands was generally conceived of in financial terms. It was the fear of the cost of paying alimony to their former wives, rather than their social position as separated husbands that could trouble them.[124]

It is significant that most of the material we have about neighbourhood involvement in violent marriages relates to the lives of working men and women, and that concerns about the social consequences of marriage separation were mainly voiced by women from the middling and upper social ranks. Of course, the social elite were arguably those who could most afford to be taxed by questions of social reputation, whereas a greater problem facing wives from the lower classes was economic survival following marriage separation. B. Seebohm Rowntree's survey of the poor in York at the end of the nineteenth century, for example, revealed that of the 15.63 percent of households below the poverty line, there were fourteen cases of women who had been separated or deserted by their husbands.[125] Yet records of marriage separation following violence also tell us about how people in the past defined 'community', and suggest that this may have differed according to social status.

Communities were collections of people who shared similar ideas and values. They thus had a moral identity, as well as any social function. In cases of marital violence, for intervention to be most effective, there had to be a degree of consensus within a community about the acceptability, or otherwise, of violence in married life. Importantly for the women who were subject to marital violence, our records reveal that membership of communities varied with social class. We have seen from occasions of intervention and sanction that working wives had those who lived nearby, both strangers and friends, as well as family, as members of their communities. Their definition and experience of community was one that was generally local and geographically confined, and depended upon interaction at a personal level. Community was closely related to neighbourhood.

In contrast, the social networks that made up the communities of middling- and upper-class women, only included neighbours if they

---

[123] LMA, DL/C/178 (1777), f.778v.
[124] See, for example, LPL, CA, Case 2391 (1667), Eee2, f.297r.
[125] As cited in, S. O. Rose, 'Widowhood and poverty in nineteenth-century Nottinghamshire', in J. Henderson and R. Wall (eds.), *Poor Women and Children in the European Past* (London, 1994), pp. 269, 287n.

were already established friends. Their communities were based upon family and friends who were of the same social status, and members of their household, chiefly their servants. It may be that their superior social status acted as a barrier to the more spontaneous intervention by neighbours experienced by women suffering marital violence lower down the social scale. Furthermore, the continuing importance of reputation meant that elite communities did not have to be defined by physical space: they could consist of the amorphous body of people known as polite or fashionable 'society'. Consciousness of belonging to this type of community meant that the marital and extra-marital behaviour of middling- and upper-class couples could be influenced by their perceptions of the attitudes of people they had never even met. When the marriage between Henrietta and Charles Howard broke down in the early eighteenth century, for example, both parties appealed to the opinion of "the world" (by which they meant both their immediate and wider social circle) to defend their actions.[126] Marital life was conducted, and decisions were made relating to it, in the stifling and restrictive atmosphere of manners and social expectations. This could act to seriously limit the ability of middle- and upper-class women to continue the same types of social interaction, and even remain members of their communities if they were forced to leave their husbands. Thus, the composition of communities did not vary over time, but according to social class.

Conclusion

Marital violence began as a struggle between two people, but it was rarely possible to contain its effects within the family and household. Community intervention was not guaranteed, but the factors that governed and limited it were not related to a lack of knowledge or concern about the married lives of others which increased over time. Families did not become more private as our period progressed. Indeed, even beyond the mid-nineteenth century, as for example Carolyn A. Conley has shown for the period 1859–80, local communities continued to be important in setting the 'values and priorities' for dealing with domestic violence.[127] What began to change by the mid-nineteenth century, as the next chapter will show, was who *within* communities was thought most responsible for dealing with the consequences of marital violence.

[126] Tague, 'Love, honor, and obedience', 102–3.
[127] Conley, *The Unwritten Law*, passim.

5   The origins of professional responses

This chapter suggests that it was the innovations of this period that began the long-term shift in popular responses to dealing with marital violence. The introduction of the 'new police' under Sir Robert Peel, the 'professionalisation' of medicine, and legislation that increased the powers of magistrates, occasionally brought practical benefits for wives with violent husbands, but more importantly they started a process of change in which responsibility for dealing with marital violence was adjusted. By the mid-nineteenth century it was becoming possible to designate marital violence as a matter that might be dealt with by the police, doctors or magistrates, rather than solely by the informal intervention of those who were related or lived nearest to the woman affected. We see only the seeds of change within the period covered by this book, not their full development. 'Amateur' assistance for wives remained important, and was never wholly replaced by the professionals. Furthermore, change was far from uniform; it was Rachael Norcott, not Mary Veitch who had as one of her witnesses a surgeon who previously treated her injuries. Nevertheless, the groundwork had been laid, and in the future it would be third parties who would be left to manage the effects of marital violence.

The period between the Restoration and the mid-nineteenth century was one of transition in the development of the professions.[1] During this period, clergymen, parish and poor law officials, constables, JPs, the police and medical practitioners were not seen as 'outsiders'. They usually resided near to the women who sought their help, and so they were members of the communities they served. As the neighbours of women who were being subjected to marital violence, it was logical that they would be called upon for assistance. In this chapter we will see that these professionals played an important part reconciling quarrelling

---

[1] For the professions in this period see, W. Prest (ed.), *The Professions in Early Modern England* (Beckenham, 1987); and P. J. Corfield, *Power and the Professions in Britain 1700–1850* (London, 1995).

couples and dealing with the consequences of marital violence, but that before the systematic recording of these interventions, the most successful endeavours by professionals could remain hidden from view. The limitations of the professions in this early period will also become clear, in particular their failure to build a body of information containing advice about the best ways to tackle the problem of marital violence. In our period this hindered the extent to which professional interventions were afforded additional value, and prevented the wholesale transferral of obligation to cope with the aftermath of marital violence from ordinary individuals to those with specialist knowledge and skills.

Clergymen

Clergymen had long been consulted for advice and to act as intermediaries and mediators at times of marital discord. Protestant clergy were often married themselves, and so could have personal experience of the trials and challenges of married life. It was clergymen who had been the authors of the first domestic conduct books that prescribed how couples should order their marriages, and most opposed violence in marriage, whatever the circumstances. Despite the post Restoration diversity of religious views, and the growth of Protestant Nonconformity, there is no evidence of a difference of attitudes among Protestants about marital violence.

Visiting parishioners, and when necessary helping them to overcome their differences was considered an essential part of the diverse role of clergymen. The visitation charges of bishops to their clergy, and instruction books written specifically for them, taught that this form of pastoral work was inseparable from their spiritual duties. Indeed, when a minister was ordained, he promised to maintain 'quietness, peace and love among all Christian people'.[2] Subsequently it was thought important ministers learned that it was only by going to parishioners in their own homes, and seeing how they conducted their lives, that they could gain a true picture of the spiritual needs of their flock. Counselling parishioners 'endears you to the People', lectured one eighteenth-century bishop.[3] The prosecution of the curate John Turner in 1706 by his church court

---

[2] *Directions given by Edmund Lord Bishop of London to the Clergy of his Diocese, in the year 1724* (London, 1724), pp. 21–4; see also, G. Herbert, *A Priest to the Temple or the Country Parson* (1652) ed. R. Blythe (Norwich, 2003), pp. 34, 38, 40–1; W. Jesse, *Parochialia; Or Observations on the Discharge of Parochial Duties* (Kidderminster, 1785); A. Oxenden, *The Pastoral Office: Its Duties, Difficulties, Privileges and Prospects* (London, 1857), p. 166; A. Russell, *The Clerical Profession* (London, 1984), chapter 8.

[3] *Directions given by Edmund*, p. 24.

for breeding 'strife and sedition amongst your neighbours and very often between man and wife by advising them to part from one another (whereas by your holy office you should be a peace maker . . .)', shows that ministers could expect to be reprimanded if they did otherwise.[4]

Quite aside from any requirement of their post to become involved, the reaction of some clergy makes it clear that it was personal conviction that compelled them to do so. Their belief that marital violence was an affront to the sanctity of marriage meant that occasionally they could not resist the opportunity of taking the moral high ground. We have seen how one minister preached at a dinner to his daughter and son-in-law about 'the deserts of a man who used his wife ill', when he suspected violence in their marriage.[5] Others challenged violent husbands more directly. The Dublin minister Henry Elphin went to speak with his next-door-neighbour, Jacob Bor, on the morning after Jacob's wife had sought shelter with him from Jacob's violence. Henry later remembered how he 'expostulated with him of the ill usage of his wife', telling Jacob 'how inconsistent' his behaviour to his wife was to 'the relation he bore to her, and the vow and covenant betwixt them made'. When this scolding made no impact, Henry tried a thinly veiled threat, telling Jacob that 'as yet' the matter was only known to Henry and Jacob's families, 'and if he pleased it need not go any further', but that if he was not reconciled with his wife, 'the whole town would ring of it'. Desperate to impress upon Jacob the seriousness of his actions, Henry was prepared to compromise any obligation to confidentiality that others may have expected him to assume. But Jacob responded that 'he did not care' who knew of his disagreements with his wife. Unable to convince Jacob of his wrong Henry left with the words 'God be with you, and restore you to a better mind'.[6]

As Henry found, the marital problems of parishioners were not easily resolved. To many clergy, responding to appeals for help from women who were subject to marital violence presented some of the most difficult and challenging work required from them. Henry Newcome recorded his meetings with a Mrs Holden, who had 'sore troubles with her husband', in his diary in February 1662. The entries are fairly cryptic, and it appears that there may have been issues of contention between Newcome and Mr Holden before she made complaint to him. A letter written by Newcome to Mr Holden, 'upon his own provocation of me

---

[4] As cited in Bailey, *Unquiet Lives*, p. 35.
[5] LMA, DL/C/179 (1783), f.410v.
[6] NA, DEL1/364 (1721), f.4–8r.

. . . about a case of the husband's authority over the wife', seems to have only made matters worse. When Mrs Holden did not attend church, Newcome concluded that, 'her husband out of rage unto me' had prevented her from coming, and 'hindered' her 'from her liberty'. 'Poor creature, she may find much affliction in it', he wrote. According to Newcome, it was only a subsequent but provident bout of pleurisy that brought Mr Holden to see the error of his ways.[7]

For other clerics, experience had taught them that it was sometimes more prudent to try and avoid becoming involved in the first place. When compared to the account given by her clergyman husband, the story related by Mary Haggitt in April 1825 describing the part that he played in the marriage of Eliza and William Carmichael Smyth, is very revealing. Mary had known William since they had attended the same school in their childhood. It was Mary's husband, the Reverend D'Arcy Haggitt, who had married William and Eliza, so when she heard that William had wrongfully confined Eliza in a private madhouse, she was 'greatly astonished and distressed'. Significantly, Mary had long been 'aware of their disagreements and quarrels', but had done nothing, for 'she could not have supposed it would have come to such a pitch as that'. But sending a wife to a madhouse was a step too far. She was 'very anxious to do something instantly', but according to Mary, her husband's response was different. In Mary's words, 'her husband felt reluctant to allow her to interfere, by reason that they had both had a good deal of trouble and anxiety on account of previous disturbances', and besides, he was then already engaged in some other of his duties. But Mary would not be discouraged, for she 'felt so strongly the miserable situation' in which Eliza was placed, 'and considered it her duty' to do something, especially as she believed that Eliza had appealed to her 'as a friend to interfere'. 'Pressing' upon her husband, he at last agreed to let her go to Bow Street and begin the proceedings by which a writ of habeas corpus would be issued to those who were confining Eliza.

Reverend Haggitt's statement was perhaps unsurprisingly different from that of his wife. He portrayed himself as very much a man of action, responding immediately to news of Eliza's confinement. As soon as he heard that she was detained he set off to visit the madhouse, 'determined to do anything that may lay in his power to affect her release'. He even claimed that he had threatened the madhouse keeper that he would 'ruin the house', because he knew that Eliza was 'perfectly

---

[7] T. Heywood (ed.), *The Diary of the Reverend Henry Newcome, from September 30, 1661 to September 29, 1663* Chetham Society, 18 (Manchester, 1849), pp. 54–9, spellings have been modernised for ease of comprehension.

in her sound mind'.[8] There are no moments of doubt or hesitation in Reverend Haggitt's account, and we may wonder whose story of events, his or his wife's is closer to the truth. Either way, Mary Haggitt's involvement in this type of parish business may suggest that a particular type of role was evolving for the minister's wife. Mary had a keen sense that it was 'her duty' to become involved in this case of marriage breakdown. In this society, it would have been regarded as only natural that the minister's wife, as a woman, should have a developed sense of sympathy and understanding for other women in distress. 'The distinguishing characteristics of the female', taught one conduct book for clergymen's wives, 'are tenderness and compassion'. Such feminine qualities in their wives must have been especially useful to clergymen when family matters were at stake.[9] Perhaps what we are seeing here is a division of labour, with the wives of ministers taking responsibility for the personal welfare of parishioners, leaving their husbands to concentrate upon spiritual matters. But as with so many areas of women's work, their efforts in this sphere went unacknowledged. According to Reverend Haggitt, it was he who took the initiative in their response to news of Eliza, and gave the order to his wife to fetch legal assistance, while he tackled Eliza's imprisonment more directly.

Of course, not all clergy were themselves able to live up to the standards of married life that they set for others. Advocating an ideal for married life was a risky business because it directed attention to the marriages of clerics. Realistically or not, parishioners could envisage their ministers and their marriages as role models to follow. Writers of prescriptive literature for clergy warned that their personal lives were of relevance if their ministry was to be significant. 'It has been said of the Pastor that he has a double self', explained one writer:

By virtue of his office, he is in one sense a public man. He has public functions to discharge . . . But if that were his only labour, which is carried on before the open glare and gaze of men, then would it be poor and ineffectual indeed. There is home work, a closet work, an inner work, which, though unseen, will be surely felt all over his parish. Like the Clock upon the Church Tower, he is the great indicator, the regulator of men's spiritual course; so that they look up to him, and are guided by his movements.

A clergyman needed to look to his 'interior self', and ensure that his household and family was in good order, his home a place where love and peace prevailed. For,

---

[8] NA, PCAP 3/2 (1834–6), ff.200–201, 213–214.
[9] *Hints to a Clergyman's Wife; Or, Female Parochial Duties Practically Illustrated* (London, 1832), pp. 1–2.

if it be known (and most assuredly the truth will ooze out) that his own temper is unsubdued – that he is sharp and hasty with his own family . . . then his words, however powerfully spoken, die away like mere gusts of wind.[10]

In the nineteenth century (when this conduct book was written), there is certainly a case for arguing that the nature of their profession gave Anglican clergymen unique opportunities to achieve the middle-class domestic ideal. Working from home, away from the competitive pressures that were perceived to be confined to the business world, clergymen were able to spend time and pay attention to developing their roles as husbands and fathers. Yet stories of Victorian clerical marriage and fatherhood by a number of historians have illustrated that all too often this potential was not realised, and that home was a place of tension and conflict rather than companionship and love.[11] Reconciling the 'inner man' with the public one could prove particularly problematic for clergymen. Because they could not divide family life from work, rather than offering a refuge, home could be a sphere where clergymen were continuously facing challenges to their self-identity.

People were shocked when clerical marriages broke down. The spot-light was on the relationships of clergy, searching out any hint of hy-pocrisy, and allowing gossip to turn rumour into public scandal. Several studies have shown that the sexual reputation of clergymen was vulner-able to scrutiny, but in a climate of criticism about marital violence, the failure of clergy to govern their wives without resort to physical correction could also be exposed.[12]

The reaction of others to Henry Young's drunken behaviour and violence to his wife in the mid-nineteenth century, demonstrates that people expected the clergy to exercise a greater degree of control over their passions than other men. Elizabeth, married to Henry, who was the vicar of Hollesley parish in Suffolk, had long endured beatings and verbal abuse from her husband, which she believed were brought on by his habitual drunkenness. But she could not tolerate him being rude to her relations. When he started insulting them in August 1855, she

---

[10] Oxenden, *The Pastoral Office*, pp. 288, 289, 291–3.

[11] Hammerton, *Cruelty and Companionship*, pp. 71, 79, 94–101; and Tosh, *A Man's Place*, pp. 68–73, 98–9, 119–20.

[12] S. Hindle, 'The shaming of Margaret Knowsley: gossip, gender and the experience of authority in early modern England', *Continuity and Change* 9, 3 (1994), 391–419; and D. Turner, "Nothing is so secret but shall be revealed': The scandalous life of Robert Foulkes', in T. Hitchcock and M. Cohen, (eds.), *English Masculinities 1660–1800* (Harlow, 1999), pp. 169–92.

pleaded with him, 'Henry remember your profession', to which he swore, 'my profession be damned and you too'. Henry's sister, Emma, tried a similar tactic, to be met with the same response. Acting as a witness for Elizabeth, rather than Henry, she described how 'very painful' it was 'to give evidence against my own brother', but that she felt 'compelled to come forward' and 'tell the truth'. She concurred with Elizabeth that it was drink that changed Henry's character, describing how he would awake calm and sober, but as the day progressed become more drunk and violent. 'I have at times remonstrated with him on such occasions', she said, 'and reminded him that he was a clergyman, but it only made him swear the more'. Henry's insulting behaviour to his family, and his violence to his wife, were represented in this case as symptoms of his inability to summon sufficient willpower to stop drinking. Without this self-control he was unfit to fulfil his role both as a husband and governor of a household, and as a minister in a parish. Even his dying father spoke to him about the 'cruelty of his conduct to his wife, and also spoke very strongly of his vice of drunkenness, and alluded to the aggravation of his conduct as being a clergyman'. It seems that everyone in Henry's family expected better behaviour of him because of his occupation. When the case of marital cruelty was heard in the church courts, it is likely that his fellow clerics would have agreed.[13]

Policing marital violence

Within every parish there were assigned churchwardens and overseers of the poor who were responsible for administering the poor laws. The historian Steve Hindle has shown how these officials were ready to intervene in marriage matters if there was the possibility that they could have consequences for ratepayers. Thus there were occasions when the marriages of the poor were delayed or even prevented because of fears that the couple would become a burden upon the parish.[14] But once marital unions were made, it became financially prudent for the parish to ensure that couples remained together. Officials dealing with the issues of settlement and vagrancy that could arise in the context of the poor laws, insisted that husbands returned home to the wives and children

---

[13] LPL, CA, Case 10404 (1855), H838/2,5, f.181–219. For other cases when clergy were accused of marital violence see, for example, LMA, DL/C/177 (1773), f.301–329; NA, DEL 1/668 (1797), f.179 and NA, DEL 7/1, f.234–239; and LPL, CA, Case 7822 (1839), D1802.

[14] S. Hindle, 'The problem of pauper marriage in seventeenth-century England', *Transactions of the Royal Historical Society* 6th series, 8 (1998), 71–89.

they had deserted.[15] Desertion often followed physical violence. In the eighteenth century, Hackney petty sessions ordered that John Wheeler should answer the 'complaint' of the churchwardens and overseers of the poor for deserting his wife and family, and for 'assaulting beating and bruising' his wife. The worry was that Wheeler's desertion left his wife and children depending upon poor relief, so that although the justices might reprimand Wheeler for his violence towards his wife, it was still in their interests for him to return to her.[16]

Punishing a violent husband by withdrawing relief was no solution when it could result in also penalising his wife and family. But continuing to support pauper husbands who were violent to their wives caused considerable discomfort for overseers. There was lengthy correspondence between the parish officers of Romford and Mundon in Essex between 1830 and 1831, for example, over the case of John Thurtell. John's letters to the overseers requesting additional cash sums and supplies of leather for his trade as a shoemaker caused alarm because it was known that even though he had previously received poor relief, he kept his wife in a destitute condition, 'almost starved', and as one overseer reported, 'the fellow beats his wife tremendously'. Despite gathering and sharing information about John, and even visiting him at home, the Essex overseers appear to have been powerless to censure his violence.[17] Instead, overseers of the poor could be left to pick up the pieces when marriages broke down irreconcilably. Overseers organised relief for wives and their children when they had been deserted and their recalcitrant husbands could not be traced, and they supervised support for those wives for whom life with violent husbands had become so intolerable that it had driven them insane. It was poor law officials who could arrange for pauper lunatics to be accommodated in private madhouses, public asylums, workhouses or houses of correction. They could also respond to orders from JPs to confine husbands whose violence had become so furious and dangerous that it was interpreted as a sign of madness.[18]

---

[15] Bailey, *Unquiet Lives*, pp. 36–7.

[16] Paley (ed.), *Justice in Eighteenth-Century Hackney*, p. 100.

[17] T. Sokoll (ed.), *Essex Pauper Letters, 1731–1837* Records of Social and Economic History, new series, 30 (Oxford, 2001), pp. 544–6. Thomas Thurtell also wrote requesting relief in 1823, and several times between 1832 and 1834, see, pp. 543–4, 547–51.

[18] A. Suzuki, 'Lunacy in seventeenth- and eighteenth-century England: analysis of Quarter Sessions records. Part I', *History of Psychiatry* 2 (1991), 440–5, and 'The household and the care of lunatics in eighteenth-century London', in P. Horden and R. Smith (eds.), *The Locus of Care: Families, Communities, Institutions and the Provision of Welfare since Antiquity* (London, 1998), pp. 155–60; Levine-Clark, 'Dysfunctional domesticity', 341–61.

Before the development of a professional police force, it was constables who probably most often had to deal with the unruly and disorderly aspects of marital violence. They were called into domestic disputes to act as peace-keepers. In October 1743 drinkers at a public house in St Paul's, London, for example, sent for a constable when Thomas Bates began striking his wife and trying to strangle her in front of them. By the time the constable arrived, 'a great mob' had gathered, and the constable with some 'other persons' managed to rescue the wife from further harm.[19] Constables were employed on a part-time, ad hoc basis, received expenses and fees for their work, and were increasingly of humble status. Along with watchmen, constables were often the first officials called to intervene. But because in many cases they were successful at restoring order and achieving an informal reconciliation between a couple, their activities are rarely recorded.[20]

The linchpin of this system of parish order and governance was the JP, or magistrate. It was his orders at the quarter or petty sessions that directed the poor law officials and constables. Until the late eighteenth century, the JP was an unpaid gentleman who saw it as his right and privilege to serve in this position. Some men acted as both JP and cleric.[21] Undoubtedly, the role of JP became more demanding over the period that this book covers. Examining the notebooks kept by some JPs indicates that dealing with cases of marital violence provided a steady proportion of their vast range of work. Because most cases were settled by the justices out of court, our records of assault hearings at the sessions may give us a picture of only the tip of the iceberg. Instruction manuals for JPs gave little advice about how to deal with cases of marital violence, other than outlining the procedures for binding violent husbands to keep the peace.[22] Like other officials who became involved in marital

---

[19] LPL, VH80/31/12 (1743).

[20] For constables see, R. D. Storch, 'Policing rural England before the police: opinion and practice, 1830–1856', in D. Hay and F. Snyder (eds.), *Policing and Prosecution in Britain 1750–1850* (Oxford, 1989), pp. 224–6; P. King, *Crime, Justice, and Discretion in England 1740–1820* (Oxford, 2000), pp. 65–75; J. M. Beattie, *Policing and Punishment in London, 1660–1750: Urban Crime and the Limits of Terror* (Oxford, 2001), chapter 3; and Bailey, *Unquiet Lives*, pp. 37–8. For watchmen see, E. A. Reynolds, *Before the Bobbies: the Night Watch and Police Reform in Metropolitan London, 1720–1830* (Basingstoke, 1998), and for an example of intervention in marital violence by a watchman see, LPL, CA, Case 821 (1823), D164, f.75.

[21] See, for example, the involvement of the Reverend William Roberts who was a Surrey JP in one case of marital violence, LPL, CA, Case 8572 (1811), H164/6.

[22] See, for example, R. Burn, *The Justice of the Peace and Parish Officer* 2 vols. (London, 1755), II, p. 520; M. Dalton, *The Country Justice: Containing the Practice, Duty and Power of the Justices of the Peace* (London, 1746), p. 271; and J. Keble, *An Assistance to Justices of the Peace, for Easier Performance of their Duty* (London, 1683), p. 193.

quarrels, JPs could themselves be attacked by violent husbands.[23] Between 3 per cent to 6 per cent of justices' time outside of the sessions courts could be spent dealing with marital complaints. A growing and urban population stretched the workload of JPs to new limits. Acts passed in 1828 and 1853 gave summary powers to justices to fine or imprison men who assaulted their wives. It is no wonder that by the terms of the 1792 Middlesex Justices Act, the first stipendiary magistrates were appointed, and that the 1835 Municipal Corporations Act permitted towns to appoint trained lawyers as stipendiary magistrates. However, by the end of our period, it was only in London that the magistracy were all paid and formally trained officials. Elsewhere in the country, the majority of justices remained gentleman volunteers.[24]

Historians have long debated why reformers were successful at passing a number of acts in parliament between 1829 and 1856 that created the 'new police', when previously there had been so much resistance to the idea of a full-time, paid and trained force. Certainly, it has convincingly been shown that the changes were not introduced because the old system was viewed as inadequate or inefficient. Indeed, there remained a sentimental attachment to the parish constable, and in some communities constables served alongside the new police until the 1870s.[25] What was more relevant to the climate of reform was mounting fear and alarm about the apparently increasing rate of crime and disorder in early nineteenth-century society. The collection of criminal statistics led the rulers of this society to believe that they were experiencing a crime wave that reflected a new lawlessness and moral laxity among the working classes. In cities crime was of such a scale that magistrates, constables and watchmen were overwhelmed with work. The new police, whose primary task was 'the prevention of crime', were expected to relieve the burden on magistrates by helping them to restore and then maintain public order.[26]

---

[23] See, for example, NA, KB1/19 part 3, Mich.13, Geo.3, no.1, affidavit of Mark Milbanke (23 November 1772).

[24] N. Landau, *The Justices of the Peace 1679–1760* (Berkeley, CA, 1984); Bailey, *Unquiet Lives*, p. 39; King, 'Punishing assault', 46; D. Philips, 'Crime, law and punishment in the Industrial Revolution', in P. O'Brien and R. Quinault (eds.), *The Industrial Revolution and British Society* (Cambridge, 1993), pp. 163–5.

[25] R. Paley, '"An imperfect, inadequate and wretched system?": Policing in London before Peel', *Criminal Justice History* 10 (1989), 95–130; 'The Old English Constable', Madden vol. 20, no. 219; D. J. V. Jones, 'The new police, crime and people in England and Wales, 1839–1888', *Transactions of the Royal Historical Society* 5th series, 33 (1983), 154–5.

[26] There is an extensive historiography on this subject. For a sample of readings, see, V. Gatrell, 'Crime, authority and the policeman-state', in F. M. L. Thompson (ed.), *The*

Of course, marital violence was not a crime in this period, but because husbands could be prosecuted for assaulting their wives, and disturbing the peace, it was a matter that could involve the new police. What was their impact in the years leading up to the first Divorce Act? Evidence suggests that in many respects the new police served the same function in cases of marital violence as the parish constable. The police could act to break up fights between married couples; hence Francis Hart was said to kick his wife along a street in Plymouth in June 1848 until the police stopped him.[27] They could also investigate women's cries and screams for help, apprehend violent husbands, and present them before magistrates at the police courts or quarter sessions. We hear the voices of London policemen through the reports they made to these courts. So, for example, policeman Thomas Holway, giving his police number and division, described how Ann Reid had come to him, 'horribly disfigured and covered with marks of violence, complaining of her husband's ill-treatment' one Saturday night in January 1856. Thomas was able to apprehend Ann's husband on the Monday night, and 'lock him up' until he was brought to the Clerkenwell police court. Sergeant Mulverney also appeared in relation to this case, and presented a medical certificate from the surgeon who had examined Ann, and which testified to her injuries.[28]

In these ways the police could serve a useful role for the wives of violent men, responding to their appeals for assistance, and acting as witnesses in the courts. But the historian Robert Storch has regarded the police in a far more negative light, arguing that policemen acted as 'domestic missionaries', imposing new controls upon working-class popular culture, and regulating drinking, animal sports, festivities and other recreational activities. Their unpopularity within working-class communities, where the police were known as the blue 'plagues', 'drones' and 'locusts', probably stemmed from these interventions, as well as their occasional and ruthless suppression of political protests. However, there is nothing to support Storch's suggestion that the police were agents in a class war between the standards of ruling-class and working-class family life.[29] Instead, the new police were usually drawn

Cambridge Social History of Britain 1750–1950 Vol. 3 (Cambridge, 1990); C. Emsley, *The English Police: A Political and Social History* 2nd edition (London, 1996); D. Taylor, *The New Police in Nineteenth-Century England: Crime, Conflict and Control* (Manchester, 1997) and *Crime, Policing and Punishment in England, 1750–1914* (Basingstoke, 1998).

[27] LPL, CA, Case 4282 (1853), H826/5.

[28] *The Times* (16 January 1856) 11e; for other examples of policemen serving similar roles see, *The Times* (16 August 1836) 6e; (3 September 1836) 5f; and (3 October 1855) 10c.

[29] R. D. Storch, 'The plague of the blue locusts: police reform and popular resistance in northern England, 1840–57', *International Review of Social History* 20 (1975), 61–90,

from the communities where they worked, were working class themselves, and shared the same cultural values, prejudices and expectations
of married life as their neighbours.[30] This explains why the police could
be prepared to tolerate occasions of charivari, when rather than relying
upon the police or magistracy to punish marital violence, communities
took the law into their own hands. Police were called to a Kent village
in 1863, for example, to find a crowd trying to duck a well known wife-
beater in the pond after he had locked his wife out of their house
following a violent argument. Although the police stopped the ducking,
they did not make any arrests. Police in northern and Welsh counties did
try to suppress charivaris, but occasional apathy towards these events, as
experienced in Kent, demonstrates that the police and the residents of
the communities they served could have more in common with each
other than is sometimes recognised.[31]

Certainly, police intervention in domestic disputes was not just
directed against violent disorder in working-class marriages. Police constable John Mobbs was called to the Young household in September
1855, to respond to the violent and drunken behaviour of the Reverend
Henry Young, whose case we discussed above. Young was clearly af-
fronted that he should be arrested, and demanded to know why he was
being charged. Mobbs explained it was because he was 'drunk and
disorderly', to which Young responded that 'he was a man of £2,000 a
year and a magistrate', as well as a clergyman, and that therefore Mobbs
'had no authority to remain in the room with him'. In this power struggle
between men of quite different social status, Mobbs appears to have
been determined to continue with his duties unabated, even when Young
threatened to see that he lost his job. Police response to marital violence
meant that even a mighty magistrate and minister could be brought
low by a humble policeman.[32]

Women's conviction that the police would act to protect them from
marital violence meant that they could use the threat of calling the police
in an attempt to control their husband's violence. Elizabeth Heathcote
successfully rid herself of the company of her estranged husband, who
came to her lodgings in 1832 to try and force her to abandon her suit for
cruelty and adultery against him, by threatening that, 'if he did not

---

and 'The policeman as domestic missionary: urban discipline and popular culture in
northern England, 1850–1880', *Journal of Social History* 9 (1976), 481–509; 'New
Police Act', Madden vol. 20, no. 217.

[30] Tomes, 'A "torrent of abuse"', 336.

[31] Conley, *The Unwritten Law*, p. 23; Storch, 'The policeman as domestic missionary',
489–90.

[32] LPL, CA, Case 10404 (1855), H838/5, ff. 39, 257–261.

immediately leave the house, she would send for a police officer to take him into custody'.[33] It was only when she was rescued by a servant, who said he would fetch a policeman, that Francis Hart ceased trying to strangle his wife in November 1847.[34]

The bitterness that some men could feel about the interference of the police in their married lives, and the belief that the police were too easily persuaded to take the woman's side in domestic disputes, was portrayed in popular ballads of the period. The nineteenth-century ballad printed in Birmingham entitled 'Mrs. Clark', for example, told the story of a man miserably married to a violent and shrewish wife. After his wife had hit him and turned him out of the house, a policeman on his beat is convinced by the wife that it was she who was the victim of marital violence, and the unfortunate husband spends the night confined in a dark cell of the police station.[35] Special constables, who after 1835 could be sworn in by magistrates, and were intended to be deployed to respond to short-term, specific local crises, could also cause resentment. A ballad about the special constables in Liverpool presented them as unnecessarily punctilious and heavy handed in their duties:

> And if a drunken husband should
> Abuse his wife by jingo,
> Call in a Special Constable
> And shove him into limbo.[36]

One detects in these ballads signs that the police could be seen by some as out of touch with the sentiments of the general populace, and too ready to carry out orders in an unthinking way. In the early years of the new police there was evident uncertainty about what role the public wanted them to fulfil. Whereas in 1830 the radical *Weekly Dispatch* protested about the 'Over Officiousness of the New Police', when a man had been charged with 'quarrelling with his own wife!', in 1834 the same paper was critical of the 'Inefficiency of the New Police', who could not be found when a husband had beaten his wife in a street with a poker. Policing family life was obviously going to require maintaining a delicate balance between vigilance and surveillance on the one hand, and respect for the demands of each community for privacy on the other. But

---

[33] NA, PCAP 3/1 (1834), f.206.

[34] LPL, CA, Case 4282 (1853), H826/5.

[35] 'Mrs. Clark', in P. Carnell (ed.), *Broadside Ballads and Song-Sheets from the Hewins MSS. Collection in Sheffield University Library: A Descriptive Catalogue with Indexes and Notes* (Sheffield, 1987), p. 4.

[36] 'The Special Constables!' Madden vol. 18, 35; Taylor, *The New Police*, pp. 30, 35–6.

if the police were viewed as 'unwelcome spectators' of working-class life, it seems that violent husbands had the most to fear.[37]

Despite some men's concerns about the favouritism that the police could exhibit towards wives, it is clear that in many ways women with violent husbands were failed by the new police. First, uneven recruitment meant that in some areas there were too few police for them to be relied upon as women's protectors. Emma Young, sister to Reverend Young, was confident that the policeman who came to arrest her brother was John Mobbs, for example, because they only had one policeman in Wells-on-the-Sea.[38] Second, the fact that there were not any women police officers until the early twentieth century, may well have acted as a disincentive to reporting violence, especially when we consider that this could require wives to disclose intimate, and sometimes sexual details of their married lives to male officers.[39]

Third, men as well as women could use the police for their own purposes, and occasionally with malicious and sinister intent. In 1828, following the wrongful confinement of his wife, Eliza, in a private madhouse, and her launch of a separation case for cruelty in the London consistory court, William Carmichael Smyth had come to a private separation agreement with his wife. But after Eliza tried to claim from him the monetary support he had promised in the agreement, William hounded her with a relentless campaign of persecution. William saw the police as a tool with which to torment his wife. He printed defamatory handbills about Eliza so that she could no longer make a living as a landlady, and 'for the further purpose of intimidating and harassing' his wife, engaged Benjamin Schofield, a police officer, to come with him to apprehend her. All he told Benjamin was that Eliza was a person 'charged with forgery and felony', and that he should bring 'hand-cuffs and pistols, as there would be a desperate struggle'. When Benjamin arrived at Eliza's house, and discovered that she was William's wife, he refused to 'interfere further in the business', even when William offered him money to do so. Instead, Benjamin remembered objecting to 'the unpleasant situation he [William] was placing me in'. William then tried at different police offices and the King's Bench to have his wife arrested for 'housebreaking', and when this did not work, he got warrants from police stations to apprehend Eliza for sending him a threatening letter. On four occasions Eliza was detained at police stations, and was once

---

[37] As cited in Clark, 'Humanity or justice?', p. 197; Storch, 'The plague of the blue locusts', 84.

[38] LPL, CA, Case 10404 (1855), H838/5, f.197.

[39] L. A. Jackson, 'Women professionals and the regulation of violence in interwar Britain', in D'Cruze (ed.), *Everyday Violence*, pp. 119–35.

'shut . . . up in a room with prisoners of the lowest description', before magistrates dismissed the charges against her. William would not give up. He even got his servant, Henry Weed, sworn in as a special constable, and through him insisted that officers at Marylebone police station release Eliza, 'for that she was his wife, and he had a right to do as he pleased with her'. He then dragged Eliza down Oxford Street, until a large crowd gathered, which had to be dispersed by the police. William accused his wife of putting his life in danger, and of fraud, so that she was confined again, first in Clerkenwell, and then in White Cross Street prison. Given William's character, it is little wonder that Eliza would have to fight him for separation all through the courts, ending finally with a decision in the Privy Council in June 1836. This allowed Eliza to live apart from her husband, and awarded her alimony. The sentence came thirteen years after she had first left her husband, during which time William had used the police and every expedient available to make Eliza's life a misery.[40]

Fortunately, few wives had such a lengthy and difficult battle to obtain their liberty from their husband's oppression. But the recoil of the policeman Benjamin Schofield at his discovery that he had been called to deal with a domestic dispute may have been more typical. For the fourth reason why married women could not depend upon the assistance of the police was because, to use Schofield's words, responding to cases of marital violence confronted them with an 'unpleasant situation' that most policemen would rather avoid. In part this was because interference could result in a husband's violence being redirected towards the police. Attacks on police when they were trying to apprehend violent husbands were not unusual, and were something that parish constables had learned to expect. When Sergeant Harrison was assaulted as he tried to apprehend James Pipkin for assaulting his wife in Middlesex during May 1851, his experience was little different from the farmer and constable of Clifton, York, who was hit in the eye by the drunken husband, John Doughty, after he was handcuffed following a marital quarrel in September 1837.[41] Policemen were at risk from injury when they intervened in all types of violent incident, but what was particularly 'unpleasant' about cases of marital violence was that because they involved violence between husbands and wives, they did not present situations that could be clearly labelled as criminal. As a result, instructions issued

[40] NA, PCAP 3/2 (1834–36), ff.185–191, 220–221, 231.
[41] LMA, Edmonton Petty Session Division: Tottenham, Enfield and Wood Green Courts, PS.E/E1/1, p. 285; York Minster Archives, Petty Sessions, F2/3/2/71 (9 September 1837).

by local police authorities, such as that in Bristol in 1880, were vague about the circumstances when police should intervene:

The police are not to interfere unnecessarily between a man and his wife who are quarrelling, and unless it is absolutely necessary to prevent serious violence to either party or public disturbance.[42]

Effectively this left individual police officers to make judgements about the nature and severity of marital violence in each case that they encountered (when was interference unnecessary, and what was serious violence?), and to decide upon how they should respond. Discretion, which had been a feature of so much seventeenth- and eighteenth-century law enforcement appears to have survived well into the nineteenth century, despite the professionalisation of policing. The result of such ambiguous guidelines, and of frustration that wives could withdraw their complaints of marital violence after police had been called, may have led to police reluctance to become involved in 'domestics', a trend that has continued until today.

By the terms of the 1853 Assaults Act persons other than the 'party aggrieved' could bring cases of marital violence to the attention of magistrates, hence widening the opportunities for the police to act as prosecutors as well as make arrests.[43] But these new powers do not appear to have been fully realised. Disinclination about playing a greater role in cases of marital violence added to a lack of clarity within police forces about when they could interfere legitimately. A prosecuting attorney in a 1859 manslaughter case, when a man was charged with the death of his wife, blamed the police for not intervening when they knew the wife was subject to violence. The wife's son and neighbour claimed that the police would not act, 'because they had not seen any blow struck'. In his summing up Justice Bramwell could see the dilemma that the police faced:

It was not required for the police to see an assault actually committed to justify them in interfering . . . it was their duty to interfere to prevent the commission of an assault. At the same time there was a good deal to be said for the police for complaints were constantly and readily made when they were supposed to have interfered in such matter too hastily.

Hesitation could be prudent when marital violence was not universally condemned. A magistrate decided in 1871 that a policeman who had

---

[42] As cited in A. Bourlet, *Police Intervention in Marital Violence* (Milton Keynes, 1990), p. 15.
[43] Doggett, *Marriage, Wife-Beating and the Law*, pp. 114–15.

stopped a husband beating his wife had interfered unnecessarily, and fined him for 'common assault'.[44]

The idea that third parties such as the police should act as prosecutors was not a new one. More than a century earlier the Westminster JPs Henry and John Fielding had encouraged the public to go to them as a first step to prosecution, and leave the apprehending of criminals to their 'Bow Street Runners', the groups of constables they employed for this purpose. Temporarily this way of policing the London streets appears to have been popular, and ordinary men and women left the responsibility for the detection and arrest of criminals to magistrates and the Runners.[45] But when it came to domestic disputes, neither Londoners nor the 'new police' in the nineteenth century were prepared to relinquish the long tradition of private prosecution. Most cases of assault continued to be privately prosecuted.[46]

The priority of many early police forces was order on the streets, and it seems to have been their intention to deal chiefly with instances of marital violence when, and if, they spilled out into these public spaces.[47] Achieving this aim would generally have allowed the police to avoid becoming embroiled in too many time consuming and complex personal disputes that were rarely readily resolved. But the demands of women in violent marriages and those who sympathised with them meant that this limited police role in cases of marital violence proved elusive. Members of communities where policemen lived and worked continued to seek more from these new professionals. Despite their failings, from the beginnings of the police force in 1829, many married women in violent relationships looked to the police for assistance. The varied response of the police is unlikely to have resulted in them serving a preventive function in reducing the incidence of marital violence. Nevertheless, their presence on the streets, occasional and decisive interventions, and witness statements in the courts may have had some bearing on the willingness of victims to prosecute. Although we do not know what proportion of the total number of assaults were directed by husbands on their wives, the Select Committee on the Police of the Metropolis found in 1834 that committals for assaults had increased by 50 per cent since the introduction of the Metropolitan police.[48] In the longer term, the role that the police played in domestic disputes may have been a

---

[44] As cited in Conley, *The Unwritten Law*, p. 76.
[45] Shoemaker, *The London Mob*, pp. 22, 40-1, 276-7, 282-3, 288, 291.
[46] Davis, 'Prosecutions and their context', pp. 413, 420.
[47] R. Smith, *Police Reform in Early Victorian York, 1835–1856* Borthwick Paper, 73 (1988), pp. 26–7; D'Cruze, *Crimes of Outrage*, p. 69.
[48] Reynolds, *Before the Bobbies*, pp. 160–1.

contributing factor to the gradual acceptance of the new police after what had been a generally hostile reception. By the mid-nineteenth century the police had become another resource for women with violent husbands, and one that could be of great value.

Medical interventions

The final group of professionals who became involved in cases of marital violence were the medical practitioners. This group included the physicians, surgeons, apothecaries, midwives, nurses and mad-doctors who tended to the injuries and illnesses that could be the result of violence. Over the course of the period of this book, specialist training, regulation and organisational consolidation enabled these practitioners to gradually develop into separate professions. Professionalisation has been studied by historians alongside medicalisation, defined as, 'the progressive expropriation of health from the public sphere and its relocation in an exclusive professional domain'.[49] The consequences for patients have been viewed in negative terms. Influenced by Michel Foucault's theories about the 'birth of the clinic', and using the case study of hospital medicine, Mary Fissell, for example, presents a picture of patients becoming increasingly alienated from their practitioners. According to Fissell, during the eighteenth century growing knowledge and confidence among medical practitioners devalued the role of patients in describing and interpreting their illnesses. Patients were 'deskilled' and depersonalised so that their narratives of illness were no longer important.[50] For the female patient, professionalisation has also been interpreted as signalling a more sustained attempt to exclude women from the practitioner role, exemplified by the rise of the man-midwife.[51] The result was that it became more likely that when women became patients, it was in a relationship that was with a male practitioner.

An examination of the role that medical practitioners played in dealing with the consequences of marital violence gives us a new way

---

[49] I. A. Burney, *Bodies of Evidence: Medicine and the Politics of the English Inquest 1830–1926* (Baltimore, 2000), p. 10.

[50] M. Foucault, *The Birth of the Clinic: An Archaeology of Medical Perception* trans, A. M. Sheridan (London, 1973); M. Fissell, *Patients, Power and the Poor in Eighteenth-Century Bristol* (Cambridge, 1991), esp. chapter 8, and 'The disappearance of the patient's narrative and the invention of hospital medicine', in R. French and A. Wear (eds.), *British Medicine in an Age of Reform* (London, 1991), pp. 92–109. See also, N. D. Jewson, 'The disappearance of the sick-man from medical cosmology, 1770–1870', *Sociology* 10 (1976), 225–44.

[51] B. Ehrenreich and D. English, *Witches, Midwives and Nurses* (New York, 1973); J. Donnison, *Midwives and Medical Men: A History of Inter-professional Rivalries and Women's Rights* (London, 1977); Wilson, *The Making of Man-Midwifery*.

of testing these theories of change. A quite different picture of the patient-practitioner relationship emerges. In the area of private practice where most cases of marital violence were handled, rather than in the hospital, the balance of power remained in the patient's favour. Women with violent husbands could find ways to make the most of their consultations with medics, and their narratives of pain and suffering remained their own. Even if medics were increasing their knowledge and status in this period, their encounters with cases of marital violence demonstrated that there were some causes of medical problems that they were powerless to mend, fix or heal. Furthermore, as we shall see, marital violence gave a context in which female medical knowledge, belonging to both midwives and amateur healers, continued to be important. In this period at least, male medical intervention in cases of marital violence did not amount to take over.

It is clear that medical practitioners were another avenue of support for wives enduring violence from their husbands. The full range of medics treated the consequences of marital violence. Ann Knibbs had medical assistance from a surgeon for two weeks in December 1796 after she was hit with a stick by her husband, for example. The surgeon let blood and cared for her while she kept to her bed. In another case, after Sarah Chance showed an apothecary the bruises she had received from her husband, she was advised to visit, 'once or twice a day to have her back bathed' by him and his wife.[52] Medics who had the same patients discussed their case histories and shared information about them. Rachael Norcott was treated by a surgeon, Thomas Woodall, after she was hit by her husband on the head with a candlestick. Thomas reported that subsequently he had heard Rachael's midwife say that Rachael was very 'cruelly used' by her husband.[53] Officials in the law courts could measure the seriousness of violence according to whether a medic had been called. Hence the judge Dr Lushington ruled in 1844 that the fact that a 'medical gentleman' was fetched for the Countess of Dysart, 'does prove that some injury had been received by the countess in the quarrel of the night proceeding'.[54]

Medics often became involved in cases of marital violence because so much of routine medical care took place in the family home in this period. Midwives who were resident in the home during pregnancy and the period of confinement that followed, and wetnurses who cared for young children, had privileged access to domestic spaces and

---

[52] LMA, DL/C/183 (1797), ff.331r, 332r; LMA, DL/C/175 (1767), f.116r.
[53] LPL, CA, Case 6659 (1666), Eee2, f.98v–99r.
[54] *Dysart v. Dysart* (1844), *English Reports* vol. 163, p. 983.

women's bodies that allowed them to detect violence. As a result, they could reveal detailed knowledge of the married lives of their patients, and be confident about the causes of violence that had led to harm. When the wife of a surgeon miscarried, the woman who acted as her midwife was sure that it had been caused by the husband's verbal abuse, which had carried on all the previous night.[55] The mere presence of medics could act as a control on violence. Two days after she had given birth, and in a 'weak condition', Ann Parry's husband attempted to force her to have sex. According to Ann, her nurse was able to prevent this incident of sexual cruelty, although it is by no means clear how she achieved this. Even in the bedroom, it seems, medical practitioners could be well placed to protect women.[56]

Medics could act as legal witnesses to marital violence. They were sometimes called to testify if it looked likely that the wife's life was endangered by their husband's violence, and were especially valuable if the wife herself was too ill to attend. The surgeon, Mr Wadd was twice called to give evidence to the Mansion House police court in October 1824 when a Mrs Lees had been hit on the head with a broken knife by her husband. He said that although he believed that there would be 'no fatal consequences' from her wounds, the mental scars from months of mistreatment would prove less conducive to healing. She was subject to 'extraordinary terrors' because of what she had experienced, he said.[57] There was a long tradition of women also acting as 'expert' witnesses in the courts as 'juries of matrons' to examine women for signs of pregnancy or recent childbirth, and as the searchers for the marks that were popularly held to be found on the bodies of witches.[58] Cases where there were claims of marital violence presented particular circumstances when female witnesses could play a similar role. In 1824, for example, Mrs Gibson believed that her 'stays' had miraculously 'protected her person from any injury', when her drunken husband had tried to stab her with a knife. The magistrate who heard her accusations of ill-treatment gave directions that she should be examined by 'a female in the house, who is generally employed on such occasions', to confirm her story.[59]

[55] LPL, CA, Case 5089 (1717), Eee12, f.32.
[56] LMA, DL/C/178 (1777), f.567r.
[57] *The Times* (7 October 1824) 3c, (11 October 1824) 3c; for other examples of medical testimony in similar cases see, *The Times* (22 July 1823) 2c; and *The Times* (16 January 1856) 11e.
[58] See, for example, T. R. Forbes, 'A jury of matrons', *Medical History* 32 (1988), 23–33; and C. Holmes, 'Women, witnesses and witches', *Past and Present* 140 (1993), 45–78.
[59] *The Times* (8 October 1824) 3d.

The experiences of medics dealing with the effects of marital violence must have been a sharp reminder to them that illness did not always have a natural or accidental cause. Incidents of marital violence may also have contributed to the evolving role of the professional medical practitioner for they presented scenarios that required more than clinical skills. Some appreciated that effective medical treatment necessitated an understanding and questioning about the familial context in which the patient lived. Indeed, patients were expected to take the lead in telling practitioners the history of their illness.[60] Hence an apothecary explained during a legal dispute heard in 1701 that he had treated a Mrs Courtney for five years before her death. She had been suffering from a 'deep melancholy', which she had told him had been caused by her husband's 'great unkindness'. Over the course of her treatment by him, Mrs Courtney had complained many times of her husband's behaviour towards her, and the apothecary claimed that he had acted on occasion as a peacemaker between wife and husband.[61] This apothecary presented himself as much a listener and counsellor as a dispenser of medicines.

But this is not to say that when practitioners discovered that marital violence was the cause of their patient's injury or illness, they were always ready to challenge the perpetrators of their patient's suffering. Many shied away from assuming this kind of responsibility for their patients. We saw in Chapter 2 how medics dealing with the mental consequences of marital violence could be more willing to subject wives to severe regimes aimed at rehabilitation, than question the cause of their distress.[62] This reluctance to search for the reasons for women's illnesses may have lain partly with the law. Under the common law doctrine of coverture, it was only husbands who could contract medics to treat their wives. Hence dealing with the consequences of marital violence could bring medics face to face with the most extreme instances of the abuse of power, but they knew that taking the moral high ground could deprive them of payment from the men who employed them. Indeed, we only know about Mrs Courtney's troubles because her husband refused to pay her apothecary after her death.[63] It was a case of divided loyalties between the needs of the patient and the demands of those who paid for medical services. The result could be that some tried to avoid confronting the ethical dilemmas that marital violence

---

[60] D. and R. Porter, *Patient's Progress*, chapter 5.
[61] As cited in Crawford, 'Patients' rights', 399–400.
[62] See above, Chapter 2, pp. 99–100.
[63] Crawford, 'Patients' rights', 382, 396–401, 409.

presented. When John Sim, a surgeon and apothecary, was requested to go to the house of Sophia Roper, he found that she was 'in such a perturbed state of mind as to be almost frantic and not at all conscious of what she did'. Sophia would later accuse her husband of sexual and physical cruelty, but when Sim treated Sophia and discovered that her condition had been provoked by her husband's treatment, he 'purposely avoided all allusion to it not wishing to interfere in family concerns'.[64] Similarly, another surgeon-apothecary in 1837 claimed that the marital quarrels that occurred when he was visiting his female patient were, 'a matter which did not concern me – and I paid no attention to what passed'.[65] Such attempts to avoid becoming involved, however, were in vain, for both medics were subsequently called to be witnesses in the marriage separation cases that followed.

The position of medics as the witnesses to the results of marital violence was certainly an unenviable one. Dealing with these incidents could be personally risky. As well as drawing medics into contact with volatile and violent men, if it was the case of male practitioner and female patient, there was always the possibility that angry husbands could turn to accuse medics of sexual impropriety with their wives. In 1669 Grace Hubbard claimed that she had to be treated by a surgeon because her philanderer husband, John, had given her VD. But the surgeon had his reputation questioned in the separation case for adultery and cruelty that followed, because John accused Grace of adultery with her practitioner. Even as medics developed mechanisms for professional regulation and training, suspicions about their practice with female patients continued. Robert Bostock, himself a retail druggist, resented having to pay his wife's medical bills, and labelled his wife's doctors her 'fancy men' in a case for marriage separation heard in 1858. Spending time with female patients could raise the suspicions of jealous husbands, especially when medical intervention required touching intimate areas of women's bodies. It is little wonder that practitioners tried to ensure that private consultations with their patients were the exception rather than the rule. But for women, this meant that disclosure of the causes of harm and injury must have been rendered even more difficult. In the 1860s James Kelly refused to allow his wife to see her doctor without him being in the room because otherwise he believed that she would discuss 'not her bodily ailments but her fancied sense of legal wrong' that she had suffered during her marriage. The notion that the

---

[64] LPL, CA, Case 7828 (1817), H272/27, 35.
[65] LPL, CA, Case 4915 (1837), H544/12/2.

sick-bed could offer women opportunities to share confidences with their practitioners was difficult to achieve under these circumstances.[66]

Fortunately, women were not solely reliant upon regular medical practitioners for medical care. Much medical knowledge was shared by lay people and medical practitioners in this period. It seems highly likely that women who were harmed by their husband's violence would have frequently resorted to self-help medicine and followed recipes for home-made cures, rather than seeking aid from others. We can assume that women also sought help from those who immediately surrounded them in their households. Wives who had been subjected to violence from their husbands could be bedridden for lengthy periods while they recovered from their injuries. Anne Ekins, for example, the wife of a Northamptonshire farmer, said that after her husband's violence she was, 'unable to exert herself in any way even to rise up or sit down in her chair or to go up and down stairs or the like without assistance for nearly six weeks'. Her husband would not allow her to seek any medical advice, so one presumes that the 'assistance' she depended upon was from her household servants. Caring for their invalid mistress must have added considerably to their burden of duties.[67]

Women also sought alternative, less conventional methods of healing than those proffered by official practitioners. This meant that medical practitioners offered no indispensable or unique role dealing with the consequences of marital violence. We have seen how women could buy magical remedies for their unhappiness, and it seems probable that some would have consulted the growing number of 'quacks', who were especially popular for the confidential treatment that they could offer for VD.[68] Some women were able to afford to go to spa towns to take their healing waters. Philippa Foulkes visited Tunbridge Wells in the summer of 1798 for seven weeks on the advice of her doctors because she had become so ill from her husband's violence, and when Elizabeth Ann Heathcote was infected by VD from her husband, she claimed that it was her doctors who told her to go to Tunbridge Wells for two months in 1832. It is little surprise that such visits were medically approved. By offering the possibility of a 'cure' without the need for intruding into

---

[66] LPL, CA, Case 4834 (1669), Ee3, f. 338v–339; Eee3, f.246v; Hammerton, *Cruelty and Companionship*, pp. 84–5, 99. For fears about the sexual impropriety of male medical practitioners see, R. Porter, 'A touch of danger: The man-midwife as sexual predator', in G. S. Rousseau and R. Porter (eds.), *Sexual Underworlds of the Enlightenment* (Manchester, 1987), pp. 206–32.
[67] LPL, CA, Case 3059 (1838), H580/5.
[68] For magical remedies see Chapter 2, p. 99; R. Porter, *Health for Sale: Quackery in England 1660–1850* (Manchester, 1989), pp. 153–5.

the personal circumstances of their patients, the spa solution temporarily let medical practitioners off the hook. Women probably viewed spa towns as offering a welcome escape from brutal husbands, recovery time and the opportunity for psychological as well as any physiological healing.[69]

Of course, we may only be gaining evidence of a fraction of the medical care that women received following marital violence. Many marriages in which women experienced violence from their husbands would have met with a medical response, but never reached the stage of marriage breakdown and legal proceedings. Amateur medical care was even less likely to be recorded, and thus it is more difficult for us to detect today. But one gains the impression from the evidence that we do have, that while many 'professional' medical practitioners adopted the 'treat and go' response to marital violence, not wishing to become any more deeply involved in these cases, it was 'amateur' practitioners who not only offered much immediate first aid, but also provided the long-term care that women often needed.

As forensic witnesses in the law courts, medical practitioners played a minor role. Medical testimony in assault cases with non-fatal injury was rarely heard in the Old Bailey before the mid-nineteenth century, and the same was true in marriage separation cases.[70] In the main, this was because it was not needed. Anyone could describe seeing black and blue bruising, cuts and bleeding without resort to specialist language or knowledge. However, there were two types of marital cruelty for which the opinions of medics could have been more useful to the courts: the 'wilful communication of venereal disease', and wrongful confinement for insanity. On occasion, judges in the church courts were very deferential to medical opinion on these matters. Without the testimony of medical practitioners, 'how is it possible that the Court, having no medical education, could deduce from the symptoms that the disease was this or that character?', asked one judge, ruling on a marital dispute about VD in 1838.[71] Prominent doctors, such as Thomas Monro (1758–1833), who served as a physician at Bethlem hospital, could also be called to testify in marriage disputes that involved questions of sanity. Their opinions could be crucial in determining whether husbands could legitimately confine their wives in public or private madhouses, and

---

[69] LMA, DL/C/186 (1802), f.463v; NA, PCAP 3/1 (1834), f.205v; for an example of a wife who was advised to visit Harrogate after threats of marital violence see, NA, PCAP 1/199 (1856), f.58.

[70] T. R. Forbes, *Surgeons at the Bailey: English Forensic Medicine to 1878* (London, 1985), pp. 198–9.

[71] *Collett v. Collett* (1838), *English Reports* vol. 163, p. 240.

there were cases in which wives were only released from such institutions when medics judged them sane.[72]

But these occasional and sensational interventions by medical practitioners into married life did little to raise their overall status as legal witnesses. For their claims to expertise were hindered in this period by limited medical certainty and consensus about the effects of VD and the methods for determining madness. So in 1708 when Lady Ashe claimed that her husband had infected her with VD, and that three of their children had subsequently been born and died of the same disease, more than six medical practitioners testified, but could agree upon neither whether Sir James Ashe had been cured of VD, nor if the children had died of a mysterious 'disorder in the blood' rather than VD.[73] Defining madness was a notoriously subjective and arbitrary process in this period. There were very limited numbers of medics who had developed a specialism in mental illness, and there was no scientific or professional language for them to describe the affliction. Thus, 'medicine had yet to formulate a distinctive – and exclusive – "way of seeing" madness'.[74] Marriage was an arena for mental illness in which medical practitioners had developed neither the tools for diagnosis nor the cure.

Cases of marital violence show us that if the period between the Restoration and the mid-nineteenth century was one of professionalisation and medicalisation, married women as patients were losers in the sense that the causes of some of their illnesses were never fully recognised. Nevertheless, it was precisely because medical practitioners never became 'experts' in the causes and effects of marital violence that lay responses and interpretations continued to carry weight. Women themselves were able to manipulate medical understandings of their bodies to their own advantage, as we saw in our earlier discussion of nervous illness and hysteria as a reaction to marital violence.[75] Ulinka Rublack's observation that, 'illnesses . . . opened up a narrative space that individuals could use to explain their disorders in terms of disordered relationships rather than just disordered physiology', is relevant for understanding women's descriptions and understandings of their illnesses across our period.[76] Changes in the training, organisation and

---

[72] LPL, CA, Case 3366 (1811), D757/503–505; Foyster, 'At the limits of liberty', 39–62.
[73] NA, DEL/1/329 (1708), ff.196v–202, 515v–516r, 521v–523, 533r–538v, 628v–633r.
[74] J. P. Eigen, '"I answer as a physician": opinion as fact in pre-McNaughton insanity trials', in M. Clark and C. Crawford (eds.), Legal Medicine in History (Cambridge, 1994), p. 171.
[75] See above, Chapter 2, pp. 122–27.
[76] U. Rublack, 'Fluxes: the early modern body and the emotions', History Workshop Journal 53 (2002), 11.

status of medical personnel had little impact on their utility for women who had been subjected to violence from their husbands. Professional medical practitioners numbered only some of those who were part of the medical marketplace available to wives in our period.

Conclusion

Until now, there has been no historical study of the role of clergy, JPs, constables, the police and medical practitioners in dealing with cases of marital violence. Although none of these officials saw responding to these types of domestic incident as their chief function, this preliminary study reveals that marital violence presented situations that could be both demanding and time consuming. It is a measure of the difficulties faced by professionals dealing with marital violence, that it is still an area that generates concern for these groups of workers today.[77] For professionals working in the period examined in this book, fears for personal safety, coupled with doubts about the extent of their authority over an area of marital conflict that was riddled with legal ambiguities, meant that intervention remained reactive rather than proactive. Frequently married themselves (James Veitch was a physician and surgeon), professional men shared the same ideas and prejudices about marital violence as their clients. Thus their condemnation of marital violence was not a given. During our period, the impression is that the general populace often wanted more from these professionals than they were prepared to deliver. Marital violence demanded a pastoral or counselling role from a range of professionals, not just the clergy. But despite increasing experience dealing with instances of marital violence there is little evidence that any group developed specialist knowledge that could mark them out as 'professionals' in this area. What individuals learned 'on the job' was not passed onto others in any systematic way.

As a result, although these officials were often regarded as senior figures in communities who commanded respect, generally their interventions in cases of marital violence were not afforded additional significance or value. When a wife faced marital violence, help was sought from whoever was closest to hand, no matter what their occupation. Getting witnesses to observe and hear about the effects of marital violence helped wives to get the story of what they had endured out, and the

---

[77] See, for example, Bourlet, *Police Intervention*; S. C. Hunt and A. M. Martin, *Pregnant Women Violent Men: What Midwives Need To Know* (Oxford, 2001); and J. Richardson and G. Feder, 'Domestic violence: a hidden problem for general practice', *British Journal of General Practice* (April 1996), 239–42.

angry reaction of some husbands to the involvement of officials shows that their wives had been successful in this aim. But the frequent reluctance of professionals to intervene when they knew that marital violence was the cause of a disturbance, and their unwillingness to assume a role of welfare that could require more probing into people's married lives, meant that it was only the disciplinary powers held by magistrates and the police that set these officials apart from the general populace. Social workers and specialist agencies of support for wives who were subject to marital violence would not develop until the twentieth century. Until at least the mid-nineteenth century, the 'professions' supplemented rather than threatened to replace amateur care for women in the community. Responsibility for dealing with the consequences of marital violence was still shared and distributed throughout communities.

The inquest into a wife's death in June 1853, serves as a chilling prediction of how attitudes were to change over the subsequent 150 years. Hannah Gray was the first witness to speak, and had been a lodger in the same house in Marylebone, London, as the woman who had died, Mary Mead, the wife of a shoemaker. Hannah described how she had heard Mary's cries on a Saturday night, and struggled to force open the door to Mary's room, which had been locked. Finally managing to enter the room, she witnessed Mary's husband, Francis, grabbing her by her hair, 'as one would a cat by the skin', and flinging her across the room. Fearful for her own life, Hannah left the room, to hear further cries through the night. Hannah did not see Mary again until Monday, when she 'found her very ill in bed. Her face was covered with bruises, and her eyes were so swollen that she could scarcely see'. Mary died that night. After she had given her testimony, *The Times* recorded that the coroner 'severely censured' Hannah, 'for not having called in the police, when she saw the deceased so brutally treated'. Hannah replied, 'that she did not consider it her business to interfere with other people's affairs'.

But, of course, Hannah *had* interfered. She reacted to Mary's screams by forcing entry into her room, stayed for long enough to establish what and who was the cause of her distress, and visited Mary again to witness the consequences. Her knowledge meant that she was bound to be one of the main witnesses in the inquest that followed. But for the coroner this was not enough. Realising that this was violence of such a 'brutal' degree that she could not personally stop it, in the coroner's view, Hannah should have called in the experts to restore order; the police. To Hannah, however, this was not 'her business', and to call in others amounted to an interference that was even more intrusive than her bursting through her fellow lodger's door.

The exchange between the coroner and Hannah betrays the emergence by this period of a divergence of views about what constituted appropriate intervention in instances of marital violence. To the coroner, amateur responses were inadequate, instead severe marital violence necessitated the involvement of the professionals. This group included medical practitioners as well as the police. Hence in the inquest presided over by the coroner, consideration was given to medical testimony. The inquest heard statements from a surgeon, Mr Nelson, who had attended Mary from the Sunday evening until her death, and a doctor from the Free Dispensary, from whom Mary had been receiving medical care for her 'weakly constitution' for several months before her death, and who was fetched by Francis on the Sunday morning.

To Hannah, however, the violent quarrel between Francis and Mary Mead was the type of dispute that should have been resolved within the boundaries of their lodging house and by its members. So after her initial investigation on the Saturday night, Hannah did nothing when she heard further cries coming from the room where Mary and Francis lived, 'as they were fellow-lodgers'. Three other lodgers spoke at the inquest, and two said that they 'took no notice of it as they imagined that he [Francis] was beating his son'. In other words, they believed that what they were hearing was legitimate correction of another family member by its patriarch. In the marital dispute that was actually taking place, Mary's family became involved. Her son was present at the time of the violence, and her brother, as well as 'an acquaintance' visited her as she lay dying on the Monday. One lodger had fetched a surgeon to treat Mary on the Sunday evening, to 'attend her', but his testimony at the inquest, when he gave details of the post mortem he had conducted, demonstrates the limitations of forensic medicine at this time. 'Witness could not say what was the nature of the violence used toward deceased', *The Times* recorded, 'but it was of a most frightful character, as the bruised condition of deceased's body evidenced'. His account was no more specialist in its language than that given by others.

Mary died surrounded by those who knew her and had witnessed what she had suffered. The violence that had been targeted against her also had an impact upon her child, fellow residents in the lodging house, her brother, friend, and the two medics who were consulted. To Hannah these were the limits of the moral community who should have contained and responded to Francis's violence. Resorting to the police was to bring in outsiders to this community who would force it to confront what nobody, even Mary, was willing to admit: that it was a husband's abuse of his authority that had caused her fatal injuries. It was far easier for everyone in Mary's acquaintance to repeat her unlikely explanation for her injuries; that she had fallen down the stairs, than to assume responsibility for ensuring that justice was done. In a period before the possibility of anonymous reporting of domestic violence to the police, it required a level of personal or individual motivation and resolve to get police assistance, which Hannah did not possess. It took Mary's death, and social distance from the victim for individuals to express a collective outrage at her suffering. The 'yells and hootings of upwards of 300 persons' were said to accompany Francis as he was conveyed to Newgate.[78]

Although the murder of Mary Mead is just one story of marital violence among many that were reported in nineteenth-century newspapers, Hannah's fatal decision not to call in extra help, believing that it was not 'her business', and the coroner's response, can be seen as marking the beginnings of a change of attitudes about intervention in marital violence. Subsequently the coroner's view that it was only the police who had the power and authority to stop and censure a husband's violence, and Hannah's belief that involving the police would amount to an unwelcome interference have combined to produce a widespread public apathy towards marital violence. In short, when marital violence became somebody's problem, in terms of it lying within their professional expertise, it ceased to be everybody's problem. It is this change in attitudes that has cost so many women their lives.

[78] *The Times* (9 June 1853) 6f.

Conclusion: The 1857 Divorce Act and its consequences

What happened to Rachael Norcott and Mary Veitch? In neither case has a sentence, or judgement upon their request for marriage separation survived. While we will never know whether they were released from the clutches of their brutal husbands, we have seen how in many ways their stories were typical of the experiences of women who resisted marital violence. The similarities of their accounts suggest the continuities of what women could endure over the period between their lifetimes. Their stories have shown us how marital violence had multiple forms, of which physical violence constituted only one damaging part. While the variability of marital violence made it difficult for lawyers to label or define, we have learned that to ordinary people who witnessed the violence directed towards Rachael and Mary, unacceptable or cruel violence depended upon the personal circumstances or characteristics of the person who was its target. As for much of this period violence was seen as a legitimate corrective to insubordinate behaviour, the conduct of Rachael and Mary also had to be assessed before any judgement of cruelty could be made. We have seen how the impact of marital violence extended beyond its intended target, to affect Rachael and Mary's children, family, friends, and neighbours. There is little evidence that the violence directed against Mary was any more private or secret than that against Rachael.

But the insights that we have gained into the lives of Rachael and Mary have also revealed some key changes in attitudes towards marital violence between the Restoration and the early nineteenth century. By the latter period the social class of the target of violence had become far more important in determining whether violence was judged to be cruel. Mary's solidly middle class and respectable background was highlighted to emphasise the unacceptability of her husband's violence, and to demonstrate the limits of her ability to cope with it. Rather than resisting violence by fighting back, as women in Rachael's generation may have done, Mary adopted a new form of response by assuming the signs of nervous illness. Husbands who defended their physical violence by arguing that it was their right to correct their wives after disobedient or 'provocative' behaviour, found that they were on less sure ground as the period progressed. The damage that inter-parental violence did to children was rarely acknowledged. However, shortly after Mary's case for separation was heard, the changes that were introduced by the terms of the first Infant Custody Act, meant that at least younger children of the middle classes would no longer have to continue to reside with their violent fathers after their parents had separated. Finally, although marital violence continued to be a matter resolved within and by communities, the development of the professions would enable some to start to argue by the mid-nineteenth century that its consequences were so serious that they could only be sufficiently dealt with by those with special powers or knowledge.

Overall what this shows us is that in the period between the marriage separation suits brought by Rachael and Mary, there had been alteration in both the popular definitions and responses to cruel violence. Levels, forms and ways of reacting to marital violence that would have been tolerated in Rachael's social circle were regarded as unbearable or repugnant in Mary's time. Emphatically, and tragically for the women concerned, this is not to suggest that in practice wives in the nineteenth century endured less or different forms of violence from their husbands than in earlier periods. But it is to argue that by this later period views and attitudes had changed to the extent that although Mary presented an account of cruelty in her marriage that rested mainly on verbal violence and threats of confinement, and Rachael focused far more on physical violence, Mary was no less likely than Rachael to have been successful in gaining a legal separation from her husband. When directed against a woman of similar middle-class status, a husband's violence, whether actual or threatened, and in whatever form, was less socially acceptable in the mid-nineteenth century than it had been two hundred years earlier.

It was in this changed cultural climate, just twenty years after Mary's case was heard in court, that the Divorce Act of 1857 was passed. By the terms of this Act, for the first time in English history husbands and wives could achieve a divorce that would allow them to remarry, without having to go through the lengthy and often costly process of seeking a divorce by private act in parliament. The unpopularity of parliamentary divorce had been reflected in the number of successful petitions: only 321 men (an average of one or two a year), and four women achieved divorce in this way between 1670 and 1857.[1] The 1857 Act

---

[1] For parliamentary divorce see, S. Anderson, 'Legislative divorce – Law for the aristocracy?', in G. R. Rubin and D. Sugarman (eds.), *Law, Economy and Society: Essays in the*

established a new civil court to hear all divorce and matrimonial business, so that no further cases would be heard in the church courts. The financial position of the separated, divorced or deserted wife was radically improved from her predecessors. A separated or divorced wife would be treated in law as a 'feme sole', or as if she was an unmarried woman, allowing her to own property, engage in contracts, and dispose of her goods in her will as she saw fit, without interference from her husband. Desertion without cause for two years or more became a new ground for separation. In addition, a wife who had been deserted could apply to a magistrate for protection of her property from her husband. Hence wives who may have feared that they did not have the economic means to leave violent or neglectful husbands were, by the terms of the Act, given assurances about how they could achieve secure financial independence following divorce or separation. The fate of children from these broken marriages was also considered. In the final decrees that the new court would make on marriages, it was determined that orders and provisions, as it deemed 'just and proper', should be made with regards to the 'custody, maintenance, and education' of children, and as a last resort, that these children should be placed under the protection of the Court of Chancery. Altogether, Stone believes, this Act represented a positive shift in attitudes towards women; 'the debates over the Divorce Act led to greater public awareness of the problems of wives, and as a result they were the main beneficiaries'.[2]

But despite this legislation, the marital status of Rachael and Mary would have been little altered by this Act, because under its terms a woman could not achieve a divorce solely on the grounds of her husband's violence. Instead, the chief ground for divorce was adultery. In the mid-nineteenth century the double sexual standard, whereby a wife's adultery was deemed more serious than her husband's was still very much alive and kicking. Thus, although a husband could divorce his wife if he proved her guilty of adultery, a wife could only divorce her husband if his adultery had been 'aggravated' by another offence. These additional offences were adultery that had involved incest, bigamy, rape, sodomy, bestiality, desertion for more than two years, or adultery 'coupled with such cruelty as without adultery would have entitled her [the wife] to a divorce *a mensa et thoro*' (separation from 'bed and

History of English Law, 1750–1914 (London, 1984), 412–44; Wolfram, 'Divorce in England', 155–86; Phillips, *Putting Asunder*, pp. 227–41; and Stone, *Road to Divorce*, chapter 10.
[2] Stone, *Road to Divorce*, p. 388.

board').[3] Hence marital violence was designated as only significant if it was accompanied by adultery, and was relegated to a subsection of male behaviour that could render men's sexual lapses transgressive, rather than being seen as an offence against the marital tie in its own right. It is true that, by the terms of the Act, marital violence could debar a husband from achieving divorce from his adulterous wife if it could be shown that his violence had 'conduced' her to be unfaithful. But this proof of violence could not allow a wife to achieve divorce from her husband. The Divorce Act stipulated that a wife whose husband was 'simply' violent but not adulterous was only entitled to a 'judicial separation', which like the divorce *a mensa et thoro*, did not allow her to remarry. If she had property her position was improved, and there was the possibility of the custody of her children, but otherwise she remained married, if living separately, to her husband. The message of this Act was clear: a husband's violence, however severe, was not alone serious enough to dissolve a marriage.

Why did the Divorce Act fail to address the position of women in violent marriages, when ideas about violence in marriage had changed so significantly over the previous two hundred years? Clearly we cannot write any simple or Whiggish history of marriage that shows how women's position and status within it improved over time. Stone's optimistic interpretation of the Act is seriously misplaced. Instead, the limitations of the Divorce Act should not come as a surprise to us, for they served to highlight and reinforce the common prejudices and problems, discussed throughout this book, which contemporaries shared and encountered whenever they were faced with marital violence.

It was inevitable that marital violence would not be included as a separate cause for divorce. This was primarily because physical violence in marriage was seen as a problem largely confined to the working classes. A key change identified as occurring within the period of this book; the increasing association of particular forms of marital violence with different social groups, hindered the effectiveness of the Divorce Act, as it would do for measures that dealt more directly with marital violence for the next 150 years. Furthermore, marital violence was

---

[3] 'An Act to Amend the Law relating to Divorce and Matrimonial Causes in England' (20 and 21 Vict; c.85); for general discussion of the passage and significance of this legislation see M. L. Shanley, '"One must ride behind": married women's rights and the Divorce Act of 1857', *Victorian Studies* 25 (1982), 355–76 and *Feminism, Marriage and the Law*, chapter 1; A. Horstman, *Victorian Divorce* (London, 1985); Phillips, *Putting Asunder*, pp. 412–22; Stone, *Road to Divorce*, chapters 11–13; and G. L. Savage, '"Intended only for the husband": gender, class, and the provision for divorce in England, 1858–1868', in K. O. Garrigan (ed.), *Victorian Scandals: Representations of Gender and Class* (Athens, Ohio, 1992), pp. 11–42.

regarded as so unwieldy and variable in practice that any attempt by reformers to confront it risked drawing them into a situation which offered no politically expedient means of escape. Marital violence continued to be such a divisive issue, that no political group, even one led by feminists, could afford to focus its efforts on seeking divorce for those who were its target. Nor, as we shall see, was divorce always regarded as the most appropriate solution to marital violence. Some went as far as to address what they regarded as the causes of marital violence, believing that if they could root out what stimulated violence, then resort to divorce on this ground would rarely be required. For most contemporaries, however, the suggestion that women would need to be placed on a more equal footing with men in marriage for the incidence of violence to decline, risked destabilising the ultimate basis of male power and authority, and hence the very institution of marriage itself. To make proof of marital violence a ground for divorce would be to create an offence against the marriage bond that was committed almost entirely by men; a fact that few wished to acknowledge. The disturbing truth about marital violence, revealed in the debates about marriage and divorce in the mid-nineteenth century, was the extent to which the threat, exercise or control of violence was cherished still as a male right and prerogative.

There is certainly much to suggest that the issue of marital violence was not dealt with in the Divorce Act because contemporaries believed they had tackled it in previous nineteenth-century legislation. Lord Ellenborough's Act in 1803 imposed the death penalty upon those who attempted to kill or inflict grievous bodily harm on others, when it could be proved that potentially lethal weapons, such as swords or knives had been used. Although contemporaries saw this as an important first step in the control of domestic violence, it had serious limitations. Like the popular 'rule of thumb', it led to discussions about the nature of the weapons that could be used by a husband against his wife. In October 1824, for example, the Lord Mayor of London felt unable to commit a husband under the terms of the Act, because he had only used a blunt or broken knife against his wife.[4]

Subsequent legislation in 1828 and 1853 was more significant in the majority of marital violence cases, where weapons were not used, and/or injury was less serious. The 1828 Offences Against the Person Act gave magistrates summary powers to try cases for common assault and battery and to impose a maximum fine of £5 or two months imprisonment on default. The use of weapons during the violent incident did not

---

[4] *The Times* (11 October 1824) 3c.

need to be proved. Violent husbands could find themselves punished under the terms of this Act, and some wives could be insistent that their husbands felt the full weight of the law. When a London magistrate tried to reconcile Martha Taylor with her journeyman husband in 1837, after he had beaten her, she would have none of it. She wanted the magistrate to bind her husband, 'neck and heels to keep the peace, or let him go to prison if he can't find bail'.[5] Despite the popularity of this Act, by the mid-nineteenth century, the conviction that marital violence was an 'evil' that was 'rapidly growing', led Mr Fitzroy, MP for Lewes to argue that the punishment imposed by the 1828 Act was inadequate. Arguing that cruelty to animals was more severely penalised than cruelty to wives, and hence introducing, 'the startling principle of English law that women are of less value than Poodle dogs and Skye terriers', Fitzroy convinced parliament in 1853 to pass the Act for the Better Prevention and Punishment of Aggravated Assaults upon Women and Children. A husband summarily convicted by magistrates under this Act could be fined £20 or imprisoned for six months with or without hard labour.[6]

The debates surrounding this legislation reveal much about the common assumptions that were made about marital violence at this time. To MPs, the 1828 and 1853 Acts were intended to deal with a working-class problem. Discussion about an amendment to the terms of the 1853 Act touched upon whether publicly flogging the violent husband would be a more suitable punishment than a fine or imprisonment. In the seven years following the 1853 Act, there were at least three further attempts to introduce bills that would have made flogging the punishment for those convicted of serious assault. There is no way that this would have been a topic for debate if MPs imagined that members of their own social class could have been subject to this penalty. Of the cases of severe marital violence that had been heard in the London police courts, and which were selected by Fitzroy to exemplify the inadequacy of existing punishment, all were from working-class marriages. Lord Lovaine, who spoke in favour of flogging, said that, 'he believed there were persons who could not be reached by any other punishment, and it was for that class only, which was so utterly degraded, that he recommended its infliction'.[7] When historians conclude that from the late eighteenth century

---

[5] As cited in, Clark, 'Humanity or justice?', p. 198; for examples of husbands being fined or imprisoned under the terms of the 1828 Act, see, *The Times* (13 October 1832) 3f; (3 September 1836) 5f; and (24 September 1836) 6f.

[6] *Hansard*, vol. 124 (10 March 1853), 1414; *The Times* (12 March 1853) 6d.

[7] *Hansard*, vol. 124 (10 March 1853), 1415–16; vol. 125 (6 April 1853), 679; Doggett, *Marriage, Wife-Beating*, pp. 106–11.

there was a sea change of attitudes towards physical violence, manifest in a growth of public intolerance for corporal punishment, they should be reminded of these discussions.

Even when the idea of flogging was dismissed by MPs, it was inconceivable that the lesser punishment of imprisonment with hard labour would have been seen as a feasible alternative if there was any possibility that impecunious middle-class men might have been its object. Outside parliament, the newly-weds, Harriet Taylor and John Stuart Mill questioned whether,

it be supposed that any amount of imprisonment without labour. . . has a deterring effect upon criminals of the class who come under the proposed enactment? What is a prison to them? A place where, probably, they are better fed, better clothed, better lodged, than in their own dwellings. . . In the case of the poor, the addition of labour is not even a punishment. Their life when at large must be one of labour. . . With the addition of labour, imprisonment to the ordinary labourer scarcely amounts to a punishment; without labour it is a holiday.

While condemning wife beating as a brutish and uncivilised form of behaviour, the Mills reserved their opprobrium for the working class. When they argued in support of flogging, they were convinced that, 'it is probably the only punishment which they would feel'. 'The law', they believed, 'has the forming of the character of the lowest classes in its own hands', and thus should teach them the moral wrongs of marital violence.[8] Indeed, when the 1853 bill became law, it was middle-class magistrates in the petty sessions and London police courts who enforced its provisions in assault cases brought by working-class wives. From a survey of local newspaper reports, Jennifer Davis has shown that, 'assault cases with middle-class prosecutors were oddities and frequently treated as such by the press', and that, more particularly, wives who charged their husbands with assault in the second half of the nineteenth century came 'predominantly from the casual poor'.[9]

Thus nineteenth-century legislation and practice reinforced the perception that marital violence was a feature of working-class life and was most dangerous when it was physical in form. Politically, it was timely and expedient to foster this belief, since it allowed the ruling classes to argue that working men did not deserve the privilege of the vote.[10] But

[8] H. Taylor Mill and J. S. Mill, *Remarks on Mr. Fitzroy's Bill for the More Effectual Prevention of Assaults on Women and Children* (London, 1853), as cited in Robson and Robson (eds.), *Sexual Equality*, pp. 94, 95, 97.

[9] Davis, 'Prosecutions and their context', p. 413, footnote 50, pp. 418–19; see also 'A poor man's system of justice', 309–35.

[10] Clark, *Struggle for the Breeches*, passim.

even for those for whom it was intended, this legislation proved unsatisfactory. For working-class women, the costs of hiring an attorney to prosecute their husbands could be prohibitive, and knowing that they could lose their husband's earnings while they served a prison sentence could discourage wives from accusing their husbands of assault. As a result, the 1853 Act was mostly used to punish men who had been violent to women and children that were unrelated to them.[11] For men, the 1853 Act, widely known as the 'Good Wives' Rod', was portrayed in popular culture as grossly unfair.[12] As the title of one ballad put it, all a wife now had to do was to make some petty complaint about her husband's behaviour, and magistrates would 'Pop him into Limbo'; the 'quod' or jail where for six months she could forget all about him. The fact that the Act had been passed under a female monarch was not lost to those with an eye for its comic potential;

> Our Queen woke up the other night, and filled the room with laughter,
> She sang aloud, in sweet delight, now petticoats is master!

With women in charge, this ballad continued, traditional gender roles were reversed, so that women became all powerful, and men were reduced to a state of subservience:

> Every married man must be, both upright and steadfast,
> Take his wife hot rolls and tea to her bedside for breakfast;
> Wash her shift and stockings too, and lace her stays by jingo,
> Or else in jail he must bewail – pop him into limbo.
>
> He must buy her lollipops and gin, and never dare by snarling,
> He must not use no other words, than duckey, dear, and darling!
> Pop goes the pots and pans – the law will give him stingo,
> Pop goes the spiteful man, for six months to limbo.[13]

According to such sentiment the 1853 Act had already gone too far, so that certainly no further legislation was needed.

This is not to say that the idea of extending the grounds of divorce to include marital cruelty was never discussed. But it was because marital violence could not be easily defined in a way that adultery could, that it remained an unpopular option for inclusion. There was a Royal

---

[11] Doggett, *Marriage, Wife-Beating and the Law*, pp. 30–1; Clark, 'Humanity or justice?', p. 203.

[12] *The Good Wife's Rod for a Bad Husband, A Copy and Explanation of the New Act for the Protection of Women* (London, 1853); M. J. Wiener, *Reconstructing the Criminal: Culture, Law, and Policy in England, 1830–1914* (Cambridge, 1990), p. 82.

[13] 'Pop him into Limbo' Madden, vol. 11, 547; for other examples of ballads that mention the terms of the 1853 Act see, 'The Late Trial of Mr and Mrs N.', Madden, vol. 14, 2; and 'My Husband Was A good for Nothing Man', Madden, vol. 14, 153.

Commission that investigated the law of divorce in 1853, the findings of which formed the basis of the subsequent legislation in 1857, and were much cited in the debates about divorce at this time. It had considered whether cruelty should be allowed as a cause of divorce, or whether at least the definition of cruelty permitting separation *a mensa et thoro* should be extended beyond, 'a reasonable apprehension of danger to life, limb, or health', to include 'mutual dislike, incompatibility of temper, neglect, severity, and repeated provocation'. But the Commissioners rejected both suggestions, resorting to the wisdom of the eighteenth-century philosophers David Hume and William Paley, and the trusty words of Sir William Scott, Lord Stowell, to support their position. Part of Scott's judgement on the *Evans* case made more than sixty years previously, was quoted by the Commissioners, and again by one MP in the House of Commons during debates in July 1857 on the Bill. According to Scott:

> though, in particular cases, the repugnance of the law to dissolve the obligations of matrimonial cohabitation may operate with great severity upon individuals; yet it must be carefully remembered, that the general happiness of the married life is secured by its indissolubility. When people understand that they *must* live together, except for a very few reasons known to the law, they learn to soften by mutual accommodation that yoke which they know they cannot shake off; they become good husbands and wives, from the necessity of remaining husbands and wives. . . In this case, as in many others, the happiness of some individuals must be sacrificed to the greater and more general good.[14]

Knowing that divorce was not an option, argued Scott, meant that people made the most of their marital relationships. It was in society's best interests that couples remained married, even if this meant that some individuals suffered and were miserable. Of course, since they were the main victims of marital violence, it was chiefly women's happiness that was at stake under this utilitarian philosophy.

With the findings of the Commission behind them, by the time the grounds for divorce came to be debated in parliament, the idea of allowing cruelty as a ground for divorce was regarded by both supporters and opponents to the Bill as something of a distraction. Those who supported reform were eager to demonstrate that the Bill did not introduce new 'rules and principles' concerning marriage, but instead only removed the 'inconveniences' of existing practice. As the attorney general explained to the House of Commons, 'the Bill embodied nothing

---

[14] *First Report of the Commissioners, appointed by her Majesty to enquire into the Law of Divorce* (London, 1853), p. 13, italics are in the original; *Evans v. Evans* (1790), *English Reports* vol. 161, p. 467; *Hansard*, vol. 147 (30 July 1857), 760, 766.

but what had been known to be the law of England for 200 years'.[15] For the Divorce Bill to become law, its engineers believed that it was necessary for it to be presented as a conservative measure, which aimed for reform rather than radical change. Since it was adultery on the part of a wife, or the 'aggravated' adultery of a husband that had been the grounds for parliamentary divorce, the Divorce Bill could be presented as only allowing minor alterations to current procedure (through adding cruelty and desertion to the list of aggravations to adultery), and as addressing the perceived social inequalities of parliamentary divorce by giving a greater number of people access to divorce. Acknowledging that marital violence could be an aggravation to adultery was regarded as concession enough. By otherwise not altering the grounds for divorce, advocates for the Act could argue that it just represented a movement of jurisdiction over divorce from parliament to the new Divorce Court. Hence supporters of the Bill included men such as Lord Brougham, founder of the Law Amendment Society, which campaigned for greater efficiency and improvements in the legal system. During debates on the Bill, its aims were contrasted, on the one hand with the success of Scottish legislation, which allowed divorce only for adultery or desertion, and on the other, with countries where divorce was permitted more easily. Compared to the northern states of Germany, argued Lord Chancellor Cranworth, where couples were said to be able to divorce because of mere 'incompatibility of temper', England's divorce reform looked very staid indeed.[16] Thus overall it can be seen that those who supported the Bill believed that it was simply not in their interests to push for more grounds of divorce to be allowed.

For opponents of the Bill, however, raising the question of marital cruelty was a useful diversionary and delaying technique. To these men, allowing divorce for more than adultery would mark only the start of a slippery slope towards permitting marriages to end for a host of trivial reasons. 'The moment they went one step beyond the case of adultery, where and when would they stop?', asked Lord Campbell.[17] Objections were voiced about the proposals to allow men and women different routes to divorce. William Gladstone, (at this stage in his career, MP for the University of Oxford), did everything in his power to prevent the Bill, and pointed out the difficulty of enforcing a law that gave women divorce if their husband's adultery was accompanied by cruelty. 'What is

---

[15] As cited in Savage, '"Intended only for the husband"', 12.
[16] *Hansard*, vol. 145 (25 May 1857), 817; vol. 146 (23 June 1857), 201, 207–08; vol. 147 (30 July 1857), 718–19, 722–3, 868.
[17] As cited in Shanley, '"One must ride behind"', 368.

the meaning of cruelty?', he asked, provocatively. Citing Scott's ruling, he gave the definition of cruelty as that which endangered 'life, limb, or health, or a reasonable apprehension of such danger'. But, Gladstone argued,

Is that the only kind of cruelty which prevails in civilized society? Is that the only kind of cruelty which finds its way into the hearts of educated and refined women? Is not the cruelty of insult just as gross, just as wicked, just as abominable as the cruelty of mere force? . . . Is it not too notorious that. . . the adulteries of the husband have not only been occasional, but continuous; not only continuous, but open. . . And is not the insult inflicted in these cases one which sends the iron into the soul as deeply, and far more sharply, than any material instrument can send it into the body?[18]

To Gladstone, what the Bill proposed was unjust because it gave women an unequal access to divorce. In his opinion, for 'educated and refined women', the 'insult' of their husband's adultery was as painful as any physical blow. But his statement that marital cruelty could be mental as well as physical in form and consequence was not introduced to argue that the grounds of divorce should be extended, but rather to show how adultery could be as damaging to women as men. Thus upholding the double sexual standard in the Bill was not justifiable. Because the sexes were equal, believed Gladstone, neither men nor women should be allowed to divorce. Furthermore, the fact that in practice violence in middle- and upper-class marriage was not confined to the assaults upon 'life, limb, or health' that Scott outlined, meant that to permit women to divorce for adultery only when it was combined with such physical violence was grossly unfair. The 'educated and refined women' of Gladstone's social class would be prevented from obtaining divorce if they 'only' suffered the cruel indignity of their husband's infidelities. According to Gladstone, 'adultery with cruelty was at present a thing almost unknown in the higher classes of society, because the cruelty mentioned in the clause did not mean moral cruelty but cruelty attended with the effect of producing bodily fear'.[19] It was because Gladstone believed that violence was experienced differently across the social scale, that he thought wives in the upper social ranks would be disadvantaged by its terms. Following Gladstone's line of thinking, it was the varied nature of marital violence, (which could range between physical violence and 'moral' or sexual insult), and so its lack of precise parameters or definition, that made it so unsuited for inclusion in any aspect of legislation dealing with the grounds of marriage and divorce.

[18] *Hansard*, vol. 147 (7 August 1857), 1275–6.
[19] *Hansard*, vol. 147 (13 August 1857), 1538.

It was late on in the discussions on the Bill, in August 1857, that one Member went as far as to suggest that cruelty should be introduced as a separate cause for divorce. Mr Henry Drummond called upon a House of Commons Committee, 'to do justice to a suffering class, whose sufferings they did not know, because. . . those who knew their sufferings were interested in concealing them'. Referring, presumably, to the 1828 and 1853 legislation, Drummond admitted that MPs 'might think that they had done much in protecting women against the brutal violence of drunken husbands', but he argued that, 'there were much more serious lacerations of heart which took place in the higher regions'. Giving examples of the cruelties endured by wives married to adulterous husbands in the exclusive neighbourhoods of Grosvenor Square and Belgravia, Drummond demanded that a new clause should be inserted into the Bill that would allow divorce for such causes. To Gladstone this was like red rag to a bull. This is just what he and other opponents to the Bill had warned would happen, he argued, if parliament relaxed the law on divorce. It was vital, he argued, that MPs did not allow themselves to be swayed by 'the fashionable opinions of the day', and resisted such attempts to introduce more causes for divorce. Otherwise the floodgates would be opened and the institution of marriage subjected to irreparable damage.[20] At least in this plea, Gladstone was heard, and members of the House of Commons Committee rejected Drummond's amendment. Branded as simply the result of a transitory, populist, liberal 'fashion', the idea that marital violence could warrant divorce was dismissed out of hand.

How did women respond to these discussions about the Divorce Act? Opinion was clearly divided. Even if women could not sit in parliament, they could still shape its proceedings. A petition signed by some sixteen thousand women was presented to the Queen against the Bill, arguing that it would enable men to divorce them more easily, leaving them in a position of social isolation and financial hardship.[21] While broadly welcoming the Divorce Bill in her *Letter to the Queen* (1855), and in two other publications provoked by it, Caroline Norton highlighted what she saw as the injustices of some of its proposals. Her conviction that women should be able to divorce their husbands on the same grounds as men, and belief that women who were separated or divorced by their husbands should have the property rights of a 'feme sole', were taken up by her friend Lord Lyndhurst in parliament. At least in the latter cause, Norton was successful in gaining an amendment to the Bill that won property

[20] *Hansard*, vol. 147 (13 August 1857), 1587–90.
[21] Wolfram, 'Divorce in England', 178.

rights for separated and divorced wives. Given her earlier efforts to alter the law on child custody, discussed in Chapter 3, she must also have been heartened by the discretionary powers given to the new Divorce Court on this issue.[22]

Despite what she achieved, in many ways Norton was deeply conservative in her views. Perhaps inevitably in the light of her own experiences, she was far more interested in improving the lot of women who had been forced to live apart from their husbands, than fighting to change the position of wives who remained in marital relationships. She was clear about the sorts of women she thought had been most oppressed by the laws on marriage and divorce, and she sought to represent their views in her writings. As she explained:

The law compels the poor man to be responsible to the community at large, for the maltreatment of his wife; by a *new law* (the necessity for which has been abundantly proved by the daily police reports). Why should it seem grievous and shocking to make new laws of restraint for gentlemen as well as poor men?

According to Norton, MPs had already dealt with the marital problems of the poor, which centred upon physical marital violence, when they passed the 1853 Assault Act. But the concerns of Norton and her social circle had not been addressed. A man's natural superiority over his wife, Norton believed, gave him a duty of protection. 'Failing her natural protector', she argued, 'the law should be able to protect'.[23] In contrast to working-class wives, what women of Norton's social class needed, she argued, was protection of their property rather than their person. Hence Norton both maintained and defended notions of class and gender difference in her writings, and did all she could to distance herself from any group that could be labelled as feminist.

Regardless of Norton's personal viewpoint, her writings did inspire feminists, and her ideas about giving women rights over their property provoked others to pursue them to far more radical ends. To many feminists, divorce only dealt with the consequences of marriage breakdown, not its cause. In this light, the Divorce Act was hardly worthy of attention because it failed to address the more fundamental problem of sexual inequality within marriage. Barbara Leigh Smith, for example, published *A Brief Summary, In Plain Language, of the Most Important Laws Concerning Women* in 1854, which was so successful that a second

---

[22] Norton, *English Laws for Women* (1854); *A Letter to the Queen* (1855); and *A Review of the Divorce Bill of 1856* (1857). For discussion of these publications, see, M. Poovey, *Uneven Developments: The Ideological Work of Gender in Mid-Victorian England* (Chicago, 1988), chapter 3.

[23] Norton, *English Laws for Women*, pp. 147, 168, 172; italics are in the original.

edition was printed in early 1856. This was highly critical of the common law doctrine of coverture, and saw this as the root of many marital difficulties and violent quarrels. Thus it was within the debates about married women's property that feminists such as Leigh Smith found a way to address the problem of economic cruelty, which, as Chapter 1 showed, played such a key role in much marital violence. Unlike Norton, Leigh Smith focused on the damaging effects of existing property law for women within marriage, and for working-class as well as middle-class women. Discussing the working class, Leigh Smith wrote,

> In that rank of life where the support of the family depends often on the joint earnings of husband and wife, it is indeed cruel that the earnings of both should be in the hands of one, and not even in the hands of that one who has naturally the strongest desire to promote the welfare of the children. All who are familiar with the working classes know how much suffering and privation is caused by the exercise of this *right* by drunken and bad men. It is true that men are legally bound to support their wives and children, but this does not compensate women for the loss of their moral right to their own property and earnings, nor for the loss of the mental development and independence of character gained by the possession and thoughtful appropriation of money.[24]

Leigh Smith recognised just why property rights were so crucial to women. Of course, it made practical sense to let wives retain what they earned so that on a day-to-day basis they could provide easily for their families. But Leigh Smith also knew that owning and disposing of money freely would have a greater significance for wives. First, it would act as an acknowledgement of women's 'naturally' better understanding as mothers of what was in the best interests of children, and so give them a special position of authority within marriage. Second, allowing women that responsibility would give them the agency, or ability to shape their own lives, which was denied to them as 'femes covert'. Finally, and for our purposes, most importantly, if women had greater equality of property rights in marriage, then the threat of a form of violence 'by drunken and bad men' would be lessened because husbands would no longer have as much opportunity to deprive their wives of the material necessities of life. Without the notion of coverture governing the oper-ation of marital relationships, men's economic cruelties would lose their force. Instead of dividing the notion of protection, as Norton did, between that needed for the person, and that for property, Leigh Smith believed that a wife's physical and mental well-being could be protected

---

[24] B. Leigh Smith (later Bodichon), *A Brief Summary, in Plain Language, of the Most Important Laws Concerning Women* (London, 1854), p. 15; italics are in the original.

through their relationship to property. By thinking about what was common to married women (their lack of property rights), rather than, as Norton thought, what differentiated them (their class), Leigh Smith was able to confront and offer a solution to the sufferings endured by so many women of her period.

Leigh Smith's writing stuck a chord with other influential middle-class women and men of the day. She formed a committee, sometimes seen as marking the start of the organised feminist movement, which aimed to reform the laws for married women. Taking their name from the location in London of their meetings, the Langham Place group of feminists established the *English Woman's Journal*, which publicised their campaigns. The committee's work attracted widespread attention. Seventy petitions were presented to parliament seeking a change in the property rights of wives in 1856, one signed by 26,000 women and men, another by such literati as Elizabeth Barrett Browning and Elizabeth Stevenson Gaskell.[25] The Law Amendment Society saw this as too good an opportunity to miss, and two Bills were introduced to the House of Commons for the reform of married women's property in February and May 1857, first by Lord Brougham, then by Sir Erskine Perry. But although Perry's Bill passed its second reading in the Commons, neither became law. In part this was because some MPs opposed any measure that they believed had been tainted by feminism; one voiced concern that they were dealing with 'the extravagant demands of the large and manly body of "strong-minded women"'.[26] At the heart of debates, however, were fears about how husbands would maintain their power in marriage if their exclusive rights to property were removed. In this light, the Divorce Bill, which was being discussed at the same time, and limited property rights to wives who had separated or divorced from their husbands, rather than giving property rights to all married women, appeared a far more attractive option. The Married Women's Property Bill was discussed no further, and fell victim to the Divorce Act, which, as Perry later remarked, 'took the wind out of our sails'.[27] The issue was not raised again until 1868, and it was only after the passing of the 1870 Married Women's Property Act that a wife's wages and property were accepted as her separate property.

---

[25] 'A Petition for Women's Rights' (1856), in A. H. Manchester, *Sources of English Legal History: Law, History and Society in England and Wales 1750–1950* (London, 1984), pp. 400–2.

[26] As cited in, Poovey, *Uneven Developments*, p. 73.

[27] As cited in, L. Holcombe, *Wives and Property: Reform of the Married Women's Property Law in Nineteenth-Century England* (Toronto, 1983), p. 93.

Feminists continued to debate the significance of marriage for women throughout the nineteenth century.[28] They represented the public and collective voice of women's resistance to violence, while, as we have seen in Chapter 2, many wives continued to resist abuse in their own homes. Mary Wollstonecraft raised the problem of marital conflict in her final novel *The Wrongs of Woman* (1798), when she told the story of a woman who was wrongfully confined in a private madhouse by her husband, and the issue was taken up by feminist groups thereafter. The radical Unitarians and Owenites in the 1830s increased awareness of the legal inequalities that married women faced, and argued that divorce should be more freely available. Their ideas were influential in working- as well as middle-class circles. However, the question of marital violence was never central to their discussion. We do not have an answer to the question posed in a letter written on 22 October 1855 by John Chapman, editor of the *Westminster Review*, to the Unitarian, Harriet Martineau: 'Can you propose any remedy for the wife-beating except divorce? The question is pressing for solutions'.[29] Any solution, as the Owenites found to their cost, when they suggested that a new model of marriage and co-operative family life was necessary, where men and women were in an egalitarian position, was likely to cause alarm. Their vision of marriages of 'nature' where couples had greater liberty to be free if affection was lacking were viewed as simply giving licence to male libertinism. As a result, feminist ideas were increasingly seen as a danger to the socialist cause.[30] When debates about the marital relationship provoked such a divergence of opinion, and caused division even within groups who were pressing for change, there was no possibility for feminists to sustain a unified campaign on the problematic issue of marital violence. Without this pressure for reform, there was little reason for MPs to believe that marital violence was an important consideration when they discussed the grounds for divorce.

There is much to support Jan Lambertz's thesis, advanced for the twentieth century, but just as applicable to the mid-nineteenth, that many feminists, while being concerned about marital violence, believed that it was strategic to focus on other issues.[31] After all, the nineteenth century was a period when the Victorian ideal of domesticity gave

[28] P. Levine, '"So few prizes and so many blanks": Marriage and feminism in later nineteenth-century England', *Journal of British Studies* 28 (1989), 150–74.

[29] As cited in, K. Gleadle, *The Early Feminists: Radical Unitarians and the Emergence of the Women's Rights Movement, 1831–51* (Basingstoke, 1995), p. 126.

[30] B. Taylor, *Eve and the New Jerusalem: Socialism and Feminism in the Nineteenth Century* (London, 1983), chapter 6.

[31] J. Lambertz, 'Feminists and the politics of wife-beating', in H. L. Smith (ed.), *British Feminism in the Twentieth Century* (Aldershot, 1990), pp. 25–8.

renewed importance to the ideal of the wife in the home, and women's role as mothers had been placed on high pedestal, as Chapter 3 showed. For feminists to suggest, by highlighting cases of marital violence, that the home was a 'dangerous place' for women, could have been viewed as an unwise tactic. For the very incidence of marital violence was a clear demonstration that the home was far from being the universal centre of women's power and authority. Abused wives who made no complaint, or began legal proceedings against their violent husbands and then withdrew them, challenged the feminist view that all women interpreted patriarchal rule as oppressive. Finally, to feminists the importance of domestic roles for women's moral and social status made it very difficult for them to imagine women living outside the institution of marriage. Most feminists were eager to stress that they did not want to challenge the institution of marriage *per se*, but rather alter the position of women within it.[32] Enabling wives to gain easier access to divorce on a wider range of grounds was not regarded as liberating for feminists, but as condemning women to an uncertain and ill-defined existence. As we saw in Chapter 4, women's lives after legal separation could be subject to the harsh cruelties of poverty and social exclusion, when women themselves could sometimes ostracise other women who were less fortunate in their marriages.

It is for these reasons that marital violence was not included as a ground for divorce in 1857, and why the injustices of the Act did not cause an immediate outcry. The terms of the Act meant that until 1923, when wives were given the right to obtain divorce for adultery on the same grounds as husbands, men procured 60 per cent of all divorces. Until then, since considerable obstacles had to be overcome by women to achieve divorce, (they had to prove some other cause that had 'aggravated' their husbands' adultery), it is testimony of their determination that 40 per cent of the total number of divorces were granted to them.[33] While the annual number of divorces rose from an average of four divorce acts achieved through parliament before 1857, to between two to three hundred from the new Divorce Court, those who achieved divorce were mainly men from the middle class or the upper ranks of the working class. Recent work has emphasised that the new Divorce Court was not a socially exclusive domain, and that the less affluent did resort to it in greater numbers than had been anticipated. However,

---

[32] This was a position that feminists still held at the end of the nineteenth century, see, L. Bland, 'The married woman, the 'new woman' and the feminist: sexual politics of the 1890s', in J. Rendall (ed.), *Equal or Different: Women's Politics 1800–1914* (Oxford, 1987), p. 147.

[33] Wolfram, 'Divorce in England', 157, n.11.

despite the fact that the cost of obtaining a divorce was significantly less than it had been previously, (around £40 to £60, rather than several hundred pounds), this was still out of the range of affordability for many working people. Furthermore, the Divorce Court remained in London, meaning that for those who resided elsewhere there were additional travel and accommodation costs to be met for both parties and their witnesses.[34] As a result, by the end of the nineteenth century, England's divorce rate was one of the lowest in Europe.

The Divorce Court also heard the cases for judicial separation that were brought by wives whose husbands were 'simply' violent, but not adulterous. Rather than being able to seek a separation *a mensa et thoro* in their local church court, the journey and expense of a trip to London was now necessary. The new court inherited both the legal precedents and personnel of the former church courts, which, theoretically, made any change in the definition of cruelty that would allow separation unlikely. In practice, according to Hammerton, significant changes in the law on matrimonial cruelty did occur, so that by 1869 judges were less insistent that physical violence needed to have taken place for cruelty to be proved. But as this book has shown, magistrates and judges had long been prepared to consider the cruelty of non-physical violence. Furthermore, the judgements made by the Divorce Court showed that legal personnel remained wedded to patriarchal notions of marriage, and their assessment of the consequences of violence was determined by the social class of its target. Thus their rulings repeated rather than created the idea that the cruelty of violence varied across the social structure.[35]

Resorting to this court for a judicial separation was very rare; in 1858–62 less than one spouse in every 100,000 of the married population took this route to end marriage. Private separation deeds, which could be drawn up by a lawyer, and agreed by mutual consent, continued to be a more popular course of action.[36] This should not surprise us when we consider the very public nature of the new Divorce Court. Members of the public could attend its hearings, whereas before 1857 couples seeking separation simply submitted written statements to be considered privately by the judges of the church courts. In the longer term, Hammerton may be correct in his assertion that the publicity surrounding the Divorce Court exposed middle-class marriage to greater critical scrutiny, and hence benefited women in general.[37] But for many individual women seeking an immediate remedy to marital violence, the

---

[34] Phillips, *Putting Asunder*, pp. 420–1; Savage, '"Intended only for the husband"', pp. 19–37; Hammerton, *Cruelty and Companionship*, pp. 103–5, 175.

[35] Hammerton, *Cruelty and Companionship*, pp. 118–33.

[36] Anderson, 'State, civil society and separation', 161–201.

[37] Hammerton, *Cruelty and Companionship*, pp. 102–3.

prospect of facing the glare of the public gaze in this courtroom must have been extremely intimidating, even to the point of deterring legal action. Indeed, it can be argued that by the terms of the 1857 Act it was only working-class wives who had been deserted by their husbands who were in a better position to seek legal redress. Protection orders to preserve their property could be obtained from any magistrate, and a legal separation was possible. However, if it was the wife rather than the husband who had deserted the marriage because of his violence, protection orders were not available.

It took the journalistic efforts of Frances Power Cobbe (1822–1904), an Anglo-Irish gentlewoman who never married, for the limitations of the Divorce Act for wives whose husbands were violent but not adulterous to be widely recognised. Her writings allow us a measure of the changes and continuities that this book has outlined. While she was interested in a wide number of feminist causes, Cobbe's focus on the problem of marital violence enabled her to demonstrate the fatal consequences of women's subordinate position in society. Her most famous article on marital violence, 'Wife-Torture in England', published in 1878, was based on her reading of statistics of the numbers of cases brought before magistrates under the terms of the 1853 Assaults Act, and the stories of these cases as reported in the press. The tone of her writing is evidence of the level of outrage that marital violence inspired by this period. Citing the horrific details of recent cases, Cobbe argued that this violence should be termed 'wife-torture' rather than 'wife-beating', because the latter conveyed only a remote notion of the extremity of cruelty involved. Female as well as male violence was recognised, as Cobbe described 'wife-beating by combat', or the incidents when both wives and husbands exchanged violence towards each other. While Cobbe did not go as far as to suggest that women's violence towards their husbands could be in self-defence, she did strike a final blow for the male defence that their wives' behaviour had provoked them to violence. If wives were scolds and drunks, she argued, it was because they had been driven to such conduct by the 'sheer misery' of living with abusive husbands.

Cobbe had no hesitation concluding that it was the popular belief in a husband's right to beat his wife, and the notion that a wife was a husband's property, that was 'the fatal root of incalculable evil and misery'. These popular attitudes were so deeply entrenched, that wives who were being attacked by their husbands 'sometimes turn round and snap at a bystander who has interfered on their behalf', Cobbe observed. Demonstrating a keen understanding of the limitations of community involvement in marital violence by this period, Cobbe knew that the result of this response by some wives was that witnesses were given a 'welcome excuse' for the 'policy of non-intervention'. In the absence of community support, legal sanctions to marital violence were no more attractive. The 'ignorant, friendless, and penniless women', who Cobbe believed were the main victims of wife-torture, were unable to achieve full divorce from the Divorce Court, and fears about what would happen to their children following separation acted as a major disincentive to judicial separation. Confronting the link between marital and child abuse in a way that had so eluded her eighteenth- and early-nineteenth century predecessors, Cobbe argued that,

the man who is. . . capable of kicking, maiming, and mutilating his wife, is even less fit to be the guardian of the bodies and souls of children than the lord and master of a woman. They are no more safe under his roof than in the cage of a wild beast.

Punishing the perpetrator of this violence with flogging was no answer, thought Cobbe, as she quite rightly realised that this would only increase the number of wives who were reluctant to prosecute or withdrew their complaints, fearful of facing even angrier husbands on their return home. What these wives needed was relief and escape from violent marriages.

Cobbe's call for legislation that would give women easier access to separation following marital violence was answered in the Matrimonial Causes Act of 1878. This gave magistrates the ability to award wives separation from husbands who had been convicted of aggravated assault; custody of children under the age of ten years of age; and weekly maintenance. The promise of escape from violent marriage in this way proved far more popular than judicial separation. In 1888, the Divorce Court granted only 39 judicial separations, while London wives alone were granted 108 separation orders by metropolitan police magistrates. Cobbe's own life story and writings, meanwhile, provided a positive example of what women could achieve outside the institution of marriage. By 1878, then, marital violence was an issue that was obtaining serious and sustained public attention, and a recognition that its causes and consequences were to be found beyond the immediate lives of couples whose marriages it affected.[38]

Yet for all that had been achieved, Cobbe's views were very much the product of their time, for although she pursued them to feminist ends,

[38] F. P. Cobbe, 'Wife-Torture in England', *The Contemporary Review* 32 (April 1878), 58, 61–2, 64, 68–85; C. Bauer and L. Ritt, '"A husband is a beating animal" Frances Power Cobbe confronts the wife-abuse problem in Victorian England', *International Journal of Women's Studies* 6, 2 (1983), 99–118; B. Caine, *Victorian Feminists* (Oxford, 1992), chapter 4; Anderson, 'State, civil society and separation', 171.

her ideas about marital violence stemmed from and reflected what had become standard nineteenth-century thinking on the subject. Cobbe, like so many of her contemporaries, was unable to break free from class-based misconceptions about marital violence. 'The dangerous wife-beater belongs almost exclusively to the artisan and labouring classes', argued Cobbe, whereas in the upper and middle classes, marital violence 'rarely extends to anything beyond an occasional blow or two of a not dangerous kind'. Despite all the evidence that this book has discussed, which shows that violence in all its forms was experienced in every social class, when marital violence came to be seen as a problem to be regulated, it was physical violence among the working classes that was the first to receive attention. The problem of upper- and middle-class women and men imposing solutions upon working-class marriage, rather than seeking answers from the working class themselves was not acknowledged. As a result, reforms were often ill-matched to patterns of working-class life.[39] Arguably the 1878 Act created a 'class apartheid', when if marriages failed, it was mainly middle- and upper-class wives who sought judicial separation from the Divorce Court, and working-class women who obtained separation orders from their local magistrate. In neither case was full divorce with the option to remarry permitted.[40]

Whereas thinkers such as Cobbe were able to see that the 'fatal root' of marital violence was how women were popularly viewed by men as inferiors and unequals, nevertheless, and perhaps inevitably, the changes that were proposed by Cobbe and others addressed the consequences instead of the causes of marital violence. The limitations of this approach were recognised by Cobbe herself. 'To a certain extent', she wrote, 'this marital tyranny among the lower classes is beyond the reach of the law, and can only be remedied by the slow elevation and civilization of both sexes'.[41] Legal change did arrive eventually. It was in 1891 that judges first declared that husbands did not have a right to beat or confine their wives; the ability of wives to gain full divorce on the grounds of cruelty or desertion was obtained in 1937; and in 1991 the illegal parameters of violence within marriage were extended when the concept of marital rape was accepted in English law. It would take a much longer process of change for ideas about the legitimacy of violence in marriage to be

---

[39] This pattern continued into the early twentieth century, see I. Minor, 'Working-class women and matrimonial law reform, 1890–1914', in D. E. Martin and D. Rubinstein (eds.), *Ideology and the Labour Movement: Essays Presented to John Saville* (London, 1979), pp. 103–24.

[40] P. Levine, *Victorian Feminism 1850–1900* (London, 1987), p. 143; O. R. McGregor, L. Blom-Cooper and C. Gibson, *Separated Spouses: A Study of the Matrimonial Jurisdiction of Magistrate's Courts* (London, 1970), p. 16.

[41] Cobbe, 'Wife-Torture', 61.

challenged and overcome. The period of this book may have marked the beginning of legislative change with regard to marital violence, but popular attitudes towards the kinds of violence endured by both Rachael Norcott and Mary Veitch have been painfully slow to alter.

There is much that Rachael Norcott and Mary Veitch would not recognise about the marriages and family lives of women today. The professions that were at their early stages of development in the Restoration to Victorian period have expanded, and new specialists such as marriage guidance counsellors, psychiatrists and social workers deal with the consequences of marital violence. In addition, and sometimes in place of the support offered to Rachael and Mary by their families, friends and neighbours, these professionals offer advice and provide accommodation via shelters and refuges. As the divorce rate soars, the social unacceptability of the separated wife is no longer an issue. Improving legal rights and employment opportunities have enabled divorced women to obtain the kinds of financial security unknown to earlier generations.

Yet there remains an alarming degree of similarity between the world inhabited by Rachael and Mary and our own. Popular confusion about the most basic questions relating to marital violence can be traced back to the period surveyed in this book. The idea that marital violence is primarily physical in form has to be countered with evidence that its verbal and sexual components can be equally damaging. Now that we have easier access to divorce, the assumption that a wife is somehow to blame for her fate if she remains with her violent husband is more readily reached. Judgements about the victims of marital violence continue to be made before its perpetrators are condemned, and explanations for violence that blame a woman's provocative behaviour remain popular. Few are willing to accept the ramifications of the idea that violence between family members is never deserved. We are little closer than our predecessors to understanding violence by women against men in marriage. The debates over child custody have gone full circle, and it is now fathers who fight for greater rights. But as violence within the family is exposed, we are still coming to terms with the impact of inter-parental violence on children. Despite our faith in the professions, theories about the causes and the most appropriate responses to male violence continue to abound. Although few men would now regard physical correction of their wives as their 'right', an unknown number of women are subject to violence in their marital relationships. In the midst of our condemnation of marital violence, wives like Rachael and Mary suffer. The legacy of the views and beliefs about marital violence that have been outlined in this book is a lengthy one.

Bibliography

UNPUBLISHED MANUSCRIPTS AND COLLECTIONS

British Library, London
Sabine Baring-Gould Collection of Ballads, 10 vols., c.1800–70.
Thomas Bell Collection of Ballads, c.1780–c.1820.

Cambridgeshire County Record Office, Shire Hall, Cambridge
Ely and South Witchford Division Minute Book (7 January 1797 to 30 December 1802).

Cambridge University Library, Cambridge
Ely Diocesan Records (EDR): Quarter Sessions Files, E47–52 (1743 to 1768).
Madden Collection of Ballads, 26 vols., for the period c.1775–c.1850.

Lambeth Palace Library, London
Court of Arches (CA): Personal Answers (Ee), Process Books (D), Depositions (Eee) for the period 1660–1800, and Nineteenth-Century Case Papers (H) for the period 1800–57. Indexed in J. Houston (ed.), *Index of Cases in the Records of the Court of Arches at Lambeth Palace Library 1660–1913*, London, 1972.
Peculiars of the Archbishop of Canterbury: Cause Papers (VH80) for the period 1686–1844.

London Metropolitan Archives, London
Edmonton Petty Session Division: Tottenham, Enfield and Wood Green Courts, Minute Book (PS.E/E1/1) for the period 5 October 1848 to 4 December 1851.
London Consistory Court: Libels and Deposition Books (DL/C) for the period 1752–1806.

National Archives, Kew
High Court of Delegates: Processes (DEL1) for the period 1702–1800.
Judicial Committee of the Privy Council: Processes (PCAP 1) and Case Books (PCAP 3) for the period 1834–56.
King's Bench (Crown Side): Affidavits (KB1) for the period 1738–82.

York Minster Archives, York
Petty Sessions records for the JPs of the Liberty of St Peter, York, Case Papers (F2/3/2/1–75) for the period 1819–38.

PRINTED PRIMARY SOURCES

The Bath Journal (1748–51)
Fog's Weekly Journal (1731–33)
Scotland on Sunday (31 March 2002)
The Scotsman (27 March 2002)
The Times (1800–57)
The Accomplished Youth: Containing a Familiar View of the True Principles of Morality and Politeness, London, 1811.
'An Act to amend the Law relating to Divorce and Matrimonial Causes in England' (20 and 21 Vict; c.85).
Andrew, D. T. (ed.), *London Debating Societies, 1776–1799*, London Record Society, London, 1994.
Anselment, R. A. (ed.), *The Remembrances of Elizabeth Freke, 1671–1714*, Camden Fifth Series, vol. 18, Cambridge, 2001.
Arden of Faversham, London, c.1591.
Blackstone, W., *Commentaries on the Laws of England*, 4 vols., Oxford, 1783.
Bond, D. F. (ed.), *The Spectator*, 5 vols., Oxford, 1965.
Brontë, A., *The Tenant of Wildfell Hall* (1848), Harmondsworth, 1994.
Burn, R., *The Justice of Peace and Parish Officer* 2 vols., London, 1755.
Burnett, J. (ed.), *Destiny Obscure: Autobiographies of Childhood, Education and Family from the 1820s to the 1920s*, London, 1982.
Carnell, P. (ed.), *Broadside Ballads and Song-Sheets from the Hewins MSS. Collection in Sheffield University Library: A Descriptive Catalogue with Indexes and Notes*, Sheffield, 1987.
Chapman, G., *A Treatise on Education*, Edinburgh, 1773.
Chappell, W. (ed.), *The Roxburghe Ballads* vols. I–III, London, 1871–80.
Cirket, A. F. (ed.), *Samuel Whitbread's Notebooks 1810–11, 1813–14*, Bedfordshire Historical Record Society, 150, Bedford, 1971.
Cobbe, F. P., 'Wife-Torture in England', *The Contemporary Review* 32 (April 1878), 55–87.
Crittall, E. (ed.), *The Justicing Notebook of William Hunt 1744–1749*, Wiltshire Record Society, 37, Devizes, 1982.
Crosley, D., *The Christian Marriage Explained*, London, 1744.
Dalton, M., *The Country Justice: Containing the Practice, Duty and Power of the Justices of the Peace*, London, 1746.
Dawburn, E., *The Rights of Infants*, Wisbech, 1805.
Day, W. G. (ed.), *The Pepys Ballads*, 5 vols., Cambridge, 1987.
Dickens, C., *The Old Curiosity Shop (1840–41)*, London, 2000.
Directions given by Edmund Lord Bishop of London to the Clergy of his Diocese, in the year 1724, London, 1724.
Dod, J. and Cleaver, R., *A Godly Forme of Householde Governement*, London, 1630.

Downame, J., *A Treatise of Anger*, London, 1609.

Ebsworth, J. W. (ed.), *The Roxburghe Ballads* vols. IV–IX, London, 1883–99.

Ellis, S., *The Wives of England, Their Relative Duties, Domestic Influences, and Social Obligations*, London, 1843.

English Reports: Ecclesiastical, Admiralty, Probate and Divorce vols. 161–4, Edinburgh and London, 1917–21.

First Report of the Commissioners, appointed by her Majesty to enquire into the Law of Divorce, London, 1853.

Fleetwood, W., *The Relative Duties of Parents and Children*, London, 1705.

Forsyth, W., *A Treatise on the Law Relating to the Custody of Infants, in Cases of Difference between Parents or Guardians*, London, 1850.

Giles, W., *A Treatise on Marriage*, London, 1771.

The Good Wife's Rod for a Bad Husband, A Copy and Explanation of the New Act for the Protection of Women, London, 1853.

Gouge, W., *Of Domesticall Duties*, 3rd edition, London, 1634.

Gude, R., *The Practice of the Crown Side of the Court of King's Bench*, London, 1828.

Halliwell, J. O. (ed.), *The Autobiography and Personal Diary of Dr Simon Forman*, London, 1849.

[Handley, Edwin Hill], 'Custody of Infants Bill', *The British and Foreign Review* 7 (July 1838), 269–411.

Hansard's Parliamentary Debates, 3rd series, vols. 124–5, 141, 145–7.

The Hardships of the English Laws in Relation to Wives, London, 1735.

Hawky's Garland, a collection printed chiefly by J. and M. Robertson, Glasgow, 1779–1816.

Haywood, E., *The History of Miss Betsy Thoughtless* (1751), ed. B. F. Tobin, Oxford, 1997.

Heale, W., *An Apology for Women*, Oxford, 1609.

Herbert, G., *A Priest to the Temple or the Country Parson* (1652), ed. R. Blythe, Norwich, 2003.

Heywood, T. (ed.), *The Diary of the Reverend Henry Newcome, from September 30, 1661 to September 29, 1663*, Chetham Society, vol. 18, Manchester, 1849.

Hints to a Clergyman's Wife; Or, Female Parochial Duties Practically Illustrated, London, 1832.

Jalland, P. and Hooper, J. (eds.), *Women from Birth to Death: The Female Life Cycle in Britain 1830–1914*, Atlantic Highlands NJ, 1986.

Jesse, W., *Parochialia; Or Observations on the Discharge of Parochial Duties*, Kidderminster, 1785.

Jones, V. (ed.), *Women in the Eighteenth Century: Constructions of Femininity*, London, 1990.

Keble, J., *An Assistance to Justices of the Peace, for Easier Performance of their Duty*, London, 1683.

Leigh Smith (later Bodichon), B., *A Brief Summary, in Plain Language, of the Most Important Laws Concerning Women*, London, 1854.

Locke, J., *Some Thoughts Concerning Education* (1693), eds. J. W. and J. S. Yolton, Oxford, 1989.

Matthews, W. (ed.), *The Diary of Dudley Ryder 1715–1716*, London, 1939.

Mead, M., *A Discourse on Marriage*, London, 1732.

The Memoirs of Mrs Catherine Jemmat, 2 vols., London, 1762–71.

[More, H.,] *Cheap Repository of Moral and Religious Tracts*, London, 1797.

Morgan, G. and Rushton, P. (eds.), *The Justicing Notebook (1750–64) of Edmund Tew, Rector of Boldon*, Surtees Society, 205, Woodbridge, 2000.

Nelson, J., *An Essay on the Government of Children*, London, 1756.

Norton, C., *English Laws for Women in the Nineteenth Century*, London, 1854, in J. O. Hoge and J. Marcus, *Selected Writings of Caroline Norton*, New York, 1978.

A Letter to the Queen on Lord Chancellor Cranworth's Marriage and Divorce Bill, London, 1855, in J. O. Hoge and J. Marcus, *Selected Writings of Caroline Norton*, New York, 1978.

A Plain Letter to the Lord Chancellor on the Infant Custody Bill, London, 1839.

A Review of the Divorce Bill of 1856 (1857).

The Separation of Mother and Child by the Law of 'Custody of Infants' Considered, London, 1838.

Observations on the Natural Claim of the Mother to the Custody of her Infant Children, as Affected by the Common Law Right of the Father, London, 1837.

Oxenden, A., *The Pastoral Office: Its Duties, Difficulties, Privileges and Prospects*, London, 1857.

Paley, R. (ed.), *Justice in Eighteenth-Century Hackney: The Justicing Notebook of Henry Norris and the Hackney Petty Sessions Book*, London Record Society, London, 1991.

Parkinson, R. (ed.), *The Autobiography of Henry Newcome*, 2 vols., Chetham Society, Manchester, 1852.

Pennington, S., *A Mother's Advice to her Absent Daughters*, 8th edition, London, 1817.

'A Petition for Women's Rights' (1856) in A. H. Manchester, *Sources of English Legal History: Law, History and Society in England and Wales 1750–1950*, London, 1984, pp. 400–2.

The Polite Present, Or the Child's Manual of Good Manners, Glasgow, 1833.

Prentiss Bishop, J., *Commentaries on the Law of Marriage and Divorce*, Boston and London, 1852.

The Proceedings of the Old Bailey (http://www.oldbaileyonline.org).

Robson, A. P. and Robson, J. M. (eds.), *Sexual Equality: Writings by John Stuart Mill, Harriet Taylor Mill, and Helen Taylor*, Toronto, 1994.

Rollins, H. E. (ed.), *A Pepysian Garland: Black Letter Broadside Ballads of the Years 1595–1639*, Cambridge, MA, 1971.

Rosenheim, J. M. (ed.), *The Notebook of Robert Doughty 1662–1665*, Norfolk Record Society, 54, 1989.

Ross, A. (ed.), *Selections from* The Tatler *and* The Spectator, Harmondsworth, 1982.

Silverthorne, E. (ed.), *Deposition Book of Richard Wyatt, JP, 1767–1776*, Surrey Record Society, 30, Guildford, 1978.

Smith, H., *A Preparative to Marriage*, London, 1591.

Snawsel, R., *A Looking-Glasse for Married Folkes*, London, 1631, ed. Amsterdam, 1975.

Sokoll, T. (ed.), *Essex Pauper Letters, 1731–1837*, Records of Social and Economic History, new series, 30, Oxford, 2001.

Sylvestre du Four, P., *Moral Instructions for Youth: Or, A Father's Advice to a Son*, London, 1742.

Taves, A. (ed.), *Religion and Domestic Violence in Early New England: The Memoirs of Abigail Abbot Bailey*, Bloomington, 1989.

Thompson, W., *The Care of Parents is a Happiness to Children: Or, The Duty of Parents to their Children, and of Children to their Parents*, London, 1710.

Vauts, M. À., *The Husband's Authority Unvail'd; Wherein it is Moderately Discussed Whether it be Fit or Lawful for a Good Man, to Beat his Bad Wife*, London, 1650.

Waddilove, A., *A Digest of Cases Decided in the Court of Arches*, London, 1849.

Webster, W., *A Casuistical Essay on Anger and Forgiveness*, London, 1750.

Whateley, W., *A Bride Bush*, London, 1623.

Wight, J., *Mornings at Bow Street: A Selection of the Most Humourous and Entertaining Reports which have Appeared in the Morning Herald*, London, 1824.

Wilkes, W., *A Letter of Genteel and Moral Advice to a Young Lady*, 8th edition, London, 1766.

Woolley, H., *The Gentlewoman's Companion; Or, a Guide to the Female Sex*, London, 1675.

Wollstonecraft, M., *The Wrongs of Woman: Or, Maria* (1798), ed. G. Kelly, Oxford, 1998.

The Young Man's Own Book. A Manual of Politeness, Intellectual Improvement, and Moral Deportment, London, 1833.

SECONDARY SOURCES

Abrams, L., 'Companionship and conflict: the negotiation of marriage relations in the nineteenth century', in L. Abrams and E. Harvey (eds.), *Gender Relations in German History: Power, Agency and Experience from the Sixteenth to the Twentieth Century*, London, 1996, pp. 101–20.

'"There was nobody like my daddy": Fathers, the family and the marginalisation of men in modern Scotland', *The Scottish Historical Review* 78, 2 (1999), 219–42.

Adler, J. S., '"My mother-in-law is to blame, but I'll walk on her neck yet": Homicide in late nineteenth-century Chicago', *Journal of Social History* 31, 2 (1997), 253–76.

Amussen, S. D., *An Ordered Society: Gender and Class in Early Modern England*, Oxford, 1988.

'"Being stirred to much unquietness": Violence and domestic violence in early modern England', *Journal of Women's History* 6, 2 (1994), 70–89.

'"The part of a Christian man": the cultural politics of manhood in early modern England', in S. D. Amussen and M. A. Kishlansky (eds.), *Political Culture and Cultural Politics in Early Modern England: Essays Presented to David Underdown*, Manchester, 1995, pp. 213–33.

'Punishment, discipline, and power: the social meanings of violence in early modern England', *Journal of British Studies* 34 (1995), 1–34.

Anderson, O., 'State, civil society and separation in Victorian marriage', *Past and Present* 163 (1999), 161–201.

Suicide in Victorian and Edwardian England, Oxford, 1987.

Anderson, S., 'Legislative divorce – Law for the aristocracy?', in G. R. Rubin and D. Sugarman (eds.), *Law, Economy and Society: Essays in the History of English Law, 1750–1914*, London, 1984, pp. 412–44.

Andrew, D. T., 'The code of honour and its critics: the opposition to duelling in England, 1700–1850', *Social History* 5, 3 (1980), 409–34.

Ariès, P., *Centuries of Childhood*, London, 1962.

'Introduction', in P. Ariès, G. Duby and R. Chartier (eds.), *A History of Private Life* vol. 3, trans. A. Goldhammer, London, 1989, pp. 1–11.

August, A., *Poor Women's Lives: Gender, Work, and Poverty in Late-Victorian London*, London, 1999.

Bailey, J., 'Breaking the conjugal vows: marriage and marriage breakdown in the north of England, 1660–1800', PhD thesis, University of Durham, 1999.

'Favoured or oppressed? Married women, property and 'coverture' in England, 1660–1800', *Continuity and Change* 17, 3 (2002), 351–72.

Unquiet Lives: Marriage and Marriage Breakdown in England, 1660–1800, Cambridge, 2003.

'Voices in court: lawyers' or litigants'?', *Historical Research* 74, 186 (2001), 392–408.

Barber, M., 'Records of marriage and divorce in Lambeth Palace', *Genealogists' Magazine* 20, 4 (1980), 109–17.

'Records of the Court of Arches in Lambeth Palace Library', *Ecclesiastical Law Journal* 3 (1993), 10–19.

Barker-Benfield, G. J., *The Culture of Sensibility: Sex and Society in Eighteenth-Century Britain*, Chicago, 1992.

Bartrip, P. W. J., 'How green was my valance?: Environmental arsenic poisoning and the Victorian domestic ideal', *English Historical Review* 109 (1994), 891–913.

Bauer, C. and Ritt, L., '"A husband is a beating animal" Frances Power Cobbe confronts the wife-abuse problem in Victorian England', *International Journal of Women's Studies* 6, 2 (1983), 99–118.

Beattie, J. M., *Crime and the Courts in England 1660–1800*, Princeton, 1986.

Policing and Punishment in London, 1660–1750: Urban Crime and the Limits of Terror, Oxford, 2001.

'Violence and society in early-modern England', in A. N. Doob and E. L. Greenspan (eds.), *Perspectives in Criminal Law*, Ontario, 1985, pp. 36–60.

Ben-Amos, I. K., *Adolescence and Youth in Early Modern England*, London, 1994.

'Gifts and favors: informal support in early modern England', *Journal of Modern History* 72 (2000), 295–338.

'Reciprocal bonding: parents and their offspring in early modern England', *Journal of Family History* 25, 3 (2000), 291–312.

Berg, M., 'Women's consumption and the industrial classes of eighteenth-century England', *Journal of Social History* 30, 2 (1996), 415–34.

Berg, M. and Eger, E., 'The rise and fall of the luxury debates', in M. Berg and E. Eger (eds.), *Luxury in the Eighteenth Century: Debates, Desires and Delectable Goods*, London, 2003, pp. 7–27.

Berry, H., *Gender, Society and Print Culture in Late-Stuart England: The Cultural World of the* Athenian Mercury, Aldershot, 2003.

'Prudent luxury: the metropolitan tastes of Judith Baker, Durham gentle-woman', in R. Sweet and P. Lane (eds.), *Women and Urban Life in Eighteenth-Century England: 'On the Town'*, Aldershot, 2003, pp. 131–56.

Biggs, J. M., *The Concept of Matrimonial Cruelty*, London, 1962.

Bland, L., 'The married woman, the "new woman" and the feminist: sexual politics of the 1890s', in J. Rendall (ed.), *Equal or Different: Women's Politics 1800–1914*, Oxford, 1987, pp. 141–64.

Boulton, J., *Neighbourhood and Society: A London Suburb in the Seventeenth Century*, Cambridge, 1987.

Bound, F., '"An angry and malicious mind"? Narratives of slander at the church courts of York, c.1660–c.1760', *History Workshop Journal* 56 (2003), 59–77.

'An "uncivil" culture: marital violence and domestic politics in York, c.1660–c.1760', in M. Hallett and J. Rendall (eds.), *Eighteenth-Century York: Culture, Space and Society*, York, 2003, pp. 50–8.

Bourlet, A., *Police Intervention in Marital Violence*, Milton Keynes, 1990.

Bowers, T., *The Politics of Motherhood: British Writing and Culture, 1680–1760*, Cambridge, 1996.

Brown, K. M., 'The laird, his daughter, her husband and the minister: unravel-ling a popular ballad', in R. Mason and N. MacDougall (eds.), *People and Power in Scotland: Essays in Honour of T. C. Smout*, Edinburgh, 1992, pp. 104–25.

Browne, A., *When Battered Women Kill*, New York, 1987.

Burke, P., *The Art of Conversation*, Oxford, 1993.

'Some reflections on the pre-industrial city', *Urban History Yearbook*, Leicester, 1975, pp. 13–21.

Burney, I. A., *Bodies of Evidence: Medicine and the Politics of the English Inquest 1830–1926*, Baltimore, 2000.

Caine, B., *Victorian Feminists*, Oxford, 1992.

Capp, B., 'English youth groups and "The Pinder of Wakefield"', in P. Slack (ed.), *Rebellion, Popular Protest and Social Order in Early Modern England*, Cambridge, 1984, pp. 212–18.

When Gossips Meet: Women, Family, and Neighbourhood in Early Modern England, Oxford, 2003.

Carter, P., 'James Boswell's manliness', in T. Hitchcock and M. Cohen (eds.), *English Masculinities 1660–1800*, Harlow, 1999, pp. 111–30.

Cavallo, S., 'What did women transmit? Ownership and control of household goods and personal effects in early modern Italy', in M. Donald and L. Hurcombe (eds.), *Gender and Material Culture in Historical Perspective*, Basingstoke, 2000, pp. 38–53.

Chaytor, M., 'Household and kinship in Ryton in the late sixteenth and early seventeenth centuries', *History Workshop Journal* 10 (1980), 25–60.

Childs, F. A., 'Prescriptions for manners in English courtesy literature, 1690–1760, and their social implications', DPhil. thesis, University of Oxford, 1984.

Clark, A., 'Domesticity and the problem of wifebeating in nineteenth-century Britain: working-class culture, law and politics', in S. D'Cruze (ed.), *Everyday Violence in Britain, 1850–1950: Gender and Class*, Harlow, 2000, pp. 27–40.

'Humanity or justice? Wifebeating and the law in the eighteenth and nineteenth centuries', in C. Smart (ed.), *Regulating Womanhood: Historical Essays on Marriage, Motherhood and Sexuality*, London, 1992, pp. 187–206.

The Struggle for the Breeches: Gender and the Making of the British Working Class, London, 1995.

'Whores and gossips: sexual reputation in London 1770–1825', in A. Angerman, G. Binnema, A. Keunen, V. Poels and J. Zirkzee (eds.), *Current Issues in Women's History*, London, 1989, pp. 231–48.

Women's Silence Men's Violence: Sexual Assault in England 1770–1845, London, 1987.

Cliffe, J. T., *The World of the Country House in Seventeenth-Century England*, London, 1999.

Cockburn, J. S., 'The nature and incidence of crime in England 1559–1625: a preliminary survey', in J. S. Cockburn (ed.), *Crime in England 1550–1800* London, 1977, pp. 49–71.

'Patterns of violence in English society: homicide in Kent 1560–1985', *Past and Present* 130 (1991), 70–106.

Conley, C., *The Unwritten Law: Criminal Justice in Victorian Kent*, Oxford, 1991.

Corfield, P. J., *Power and the Professions in Britain 1700–1850*, London, 1995.

Coster, W., *Baptism and Spiritual Kinship in Early Modern England*, Aldershot, 2002.

Crawford, C., 'Patients' rights and the law of contract in eighteenth-century England', *Social History of Medicine* 13, 3 (2000), 381–410.

Cressy, D., 'Kinship and kin interaction in early modern England', *Past and Present* 113 (1986), 38–69.

'Purification, thanksgiving and the churching of women in post-Reformation England', *Past and Present* 141 (1993), 106–14.

Cunningham, H., *Children and Childhood in Western Society Since 1500*, London, 1995.

'Histories of childhood', *American Historical Review* 103 (1998), 1195–208.

D'Cruze, S., '"A little, decent-looking woman": violence against nineteenth-century working women and the social history of crime', in A-M. Gallagher, C. Lubelska and L. Ryan (eds.), *Re-presenting the Past: Women and History*, London, 2001, pp. 63–86.

Crimes of Outrage: Sex, Violence and Victorian Working Women, London, 1998.

(ed.), *Everyday Violence in Britain, 1850–1950: Gender and Class*, Harlow, 2000.

'Introduction. Unguarded passions: violence, history and the everyday', in S. D'Cruze (ed.), *Everyday Violence in Britain, 1850–1950: Gender and Class*, Harlow, 2000, pp. 1–24.

Dabhoiwala, F. N., 'Prostitution and police in London, c.1660–c.1760', DPhil. thesis, University of Oxford, 1995.

Davidoff, L. and Hall, C., *Family Fortunes: Men and Women of the English Middle Class 1780–1850*, London, 1987.

Davidson, T., 'Wifebeating: a recurring phenomenon throughout history' in M. Roy (ed.), *Battered Women: A Psychosociological Study of Domestic Violence*, New York, 1977, pp. 2–23.

Davis, J. S., 'A poor man's system of justice: the London police courts in the second half of the nineteenth century', *Historical Journal* 27, 2 (1984), 309–35.

'Prosecutions and their context: the use of the criminal law in later nineteenth-century London', in D. Hay and F. Snyder (eds.), *Policing and Prosecution in Britain 1750–1850* (Oxford, 1989), pp. 397–426.

Davis, N. Z., *Society and Culture in Early Modern France*, Stanford, 1975.

Digby, A., *Making a Medical Living: Doctors and Patients in the English Market for Medicine*, Cambridge, 1994.

Dobash, R. and Dobash, R., *Violence Against Wives: A Case Against the Patriarchy*, New York, 1979.

Women, Violence and Social Change, London, 1992.

Doggett, M. E., *Marriage, Wife-Beating and the Law in Victorian England*, Columbia, South Carolina, 1993.

Dolan, F. E., *Dangerous Familiars: Representations of Domestic Crime in England, 1550–1700*, Ithaca, 1994.

Donahue, C., 'Proof by witnesses in the church courts of medieval England: an imperfect reception of the learned law', in M. S. Arnold, T. A. Green, S. A. Scully and S. D. White (eds.), *On the Laws and Customs of England*, Chapel Hill, 1981, pp. 127–58.

Donnison, J., *Midwives and Medical Men: A History of Inter-professional Rivalries and Women's Rights*, London, 1977.

Doolittle, M., 'Close relations? Bringing together gender and family in English history', *Gender and History* 11, 3 (1999), 542–54.

Duncan, G. I. O., *The High Court of Delegates*, Cambridge, 1986.

Eales, J., 'Gender construction in early modern England and the conduct books of William Whateley (1583–1639)', in R. N. Swanson (ed.), *Gender and Christian Religion*, Studies in Church History, 34, Woodbridge, 1998, pp. 163–74.

Earle, P., *A City Full of People: Men and Women of London 1650–1750*, London, 1994.

The Making of the English Middle Class: Business, Society and Family Life in London 1660–1730, London, 1989.

Ehrenreich, B. and English, D., *Witches, Midwives and Nurses*, New York, 1973.

Eigen, J. P., "I answer as a physician': opinion as fact in pre-McNaughtan insanity trials', in M. Clark and C. Crawford (eds.), *Legal Medicine in History*, Cambridge, 1994, pp. 167–99.

Elias, N., *The Civilizing Process: The History of Manners*, trans. E. Jephcott, Oxford, 1978.

Emsley, C., *Crime and Society in England, 1750–1900*, 2nd edition, Harlow, 1996.

The English Police: A Political and Social History, 2nd edition, London, 1996.

Erickson, A. L., *Women and Property in Early Modern England*, London, 1993.

Faller, L. B., *Turned to Account: The Forms and Functions of Criminal Biography in Late Seventeenth- and Early Eighteenth-Century England*, Cambridge, 1987.

Ferraro, J. M., 'The power to decide: battered wives in early modern Venice', *Renaissance Quarterly* 68, 3 (1995), 492–512.

Finn, M., 'Men's things: masculine possession in the consumer revolution', *Social History* 25, 3 (2000), 133–55.

'Women, consumption and coverture in England, c. 1760–1860', *Historical Journal* 39, 3 (1996), 703–22.

Fissell, M., 'The disappearance of the patient's narrative and the invention of hospital medicine', in R. French and A. Wear (eds.), *British Medicine in an Age of Reform*, London, 1991, pp. 92–109.

Patients, Power and the Poor in Eighteenth-Century Bristol, Cambridge, 1991.

Fletcher, A., *Gender, Sex and Subordination in England 1500–1800*, London, 1995.

'Prescription and practice: Protestantism and the upbringing of children 1560–1700', in D. Wood (ed.), *The Church and Childhood*, Studies in Church History, 31, Oxford, 1994, pp. 325–46.

'The Protestant idea of marriage in early modern England', in A. Fletcher and P. Roberts (eds.), *Religion, Culture and Society in Early Modern Britain: Essays in Honour of Patrick Collinson*, Cambridge, 1994, pp. 161–81.

Flint, C., *Family Fictions: Narrative and Domestic Relations in Britain, 1688–1798*, Stanford, 1998.

Forbes, T. R., 'A jury of matrons', *Medical History* 32 (1988), 23–33.

Surgeons at the Bailey: English Forensic Medicine to 1878, London, 1985.

Forster, M., *Significant Sisters: The Grassroots of Active Feminism 1839–1939*, London, 1984.

Foucault, M., *The Birth of the Clinic: An Archaeology of Medical Perception*, trans., A. M. Sheridan, London, 1973.

Foyster, E., 'At the limits of liberty: married women and confinement in eighteenth-century England', *Continuity and Change* 17, 1 (2002), 39–62.

'Boys will be boys? Manhood and aggression, 1660–1800', in T. Hitchcock and M. Cohen (eds.), *English Masculinities 1660–1800*, Harlow, 1999, pp. 151–66.

'Creating a veil of silence? Politeness and marital violence in the English household', *Transactions of the Royal Historical Society* 6th series, 12 (2002), 395–415.

'Male honour, social control and wife beating in late Stuart England', *Transactions of the Royal Historical Society* 6th series, 6 (1996), 215–24.

Manhood in Early Modern England: Honour, Sex and Marriage, Harlow, 1999.

'Marrying the experienced widow in early modern England: the male perspective', in S. Cavallo and L. Warner (eds.), *Widowhood in Medieval and Early Modern Europe*, Harlow, 1999, pp. 108–24.

'Parenting was for life, not just for childhood: the role of parents in the married lives of their children in early modern England', *History* 86 (2001), 313–27.

'Silent witnesses? Children and the breakdown of domestic and social order in early modern England', in A. Fletcher and S. Hussey (eds.), *Childhood in Question: Children, Parents and the State*, Manchester, 1999, pp. 57–73.

Gammon, J. D., '"A denial of innocence': female juvenile victims of rape and the English legal system in the eighteenth century', in A. Fletcher and S. Hussey (eds.), *Childhood in Question: Children, Parents and the State*, Manchester, 1999, pp. 74–95.

'Ravishment and ruin: the construction of stories of sexual violence in England, c.1640–1820', PhD thesis, University of Essex, 2000.

Gatrell, V. A. C., 'Crime, authority and the policeman-state', in F. M. L. Thompson (ed.), *The Cambridge Social History of Britain 1750–1950* vol. 3, Cambridge, 1990, pp. 243–310.

'The decline of theft and violence in Victorian and Edwardian England', in V. A. C. Gatrell, B. Lenman and G. Parker (eds.), *Crime and the Law: The Social History of Crime in Western Europe since 1500*, London, 1980, pp. 238–369.

George, M. J., 'Riding the donkey backwards: men as the unacceptable victims of marital violence', *Journal of Men's Studies* 3, 2 (1994), 137–59.

Gillis, J. R., *For Better, For Worse: British Marriages, 1600 to the Present*, Oxford, 1985.

Gleadle, K., *The Early Feminists: Radical Unitarians and the Emergence of the Women's Rights Movement, 1831–51*, Basingstoke, 1995.

Gordon, L., *Heroes of Their Own Lives: The Politics and History of Family Violence*, London, 1989.

Gowing, L., *Common Bodies: Women, Touch and Power in Seventeenth-Century England*, New Haven and London, 2003.

Domestic Dangers: Women, Words, and Sex in Early Modern London, Oxford, 1996.

Griffiths, P., *Youth and Authority: Formative Experiences in England 1560–1640*, Oxford, 1996.

Hammerton, A. James, *Cruelty and Companionship: Conflict in Nineteenth-Century Married Life*, London, 1992.

'Victorian marriage and the law of matrimonial cruelty', *Victorian Studies* 33, 3 (1990), 269–92.

Hearn, J., 'Men's violence to known women: historical, everyday and theoretical constructions', in B. Fawcett, B. Featherstone, J. Hearn and C. Toft (eds.), *Violence and Gender Relations: Theories and Interventions*, London, 1996, pp. 22–37.

Herrup, C. B., 'Law and morality in seventeenth-century England', *Past and Present* 106 (1985), 102–23.

Hester, M., Pearson, C. and Harwin, N., *Making an Impact: Children and Domestic Violence: A Reader*, London, 2000.

Heywood, C., *A History of Childhood*, Oxford, 2001.

Hindle, S., 'The problem of pauper marriage in seventeenth-century England', *Transactions of the Royal Historical Society* 6th series, 8 (1998), 71–89.

'The shaming of Margaret Knowsley: gossip, gender and the experience of authority in early modern England', *Continuity and Change* 9, 3 (1994), 391–419.

Holcombe, L., *Wives and Property: Reform of the Married Women's Property Law in Nineteenth-Century England*, Toronto, 1983.

Holmes, C., 'Women, witnesses and witches', *Past and Present* 140 (1993), 45–78.

Horder, J., *Provocation and Responsibility*, Oxford, 1992.

Horstman, A., *Victorian Divorce*, London, 1985.

Houston, R., 'Madness and gender in the long eighteenth century', *Social History* 27, 3 (2002), 309–26.

Hufton, O., *The Prospect before Her: A History of Women in Western Europe, Volume One: 1500–1800*, London, 1995.

Hurl-Eamon, J., 'Domestic violence prosecuted: women binding over their husbands for assault at Westminster quarter sessions, 1685–1720', *Journal of Family History* 26, 4 (2001), 435–54.

Humfrey, P. M., "I saw, through a large chink in the partition ...' What the servants knew', in V. Frith (ed.), *Women and History: Voices of Early Modern England*, Toronto, 1995, pp. 51–80.

Hunt, M., 'Wife beating, domesticity and women's independence in eighteenth-century London', *Gender and History* 4, 1 (1992), 10–33.

'Wives and marital "rights" in the Court of Exchequer in the early eighteenth century', in P. Griffiths and M. S. R. Jenner (eds.), *Londinopolis: Essays in the Cultural and Social History of Early Modern London*, Manchester, 2000, pp.107–29.

Hunt, S. C. and Martin, A. M., *Pregnant Women Violent Men: What Midwives Need To Know*, Oxford, 2001.

Ingram, A., *The Madhouse of Language: Writing and Reading Madness in the Eighteenth Century*, London, 1991.

Ingram, M., 'Child sexual abuse in early modern England', in M. J. Braddick and J. Walter (eds.), *Negotiating Power in Early Modern Society: Order, Hierarchy and Subordination in Britain and Ireland*, Cambridge, 2001, pp. 63–84.

Church Courts, Sex and Marriage in England, 1570–1640, Cambridge, 1987.

'"Scolding women cucked or washed": a crisis of gender relations in early modern England?', in J. Kermode and G. Walker (eds.), *Women, Crime and the Courts in Early Modern England*, London, 1994, pp. 48–80.

Jackson, L. A., *Child Sexual Abuse in Victorian England*, London, 2000.

'The child's word in court: cases of sexual abuse in London, 1870–1914', in M. L. Arnot and C. Usborne (eds.), *Gender and Crime in Modern Europe*, London, 1999, pp. 222–37.

'Women professionals and the regulation of violence in interwar Britain', in S. D'Cruze (ed.), *Everyday Violence in Britain, 1850–1950: Gender and Class*, Harlow, 2000, pp. 119–35.

James, T. E., 'The Court of Arches during the 18th century: Its matrimonial jurisdiction', *American Journal of Legal History* 5 (1961), 55–66.

Jewson, N. D., 'The disappearance of the sick-man from medical cosmology, 1770–1870', *Sociology* 10 (1976), 225–44.

Jones, D. J. V., 'The new police, crime and people in England and Wales, 1839–1888', *Transactions of the Royal Historical Society* 5th series, 33 (1983), 151–68.

Jones, J., "She resisted with all her might': sexual violence against women in late nineteenth-century Manchester and the local press', in S. D'Cruze (ed.), *Everyday Violence in Britain, 1850–1950: Gender and Class* (Harlow, 2000), pp.104–18.

Jordanova, L., 'New worlds for children in the eighteenth century: problems of historical interpretation', *History of the Human Sciences* 3 (1990), 69–83.

Kelly, H. A., 'Rule of thumb and the folklaw of the husband's stick', *Journal of Legal Education* 44, 3 (1994), 341–65.

Kennedy, G., *Just Anger: Representing Women's Anger in Early Modern England*, Carbondale and Edwardsville, 2000.

King, P., *Crime, Justice, and Discretion in England 1740–1820*, Oxford, 2000.

'Newspaper reporting, prosecution practice and perceptions of urban crime: the Colchester crime wave of 1765', *Continuity and Change* 2, 3 (1987), 423–54.

'Punishing assault: the transformation of attitudes in the English courts', *Journal of Interdisciplinary History* 27, 1 (1996), 43–74.

Kowaleski-Wallace, E., *Consuming Subjects: Women, Shopping, and Business in the Eighteenth Century*, New York, 1997.

Kugler, A., 'Constructing wifely identity: prescription and practice in the life of Lady Sarah Cowper', *Journal of British Studies* 40 (2001), 291–323.

Lake, P., 'Deeds against nature: cheap print, Protestantism and murder in early seventeenth-century England', in K. Sharpe and P. Lake (eds.), *Culture and Politics in Early Stuart England*, Basingstoke, 1994, pp. 257–83.

Lambertz, J., 'Feminists and the politics of wife-beating', in H. L. Smith (ed.), *British Feminism in the Twentieth Century*, Aldershot, 1990, pp. 25–43.

Landau, N., 'Appearance at the quarter sessions of eighteenth-century Middlesex', *London Journal* 23, 2 (1998), 30–52.

The Justices of the Peace 1679–1760, Berkeley, CA, 1984.

Langford, P., *Englishness Identified: Manners and Character 1650–1850*, Oxford, 2000.

Laurence, A., 'Women's psychological disorders in seventeenth-century Britain', in A. Angerman, G. Binnema, A. Keunen, V. Poels and J. Zirkzee (eds.), *Current Issues in Women's History*, London, 1989, pp. 203–19.

Leneman, L., ' "A tyrant and tormentor": violence against wives in eighteenth- and early nineteenth-century Scotland', *Continuity and Change* 12, 1 (1997), 31–54.

Levene, A., 'The origins of the children of the London Foundling Hospital, 1741–1760: a reconsideration', *Continuity and Change* 18, 2 (2003), 201–35.

Levine, P., ' "So few prizes and so many blanks": Marriage and feminism in later nineteenth-century England', *Journal of British Studies* 28 (1989), 150–74.

Victorian Feminism 1850–1900, London, 1987.

Levine-Clark, M., 'Dysfunctional domesticity: female insanity and family relationships among the West Riding poor in the mid-nineteenth century', *Journal of Family History* 25, 3 (2000), 341–61.

Lewis, J. S., *In the Family Way: Childbearing in the British Aristocracy, 1760–1860*, New Brunswick, NJ, 1986.

Lucal, B., 'The problem with "battered husbands"', *Deviant Behavior: An Interdisciplinary Journal* 16 (1995), 95–112.

McCray Beier, L., *Sufferers and Healers: The Experience of Illness in Seventeenth-Century England*, London, 1987.

McGregor, O. R., Blom-Cooper, L. and Gibson, C., *Separated Spouses: A Study of the Matrimonial Jurisdiction of Magistrate's Courts*, London, 1970.

McGowen, R., 'Punishing violence, sentencing crime', in N. Armstrong and L. Tennenhouse (eds.), *The Violence of Representation: Literature and the History of Violence*, London, 1989, pp. 140–56.

McKendrick, N., Brewer, J. and Plumb, J. H., *The Birth of a Consumer Society: Commercialisation in the Eighteenth Century*, London, 1982.

Macdonald, M., *Mystical Bedlam: Madness, Anxiety and Healing in Seventeenth-Century England*, Cambridge, 1991.

Macdonald, M. and Murphy, T. R., *Sleepless Souls: Suicide in Early Modern England*, Oxford, 1990.

Macfarlane, A., *The Origins of English Individualism: The Family, Property and Social Transition*, Oxford, 1978.

Martin, A. L., *Alcohol, Sex, and Gender in Late Medieval and Early Modern Europe*, Basingstoke, 2001.

Meldrum, T., *Domestic Service and Gender 1660–1750: Life and Work in the London Household*, Harlow, 2000.

Melville, J. D., 'The use and organisation of domestic space in late seventeenth-century London', PhD thesis, University of Cambridge, 1999.

Mendelson, S., and Crawford, P., *Women in Early Modern England*, Oxford, 1998.

Minor, I., 'Working-class women and matrimonial law reform, 1890–1914', in D. E. Martin and D. Rubinstein (eds.), *Ideology and the Labour Movement: Essays Presented to John Saville*, London, 1979, pp. 103–24.

Moore, S. T., '"Justifiable provocation": Violence against women in Essex County, New York, 1799–1860', *Journal of Social History* 35, 4 (2002), 889–918.

Morris, P., 'Defamation and sexual reputation in Somerset, 1733–1850', PhD thesis, University of Warwick, 1985.

Morris, V. B., *Double Jeopardy: Women Who Kill in Victorian Fiction*, Lexington, Kentucky, 1990.

Murphy, T. R., '"Woful childe of parents rage": Suicide of children and adolescents in early modern England, 1505–1710', *The Sixteenth Century Journal* 17, 3 (1986), 259–70.

Nevill, M., 'Women and marriage breakdown in England, 1832–57', PhD thesis, University of Essex, 1989.

Newburn, T. and Stanko, E. A., 'When men are victims: the failure of victimology', in T. Newburn and E. A. Stanko (eds.), *Just Boys Doing Business? Men, Masculinities and Crime*, London, 1994, pp. 153–65.

Oldham, J., 'Law reporting in the London newspapers, 1756–1786', *American Journal of Legal History* 31 (1987), 177–206.

Oppenheim, J., *"Shattered Nerves": Doctors, Patients, and Depression in Victorian England*, Oxford, 1991.

Paley, R., '"An imperfect, inadequate and wretched system?": Policing in London before Peel', *Criminal Justice History* 10 (1989), 95–130.

Pedersen, S., 'Hannah More meets Simple Simon: Tracts, chapbooks, and popular culture in late eighteenth-century England', *Journal of British Studies* 25 (1986), 84–113.

Pelling, M., 'Child health as a social value in early modern England', *Social History of Medicine* 1 (1988), 135–64.

Pennell, S., 'Consumption and consumerism in early modern England', *Historical Journal* 42, 2 (1999), 549–64.

Perry, R., 'Colonizing the breast: sexuality and maternity in eighteenth-century England', *Journal of the History of Sexuality* 2, 2 (1991), 204–34.

Philips, D., 'Crime, law and punishment in the Industrial Revolution', in P. O'Brien and R. Quinault (eds.), *The Industrial Revolution and British Society*, Cambridge, 1993, pp. 156–82.

Phillips, R., *Putting Asunder: A History of Divorce in Western Society*, Cambridge, 1988.

Pollock, L. A., 'Childbearing and female bonding in early modern England', *Social History* 22, 3 (1997), 286–306.

'Embarking on a rough passage: the experience of pregnancy in early-modern society', in V. Fildes (ed.), *Women as Mothers in Pre-Industrial England: Essays in Memory of Dorothy McLaren*, London, 1990, pp. 39–67.

Forgotten Children: Parent-Child Relations from 1500 to 1900, Cambridge, 1983.

'Living on the stage of the world: the concept of privacy among the elite of early modern England', in A. Wilson (ed.), *Rethinking Social History*, Manchester, 1993, pp. 78–96.

'Parent-child relations', in D. I. Kertzer and M. Barbagli (eds.), *The History of the European Family*, vol. 1: *Family Life in Early Modern Times 1500–1789*, London, 2001, pp. 191–220.

Poovey, M., *Uneven Developments: The Ideological Work of Gender in Mid-Victorian England*, Chicago, 1988.

Porter, R. and Porter, D., *In Sickness and In Health: The British Experience 1650–1850*, London, 1988.

Patient's Progress: Doctors and Doctoring in Eighteenth-Century England, Oxford, 1989.

Porter, R., 'The body and the mind, the doctor and the patient: negotiating hysteria', in S. L. Gilman, H. King, R. Porter, G. S. Rousseau and E. Showalter, *Hysteria Beyond Freud*, Berkeley, 1993, pp. 225–85.

Health for Sale: Quackery in England 1660–1850, Manchester, 1989.

'Madness and the family before Freud: the view of the mad-doctors', *Journal of Family History* 23, 2 (1998), 159–72.

'Rape – Does it have a historical meaning?', in S. Tomaselli and R. Porter (eds.), *Rape: An Historical and Social Enquiry*, Oxford, 1986, pp. 216–79.

'A touch of danger: The man-midwife as sexual predator', in G. S. Rousseau and R. Porter (eds.), *Sexual Underworlds of the Enlightenment*, Manchester, 1987, pp. 206–32.

Prest, W. (ed.), *The Professions in Early Modern England*, Beckenham, 1987.

Reay, B., 'Kinship and the neighbourhood in nineteenth-century rural England: the myth of the autonomous nuclear family', *Journal of Family History* 21, 2 (1996), 87–104.

Reynolds, E. A., *Before the Bobbies: the Night Watch and Police Reform in Metropolitan London, 1720–1830*, Basingstoke, 1998.

Richardson, J. and Feder, G., 'Domestic violence: a hidden problem for general practice', *British Journal of General Practice* (April 1996), 239–42.

Robb, G., 'Circe in crinoline: domestic poisonings in Victorian England', *Journal of Family History* 22, 2 (1997), 176–90.

Rose, S. O., 'Widowhood and poverty in nineteenth-century Nottinghamshire', in J. Henderson and R. Wall (eds.), *Poor Women and Children in the European Past*, London, 1994, pp. 269–91.

Ross, E., '"Fierce questions and taunts": married life in working-class London, 1870–1914', *Feminist Studies* 8 (1982), 575–602.

Rousseau, G. S., 'Towards a semiotics of the nerve: the social history of language in a new key', in P. Burke and R. Porter (eds.), *Language, Self and Society*, Oxford, 1991, pp. 214–75.

Rublack, U., 'Fluxes: the early modern body and the emotions', *History Workshop Journal* 53 (2002), 1–16.

'Pregnancy, childbirth and the female body in early modern Germany', *Past and Present* 150 (1996), 84–110.

Russell, A., *The Clerical Profession*, London, 1984.

Savage, G., '"Intended only for the husband": gender, class, and the provision for divorce in England, 1858–1868', in K. O. Garrigan (ed.), *Victorian Scandals: Representations of Gender and Class*, Athens, Ohio, 1992, pp. 11–42.

'"The wilful communication of a loathsome disease": Marital conflict and venereal disease in Victorian England', *Victorian Studies* 34, 1 (1990), 35–54.

Schlereth, T. J., *Cultural History and Material Culture: Everyday Life, Landscapes, Museums*, Charlottesville, 1990.

Shanley, M. L., *Feminism, Marriage, and the Law in Victorian England, 1850–1895*, London, 1989.

'"One must ride behind": married women's rights and the Divorce Act of 1857', *Victorian Studies* 25 (1982), 355–76.

Sharpe, J. A., *Crime in Seventeenth-Century England: A County Study*, Cambridge, 1983.

'Debate. The history of violence in England: some observations', *Past and Present* 108 (1985), 206–15.

Defamation and Sexual Slander in Early Modern England: The Church Courts at York Borthwick Papers, 58, York, 1980.

'Domestic homicide in early modern England', *Historical Journal* 24, 1 (1981), 29–48.

Sharpe, P., 'Dealing with love: the ambiguous independence of the single woman in early modern England', *Gender and History*, 11, 2 (1999), 209–32.

Shepard, A. and Withington, P. (eds.), *Communities in Early Modern England: Networks, Place, Rhetoric*, Manchester, 2000.

Shoemaker, R. B., 'The decline of public insult in London 1660–1800', *Past and Present* 169 (2000), 97–131.

Gender in English Society 1650–1850: The Emergence of Separate Spheres? London, 1998.

The London Mob: Violence and Disorder in Eighteenth-Century England, London, 2004.

'Male honour and the decline of public violence in eighteenth-century London', *Social History* 26, 2 (2001), 190–208.

'Reforming male manners: public insult and the decline of violence in London, 1660–1740', in T. Hitchcock and M. Cohen (eds.), *English Masculinities 1660–1800*, Harlow, 1999, pp. 133–50.

'The taming of the duel: masculinity, honour and ritual violence in London, 1660–1800', *Historical Journal* 45, 3 (2002), 525–45.

Shore, H., 'Home, play and street life: causes of, and explanations for, juvenile crime in the early nineteenth century', in A. Fletcher and S. Hussey (eds.), *Childhood in Question: Children, Parents and the State*, Manchester, 1999, pp. 96–114.

Showalter, E., *The Female Malady: Women, Madness, and English Culture, 1830–1980*, London, 1987.

Slatter, D. M., 'The records of the Court of Arches', *Journal of Ecclesiastical History* 4 (1953), 139–53.

'The study of the records of the Court of Arches', *Journal of the Society of Archivists* 1 (1955), 29–31.

Smith, R., 'The boundary between insanity and criminal responsibility in nineteenth-century England', in A. Scull (ed.), *Madhouses, Mad-Doctors, and Madmen: The Social History of Psychiatry in the Victorian Era*, London, 1981, pp. 363–84.

Smith, R., *Police Reform in Early Victorian York, 1835–1856* Borthwick Paper, 73 (1988), pp. 1–48.

Smith-Rosenberg, C., 'The hysterical woman: sex roles and role conflict in 19th century America', *Social Research* 39 (1972), 652–78.

Sommerville, M. R., *Sex and Subjection: Attitudes to Women in Early-Modern Society*, London, 1995.

Spufford, M., *Small Books and Pleasant Histories: Popular Fiction and its Readership in Seventeenth-Century England*, Cambridge, 1981.

Staves, S., *Married Women's Separate Property in England, 1660–1833*, London, 1990.

'Money for honour: Damages for criminal conversation', *Studies in Eighteenth Century Culture* 11 (1982), 279–97.

Stone, L., *The Family, Sex and Marriage in England 1500–1800*, London, 1977.

'Interpersonal violence in English society 1300–1980', *Past and Present* 101 (1983), 22–33.

'Money, sex and murder in eighteenth-century England', in I. P. H. Duffy (eds.), *Women and Society in the Eighteenth Century*, Bethlehem, Penn., 1983, pp. 15–28.

'Only women', *The New York Review of Books* (11 April, 1985), 21–3.

'A rejoinder', *Past and Present* 108 (1985), 216–24.

Road to Divorce: England 1530–1987, Oxford, 1990.

Uncertain Unions and Broken Lives: Intimate and Revealing Accounts of Marriage and Divorce in England, Oxford, 1995.

Storch, R. D., 'The plague of the blue locusts: police reform and popular resistance in northern England, 1840–57', *International Review of Social History* 20 (1975), 61–90.

'The policeman as domestic missionary: urban discipline and popular culture in northern England, 1850–1880', *Journal of Social History* 9 (1976), 481–509.

'Policing rural England before the police: opinion and practice, 1830–1856', in D. Hay and F. Snyder (eds.), *Policing and Prosecution in Britain 1750–1850*, Oxford, 1989, pp. 211–66.

Suzuki, A., 'The household and the care of lunatics in eighteenth-century London', in P. Horden and R. Smith (eds.), *The Locus of Care: Families, Communities, Institutions and the Provision of Welfare since Antiquity*, London, 1998, pp. 153–75.

'Lunacy in seventeenth- and eighteenth-century England: analysis of Quarter Sessions records. Part I', *History of Psychiatry* 2 (1991), 437–56.

Tadmor, N., *Family and Friends in Eighteenth-Century England: Household, Kinship, and Patronage*, Cambridge, 2001.

Taylor, B., *Eve and the New Jerusalem: Socialism and Feminism in the Nineteenth Century*, London, 1983.

Taylor, D., *Crime, Policing and Punishment in England, 1750–1914*, Basingstoke, 1998.

The New Police in Nineteenth-Century England: Crime, Conflict and Control, Manchester, 1997.

Thomas, K., 'Age and authority in early modern England', *Proceedings of the British Academy* 62 (1976), 205–48.

Religion and the Decline of Magic: Studies in Popular Beliefs in Sixteenth- and Seventeenth-Century England, London, 1971.

Thompson, E. P., *Customs in Common*, London, 1991.

Tomes, N., 'A "torrent of abuse": crimes of violence between working-class men and women in London, 1840–1875', *Journal of Social History* 11, 3 (1978), 328–45.

Tosh, J., 'Authority and nurture in middle-class fatherhood: the case of early and mid-Victorian England', *Gender and History* 8, 1 (1996), 48–64.

A Man's Place: Masculinity and the Middle-Class Home in Victorian England, New Haven and London, 1999.

'The old Adam and the new man: emerging themes in the history of English masculinities, 1750–1850', in T. Hitchcock and M. Cohen (eds.), *English Masculinities 1660–1800*, Harlow, 1999, pp. 217–38.

Trumbach, R., *Sex and the Gender Revolution, Volume One: Heterosexuality and the Third Gender in Enlightenment London*, Chicago, 1998.

Turner, D., *Fashioning Adultery: Gender, Sex and Civility in England*, Cambridge, 2002.

'"Nothing is so secret but shall be revealed': The scandalous life of Robert Foulkes', in T. Hitchcock and M. Cohen (eds.), *English Masculinities 1660–1800*, Harlow, 1999, pp. 169–92.

Vickery, A., *The Gentleman's Daughter: Women's Lives in Georgian England*, London, 1998.

'Golden age to separate spheres? A review of the categories and chronology of English women's history', *Historical Journal* 36, 2 (1993), 383–414.

'Women and the world of goods: a Lancashire consumer and her possessions, 1751–81', in J. Brewer and R. Porter (eds.), *Consumption and the World of Goods*, London, 1993, pp. 274–301.

Waddams, S. M., *Sexual Slander in Nineteenth-Century England: Defamation in the Ecclesiastical Courts, 1815–1855*, Toronto, 2000.

Walker, G., 'Expanding the boundaries of female honour in early modern England', *Transactions of the Royal Historical Society* 6th series, 6 (1996), 235–45.

Crime, Gender and Social Order in Early Modern England, Cambridge, 2003.

'Rereading rape and sexual violence in early modern England', *Gender and History* 10, 1 (1998), 1–25.

Warner, J. and Lunny, A., 'Marital violence in a martial town: husbands and wives in early modern Portsmouth, 1653–1781', *Journal of Family History* 28, 2 (2003), 258–76.

Weatherill, L., 'A possession of one's own: women and consumer behavior in England, 1660–1740', *Journal of British Studies* 25 (1986), 131–56.

Whyman, S. E., *Sociability and Power in Late-Stuart England: The Cultural World of the Verneys 1660–1720*, Oxford, 1999.

Wiener, M. J., 'Alice Arden to Bill Sikes: Changing nightmares of intimate violence in England, 1558–1869', *Journal of British Studies* 40 (2001), 184–212.

'Domesticity: a legal discipline for men?', in M. Hewitt (ed.), *An Age of Equipoise? Reassessing Mid-Victorian Britain*, Aldershot, 2000, pp. 155–67.

Men of Blood: Violence, Manliness, and Criminal Justice in Victorian England, Cambridge, 2004.

Reconstructing the Criminal: Culture, Law, and Policy in England, 1830–1914, Cambridge, 1990.

'The sad story of George Hall: adultery, murder and the politics of mercy in mid-Victorian England', *Social History* 24, 2 (1999), 174–95.

'The Victorian criminalization of men', in P. Spierenburg (ed.), *Men and Violence: Gender, Honor, and Rituals in Modern Europe and America*, Ohio, 1998, pp. 197–212.

Wilson, A., 'The ceremony of childbirth and its interpretation', in V. Fildes (ed.), *Women as Mothers in Pre-Industrial England: Essays in Memory of Dorothy McLaren*, London, 1990, pp. 68–107.

The Making of Man-Midwifery: Childbirth in England, 1660–1770, Cambridge, MA, 1995.

Wiltenburg, J., *Disorderly Women and Female Power in the Street Literature of Early Modern England and Germany*, Charlottesville, 1992.

Wolfram, S., 'Divorce in England 1700–1857', *Oxford Journal of Legal Studies* 5, 2 (1985), 155–86.

Wright, D. C., '*De Manneville v. De Manneville*: Rethinking the birth of the custody law under patriarchy', *Law and History Review* 17, 2 (1999), 247–307.

'On judicial agency and the best interests test', *Law and History Review* 17, 2 (1999), 319–24.

Wrightson, K., *Earthly Necessities: Economic Lives in Early Modern Britain*, London, 2000.

'Household and kinship in sixteenth-century England', *History Workshop Journal*, 12 (1981), 151–8.

'The politics of the parish in early modern England', in P. Griffiths, A. Fox and S. Hindle (eds.), *The Experience of Authority in Early Modern England*, Basingstoke, 1996, pp. 10–46.

Wynne Smith, L., 'Women's health care in England and France (1650–1775)', PhD thesis, University of Essex, 1989.

Yeo, E. J., 'The creation of 'motherhood' and women's responses in Britain and France, 1750–1914', *Women's History Review* 8, 2 (1999), 201–16.

Yllö, K. and Bograd, M., 'Foreword', in K. Yllö and M. Bograd (eds.), *Feminist Perspectives on Wife Abuse*, London, 1988, pp. 7–9.

Index